Opening Scripture

# OPENING SCRIPTURE

*Bible Reading and Interpretive Authority
in Puritan New England*

LISA M. GORDIS

THE UNIVERSITY OF CHICAGO PRESS
CHICAGO AND LONDON

Lisa M. Gordis is assistant professor of English at Barnard College, Columbia University.

The University of Chicago Press, Chicago 60637
The University of Chicago Press, Ltd., London
© 2003 by The University of Chicago
All rights reserved. Published 2003
Printed in the United States of America
12   11   10   09   08   07   06   05   04   03       1   2   3   4   5

ISBN: 0-226-30412-4 (cloth)

Library of Congress Cataloging-in-Publication Data

Gordis, Lisa M.
   Opening Scripture : Bible reading and interpretive authority in Puritan New England /
Lisa M. Gordis.
      p. cm.
   Includes bibliographical references and index.
   ISBN 0-226-30412-4 (cloth : alk. paper)
   1. Bible—Criticism, interpretation, etc.—New England—History—
17th century. 2. Bible—Homiletical use—History—17th century. 3. Puritans—
New England. I. Title.

BS500 .G67 2002
220.6'0974409032—dc21

                                                                    2002006715

In memory of my grandfathers, Robert Gordis and Harry Witztum, who shared with me their love of the biblical text.

# CONTENTS

Though it is hardly unusual for authors to thank those who have supported them and their work, I feel unusually lucky in the long list of people and institutions who have nurtured this book over the years. The project was born in several classrooms where I thought I was simply fulfilling distribution requirements for my undergraduate major. Instead, the teaching of Drew McCoy, Alan Heimert, Walter Hughes, and Janice Knight fostered an intellectual interest that has given me many years of great pleasure.

At UCLA, I had the good fortune to study with Martha Banta, Barbara Packer, Jonathan Post, Karen Rowe, and Debora Shuger, who proved that it is possible to combine brilliance in teaching and in scholarship. I am particularly indebted to Michael J. Colacurcio, whose keen mind and great kindness have helped to shape not only this book, but also my sense of myself as a scholar and teacher.

At Barnard College, I have found thoughtful and supportive colleagues in James Basker, Christopher Baswell, Elizabeth Dalton, Pat Denison, Peggy Ellsberg, Mary Gordon, Maire Jaanus, Monica Miller, Remington Patterson, Caryl Phillips, Cary Plotkin, Quandra Prettyman, Claudia Rankine, and Maura Spiegel. I am especially grateful to those who read portions of this book as it developed: Rachel Adams, Ross Hamilton, Jennie Kassanoff, Paula Loscocco, Peter Platt, Anne Lake Prescott, Bill Sharpe, Timea Szell, Margaret Vandenburg, Nancy Woloch, and the members of the 1998 Willen Seminar in

American Studies. This book has benefited as well from discussion with Barnard historians Mark Carnes, Robert McCaughey, Rosalind Rosenberg, Herb Sloan, and Lisa Tiersten, from the collegial support of Columbia early Americanists Andrew Delbanco and Robert Ferguson, and from the sharp responses of Barnard and Columbia students.

The members of the Seminar on Religion and Society at Princeton University, especially Robert Wuthnow, John Wilson, and Leigh Schmidt, helped me to reconceive and reshape my argument in important ways. Discussion at David D. Hall's 1998 American Antiquarian Society summer seminar in the History of the Book helped to clarify my sense of where the book needed to go.

Many other colleagues and friends have been generous with both advice and support. I am especially grateful to Joanna Brooks, Jessie Schindler Cheney, Nan Cohen, Pat Crain, Michael Ditmore, Kris Fresonke, Beth Frost, Bill Gleason, Allegra Goodman, Sandra Gustafson, Derek Hackett, Megan Isaac, Rebecca Jaffe, Lois Leveen, James Najarian, Meredith Neuman, Mary O'Connor, Lauren Osborne, Marilynn Richtarik, Geoff Sanborn, Emily Schiller, Eric Murphy Selinger, Julianne Shanblatt, Michele Sullum, Michele Lise Tarter, Michael P. Winship, and Lewis Yelin.

Several institutions have provided financial support for this project. I thank the UCLA English Department, the U.S. Department of Education Jacob Javits Fellowship Program, Barnard College, the Gilder Foundation, the National Endowment for the Humanities, the Princeton University Center for the Study of American Religion (now the Center for the Study of Religion), and the Folger Shakespeare Library, not only for defraying the expenses of research and manuscript preparation, but also for the great gift of time for research and writing.

My research was aided by the staffs of UCLA's Powell Library, Young Research Library, English Reading Room, and William Andrews Clark Memorial Library; the Henry Huntington Library; the History of Medicine Library at Johns Hopkins University; the Barnard College Library and Butler Library at Columbia University; the New York Public Library; Firestone Library at Princeton University; Speare Library at Princeton Theological Seminary; Burke Library at Union Theological Seminary; the Library of Congress; the Folger Shakespeare Library; McKeldin Library and the Shady Grove Library and Media Center at the University of Maryland; and the Montgomery County Public Libraries.

I thank as well the people who helped to make my manuscript into this book. Alan Thomas offered sage counsel with great kindness. I am also grateful for the work of Leslie Keros, Randolph Petilos, and Mark Heineke at the University of Chicago Press, and for the thoughtful attention of David Bemelmans, Stanley Szuba, Martin White, and the anonymous reviewers of the manuscript.

Finally, my family has encouraged me from this project's inception. That many of them are teachers and scholars in their own right has been tremendously helpful, but I am most grateful for their love, their encouragement, and their faith that this book would someday be finished. I thank Ira and Sara Saiger, Miriam and George Saiger, Bronia Witztum, Elana Gordis and Mitchell Earleywine, and Felice and David Gordis. My deepest thanks are reserved for Aaron Saiger, who attended to details of my argument even after his own long days and who learned to laugh at Thomas Hooker's jokes, and for our daughter Yael Margalit, who quietly drew beautiful pictures during several crunch periods, and who fills our lives with color and joy. Our new daughter Hannah Tzivia was born in time to make proofreading a noisy adventure. I am grateful for her frequent naps and more grateful for her safe arrival and her already winning smile.

# Opening the Text

In one account of the Antinomian Controversy, John Winthrop worried that the Massachusetts Bay Colony's religious disputes would erupt into violence, "like him who when he could not by any sentence in the Bible confute an Heretick, could make use of the whole booke to break his head."[1] The image resonates with later views of New England Puritans, from early-twentieth-century condemnations of Puritan anti-intellectualism and illiberalism by writers such as Vernon Louis Parrington, H. L. Mencken, and William Carlos Williams to Darren Staloff's more recent account of Puritan magistrates and ministers using the Bible as a "tool" for "cultural domination."[2] Yet a closer look at this seventeenth-century image reveals a more complex picture. Winthrop opposes the use of "the whole booke" as a physical weapon to the more legitimate use of biblical "sentence[s]" to "confute" heresy, suggesting the slipperiness of scriptural proof by highlighting the tension between scripture's real meaning and its appropriation by those in authority. Indeed, though Winthrop describes an orthodox figure wielding the book as a cudgel in the face of interpretive impasse, his appropriation of the image reverses its thrust: he writes as a member of the reigning orthodoxy, fearful that dissenters will exchange "the sword of the Spirit" for "a sword of steele," producing "a tragicall and bloudy issue" (*Short Story*, 294). As he uses the image, book-as-cudgel and interpretive authority change hands: it is the heretic who cannot find scriptural warrant for his activity, and turns instead to physical violence.

This reversal reflects Winthrop's own altered status in New England. Having learned to marshal scripture to his cause as an English dissenter, he found himself a member of Massachusetts Bay's ruling party. The uneasiness of the image—the jarring opposition of "Heretick" and dissenter—suggests how uncomfortably Winthrop's new role fit the biblical practices he and his colleagues had learned in England and brought with them to the new world. For underlying Puritan approaches to the Bible was a distrust of human interpretive authority, and a reliance instead on scripture as an account of God's will. Consequently, Puritan interpretive practices privileged techniques that theoretically allowed the Bible to interpret itself. Puritan ministers presented their preaching as prophecy, emphasizing that they merely "opened" God's word with God's assistance. And many New England migrants believed that the Holy Spirit would enable their community of saints to reach consensus about God's will as revealed in scripture, making the imposition of human interpretive authority unnecessary. This book explores these beliefs and practices and their consequences, both for New England's literary culture and for the interpretive controversies that troubled New England's first generations.

Puritan biblical culture in New England was characterized not by the closed fists and closed minds envisioned by Parrington, but rather by interpretive fluidity that was both generative and troubling, producing both a flowering of richly intertextual literature and a series of divisive interpretive controversies. Puritan theorists saw the Bible not as a closed book, but as an open text, a locus for ongoing interaction between God and his chosen saints. Clergy and laity often described that interaction as "opening," not coincidentally the word used by more radical Protestants to describe an experience of divine revelation. In the preaching manuals most popular among Puritan ministers, William Perkins defined "interpretation" as "the *Opening* of the wordes and sentences of the Scripture, that one entire and naturall sense may appeare," while Richard Bernard called on *The Faithfvll Shepheard* "to resolue his Scripture, to laie it open to the hearers."[3] And as she stood before the General Court, Anne Hutchinson proclaimed: "The Lord knows that I could not open scripture; he must by his prophetical office open it unto me"; in her experience of revelation, God "open[ed]" the text to her.[4] Such language is appropriate to the interpretive fluidity generated by Puritan theories of reading and exegesis. Reading, interpreting, and preaching the Bible constituted a process whereby the text's meaning was unfolded in complex interactions among reader, author, and text. Such interactions were necessitated by the fallen state of the human reader, to whom the divinely authored (and thus perfect) biblical text might *seem* unclear at points. The process of conversion, the transformation of God's elect by God's intervention in their lives, would transform them as readers as well, enabling them to read and understand God's will as revealed in God's word. Moreover, the saints' reading process could include active divine involvement, as the Holy Spirit assisted them in their reading, offering them direct access to the text and to its Author's meanings. Additional assistance was provided by Puritan ministers, who interpreted the text to the laity. Their preaching, too, was divinely enabled; ideally, it was not merely preaching, but also "prophesying." Thus, for the Puritan reader, the biblical text offered indirect and mediated contact with God's revelation, and also, potentially, direct access to God as both author and interpreter.

Privileging God as author and interpreter, Puritan interpretive strategies minimized the role of the human interpreter, relying on methods that in theory allowed the text to interpret itself. Preaching manuals instructed exegetes to examine the context of each passage to reveal God's intentions, and then "collate" or collect comparable passages that could be compared and contrasted with the passage in question. This process of collation, which necessarily severed the collated verses from their contexts, opened out the interpretive process and offered great interpretive flexibility. Because interpreters could bring both similar and different passages to illuminate their texts, collation allowed them to adapt the texts to address a range of concerns, even as they were ostensibly merely "opening" the meanings of the texts themselves. In the process, collation fostered rich intertextual artistry, both in sermons and in other texts by Puritan writers. Puritan theorists, however, were ambivalent about the skill and artistry required to wield these interpretive tools. While they were attentive to the training, knowledge, and skill required to collate both properly and effectively, they nevertheless insisted that the only interpretive assistance truly necessary was the assistance of the Holy Spirit.

Puritan wariness of human interpretive authority had consequences beyond the literary realm as well. Puritan migrants believed that God's will, as presented in scripture, should guide the saints not only in their spiritual lives, but also in their broader colonial project. So even as the interpretive fluidity produced by Puritan theories of exegesis enabled Puritan writers to produce texts of pleasure and spiritual succor, that fluidity also contributed to the controversies that threatened to destroy the holy community in Massachusetts Bay. Indeed, the colony very soon faced a crisis in literary theory. Both New England preaching and the events that shook the community—the troubling figure of Roger Williams, the strife of the Antinomian Controversy, and the reluctant compromises of the Halfway Covenant—were symptoms of that crisis. Puritan theories of reading and exegesis sparked a flowering of sermon literature so engaging to its audience that the magistrates found it necessary to limit public lectures in order to accomplish the work of building a colony.

Those same interpretive theories described a relationship between the divinely authored text and its imperfect human interpreters that unsettled human interpretive authority and stymied hopes for interpretive consensus. Indeed, for New England Puritans, the openness of their approach to the biblical text rendered "the sword of the Spirit" double-edged, enlivening and disrupting their religious, cultural, and political life.

In arguing for a more fluid view of Puritan interpretive practices, and thus of Puritan interpretive authority, I join a line of scholars who have insisted on a subtler account of New England Puritanism. Perry Miller answered the charges of Parrington and Mencken, demonstrating that the "New England mind" was not small and closed, but rather that New England Puritans inhabited the same rich intellectual world and "respond[ed] to the same impulses as their philosophical contemporaries."[5] Miller's account of "orthodoxy in Massachusetts" has subsequently been opened outward, as scholars have offered a fuller picture of a more diverse and less unitary religious scene in New England.[6] Geoffrey F. Nuttall, for example, elaborated the role of the Holy Spirit in Puritan faith, connecting orthodox Puritanism with more radical Protestant groups.[7] Philip Gura has demonstrated that New England's orthodoxy competed for the colonists' allegiances with a variety of more radical Protestant movements.[8] And David D. Hall has described the range of religious practices that New England's migrants imported and developed along with Puritan orthodoxy.[9] The current trend among scholars of English Puritanism has been to see not a single coherent Puritan faith, but rather a loosely organized and variously unified movement of radical Protestants who shared some positions.[10] Applying this approach to the New England scene, Janice Knight has replaced Miller's version of "orthodoxy in Massachusetts" with an account of two competing orthodoxies battling for control in early New England.[11] Michael P. Winship has traced divisions within the Boston church itself, demonstrating that "the unity of the godly in the Boston church was a painfully achieved and easily disrupted accomplishment."[12] Moreover, he has asserted that scholars of New England Puritanism must "fully come to grips with the Collinsonian sea change," going so far as to ask "Were there any Puritans in New England?"[13]

That it has taken so long for scholars to understand the fluidity of the religious situation in early New England is partly the result of New England Puritans' desire for consensus, a desire which scholars have sometimes mistaken for actual religious unity. Sacvan Bercovitch explores this desire in *The Rites of Assent*, identifying consensus as an enduring myth of American identity.[14] He suggests that America's "corporate identity" is "built on fragmentation and dissent: a hundred sects, factions, schools, and denominations, each aggressively different from the others, yet all celebrating the same mission"

(29–30). Bercovitch finds that "[t]his *concordia discors*" functions "partly to mystify or mask social realities" (29–30). Yet he also finds that "it denoted something equally real: a coherent system of symbols, values, and beliefs, and a series of rituals designed to keep the system going" (29–30). This myth, explains Bercovitch, was "established" in the antebellum north: "there the rituals of God's country were constructed and sanctified" (29–30). Bercovitch's understanding of consensus is useful, especially for his articulation of the gap between the "myth" of consensus and actual unanimity. Bercovitch's account of this myth and its function moves outward chronologically, thematically, and in scope, from early New England to the practices of late-twentieth-century American studies. My study, however, looks backward, suggesting that the roots of Puritans' desire for consensus and the frustration of that desire lay in the approach to the Bible that they imported from England. It thus responds to the challenge of scholars such as Nathan O. Hatch and Mark A. Noll, who have affirmed the pervasiveness of the Bible in American popular and literary culture while calling for scholars to demonstrate "that the actual use of the Bible in American life has been attended with considerable complexity and decided ambiguity."[15]

I argue that a full understanding of New England's religious and cultural life depends on understanding the vexed theory of reading and interpretation that guided Puritan Bible reading, and thus shaped not only Puritan preaching, but also both Puritan literature and church polity. My first chapter lays this theoretical foundation by examining the texts that shaped Puritan ministers' understandings of the Bible and of their role as preachers. Drawing its title from William Perkins's popular preaching manual *The Arte of Prophecying* (1592), chapter 1 explores the uneasy equilibrium that ministers strove to maintain as they interpreted the Bible to their congregations. Preaching was on the one hand an "arte" requiring human skill and learning. On the other hand, it was "prophecying," a divinely enabled activity in which the minister "opened" the text of God's word to the congregation, drawing not on his own resources but on the assistance of the Holy Spirit. Balancing Reformed belief in the clarity of the biblical text and the Holy Spirit's role in "opening" that text to the regenerate reader, Puritan ministers sought to efface themselves from their own sermons, treating preaching as a fuller form of reading and privileging interpretive techniques that would theoretically allow the text to interpret itself. In their sermons, they "opened" texts by discussing "the circumstances of the place propounded," or the context of the passage, and by "collating" related passages from other parts of the Bible. Though they supplemented the Holy Spirit's assistance with a wide variety of human interpretive aids, ministers were advised to conceal such preparation from their congregants. Instead, preaching manuals suggested that ministers make their own efforts—both their learning and their intertextual artistry—seem as transparent as possible to the power of the text itself, acknowledging publicly only the role of the Holy Spirit.

This emphasis on transparency complicated both the reading practices of the laity and the relationships between ministers and their congregants. In sermons and other texts of piety, laypeople were exhorted to read the Bible on their own, imitating their ministers' interpretive methods. But lay reading was theoretically handicapped, for most lay readers lacked the tools which the preaching manuals required for proper interpretation. Moreover, because the ministers were advised to conceal their use of these tools from their flocks, the congregants had no reason to suspect the limitations of their own readings. In theory, the assistance of the Holy Spirit would overcome the laity's deficiencies. But that assistance could not be taken for granted, for even in New England Puritan divines did not expect to face congregations composed entirely of individuals who had experienced religious conversions, thereby becoming divinely enabled readers. Thus, as they preached sermons and exhorted their congregants to read the Scriptures, New England ministers were encouraging them to do what they believed many of those congregants—lacking both academic skills of interpretation and the necessary guidance of the Holy Spirit—could not be expected to do competently. At the same time, by presenting their own subtle interpretive activity as straightforward, ministers led their congregants to feel empowered as readers. It is hardly surprising, then, that New England congregants—among them Anne Hutchinson—took the ministers at their word, evaluating sermons and disputing the ministers' readings of the biblical text, while asserting the authority of their own interpretations.

For all the ministers minimized their own artistry, attempting to see their work as prophetic, I emphasize human artistry in my treatment of Puritan preaching, and indeed, in my readings of Puritan texts more generally. I contend that Puritan writers, readers, and auditors found not only piety, but also aesthetic pleasure, in the manipulation of the biblical text. While Puritanists have been eager to explicate the intellectual projects of American Puritanism, and more recently to describe the politics of American Puritanism as well, as a group we have been oddly ambivalent about the literary status of the texts that we study, all too ready to accept the judgments of critics like Mencken and their modern counterparts. We have too often felt embarrassed by the pleasure we take in Puritan texts, from the complex images of John Cotton's sermons to the gloomy glee of Michael Wigglesworth's epic *The Day of Doom*.[16] Part of my project here is to illuminate the pleasures these texts hold, not only for their seventeenth-century readers, but for us as well.

In chapters 2–4, I explore the responses of three New England ministers to the guidance of preaching manuals by examining their use of the Bible in sermons and treatises. While the sermons represent the individual ministers' applications of sermon theory, the distinction between theory and practice is hardly tidy. The sermons I consider are often themselves theoretical, offering not only interpretations of specific passages, but also guidance on Bible reading more generally.[17] To represent this first generation of New England preaching, I have chosen John Cotton, Thomas Shepard, and Thomas Hooker, three of the ministers most renowned for their preaching in their own day, all of whom had significant preaching careers in both old and New England. I have selected them as well for the diversity of their approaches to the biblical text, not only in their preaching methods, but also in the nature of the interactions they prescribe between reader and text. Such differences are significant for several reasons. First, they demonstrate how the fluidity of the method described by the preaching manuals produced dramatically varied approaches to reading, interpretation, and audience—differences that eventually posed serious problems for this community of readers. Second, each minister modeled an approach that had potentially disruptive elements, and these elements in fact proved disruptive when adopted by lay readers such as Anne Hutchinson. Finally, the variations in the ministers' approaches challenge scholarly views of Puritan preaching as monolithic and formulaic. Instead, they testify to the diversity of the ministers' biblical appropriations and preaching styles, which contributed to their aesthetic appeal.

Most popular of his generation was John Cotton, who followed Perkins's guidelines most closely. In chapter 2, I examine Cotton's efforts to balance the demands of "arte" and "prophecy." As Perkins had advised, Cotton downplayed his own artifice, treating his sermons not as performances, but as fuller alternatives to "bare reading." Bare reading, in Cotton's view, could not be efficacious for the unconverted; only the preached word could carry grace to the unbeliever. Though he claimed this important role for his preaching, however, Cotton presented his intricately constructed sermons as straightforward explications of the biblical text. The deceptive straightforwardness of Cotton's exegesis lent power to his careful arguments, making them seem to emerge inevitably from the text rather than from his own interpretive artistry. Such sermons also made the techniques of exegesis available to Cotton's auditors, who took seriously his exhortation to evaluate their ministers' preaching. It is no coincidence, I suggest, that Cotton stood so close to the center of the interpretive controversies that plagued early New England.

Though Cotton's preaching has been most closely associated with the tensions that developed in Massachusetts Bay, the sermons of his colleagues also presented complex and potentially unsettling models of reading. In chapter 3, I examine Thomas Shepard's use of both the biblical text and the sermon itself as vehicles for intimacy with the divine. Shepard maintained that the Holy Spirit could actually inhabit the text being preached, so that proper listening to sermons offered the possibility of mystical contact with Christ. By constructing his sermons as collages of biblical language, Shepard hoped that the Holy Spirit would inhabit the words he was quoting and enter the hearts of the congregation. He thus urged regenerate readers who felt themselves alienated from God to experience intimacy with the Holy Spirit through the text itself; indeed, he suggested that they hear the voice of the Spirit speaking to their souls through the Scriptures. Such mystical contact closely resembles what Anne Hutchinson described as "immediate revelation." Little wonder, then, that Shepard remained silent when Hutchinson's revelations were discussed at her trial.

Thomas Hooker, too, urged his auditors to hear the Scriptures speaking directly to them, its verses providing multiple voices engaged in dramatic debates over the state of their souls. In chapter 4, I explore Hooker's emphasis on what he called "particular application," the application of biblical texts to the lives of individual Christians. Though Hooker's applications often stressed the recognition of sin, in addressing himself to as-yet unconverted auditors, he encouraged them to apply the text's promises to themselves as well. In fact, Hooker made his reputation by comforting a despairing parishioner; the sermon that emerged from this episode advised the "Poor Doubting Christian" how to find comfort in the Bible's words. To diminish the distance between the Christian and the biblical text, Hooker urged his listeners to insert themselves into biblical dialogues. They were to identify, for example, with a sinful King David, but then switch roles to "play the part of Nathan" and rebuke themselves for their sins. By encouraging this identification with biblical sinners, Hooker hoped that his auditors would learn to see themselves as redeemed Christians as well. Hooker's experimental and affective approach followed Perkins in minimizing human learning, but directed greater attention toward the individual reader, and toward the impact of the text on the reader. And though Hooker did not attend Anne Hutchinson's trials, Hutchinson was criticized for citing his preaching with approval, while other ministers doubted that Hooker could really have said so shocking a thing as Hutchinson reported. (He had.)

In chapter 5, I consider the impact of the ministers' models on New England's laity. Drawing on David D. Hall's rejection of "the conception of two separate religions, one rooted in folk ways of thinking, the other maintained by the clerics and their bourgeois allies," I examine the shared and intersecting interpretive practices of clergy and laity.[18] Intense enthusiasm for sermons led John Winthrop in 1639 to lament:

There were so many lectures now in the country, and many poor persons would usually resort to two or three in the week, to the great neglect of their affairs, and the damage of the public. The assemblies also were (in divers churches) held till night, and sometimes within the night, so as such as dwelt far off could not get home in due season, and many weak bodies could not endure so long, in the extremity of the heat or cold, without great trouble, and hazard of their health.[19]

Eagerly absorbing the sermons of their ministers, New England's Puritan laity adopted their ministers' methods. They listened to their ministers preach, took notes, and discussed the sermons in other private meetings. They read the Bible themselves as they worked out their spiritual perplexities, following their ministers' advice and imitating their practices. And they incorporated the Bible into their own writings, finding in its words a rich language of allusion and a source of literary artistry. I argue that their artistry, like the preaching of the ministers, reveals again the double-edged quality that the "sword of the Spirit" had for Puritan writers, fostering literary creativity even as it unsettled the biblical text.

In the book's final chapters, I turn to the varied documents of New England's early controversies to consider even more unsettling consequences of Puritan literary theory. Again, I treat the division between theory and practice as fluid: while the controversies that threatened to tear the community apart were multifaceted—encompassing theological, political, economic, and gender issues—they were also theoretical debates about the nature of reading, interpretation, and revelation. Puritan migrants to Massachusetts Bay attempted to build a society around their understanding of the Bible, lavishing enormous amounts of effort on fundamentally literary questions about the nature of reading and the proper forms of interpretation. The texts of their debates reveal a great deal about Puritan theories of reading, for participants were often aware that they had both local and distant audiences, and saw themselves as establishing ground rules for the new community.

In chapter 6, I situate the controversies that swirled around Roger Williams within the context of Puritan theories of biblical clarity, interpretive authority, and interpretive consensus. The ministers who traveled to New England in the 1630s assumed that "the scripture [had] given full direction for the right ordering of" church and society. They were uneasy with the intervention of human interpreters, to whom their opponents in the English church granted wider range. Expecting consensus to emerge naturally, or rather supernaturally, with the Holy Spirit enabling regenerate readers and helping them to perceive God's will, Puritan leaders found dissent to be troubling not only practically, but theoretically. Given the clarity of the Scriptures and the aid of the Spirit, they contended that misreadings (among them Williams's position on the separation of church and state) revealed willful human resistance to the interpretive assistance of the Spirit. Citing both scripture and Christian history, Williams countered that in this world, all interpretation was fumbling in fog and darkness. He thus challenged the project of the scriptural commonwealth, not only by demonstrating how elusive interpretive consensus would be, but also by insisting that dissent was normative.

Though Williams's critics insisted that the clarity of scripture would convince any dissenter, they were dismayed by the obstinacy of dissenters in the Antinomian Controversy (1636–38). Chapter 7 suggests that this controversy was shaped at least in part by Puritan theories of private reading, revelation, and interpretive consensus. From the earliest days of the controversy, participants attempted to minimize their disagreements, insisting that "free and open" discussion would help them resolve their dispute, or, better yet, understand that they did not disagree after all. I consider Anne Hutchinson's fate in the context of these attempts to contain dissent, analyzing what made her so threatening to the community's leaders. I argue that the "immediate revelations" that Hutchinson described to a shocked General Court were less radical than the reaction they elicited might suggest. Indeed, her revelations closely resembled models of scripture reading advocated by Calvin, Cotton, Hooker, and Shepard. Reactions to Hutchinson's revelations were shaped in part by the more radical claims made by some of her followers and allies, who demonstrated what a slippery slope an orthodox theory of Spirit-assisted reading could generate. That their errors could be traced through Cotton to Calvin himself made them more alarming, rather than less, and raised the stakes involved in the resolution of the crisis.

The controversies around Roger Williams and the Antinomian dissent led to subtle changes in New England Puritan approaches to interpretive authority. The book's epilogue considers these changes as they were reflected in debates about infant baptism that culminated in the Halfway Covenant of 1662. In the wake of the Antinomian Controversy, one might have expected the clergy to clamp down on lay power. However, the ministers left considerable power over church polity in the hands of the laity, instead asserting their authority through heightened emphasis on their own interpretive skill. In a departure from earlier preaching manuals, New England's second generation of ministers grounded their authority in learning and expertise, emphasizing the need for academic training along with the assistance of the Holy Spirit. Indeed, they often lamented that lay readers had taken Reformed claims of scriptural clarity and accessibility so much to heart that they failed to recognize their own interpretive limitations.

In debating questions of church policy, ministers placed decreasing emphasis on a consensus of individual lay and clerical readers, and greater emphasis on the authority conferred by interpretive expertise. They did so hesitantly and reluctantly. This was no exuberant grasp of power, but rather a chastened and qualified attempt to create an orderly interpretive community when the assumptions on which their plans had rested failed them, when the Holy Spirit proved insufficient as a unifying force. James F. Cooper Jr. suggests that New England church polity developed to address the problem of failed consensus in a community that clung to consensus as an ideal, and relinquished it only when they could not make it viable in purest form.[20] Similarly, debates over the extension of baptism to the grandchildren of church members reveal the ministers' asserting not the power to impose their will, but instead an interpretive expertise to which the less-trained laity should defer. For them, this represented a great failure of the community reading "in the Spirit." Even more than the decline in church membership, it reflected the failure of what they had thought would be most exceptional about the New England communities. And though we may not be sorry that their aspirations failed, we should appreciate the poignancy of the realization for them, all the more since it began to dawn so soon, was resisted so fiercely, and ultimately was accepted in such a short time.

## CHAPTER 1

# "Humane Skill" and
# "The Arte of Prophecying"

The preaching manuals that Puritan ministers consulted did more than instruct them in crafting sermons. They presented Reformed theories of Bible reading and exegesis, teaching their readers how to read the biblical text, how to interpret it, and how to teach it to their congregants. These were difficult tasks, and their challenges were heightened by the caution that John Calvin had sounded in *The Institutes of Christian Religion*. Though it was necessary to take the minister's role seriously, Calvin warned ministers to recognize that not they but God would grant faith to their congregants: "God, in ascribing to himself illumination of mind and renewal of heart, warns that it is sacrilege for man to claim any part of either for himself."[1] Many Reformed theologians offered similar advice, emphasizing the perfection of the text and the role of the Holy Spirit as primary interpreter. The role of mediating human interpreters was carefully circumscribed.

The use of the term "prophesying" for preaching emphasized this sense of limited human role: the minister should focus on "opening" God's word rather than creating his own. Indeed, warned Richard Bernard in his popular preaching manual, being "tied vnto" one's own language "curbes the good motions of the spirit."[2] Puritan theorists like Bernard emphasized God's role in Puritan preaching, insisting that the "spirit of God" participates in the preaching of God's word, and assists the minister both in preparing his sermons and in preaching them (82). Puritan preachers defined their preaching style against Anglican sermons, which they saw as emphasizing human wit and artistry at great spiritual cost. In the words of one Puritan polemic, Anglican preaching offered "a cunning framed method, by excellencie of wordes and intising speeches of man's wisdom, to beguile and bewitch the verie Church of God."[3] In contrast, Puritan theorists stressed "plainness," leading their opponents to condemn "dunsticall sermons" preached by "sectaries . . . in ditches and other Conuenticles when they leape from the Coblers stall to their pulpits" with "no eloquence but Tantologies [sic], to tye the eares of your Auditory unto you: no inuention but here is to be noted, I stole this note out of Beza or Marlorat: not wit to moue, no passion to urge, but onely an ordinary forme of preaching, blowen up by use of often hearing and speaking."[4]

Perry Miller offers a less polemical account of the distinctions between Puritan and Anglican preaching, finding the "[o]pposition between the metaphysical and the Puritan sermon . . . a matter both of form and style."[5] He emphasizes distinctions of form, finding "the Anglican sermon . . . much more an oration, much closer to classical and patristic eloquence, while the Puritan work is mechanically and rigidly divided into sections and subheads, and appears on the printed page more like a lawyer's brief than a work of art" (332). Miller's description of Anglican preaching emphasizes artistry, music, and movement: "The Anglican sermon," explains Miller, "is constructed on a symphonic scheme of progressively widening vision; it moves from point to point by verbal analysis, weaving larger and larger embroideries about the words of the text. . . . The Anglican sermon opens with a pianissimo exordium, gathers momentum through a rising and quickening tempo, comes generally to a rolling, organ-toned peroration" (332–33). In contrast, Miller finds the Puritan sermon practical and businesslike, but also a bit flat:

> The Puritan sermon quotes the text and "opens" it as briefly as possible, expounding circumstances and context, explaining its grammatical meanings, reducing its tropes and schemata to prose, and setting forth its logical implications; the sermon then proclaims in a flat, indicative sentence the "doctrine" contained in the text or logically deduced from it, and proceeds to the first reason or proof. Reason follows reason, with no other transition than a period and a number; after the last proof is stated there follow the uses or applications, also in numbered sequence, and the sermon ends when there is nothing more to be said. . . . [T]he Puritan begins with a reading of the text, states the reasons in an order determined by logic, and the uses in an enumeration determined by the kinds of persons in the throng who need to be exhorted or reproved, and it stops without flourish or resounding climax. Hence it was accurately described in contemporaneous terms as "plain," and

the Puritan aesthetic led Puritans to the conclusion that because a sermon was plain it was also profitable. (332–33)

Though Miller presents the contrast between Puritan and Anglican preaching in quite definite terms and emphasizes the connection between preaching styles and partisan allegiances, he nonetheless acknowledges that allegiances and preaching style did not always fall into neat categories: "[T]here were Anglicans like Ussher who preached in a mode very similar to the Puritan, and there were moderate Puritans like Henry Smith or Thomas Adams whose works seem to us almost `metaphysical'" (332). As scholars of English Puritanism have recently stressed, distinctions between Puritans and Anglicans in sixteenth- and seventeenth-century England were often both subtle and complex.[6]

The plainness of Puritan preaching is itself more complicated than Puritan polemics suggest.[7] Certainly, as William Ames explained, Puritans believed that preaching should include "no show of human wisdom or mixture of carnal affections; it should manifest itself throughout as the demonstration of the Spirit."[8] Yet as the title of William Perkins's *The Arte of Prophecying* suggests, Reformed theologians saw preaching as an "arte" as well, one that required human labor even though it was "not of humane skill."[9] Bernard noted that preaching "is indeed a very hard worke to be performed, though to the unskilfull it seeme easie" (*Faithfvll*, sig. A3r). As Puritan ministers in early New England prepared to preach to their congregations, they strove to balance their sense of themselves as prophets with their sense of themselves as skilled craftsmen, even as they insisted that the biblical text was accessible to ordinary Christians. Preaching thus required ministers to negotiate complex interactions among the biblical text, the minister, the Holy Spirit, and the congregation. The stakes were high; many Puritans believed that the preached word was the most common means God used to offer his grace to the elect, so negotiating these interactions properly was vital. For guidance, Puritan ministers turned to preaching manuals such as Perkins's *The Arte of Prophecying* (1592) and Bernard's *The Faithfvll Shepheard* (1607). These texts offered copious advice, but they hardly eliminated the challenges of the minister's role. In fact, an examination of Reformed preaching manuals reveals the complexities inscribed in Puritan theories of reading, exegesis, and preaching, and illuminates ways in which these complexities contributed both to the flowering of the Puritan sermon and to interpretive controversy in New England.

789

## THE SERMON MANUALS

The challenges of Puritan exegesis and its communication are revealed by the various sermon manuals and rhetorics that New England ministers consulted. Believing in the importance of the preached word as a vehicle for God's grace, prominent divines composed manuals advising would-be ministers how to shape the most effective sermons possible. And the ministers, faced with the difficult task of composing numerous and lengthy sermons for an eager and demanding audience, found helpful if not always straightforward advice in the various manuals available.[10] New England ministers consulted many texts, including the sections on sacred rhetoric in Johann Heinrich Alsted's *Encyclopaedia scientiarum omnium,* and in Bartholomäus Keckermann's *Opera omnia quae extant,* as well as Keckermann's separately published *Rhetoricae ecclesiasticae.*[11] They also referred to Lutheran rhetorics, including Niels Hemmingsen's *Pastor,* translated as *The Preacher* in 1574, and Andreas Hyperius's *De formandis concionibus,* translated as *The Practis of Preaching* in 1577.[12] Nor did they ignore the insights of earlier reformers, found in works such as Philip Melanchthon's *De officiis concionatores* and Erasmus's *Ecclesiastes,* as well as in more general works of Reformed doctrine.[13] And they were, of course, familiar with a wide range of general rhetorics.[14]

But the two texts most influential among New England ministers were Perkins's *The Arte of Prophecying* and Bernard's *The Faithfvll Shepheard.* Of the two, *The Arte of Prophecying* is now better known, and was probably somewhat more widely used in its own day. Written by "the most widely known theologian of the Elizabethan church," who "by the end of the sixteenth century . . . had replaced Calvin and Beza near the top of the English religious best-seller list," Perkins's concise guide to preaching was "the manual that every nonconforming preacher studied," and which "set the pattern for Puritan manuals and practices."[15] And Bernard's *The Faithfvll Shepheard,* which built on the method and concerns described by Perkins, was one of the best read preaching manuals in New England, "widely read in edition after edition."[16]

Together, these texts by Perkins and Bernard demonstrate the basic assumptions of Puritan exegesis and the tensions between preaching as prophesying and preaching as art. Perkins emphasized the centrality of exegesis to sermon theory. He focused closely on the biblical text, stressing issues of interpretation over issues of presentation, in keeping with Puritan emphasis on preaching what Perry Miller called "the unadulterated word."[17] While "prophecying" was "the matter" of Perkins's text, he devoted much of his preaching manual to a detailed discussion of "the Word of God" itself, describing the content of the various biblical books and commenting on their importance.[18] In his thirty-two-page text, the first twenty-one pages are devoted to the theory of exegesis. Only after covering this material thoroughly did Perkins arrive at uses and applications, and only there did he consider the practical matters of audience, memory, and prayer accompanying preaching (752–62). Perkins's emphasis suggests that in his view, proper exegesis was the bulk of the minister's task, that once one had properly interpreted the text, the shaping of the sermon was a relatively simple matter.

In *The Faithfvll Shepheard,* Bernard built on Perkins's text, apparently finding it too theoretical to provide sufficient guidance. As Bernard's title reveals, he focused more closely on the minister as interpreter and teacher, rather than on the process of teaching and interpretation itself. He was more concerned than Perkins with the minister's personal impact on the congregation, extending his concern even to the minister's appearance, and requiring "a comely countenance not lumpish" (*Faithfvll,* 88). Bernard noted in his initial comments that the minister's responsibility was "the preaching of Gods word, . . . an vnfolding therof to the peoples capacity, with words of exhortation applied to the conscience, both to enforme and reform" (sig. A3r). The word remained at the center, but the minister's presentation of the word framed it. Bernard's text mirrors this structure; he organized his treatise around the experience of the minister, and around the order of occurrences on an occasion of preaching. He began with the importance of the ministry, considered the minister's calling, prayer before the sermon, and then finally the text of the scripture selected for the sermon.

Even then, Bernard's advice was more practically oriented than Perkins's, considering such issues as appropriate language and choosing a text "fit for the hearers" (18). Only having addressed these topics did Bernard explain how to "open" the text; and once more, his discussion maintained a practical focus. He presented not merely a general theory of exegesis, but a guide to opening a text "to the hearers" (20). Though he shared Perkins's sense of the text's centrality, Bernard was attentive to the fact that a minister could not remain entirely transparent. As an imperfect human being, the minister would have both blemishes and virtues. His failings could enrich his preaching, for he could draw on the understanding of sin he had gained in his own experience to render his preaching more effective (73–74). On the other hand, his personal attributes, from appearance and voice to virtues, would be noted by the congregation, who would hear his preaching through these filters. Though a minister's sermons would focus on the biblical text, "Common people respect more a good teachers life, then his learning, and reuerence his person, and not his preaching so much" (93). To negotiate his own role, the minister must be aware of this tendency, exploiting its potential but attending to its dangers as well. For Bernard agreed with Perkins that the text, and not the minister, should remain at the center of the minister's preaching.

## FAITH IN CLARITY AND THE EXPERIENCE OF OBSCURITY

Because they agreed that the Bible stood at the center of Puritan preaching, Perkins and Bernard devoted large portions of their preaching manuals to the methods of exegesis. Drawing on the tradition of Reformed exegesis, they asserted the perfection of the biblical text.[19] The Bible as a whole was unified and coherent. Calvin located the source of this unity in scripture's divine authorship; the Holy Spirit testifies to the unity of scripture, for "He is the Author of the Scriptures: he cannot vary and differ from himself."[20] Like Calvin, Perkins asserted the coherence of the Bible—"the consent of all the parts of the Scripture" (736). Despite the seeming variety of the biblical text, Perkins summarized the import of scripture concisely:

> The Summe of the Scripture is contained in such a syllogisme (or forme of reasoning, as this which followeth.) *The true Messias shall be both God and man of the seede of Dauid; he shall be borne of a Virgin; he shall bring the Gospell forth of his Fathers bosome; he shall satisfie the Law; he shall offer vp himselfe a sacrifice for the sinnes of the faithfull; he shall conquer death by dying and rising againe; he shall ascend into heauen; and in his due time he shall returne vnto judgement. But Iesus of Nazaret the Sonne of Mary is such a one: He therefore is the true Messias.* (732)

All parts of the Bible, in Perkins's formulation, work to prove this syllogism. In its very simplicity, this proposition left Reformed exegetes with a daunting task—to offer their own interpretation of a text that was itself already perfect and coherent. God had communicated his will in this divinely perfect text, and now they as merely human interpreters hoped to illuminate God's will to their congregants. The risk of presumption seemed high indeed. Little wonder that Calvin cautioned the minister to remember the relative unimportance of his own role.

The precariousness of the interpreter's position was intensified by the belief that each text had a single, clear, and literal meaning.[21] No interpretive pluralists, Reformed exegetes (among them New England's first ministers) believed that each verse communicated a particular aspect of God's will, and that it did so clearly—though to fallible human readers, this clarity might not be immediately evident. Martin Luther had asserted the clarity of this divine and perfect text energetically, proclaiming "that Scripture, without any gloss, is the sun and the sole light from which all teachers receive their light, and not the contrary."[22] But other reformers qualified Luther's assertion, disagreeing about how clear the biblical text was to imperfect human beings. Erasmus, for example "took a skeptical view of man's ability to understand and apply Scripture."[23] And Calvin, though he insisted that "Scripture, gathering up the otherwise confused knowledge of God in our minds, having dispersed our dullness, clearly shows us the true God," nevertheless "realized that [scripture] was not so clear that it needs no explanation. On the contrary, it was to this task that he devoted his life."[24]

As they composed their sermon manuals, Perkins and Bernard took into account both Luther's insistence on the Bible's clarity and their own empirical knowledge that the biblical text did not always seem as clear to them as Luther's polemical texts argued. Perkins, in fact, never asserted the clarity of scripture in *The Arte of Prophecying*, for all that he insisted upon the Bible's "excellencie," "perfection," "sufficiencie," and "puritie" (731). He did insist that "euery article and doctrine concerning faith and maners, which is necessarie vnto saluation, is very plainely deliuered in the Scriptures." Nevertheless, he found that in the biblical text, "Places are either Analogicall and plaine, or Crypticall and darke" (740). While the text as a whole might be, as Luther asserted, "without any gloss, . . . the sun and the sole light," Perkins found justification for metaphors of darkness to describe some passages.[25]

Unlike Perkins, Bernard did make a Lutheran assertion of scriptural clarity. Having instructed the preacher to paraphrase the biblical text, he suggested that there were exceptions to this rule. Namely, this "thing is not to be done where the words are plaine without any obscuritie in them" (*Faithfvll*, 26). But the order of Bernard's instructions suggested that this kind of clarity might be the exception. Having started with the practical need for paraphrase, Bernard found himself on theoretically (or at least doctrinally) delicate ground, and carefully qualified his use of the term "obscuritie." Like Perkins, he found that "euerie Scripture is either plainly set downe, and the words to be taken properly as they lie in the letter: (So is euery doctrin of Faith and meners necessary to saluation set downe) which needs no explication of words, but inlarging of the matter: or else obscurely; and this needs an exposition" (26). Nevertheless, Bernard insisted, "No Scripture is in itselfe obscure, but that wee want eie-sight to behold what is therein conteined. The Sunne is euer cleere, though wee through our blindnesse cannote see the shining; or for that some dark clouds hinder our sight, which are to be remooued, that we may looke vpon it" (26). The biblical text might be a source of clarity and divine light, but for the human reader, Perkins and Bernard insisted, finding that light could be difficult.

## HIGH STAKES AND LITERAL MEANING

Finding each biblical text's single, stable meaning was rendered more difficult by the Reformed commitment to "naturall sense" or "literal" meaning, for these terms were used to describe a mode of interpretation more complex than might at first be thought. In *The Arte of Prophecying,* Perkins defined "interpretation" as "the *Opening* of the wordes and sentences of the Scripture, that one entire and naturall sense may appeare" (737). Denying the interpreter's subjectivity, Perkins saw the exegete as "open[ing]" what already existed to his reader or listener, rather than actively interpreting. Bernard, too, asserted that "There is but one true and naturall sense of euerie place, which is the literall sense, that which the holie Ghost principally intendeth there: and accordingly can there be giuen but one true and right interpretation of the words and sentence" (28). Because the scripture was God's word, and because there was a single legitimate interpretation "of euerie place," the stakes were high in the interpretive process. An interpreter's task was to isolate the one correct meaning, if he was to identify properly "that which the holie Ghost principally intendeth" (28). And Bernard stated firmly that that meaning was the "literall sense" (28).

But this hardly cleared up all interpretive problems. The word "literal" itself was a polemical term, marshaled against the pattern of fourfold interpretation prevalent in medieval exegesis.[26] Reformed exegetes could trace their rejection of the fourfold sense of scripture to Luther, who dismissed "the literal, the allegorical, the anagogical, and the tropological, for which there is no foundation whatever."[27] Perkins and Bernard echoed this rejection emphatically, with Perkins calling for the "deuice of the fourefold meaning of the Scripture" to "be exploded and reiected," and italicizing his assertion that *"There is one only sense, and the same is the literal"* (737).

But even in Luther's impassioned *Answer to the Superchristian, Superspiritual, and Superlearned Book of Goat Emser of Leipzig with a Glance at His Comrade Murner,* the distinction between literal and other readings was muddied. Luther noted that the term "literal" was far from adequate, pointing out that this meaning was "therefore not well named the literal sense, for by letter Paul means something quite different. They do much better who call it the grammatical, historical sense. It would be well to call it the speaking or language sense as St. Paul does in I Corinthians xiv, because it is understood by everybody in the sense of the spoken language" (353). But even this was not quite what Luther meant. For despite his insistence upon this "speaking or language sense," he nevertheless in his next sentence allowed for "hidden meanings . . . called mysteries" that were revealed by the Spirit (353). Even Luther's rejection of allegory was oddly qualified. While he called "the interpretation of obscure passages and allegories . . . a merry chase," preferring instead "to be at home in Scripture, and, as St. Paul says, able to contend with abundant clear passages, without any glosses and commentaries, as with a bared and drawn sword," Luther's next sentence offered an allegorical reading. "This," he asserted, "is the significance of the golden spears in Solomon's temple. Then the adversary, convinced by the clear light, must see and confess that the words of God stand alone and need not the explanation of man" (334–35). As this was hardly the "grammatical" or "historical" sense of the spears in Solomon's temple, it would seem that even for Luther, the literal sense had a surprisingly unliteral flexibility.[28]

English reformers, among them Perkins and Bernard, waffled similarly even as they insisted on literal meaning. Perkins, after asserting that the only true sense is the literal, nevertheless expanded his definition to include the three other means of interpretation: "An allegorie is onely a certaine manner of vttering the same sense. The Anagoge and Tropologie are waies, whereby the sense may be applied" (737).[29] Perkins instructed his students that the *"natiue (or naturall) signification of the words"* was to be set aside if it *"doe manifestly disagree with, either the analogy of faith, or very perspicuous places of the Scriptures"* (740). Bernard summarized the approach quite neatly, by identifying the "literall sense" with "that which the holie Ghost principally intendeth" (28). The proper interpretation was that which accorded with the analogy of faith: *"Sensus proprius & genuina interpretatio,* is that which makes the place to agree to the chiefe purpose and scope of the holie Ghost intended in that same place of Scripture" (28).

Bernard never explicitly qualified his definition of the literal sense—he never asserted that the literal could include the tropological, anagogical, or allegorical senses. He did, however, assert that some scriptures "are not to be taken literally, but figuratively," and went so far as to explain "how wee may make an Allegorie, which is not simplie vnlawfull; for the Apostle doth allegorize, *1.Cor. 9.9*" (31, 53). Though Bernard suggested that allegories be used "briefly, and . . . not too often," he shared with Perkins a fluid and flexible allegiance to literal meaning (53).

Both Perkins and Bernard explained how to determine whether one should look beyond the literal reading of a given biblical text. Perkins considered the analogy of faith and the argument of other parts of scripture sufficient reason for rejecting the literal interpretation, defining "the analogie of faith" as "a certain *abridgement* or *summe* of the Scriptures, collected out of most manifest & familiar places" (737). Perkins's method required foreknowledge; one could not interpret properly without knowing already what the text ought to mean as well as what it could not mean. And that foreknown meaning was authoritative; although Perkins enumerated neither the details nor the arbiter of the analogy of faith, the "certain" interpretation it included carried enough authority to outweigh biblical passages that seemed to contradict it.

Recognizing that Perkins's construction left room for interpretive conflict, Bernard, always the more practical of the two, spelled out clearly the components of the analogy of faith. Most vague was the first element, "the principles of Religion," but from then on the criteria were familiar and seemingly straightforward: "the points of the Catechisme set downe in the Creed, the Lords Praier, the ten Commandements, and the doctrine of Sacraments" (28). Eventually, even the meaning of the Ten Commandments would fall into dispute in New England.[30] Nevertheless, Bernard's more specified analogy of faith provided the would-be interpreter with a more useable interpretive guideline than Perkins's.

Bernard also expanded the list of factors that could displace a literal reading considerably beyond the analogy of faith and the argument of other parts of scripture: the Scriptures cannot be read literally "if the words carrie a shew of any thing against the analogie of faith, or against the Scriptures, or against the scope of the Scripture, or against common good, or against the light of nature, conteining anie absurditie or shew of euill" (31). The grounds for dismissal of the literal meaning, in Bernard's own words the "one true and naturall sense of euerie place," had become surprisingly broad, and surprisingly human. Bernard's explicit introduction of criteria external to scripture, and even external to theology itself, is especially striking in his discussion of Matthew 26:26, which he marshaled as an example of a passage that could not be read literally: "This is an obscure Scripture, & cannot be meant literallie as the Papists expound them; as if Christ had said; This bread is my naturall bodie, borne of the virgin *Marie* my mother, by transubstantiation; for it is absurd and too grosse a conceit" (32). Although Calvin, too, called the literalist reading "absurd," he took the opposing position seriously enough to dismantle it step by step.[31] Bernard, on the other hand, was brief and dismissive, and his labeling of the opposing position a "grosse . . . conceit" suggests a greater confidence in human abilities to distinguish absurdity and "grosseness" from mystery.[32] He referred neither to other sections of the Bible nor to the analogy of faith, but instead to his own judgment as a reader of scripture.

The Reformed insistence on literal meaning, then, boiled down in practice to an insistence on a meaning consistent with orthodox doctrine. The same exegetes who supported "sola scriptura" as a standard freely admitted that all was found in scripture only if one knew in advance what the Bible meant. And while interpretive circularity may be unsurprising in a religious hermeneutic, the willingness of exegetes to declare that circularity as an interpretive rule does seem surprising, especially in exegetes so uncomfortable with institutional mediation of biblical interpretation.

## Divine and Human Interpretive Assistance

Rather than emphasizing human interpretation, Puritan exegetes stressed instead the assistance of the Holy Spirit, who enabled the human reader to understand the divine text. Perkins asserted that "The Elect hauing the Spirit of God" could "discerne the voyce of Christ speaking in the Scriptures"; for them, "the holy Ghost" was "the principall interpreter of the Scripture" (734, 737). In his understanding of Spirit-enabled reading, Perkins drew on Calvin's assertion that one could not hope to understand even scriptural clarity without the illumination of the Holy Spirit: "Indeed, the Word of God is like the sun, shining upon all those to whom it is proclaimed, but with no effect among the blind. Now, all of us are blind by nature in this respect. Accordingly, it cannot penetrate into our minds unless the Spirit, as the inner teacher, through his illumination makes entry for it."[33] Divine illumination from within the reader thus closed the gap between reader and author.

In postulating that proper reading resulted not from the Christian's own efforts but rather from the light of the Spirit within him, Perkins and Bernard denied the problem of subjective and potentially erring reading by erasing themselves as subjects.[34] They considered themselves not interpreters so much as conduits of the Holy Spirit's interpretive power. Bernard treated even human logic as "an especiall handmaid by the assistance of Gods spirit" (25).[35] In a reversal of Roland Barthes's later proclamation that "the birth of the reader must be at the cost of the death of the Author," Perkins and Bernard posited instead that it was the reader who must die—to the world—to experience his own rebirth as a Christian and thus as an enabled reader.[36] For them, the "Author-God" of Barthes's account was not only alive, but potentially present (146). The spiritual death of the subjective and erring reader would allow direct and even intimate access to Authorial intention; to a reader enabled by divine grace, "the minde and meaning of the H Ghost" were in fact knowable (*Arte*, 738).

The presence of the divine interpreter ought to resolve all hermeneutical problems, and render all "obscurities" clear. But few readers could depend on moments of intense clarity, like that described confidently by Anne Hutchinson in her examination before the General Court.[37] So Perkins and Bernard provided would-be exegetes with guidance to supplement the assistance of the Holy Spirit. Both were attentive to the delicacy of the minister's role; in "opening" the text to their congregants, ministers risked implying that human exegetes could make God's word clearer than He could. Consequently, Perkins and Bernard emphasized techniques that minimized the minister's role and privileged interpretive tools that, at least in theory, allowed the text to interpret itself.

Specifically, they relied on reading the verse in context ("the circumstances of the place propounded") and collation ("the comparing of places altogether") as their primary interpretive methods (*Arte*, 737). Perkins asserted firmly, "The supreame and absolute meane of interpretation is the Scripture it selfe" (737). And for Perkins, "The meanes subordinated to the Scripture are three; the Analogie of faith, the circumstances of the place propounded, and the comparing of places altogether" (737). The analogy of faith set the interpretive limits, and within those limits, "the circumstances of the place propounded" and "the comparing of places altogether" were the interpreter's tools.

Using these tools, the interpreter's first step was to examine a text in its context, or according to "the circumstances of the place propounded" (737). Perkins listed questions to be asked of a text: "*Who? to whom? upon what occasion? at what time? in what place? for what end? what goeth before? what followeth?*" (737–38). In *The Faithfvll Shepheard*, Bernard repeated Perkins's list, but expanded on the question of "end." Probably drawing on Matthaeus Flacius Illyricus's *Clavis scripturae sacrae* (1567), Bernard distinguished "between the words of a text and its purpose, or *scopus*": "We may not onely looke vpon one word and sentence, and thereupon iudge of all: the scope must withall bee diligently attended vnto, wherefore the words are spoken."[38] Nor was this "wherefore" a straightforward one; Bernard's earlier use of the term "scope" reveals that he meant not the purpose for which a particular biblical personage speaks certain words, but rather the intention of the "holie Ghost . . . in that same place of Scripture" (28). The "circumstances of the place" thus transcended the immediate textual context and required the interpreter to have insight into the will of the divine author. Once again, the human interpreter's role was presented as secondary to God's will, both as articulated in the text and as interpreted by the Holy Spirit.

Having considered the "circumstances of the place propounded," the exegete then turned to the interpretive tool most influential in Puritan writing, "the collation or comparing of places together" (*Arte*, 738). In collation, different texts "are set parallels one beside an other, that the meaning of them may more euidently appeare" (738). Collation reflects belief in both the unity and the self-interpretive capacity of the Bible. Since the unity of scripture precludes self-contradiction, Calvin deemed the use of biblical texts to clarify each other a strong and safe interpretive tool.[39] And Luther cited not only his belief in scriptural self-sufficiency, but also interpretive precedent: "[A]ll the fathers concede their own obscurity and illumine Scripture by Scripture alone. And that is the true method of interpretation which puts Scripture alongside of Scripture in a right and proper way; the father who can do this best is the best among them."[40] In theory, these exegetes asserted, collation allows scripture to interpret itself, limiting the involvement of the human interpreter.

But Perkins's rhetoric reveals his awareness of the human interpreter nevertheless. He compared exegetes practicing collation to "Artificers beeing about to compact or ioyne a thing together," who "are wont to fit all the parts amongst themselues, that one of them may perfectly agree with each other" (738). Bernard's description, too, conceded that the interpreter was more than a passive conduit. While the scripture was ostensibly interpreting itself, Bernard nonetheless noted that not "euerie text requires . . . this much trouble," recognizing the human interpretive effort expended in this process (31).

In New England, the human interpreter's role was enlarged by the fluidity of the seventeenth-century biblical text itself. In the first half of the seventeenth century, allegiances to particular biblical translations were shifting, as the ministers gradually moved from a Genevan standard to more frequent use of the Authorized Version.[41] As Harry S. Stout explains, "[T]he Geneva Bible was a *popular* Reformation document," its commentaries and glosses emphasizing "the person and work of Jesus Christ" and "personal salvation and eternal life," and ignoring "technical disputes . . . common among English and Continental Churchmen."[42] The Authorized Version of 1611, on the other hand, was "an establishment Bible of impeccable social and intellectual credentials" (25). Stout suggests that this was a Bible better suited to "building an entire social order according to scriptural blueprint," and thus finds it unsurprising that Puritans often shifted their allegiances from "the Geneva Bible . . . [which had] served well the purpose of an embattled religious minority" as their "numbers and influence" grew (25–26).

As Michael Ditmore reveals in his shrewd analysis of Anne Hutchinson's revelations, these changing biblical allegiances complicated debates over the biblical text.[43] But shifting textual allegiances did not always divide sharply. Stout notes that Puritan writers often drew on different translations to reflect different emphases, citing John Winthrop's *Modell of Christian Charitie* to demonstrate "how the Puritan leaders" drew on multiple Bible translations to "[fuse] the original concern with personal salvation to the novel task of model society building" (27–28). Issues other than theology and ideology affected this process as well. For example, Christopher Hill notes that the popularity of the Geneva Bible was undercut by the costliness of printing its "elaborate notes and apparatus," which eventually "priced it out of the market."[44]

Nor were competing printed translations the only complications to the notion of an authoritative biblical text. In addition to the Geneva and Authorized versions, Puritan writers learned in Hebrew and Greek often provided their own translations of biblical passages. Sometimes they pasted together portions of Geneva and Authorized translations (or other versions), and at other times they bypassed them altogether. In fact, standardized translation was itself a matter of theoretical debate. In a tract dealing with set forms of prayer, John Cotton found it necessary to consider whether reliance on a particular biblical translation constituted dependence on a set form.[45] He argued that since "the reading of *Scripture* in the Church is an ordinance of God," as is "the reading of it in a tongue which the people understandeth, . . . therefore it is an ordinance of God that the Word be read in some translation" (11). Nevertheless, he considered it admirable for "Every Minister that hath understanding of the originall languages where in the *Scripture* was written out to make use of his own gift in examining the truth of the translation which he readeth unto the Church" (12). Bernard, on the other hand, cautioned against taking this too far, and indulging in quibbling criticism of existing translations.[46]

Even those for whom unfixed translation was not a major ideological concern often produced their own idiosyncratic quotations from biblical passages. Studying multiple Bible versions and preaching from memory, often with only minimal notes, many ministers included numerous "quotations" that were not drawn from a single translation, but instead blended published translations with their own formulations.[47] Such passages were often shaped by their writers' individual views and emphases, emerging from a more active interaction between the reader/writer and the biblical text than their status as quotations might suggest.

Indeed, collation as described by Perkins and Bernard was an expansive and flexible interpretive category, and it became the primary exegetical tool of the New England divines. Perkins divided collation into two categories. The first was "the comparing of the place propounded with it selfe cited and repeated else-where in the holy writ," in other words, an examination of biblical repetition (738). In examining instances of repetition, Perkins instructed the would-be exegete to consider the purposes of both exact repetition and repetition with variations.[48] Most notable among these variations were those that were "circumscriptive: or for limitation sake, that the sense and sentence of the place might be truely restrained, according as the minde and meaning of the H Ghost was," and those in which "some things are omitted for breuitie sake: or because they doe not agree with the matter at hand" (738–39). In both cases, Perkins cited examples in which New Testament repetitions "clarify" texts of the Old Testament, and used his understanding of variations to buttress his view of testamentary unity.

What Perkins called the second kind of collation was simply comparison of the verse in question to other verses, "either like or vnlike" (739). The exegete might use almost any other biblical text on the basis of similarity or difference in phrasing or meaning (739–40). Seemingly uncomfortable with the interpretive freedom generated by comparing "vnlike" texts, Bernard separated similar and dissimilar verses into two distinct categories, and offered some cautions about the latter (30). He reminded his readers that "discord is not in Scripture, neither one place contrarie to another, albeit through ignorance it seeme so to vs; but it is not so indeed" (30). Moreover, Bernard expanded further on his examples. For instance, Perkins was content to quote the seemingly contradictory Romans 3:28 and James 2:24, trusting his reader's ability to resolve the tension between the assertion in Romans that "a man is iustified by faith without the workes of the Law," and the parallel assertion in James that "of workes a man is iustified; & not of faith onely" (740). Betraying anxiety that Perkins's conciseness might lead readers astray, Bernard carefully resolved the contradiction, explaining that Paul and James are not speaking of the same thing at all. Paul is "speaking of faith iustifiying before God: and *Iames* of faith iustifying before men" (31). Bernard conceded that collation could raise difficult questions, and that answering those questions according to the analogy of faith was not always easy.

The texts of *The Arte of Prophecying* and *The Faithfvll Shepheard* themselves reveal another important consequence of collation for Puritan texts. Collation tends to open exegesis outward, provoking digressive discussions of the collated texts. This practice meant that in a sermon on a given text, any other biblical text could be not only cited, but discussed at some length. John Cotton's sermons dramatize this most fully, for Cotton brings not only verses but whole sections of other biblical texts into play, enriching and complicating sermons (and even sermon series) that focus ostensibly on one short verse.[49] This has not only artistic, but also didactic functions, for it keeps more texts circulating in the listeners' consciousness.

But collation generates other sorts of fluidity as well. In a 1970 article, Stefan Morawski explores "The Basic Functions of Quotation," offering a taxonomy of quotation and its literary and linguistic functions.[50] Morawski is not especially interested in quotation from authoritative sources; and in distinguishing between what he calls the authoritative function of quotation and its erudite, stimulative-amplificatory, and ornamental functions, he ignores instances of overlap between his categories. Identifying quotation from an authoritative text, including "the fathers of the church referring either to the Bible or their predecessors," with an "appeal to authorities," he condemns "[t]he quotation which functions by virtue of an authoritative validity accepted by both writer and reader" as "evidence of both intellectual torpor and emotional-ritual assiduity" (692–93).

In fact, though, Puritan manipulation of collated biblical quotations fulfills all of the functions Morawski outlines. While the interpretive authority of the biblical text is foremost, quotation from that text in the sermons demonstrates the minister's skill, amplifies the original text, and ornaments the presentation. Despite his lack of interest in quotations that retain their authoritative status, Morawski's discussion of the "stimulative-amplificatory function" illuminates the way collation produces interpretive fluidity. In interpreting its "classical texts," Morawski explains, "[e]very period of history approaches its heritage anew. By rearranging and regrading the basic elements of this legacy, it also gives it a slightly altered meaning. In such a restructuralization of a particular philosophical theory the quotation plays a double role: it both continues and breaches the tradition, that is, uncovers angles of inquiry which were unknown or forgotten"(694). By quoting from other portions of the biblical text, one reasserts their authoritative status. At the same time, by bending them to one's interpretive project, one alters the meaning of those texts slightly.

Morawski's observation can be rendered in terms of Perkins's and Bernard's own interpretive rules. Both Perkins and Bernard asserted the importance of context to understand the verse in question; in fact, context was given precedence over collation in the order of interpretation. But collated verses were necessarily severed from their own contexts. Generally, the contexts of the collated verses were given at best slight attention; more often they were ignored. So the meaning of collated verses, according to the system's own rules, could be misinterpreted. At the very least, it was destabilized. Perkins addressed this risk, cautioning "that collections ought to be right and sound, that is to say, drawn from the genuine and proper meaning of the Scripture. If otherwise, we shall draw any doctrine from any place" (751). In other words, collation potentially leads to something like interpretive freeplay.

Bernard's comments on the problems of excessive quotation reflect his discomfort with the possible consequences of collation. He forcefully condemned the proliferation of quotations in some ministers' preaching:

> a new vpstart quoting of Scripture now vsed, Chapter and Verse for euerie word: It is an irreuerent abuse, a superfluous and prophane tossing of the Scriptures, without profit to the hearers; whose vnderstanding can neither conceiue them, nor memorie beare them away. Pride the inuentor, to publish the excellencie of memorie, seeking praise from Gods gift, and making

admirable his naturall worke by abusing his word, like *Iudas* in shew of loue to kisse him, whilest in kissing they betray him. (58)

Though ostensibly collation allowed scripture to interpret itself, Bernard recognized that ministers might "abuse" God's word, rather than opening it, emphasizing their own "excellencie of memorie" and skill at "naturall worke" (58). Those who did so were "irreuerent" prideful upstarts, Judases who betrayed God, "God's gift," and their congregations.

Richard Sibbes, too, cautioned against overemphasizing the importance of biblical language. Those who mistake understanding of scriptural logic and rhetoric for "the things themselves," he warned, "stick in the stile."[51] In *The Sword of the Spirit*, John Knott suggests that "Sibbes displays a typically Puritan reluctance to attach excessive importance to the language of the Bible," carefully preserving "the distinction between the text and the Word itself, insisting that Scripture is but the 'modus' for conveying the Word (1:197)" (51). But the extent of that reluctance is unclear; Knott places it between the argument that biblical words are mere "husks, to be discarded to get at kernels of meaning" and "the kind of absorption in the text that one finds in Donne" (51). This range is broad, to say the least, and the texts of the colonial ministers suggest that many Puritan writers stood closer to Donne's side of the continuum than to the huskers at the other end.

Thomas Shepard's sermons often include the obsessive quotation to which Bernard objected so strenuously. In *The Sound Believer*, for example, Shepard often strings together biblical quotations to compose his text:

> Consider the glory of the place: the Jews did and do dream stil of an earthly kingdom, at the coming of their Messiah; the Lord dasheth those dreams, and tells them "his kingdom is not of this world," and that he "went away to prepare a place for them, that where he is, they might be," (John xiv. 2, 3,) and "be with him to see his glory." (John xvii. 23, 24.) The place shall be the third heaven, called our father's house, built by his own hand with most exquisite wisdom, fit for so great a God to appear in his glory (John xiv. 2, 3) to all his dear children; called also a "kingdom." (Matt. xxv. 31,) "Come ye blessed, inherit the kingdom prepared for you," which is the top of all the worldly excellency, called also "an inheritance," (1 Pet. i. 3,) which the holy apostle infinitely blesseth God for . . . .[52]

Certainly Shepard did not mean to commit "an irreuerent abuse"; rather, his appropriation of scriptural language to describe things that he had not seen seemed to him pious and humble, an attempt to place God's words, rather than his own, in the ears of his listeners.[53]

But in practicing the art of collation, stringing texts together to construct his own, the skilled minister-exegete might call attention to his own virtuosity. And such virtuosity was often noted and praised, both by colleagues among the clergy and by lay auditors. Samuel Danforth, for example, was reputed to have "fed his flock" with sermons that "were elaborate and substantial; he was a notable *text-man*, and one who had more than forty or fifty scriptures distinctly quoted in one discourse."[54] In his biography of John Cotton, John Norton reported that "It was wont to be said, *bonus textuarius est bonus Theologus:* A good Text-man is a good Divine."[55] When Cotton Mather praised George Phillips as "Mighty in the Scriptures," he demonstrated the emphasis that Puritan readers placed on virtuosic scriptural fluency, as well as the playfulness that such fluency could inscribe (*Magnalia*, 1:376). Mather noted that Phillips could locate *"any* text, without the help of concordances" (1:378). As he praised Phillips's scriptural skills, he demonstrated his own scriptural prowess by casting his praise in the language of Acts 18:24.[56] In doing so, Mather winked at his reader, affirming Phillips's skills but calling attention to his own scriptural virtuosity as well. The technique of collation, then, often called attention to the role of the human interpreter, even as it ostensibly left the act of interpretation to the Holy Spirit.

Though the Holy Spirit offered the most important interpretive assistance, Reformed preaching manuals advised supplementing this spiritual guidance with a wide variety of human interpretive aids. Bernard found that for a minister to interpret *"faithfully and soundly," "by necessarie consequent"* from the method he laid out, that minister needed *"much knowledge"* (35). A "diuersitie of knowledge in seuerall things which many brings with him to the reading of Scripture," Bernard argued, "are as many candles to giue light to see into his text" (36). Bernard outlined that "diuersitie of knowledge" over seven pages, ranging from grammar and languages, to "Rhetoricke," and "the rest of the Liberall Sciences," including "naturall Philosophie, Oeconomickes, Ethicks, Politiques, Geographie, Cosmographie: . . . Antiquities, . . . Histories," and, of course, theology (35–37). Without such knowledge, Bernard asserted, "no man can worke cunningly vpon euerie text, if he want the instrument, (that is) the skil of that arte which should help him therein" (36). In support of such "arte," the minister required an extensive library, including works on "Husbandrie" and even "Histories of Iewish customes," as well as multiple biblical translations and theological texts (38–42). And finally, of course, Bernard reminded his readers that "a Minister besides all these helpes, must haue to rule and direct him in these subordinate meanes, the holie spirit of God, the onely true interpretour of the Scriptures; which are his owne words; who is the spirit of trueth, leading and guiding all his in the same; without which men for all the meanes, may runne into errours, and grow into heresies" (42). In Perkins's formulation, however, reliance on such an extensive library was not to be acknowledged to the laity. In opening the text to their congregations, ministers were to stress the assistance of the Spirit, not the scholarly labor involved in producing their readings.[57]

Indeed, when presenting the Bible to their congregations, the ministers were advised by Perkins and Bernard to downplay the labor of exegesis. Perkins's ministerial reader was advised to "vnderstand that the Minister may, yea & must priuately vse at his libertie the artes, philosophy, and varietie of reading, whilest he is in framing his sermon" (759). The difficulties of exegesis required these interpretive aids. "But," Perkins cautioned, "he ought in publike to conceale all these from the people, and not to make the least ostentation. *Artis etiam celare artiam; it is also a point of Art to conceale Art*": "*Humane wisedome* must be concealed, whether it be in the matter of the sermon, or in the setting forth of the words: because the preaching of the word is the *Testimonie of God, and the profession of the knowledge of Christ,* and not of humane skill: and againe, because the hearers ought not to ascribe their faith to the gifts of men, but to the power of Gods word" (759). The minister should, in Perkins's formulation, make his own efforts seem as transparent as possible to the power of the text itself, acknowledging publicly only the assistance of the Holy Spirit.

Stanley Fish suggests that, in effacing the preacher and privileging the Holy Spirit, "the Puritan sermon," though "self-effacing in style," is actually "self-glorying (in two directions) in effect, for by making no claim to be art, it makes the largest claim of all, that it simply tells the truth. The Anglicans may *display* language, but it is the Puritans who take *pride* in language, because it is the Puritans who take language seriously."[58] Indeed, this is the paradox of the minister as prophet and craftsman. If the minister's self-effacement is successful, he has become not only a skilled artisan but also a true prophet and conduit for the Holy Spirit, a role that is no less important for its ostensible transparency.

## Sermon Structure and the Illusion of Transparency

Perkins and Bernard advised Puritan ministers to structure their sermons in ways that minimized the impression of their own artistry as well. This advice has drawn considerable scholarly attention. Indeed, the best-known section of *The Arte of Prophecying* is Perkins's final summary of sermon structure, which appears almost as an afterthought to the text. Having explained the process of interpretation, Perkins advised ministers what to do once they had succeeded in interpreting the text properly. Between the concluding "*Trin-*

*uni Deo gloria"* at the end of his final page and the list of "Writers which lent their helpe to the framing" of his text, Perkins provided brief guidelines on structuring sermons in accordance with Ramist principles, "The Order and Summe of the sacred and onely methode of *Preaching*":

1. To read the Text distinctly out of the Canonical Scriptures.
2. To give the sense and understanding of it being read, by the Scripture it selfe.
3. To collect a few and profitable points of doctrine out of the natu- rall sense.
4. To apply (if he have the gift) the doctrines rightly collected to the life and maners of men, in a simple and plaine speech.
   The Summe of the Summe.
   Preach one Christ by Christ to the Praise of Christ. (762)[59]

Though Miller acknowledged that "[e]ven the division into doctrine, reasons, and uses was not absolutely obligatory," Puritanists have often taken Perkins too much at his word, seeing these guidelines as strict rules formulating an inflexible structure and leaving little room for artistry.[60] Everett Emerson, for example, describes Thomas Hooker as "pour[ing] his sermons into a mould which had been prepared by" Perkins and Ames.[61] And Edward Davidson argues that "sermons delivered in the New England churches throughout the seventeenth and well into the eighteenth century were formulaic," and that this formulaic quality rendered "the inscrutable . . . regular" and "turned" the "threatening . . . into numbers and order."[62] While Davidson sees this for- mulaic quality as in some ways beneficial, other scholars have assessed it less generously. J. W. Blench, for example, notes that "this form becomes un- bearably tedious to the modern reader after but a few pages," although he concedes that "it does not inevitably lead to dullness."[63]

More recent scholarship about Puritan sermons has focused on the im- plementation of these guidelines, recognizing the fluidity with which minis- ters applied them. Most significantly, Teresa Toulouse illuminates some of the conflicts inherent in Perkins's form, emphasizing the tensions between art and prophecy, between preaching to the elect and preaching to the unre- generate, and between passivity and voluntarism. She argues that the struggle with these tensions causes Perkins's model, and even more so the sermons of those who use that model, to draw "attention from the scriptural text and place it on" the section of the sermon dealing with uses.[64] And other scholars have noted more generally that "[t]he Puritan sermon . . . is more open- ended than its schematic presentation of reasons and uses might seem to im- ply," and that sermons were rarely developed as simply as Perkins's guidelines might suggest.[65] While many sermons did not follow Perkins's structural guidelines precisely, however, they drew on them in ways that remained true to the guidelines' purpose: privileging the text over the minister, and rendering the minister and his labor as transparent as possible to the biblical text and to God's word.

## Concealed Art and the Lay Reader

The ministers' effort to minimize attention to their labor complicated both the reading practices of the laity and relations between ministers and their congregations. In sermons and in other texts of piety, laypeople were exhorted to read the Bible on their own, imitating their ministers' exegesis and even evaluating it. Ministers expected their preaching to guide this reading, and many among the laity were eager to meet that expectation; the main activity of seventeenth-century English Protestant conventicles was repetition of the minister's sermon, or at least of its main outlines.[66] But lay readers were expected as well to read beyond the verses that their ministers had discussed. The compilers of the Geneva Bible provided readers with a table advising "How to take profite in reading of the holy Scriptures," suggesting that people read the Bible at least twice daily.[67] In *The Practise of Pietie*, Lewis Bayly offered the Christian a schedule, according to which, by reading three chapters a day and six on the last day of the year, he could read the Bible through each year.[68] John Cotton had even exhorted his congregants in Old Boston to "goe home" from church "and consider whether the things that have been taught were true or no; whether agreeable to the holy Scriptures or no."[69]

It was assumed, then, that in addition to the mediated encounter with the biblical text offered by the sermon, the faithful reader would study the Bible independently. But the laity's attempts at exegesis were necessarily handicapped, at least according to the clergy's assumptions. Bernard cautioned ministers not to overestimate the skills of the unlearned: "For there is nothing so cleere, but euen the maine points of Christianitie needeth opening . . . to such as be uncatechised, and not instructed in the common tearmes of Religion as God, Sauiour, Law, Gospell, Faith, Repentance, Flesh, Spirit, and so foorth" (32). Acknowledging "how hard a thing it is to vnderstand the holy Scriptures, and what errors, sects and heresies grow dayly for lack of the true knowledge thereof," the Geneva Bible editors provided their readers with marginal glosses.[70] Christopher Hill notes as well that "[u]nofficial guides to interpretation of the Bible, Biblical dictionaries and concordances, versifications of Scripture, were published in significant numbers in the early seventeenth century: they were clearly in demand, especially by the 'middling sort.'"[71]

But the glosses and guides hardly provided the average reader with all the knowledge that Perkins and Bernard deemed necessary for proper understanding. Moreover, because the ministers were advised to conceal their use of these tools from their congregants, the congregants could not even recognize the limitations of their own readings.

In fact, ministers were advised to avoid material that might call attention to the difficulties of interpretation. Bernard, for example, advised his readers:

> Obscure Scriptures about which must necessarilie arise questions of controuersies, leaue for Schooles, and handle not amongst the common people and vulgar sort. Common assemblies are not meet either to heare or iudge of controuersies; yet it is a fault of many Preachers, who vse commonly in euery Sermon, to raise vp one point or other in disputation, about which they spend the most of their time, often without iust occasion or necessarie cause: but the fruit of these mens labors is in their hearers contention, talk about words, quiddities and vain ostentation; but not faith working by loue and holie sanctification. (18)

Complexities of interpretation should be left to the "Schooles," warned Bernard. Such topics would only confuse the laity and ensnare them in controversy, for they lacked the learning necessary to understand such issues. On the other hand, the strategy that Bernard advised left the laity untrained in controversy itself, making the interpretive process seem easier and more straightforward than it was. If a minister followed Bernard's advice, his congregants might fail to understand how much their lack of learning affected their interpretive abilities.

Even the assistance of the Spirit, which ministers were advised to acknowledge, and indeed emphasize, could not be taken for granted. For Puritan divines did not assume that their congregants were necessarily reading in the Spirit. Perkins and Bernard described six different types of audiences a preacher might face: the ignorant and unteachable, the teachable yet ignorant, those with some knowledge who are not yet humbled, those who are humbled, those who believe, and those who are fallen.[72] But the audience ministers must expect to face, asserted Perkins and Bernard, was a "mingled people" or those "mixt of all," from the defiantly unregenerate to the believing pious (*Arte*, 756; *Faithfull*, 11). Even in New England, where many hoped that the defiantly unregenerate would be few, ministers had to assume that their audiences would be at least in part unregenerate. The ministers' responsibility to this portion of their flock was in some ways greater. For the elect, as noted above, are divinely enabled: they "doe first discerne the voyce of Christ speaking in the Scriptures. Moreouer, that voyce, which they doe discerne, they do

approue, and that which they doe approue, they doe beleeue. Lastly, beleeu-
ing they are (as it were) sealed with the seale of the Spirit" (*Arte*, 734).
Preaching is not superfluous for them, as Puritans believed that the elect were
most likely to discern Christ's voice in scripture when hearing it preached,
rather than merely reading it. But for those listeners who could hear only
the minister preaching, and not Christ's voice, the minister's interpretation of
scripture was especially vital. As Toulouse notes, "[I]f Perkins acknowledges
the sole power of the Spirit to infuse spiritual knowledge within an already
justified soul, he also recognizes the practical, pastoral responsibilities of the
preacher to an entire community of listeners" (16). She identifies Perkins's
recommended sermon form as his attempt to negotiate "between his sense of
a congregation's incapacity before God and his need to give them some voluntary responsibility in matters of salvation": "Perkins wishes the Spirit to
speak through his words in a special way for the elect and at the same time
desires to persuade his entire congregation to moral behavior" (21).

While effective preaching might foster moral behavior, it could not itself
transform the "unteachable" into Spirit-enabled readers. In preaching their
sermons and exhorting their congregants to read the scriptures, then, New
England's ministers were asking at least some of their auditors to do the impossible. Facing congregants who lacked both academic skills of interpretation and the necessary guidance of the Holy Spirit, the ministers could not
expect them to be competent Bible readers. Yet in downplaying the complexity of the interpretive process, and in urging them to read their Bibles, the
preaching clergy encouraged their congregants to feel empowered as readers.
It is hardly surprising that such instruction led to an unruly laity, as some of
those congregants (among them Anne Hutchinson) took the ministers at their
word, evaluating their ministers' sermons, disputing the ministers' readings
of the biblical text, and asserting the authority of their own interpretations.

Though this system of reading produced problems for New England Puritans, it also generated a complex and fertile literary culture centered around
the Bible. Rather than becoming an "enclosing arena" restricting expression,
as some scholars propose, the biblical text provided a rich system of reference
that fostered the colony's most prided literary productions—the sermons of
its foremost ministers, who would demonstrate the fluidity and flexibility of
the Puritan approaches to reading in sermons as varied as they were popular.[73] In part because the guidelines offered by Perkins and Bernard failed to
render Bible reading and sermon crafting simple and straightforward, ministers such as John Cotton, Thomas Hooker, and Thomas Shepard succeeded in
producing sermons that transcended any simple guidelines, sermons that ab-
sorbed the colonists deeply enough to make John Winthrop consider their at-
tendance at lengthy lectures two or three times a week excessive and "to the

great neglect of their affairs, and the damage of the public."[74] The tremendous popularity of these sermons was due in part, of course, to the piety of many New England migrants. But it was due also to the entertainment that the sermons provided, and especially to the "arte" with which the colony's sermonic stars negotiated the complexities of "prophecying."

## CHAPTER 2

# John Cotton: Reading, Preaching, and the Rhetoric of Inevitability

In New England's first generation, the minister who worked most closely with William Perkins's guidelines as he strove to maintain the balance between "prophecying" and "arte" was John Cotton (1584–1652).[1] In both old and New England, Cotton enjoyed tremendous acclaim for his preaching and for his biblical scholarship, activities he understood to be closely related. Cotton's understanding of preaching blurred the lines between preaching and reading: preaching *was* for him a biblically prescribed form of reading, and "opening" the text was an integral part of full and efficacious reading. But despite Cotton's insistence on the importance of the preached word, he strove in his preaching to minimize his own presence, and to present his sermons as careful readings of the text. Moreover, though he stressed the limits of the unpreached word, he often sent his auditors home to read on their own, empowering them as interpreters despite their limitations.

## Reading and the Preached Word

Cotton's preaching was shaped by his sense of the limits of what he called "bare reading."[2] In the Word, Cotton argued, Christians could "finde their hearts confirmed, and established in the faith," for the "mighty power of God that accompanies the word of God read" works "to strengthen men in the faith" (*CTF*, 200). Indeed, "the Word oftner read, full yieldeth

us more knowledge, new comfort, &c."[3] However, these benefits applied only
to "such as beleeve already" (*CTF*, 200). Facing a mixed audience, Cotton cautioned that those who had not received faith could not receive Scripture's full
benefits by reading on their own: "men that beleeve not," even if they "read the
Word of God over again and againe," will "receive little instruction from what
they read, little admonition, little stirred up to any goodnesse" (*CTF*, 181).
They may gain some "knowledge," but "that knowledge" will not "reach . . . to
salvation" (*CTF*, 187). "*Faith*," Cotton asserted emphatically, "*comes* not by
reading, but by *hearing*" (*CTF*, 181).

To achieve its full power, God's word must be preached, for the preached
Word carries with it the possibility of grace. In answer to the question "how
shall I get a spirit of Grace?" Cotton includes in his answers "by a diligent
hearing the Word of God, *Gal.*3.2. implying, that he doth usually breathe the
Spirit by the breath of his Word."[4] Even "carnall man," argues Cotton, can receive tremendous spiritual benefit from the preached word: "whatever is expounded to them from this Word, may be effectuall to bring them to salvation" (*CTF*, 187).

Cotton's sermons reflect his sense of preaching's relationship to reading.
Because the minister's job was to "expound" the Word, Cotton structured his
sermons as step-by-step explications, suggesting that his preaching was
merely a fuller kind of reading, and that his positions grew naturally and
inevitably out of the biblical text itself. Teresa Toulouse observes that Cotton
"seems hardly interested in developing an 'argument,'" that he appears more
interested in having "his hearers become involved in the dynamic richness of
God's revelation."[5] And Janice Knight notes that in Cotton's preaching, "[t]he
order of the biblical passage rather than the logic of a predetermined doctrinal message shapes the sermon. The appeal is to God's reason rather than to
mechanical, human logic. The preacher makes himself a passive vessel through
which the Spirit flows from Bible to saint—he is 'a conduit to convey.'"[6] But
the process by which Cotton inexorably unfolds the text's "dynamic richness" is itself, at least in part, a carefully crafted argumentative strategy, one
rooted in Reformed theories of reading, and reinforcing Reformed belief in
the coherence and unity of the biblical text, in "the consent of all the parts of
the Scripture."[7] The fluidity of collation as an interpretive tool, however, allowed Cotton great flexibility. Though his sermons offered close readings
of his chosen texts, Cotton's collations allowed him to build arguments that
seemed to emerge naturally out his sermons, creating a sense of interpretive
inevitability.

Cotton's discussion of reading in *Christ the Fountaine of Life* shows how
he used collation to build an argument. The text of the twelfth sermon in this
series is 1 John 5:13: "These things have I written unto you that beleeve on

the name of the Son of God, that ye may know that ye have eternall life, and that ye may beleeve on the name of the Son of God" (177). Though this text does not explicitly address reading, Cotton's "opening" of it uses the text "written unto" believers to anchor a discussion of the Word's efficacy. Because "these things" are addressed to believers, Cotton argues that for unbelievers, "bare reading" cannot beget faith, though the Spirit may offer grace through the preached Word (183).

Cotton develops his argument through collation, introducing potential objections and then weaving them into his discussion. First he introduces an objection based on a passage from Deuteronomy: "*You say, But sometimes God hath been pleased to blesse in old time the reading of the Word to the conversion of soules; and therefore why may we not expect the like blessing upon the reading of the Gospell in these days, as well as the Law in former times?*" (181–82). Cotton's imagined interlocutor cites a biblical passage: "*in* Deut.31.11,12,13. (*A place much stood upon in this case) it was commanded there that the people* should come up to Jerusalem, *and there the* Law should be read before them, vers. 11. that they may heare, and learne, and se e, [sic] verse 12. and their children that knew not the Lord, may learne to feare the Lord their God" (181–82).[8] He bases his objection on this passage, arguing that it testifies to the efficacy of reading "the Law" even for the ignorant in biblical times: "*Where you see, God blessed the reading of the Law, not only for the benefit of them that knew it before, but their children also, that knew not any thing, may learn to feare the Lord*" (182). And if the Law could teach the ignorant, how much more efficacious must the Gospel be, asks Cotton's imagined interlocutor: "*And if God did so blesse the reading of the Law in former times, as a notable instrument to bring on them to beleeve that never knew any thing of Gods word before? Surely one would expect that the Gospel, which of the two, is rather* the ministration of the spirit *then of the letter, or then the Law, that it should be as mighty this way for the begetting of Gods fear in men, as ever the Law was*" (182). Thus Cotton introduces an objection to his argument by imagining an interlocutor who can cite scripture to demonstrate that even unbelievers can receive faith from the read word (182).

Of course, this is not simply an objection; the quoted verse is also a text that Cotton incorporates deliberately into his argument. First, he addresses the objection apparently embodied in the text, appealing to the "circumstances of the place propounded," the larger context of the cited text. He notes that the cited verses describe a special occasion, rather than an ordinary instance of reading: "You shal not read that this was the benefit or blessing that God did accompany the Law withal, in ordinary reading of the same; But this was a solemn reading, once in seven yeares, and no oftener, or once in fifty years" (182). He backs this assertion up by appealing to the text's context, asking his listener to consider previous verses: "It was a reading at the feast of Tabernacles, in the yeare of solemnity, as verse 10,11,to 13. In a time of solemne release, that was once every seven years" (182).[9] This, he explains, was a special case, a "solemne reading," in which "God gave a more than ordinary blessing to little children those poore ignorant things that usually come to the Congregation, and heare much, but learn little" (182). The unsuccessful hearing of "those poore ignorant things" must be taken as the model for unbelieving readers, who cannot hope to benefit from ordinary reading of the Scriptures.

Having refuted the objection suggested in this passage, Cotton weaves the verse into his own argument, rather than leaving the defeated objection hanging. Reading the passage typologically, he recasts the passage from Deuteronomy as textual support for his own view of reading. Having explained the special circumstances of the reading described in Deuteronomy, Cotton asks, "And what was the reason that then it [this reading] shoulde have such a more then ordinary blessing?" (182). His answer is that "this year of Release was the acceptable year of the Lord, which typed out to them, the year of release by the Lord Jesus Christ: For he was crucified in one of these seventh years. In the year of Jubilee; And to make it a type and shadow of what benefit we should have by reading the Word, when we should be released from our sinnes by faith in his blood" (182). In Cotton's interpretation, the Deuteronomic reading is efficacious because it takes place in the year of release, in the sabbatical or jubilee year. This teaches, therefore, that "reading the Word" can only be similarly efficacious when spiritual release has already occurred—only when the reader or hearer has already been "released . . . by faith in his blood" (182). This, Cotton argues, is the reason for the Deuteronomic reading: "to shew you, that men that are come to a yeare of release from all their sins by Christ, they shall heare and know, and though they know nothing before, now they shall never read but with some profit, and some growth in Gods feare" (183). Thus the text offered ostensibly in objection returns to prove Cotton's initial position, that nonbelievers cannot truly benefit from "bare reading" of the word. In the process, Cotton emphasizes the coherence of the biblical text—even texts that seem to contradict one another ultimately agree. Moreover, since all texts, even those marshaled in objections, support Cotton's position, that position seems to emerge naturally and inevitably from the biblical text.

Nor does Cotton return to his initial text at this point. Instead, he uses the passage from Deuteronomy to explain what "reading" means. Cotton notes that "when [the biblical author] . . . there speakes of reading, he speakes not of bare reading" (183). Rather, "reading is some times put for all that expounding and applying, that did ordinarily accompany their reading at such a time" (183). For Cotton, "reading" really means opening the text to the congregation, which he demonstrates by appealing to yet another text:

> for it was at the same feast that *Nehemiah* speakes, chap. 8. last. It is said, chap 8. 4. to 8. there was a Pulpit of Wood; and in vers. 8. it is said, *They did read distinctly in the Law, and caused the people to understand the meaning of it;* so that it was not a meere outward and bare reading of the letter, but an opening of the sence, and such a kinde of applying it to the hearts of the people, that the people went away much rejoycing, because they understood the Law that was read unto them. (183)[10]

Cotton, then, defines efficacious reading as preaching. The preaching minister is not performing for his congregation; he is simply "reading" the text in scriptural terms, "opening" its sense to his congregation, and "applying it to [their] hearts" (183). Only this preached reading, in which the text is both opened and applied, can be efficacious for nonbelievers.

Having integrated the passage from Nehemiah into his sermon, Cotton draws one more point from it before picking up the main thread of his argument. Returning thematically to an earlier "digression" in his sermon, Cotton uses the text from Nehemiah to demonstrate that belief should be a joyous experience: "the people went away much rejoycing, because they understood the Law that was unto them, and many of them could not but joy and rejoyce in it, as you see from vers. 8 to the end of the 12th and when they had so done the people went away rejoycing, and he said to them, *Goe your way home, eate the fat, and drinke the sweet, &c.* vers. 10" (183). As Cotton understood the reading process, joy at comprehension was inevitable: "they could not but joy and rejoyce in it." For Cotton, the preached word serves as a conduit for grace, which in turn enhances reading ability and brings joy.

Cotton's understanding of the reading process thus complemented his soteriology, in which conversion was a divine transformation accompanied not by profound anxiety, but by joy. For those who preached doubt and anxiety, rather than joy and comfort, Cotton had strong words. In fact, he associated such preaching with the scourge of Catholicism, identifying belief in the unknowability of salvific status as a "Popish doctrine" (*CTF,* 190).[11] Preaching in England against that doctrine, he compared the Catholic Church's belief that "it [is] impossible for a man to know that he is in an estate of grace" to a "harlot['s]" inability to assert confidently who has fathered her children (*CTF,* 190). Because she "hath mixed her selfe with so many Idols and abominations," the harlot can teach her children only to "hope such an one is [their] Father, but count it presumption to say, [they] know it" (190). Rather than associating doubt with humility, Cotton thus associated it with spiritual looseness and with the evils of Rome. Later, faced with co-religionists in New England who were nevertheless anxious about the status of their souls, Cotton was similarly impatient, if more restrained in his rhetoric.[12]

Cotton's own conversion experience, however, was not uniformly joyful. Having been moved by the preaching of Richard Sibbes, Cotton suffered through the initial stages of his conversion. As John Norton reports:

> Hearing Doctor *Sibbs*, (then Mr *Sibbs*) preaching a Sermon about Regeneration, where he first shewed what Regeneration was not, when opening the State of a Civil man, he saw his own condition fully discovered, which through mercy did drive him to a stand, as plainly feeling himself to have no true grace, all his false hopes and grounds now failing him: And so he lay a long time in an uncomfortable despairing way.[13]

But just as Sibbes's preaching provoked his despair, Cotton found that God worked through Sibbes's preaching to heal it. His despair continued "till it pleased God to let in some word of Faith into his heart, to cause him to look unto Christ for healing, which word (if memory faileth not) was dispensed unto him by Doctor *Sibbs*" (13). Thereafter, Cotton expressed confidence in his spiritual health, asserting that he had seen God's mercy and felt "saving-grace" through Christ, such that he experienced "Heav'n on Earth."[14] As Cotton understood the process, God let faith into the believer's heart in the form of a "word," which was "dispensed" by a minister. Though the minister served as a spiritual physician here, the fact that he was merely a conduit for Christ as the true healer is emphasized both by Cotton's shaky recollection of the minister's identity and by Sibbes's presence only as the agent by whom the Word, as subject, "was dispensed." Moreover, Cotton's description stresses that spiritual health is the end point of this process; though the Word might initially wound, ultimately it would also produce "healing." In Cotton's view, a conversion that yielded only anxiety was not a genuine conversion at all, and such anxiety should not be the goal of a minister's preaching.

In *Christ the Fountaine of Life*, Cotton demonstrates this dynamic in his reading of the text from Nehemiah, emphasizing the overwhelming joy of the people, who "could not but joy and rejoyce in it, as you see from vers. 8 to the end of the 12th" (183). Cotton does not discuss these verses fully, but instead relies on his auditors' familiarity with the text, without reminding them of the chapter's ninth verse, which reports that Nehemiah, Ezra, and the Levites instructed the people "mourn not, nor weep. For all the people wept, when they heard the words of the law" (Neh. 8:9). Joy, as the cited but glossed-over text records, was hardly inevitable. For many, divine knowledge seemed to bring pain. But the text itself offers a corrective. When the people weep, they receive instruction, and Cotton calls his auditors' attention to verse 10, suggesting that though joy may not be inevitable, it is teachable:

> Then he said unto them, Go your way, eat the fat, and drink the sweet, and send portions unto them for whom nothing is prepared: for *this* day *is* holy unto our Lord: neither be ye sorry; for the joy of the LORD is your strength. So the Levites stilled all the people, saying, Hold your peace, for the day *is* holy; neither be ye grieved. And all the people went their way to eat, and to drink, and to send portions, and to make great mirth, because they had understood the words that were declared unto them. (Neh. 8:10–12)

The people can be taught to rejoice in their understanding, rather than to suffer tremendous bouts of anxiety over it. The role of the teacher and preacher is to offer God's word, and through it faith, and to instruct the people in its proper acceptance. In "opening" these verses from Nehemiah, Cotton asserts the minister's interpretive authority not only over the biblical text, but, at least on some level, over the responses of his congregants as well.

Cotton closes his treatment of the passages from Deuteronomy and Nehemiah, as well as the "reasons" section of his sermon, with the claim "that God hath either never so farre forth blessed the reading of the Word, as to bring on unbeleevers to Christ" (183). In his thoroughness, Cotton allows for an exception: "either never, or if he have, it is at some solemne extraordinary feast, once in seven, or once in fifty yeares, which was their great Jubilee, to make knowne to his Church what in after times it should be, when they knew Christ" (183). But even this exception connects the passages from Deuteronomy and Nehemiah, reinforcing Cotton's point about the extraordinariness of an occasion when bare reading might be efficacious.

Though Cotton presented his preaching as fleshed-out reading of the text, he thus built careful arguments into that "reading," opening the text in very pointed ways. While the initial text provided Cotton's focus, he unfolded it purposefully and strategically, building a careful argument by collating verses and considering the circumstances of the places propounded. But the seemingly digressive and text-centered structure drew attention away from Cotton as advocate; in Perkins's terms, Cotton's artistry was concealed, turning attention away from the preacher and focusing it on the text itself and upon the Spirit. Sometime adversary John Wilson praised Cotton's preaching, for example, noting that "Mr. Cotton preaches with such authority, demonstration, and life, that methinks, when he preaches out of any prophet or apostle, I hear not him; I hear that very prophet and apostle; yea, I hear the Lord Jesus Christ himself speaking in my heart."[15] As Perkins and Bernard had prescribed, this listener heard not Cotton, but Christ, when Cotton preached.

Cotton had rendered himself nearly transparent to the Word and the Spirit,
so that Wilson experienced the direct presence of Christ in his heart.[16] For
Cotton, such preaching was the reading through which the Holy Spirit offered grace to the unconverted and comfort to believers.

## EXTENSIVE PREACHING

Because Cotton believed that only the preached word could be efficacious for
the unconverted, he strove to preach the biblical text thoroughly and comprehensively. More than many other ministers, Cotton was committed to
covering the complete biblical text in his sermons, as if this would make the
means most completely available to his congregants. He balanced his desire
to cover the full text with his desire to unfold fully each verse on which he
preached, and consequently moved his sermons through the particular biblical verses on which he preached with relative dispatch. Though to modern
readers Cotton's sermons seem to linger over verses at great length, as Babette Levy notes, "Thomas Hooker spent nearly a year on *Acts* 2:37, and
Thomas Shepard, after four years on *Matthew* 25:1–13, congratulated himself that he had not, after the fashion of Papist commentators, squeezed the
last bit of meaning out of it."[17] Cotton, on the other hand, preached over multiple texts in an almost encyclopedic fashion. While he often devoted multiple sermons to a single verse, he nevertheless moved fairly steadily through
the biblical corpus.[18] Norton reports that in the course of his Sabbath lectures
in England, Cotton "preached over the first six Chapters of the Gospel of
*John;* the whole book of *Ecclesiastes,* the Prophesie of *Zechariah,* and many
other Scriptures, and when the Lords Supper was administred (which was
usually every moneth,) he preached upon I *Cor.* II. and 2 *Chron.* 30. *per to-
tum,* and some other Scriptures concerning that Subject."[19] Cotton preached
during the week as well: "On his Lecture days, he preached thorough the
whole First and Second Epistles of *John,* the whole book of *Solomons Song,*
the Parables of our Saviour set forth in *Matthews* Gospel to the end of Chapter 16. compairing them with *Mark* and *Luke*" (17).

Nor did Cotton merely repeat the cycles of his British sermons after his
arrival in New England. Rather, he attempted to be comprehensive—to
preach the entire biblical text—in this setting as well:

In the course of his Ministry in *New-Boston,* by way of Exposition, he
went through the Old-Testament unto *Isa.*30. the whole New-Testament
once through, and the second time unto the middle of *Heb.*11. Upon Lords
days and Lecture-days, he preached through the *Acts of the Apostles, Hag-*

*gai, Zechary, Ezra, the Revelation, Ecclesiastes, Canticles,* the Second and
Third Epistles of *John,* the Epistle of *Titus,* both the Epistles of *Timothy,* the
Epistle to the *Romans,* with other Scriptures. (22–23)

Cotton Mather reports that John Cotton in fact succeeded in preaching over
the entire text of the Bible, asserting that he "went over the Old Testament
once, and a second time as far as the thirtieth chapter of Isaiah" (*Magnalia,*
1:271). Because Mather's account is so closely based upon Norton's description, I am inclined to trust Norton's more conservative estimate of the scope
of Cotton's preaching.

Even by that estimate, however, the scope is impressive. And even having
preached so comprehensively, Cotton felt pressure to cover more of the biblical text at the end of his life. Norton reports that during his last illness, Cotton continued to preach "whilst his strength failed" (43). On November 18,
1652, Cotton "took in course for his Text the 4 last verses of the Epistle to
*Timothy*" (43). As this was an unusually long passage for him to preach
upon, Cotton explained that "otherwise, he should not live to make an end of
that Epistle" (43). To the end, Cotton strove to balance careful and complete
explication with full coverage of the biblical text.

## COLLATION, EXPLICATION, AND REINTEGRATION

Beyond preaching over the text sequentially, Cotton enhanced the comprehensiveness of his sermons through collation. His sermons seem thorough,
even exhaustive, not only because he explicates his initial text so fully, but
also because he addresses as well the "circumstances"—the initial contexts—
of the collated texts. As in the examples above, Cotton did not merely cite
other texts briefly. Instead, he discussed collated texts at length, using them
to develop major points of his argument.

Cotton's attempts to balance collation and circumstances can make his
sermons seem digressive and occasionally confusing. But Cotton's firm an-
choring of his digressions and his continual return to his initial text ultimately maintain the unity of most of his sermons. The result is a balancing
act that holds his audience in suspense, dazzling them with his virtuosity:
how many texts can he deal with fully without losing his focus? How many
different texts and contexts can he keep circulating? His sermons made
greater demands on auditors than those of the other ministers, perhaps; Alan
Heimert and Andrew Delbanco assert that Cotton "demanded ceaseless men-
tal effort from his listeners."[20] But such sermons found eager audiences—
congregants who enjoyed the intricacies of Cotton's preached exegesis—as

may be surmised from the spiritual revival that the Boston church experienced following Cotton's arrival.[21]

To see how Cotton weaves digressions into an elaborate whole, we return briefly to the twelfth sermon of *Christ the Fountaine of Life.* This sermon represents Cotton at his most thorough, and seemingly at his most digressive. At the same time, it demonstrates Cotton's method, the artistry with which he reintegrates his digressions, weaving them into an elaborate whole. In addition, this text lends itself especially well to a study of Cotton's preaching style. The published version of this early sermon series maintains marks of orality better than do most seventeenth-century sermon texts, dividing the text into sermons, rather than into chapters, for example. This is especially useful, since Cotton's artistry, at its most effective, produces a unified and interconnected whole within each sermon.

The text of this sermon, once again, is 1 John 5:13, though in this twelfth sermon, Cotton preaches only on the first two-thirds of the verse, leaving the final clause to be addressed in Sermon 13. Cotton opens quite straightforwardly, examining the circumstances of the place propounded—the context of his text from 1 John:

> Wee are now come to enter upon the beginning of the conclusion of this whole Epistle, wherein the Apostle rehearseth the intention and scope of the whole fore-past Epistle; the persons and subjects to whom he writes, and the end and scope of his writing: *These things have I written unto you;* To whom? *To you that beleeve on the name of the Sonne of God.* And he intends a double end:
>
> First, *That you may know that you have eternall life.*
> Secondly, *That you may beleeve on the Name of the Sonne of God.* (177)

Cotton frames his sermon in terms of both his text's place in the biblical epistle and the biblical author's intention. His first step is to set the text in context, after which he proceeds to break it down into workable parts. In the term used by William Perkins and Richard Bernard, he is beginning to "divide" the text.[22]

Cotton's approach purports not to appropriate the biblical text to the minister's purpose, but simply to unfold and explain it. In contrast, Thomas Hooker frames the opening of *The Sovles Preparation for Christ* in terms of his own argument about preparation: "In this great worke of preparation for Christ, observe two things. First, the dispensation of the worke of Grace on Gods part, hee pulls a sinner from sinne to himselfe; and secondly, the frame and temper of spirit, that God workes in the hearts of those that he doth draw: and that makes it selfe knowne in two particulars; partly in Contrition, and partly in Humiliation."[23] The biblical text of Hooker's sermon, printed immediately below his title on this first page, is Acts 2:37, but Hooker does not overtly connect his argument to that text until the third printed page of his sermon. Cotton holds himself closer to the biblical text, apparently allowing it to shape his argument.

But Cotton's commitment to thorough exposition of the verse's context immediately tempts him toward what seems like a digression. As if unable to resist reading ahead, Cotton adds: "Now to encourage to this latter end that *John* aimes at; beleeving on the name of the Sonne of God, he propounds three motives, in the 15, 16, 17. verses; amongst which the last of them is a promise of prevailing with God for pardon, and a prevention of falling into the great sinne, and so propoundeth certaine encouragements to the end of the Chapter" (177).[24] Since Cotton does not immediately discuss these "encouragements," but moves instead to a consideration of "the first part of" the verse, his need to mention these three verses here might warrant the accusation that he has lost his focus (177). But to an audience steeped in the biblical text, the biblical reference would not be as confusing as it is to many modern readers. Moreover, by mentioning these verses here—verses that emphasize the possibilities of forgiveness and of confidence in divine acceptance—Cotton establishes an emphasis to which he will return at various points during the sermon, one basic to his soteriology. Several times during his sermon, Cotton's exegesis will emphasize that an individual's spiritual state is in fact knowable, and that conversion should be accompanied by comfort and joy, rather than anxiety and fear. At those points, the echoes of these verses will add authority and richness to Cotton's argument.

Thus what initially appears a digression or loose end is ultimately incorporated into Cotton's argument, adding richness to his case by layering it with echoes of other texts. Such apparent digressions carried aesthetic value as well as argumentative value: Cotton's auditors wondered where this seeming digression would lead, how long he would leave it hanging before it became clear that it indeed fit into his argument, and how many additional texts would be introduced and interwoven in the process.[25] Without discounting the appeal of Cotton's imagery or the intellectual appeal of his tendency toward paradox, I argue that those images and paradoxes were anchored in a structure of collation, expansion, and incorporation, and that this structure kept the audience engaged and entertained.[26]

Cotton's sermons were unified not only on a thematic level, but also on the level of language. Throughout his sermons, Cotton punctuated his collations and explications with returns to the initial text, tying the sermon together both by insisting on the thematic centrality of the verse and by repeating its language. In the twelfth sermon of *Christ the Fountaine of Life*, for example, Cotton quotes the full text of 1 John 5:13 at the sermon's opening. After dividing the verse into parts, he begins his unfolding. But repeatedly throughout the sermon, he quotes all or part of the verse again, using the repetition almost as a refrain. Knight argues that Cotton's use of repetition creates a sense of "stasis or complacency" in the listener, and produces "an almost hypnotic effect."[27] She argues that "in marked contrast to the salvation plots of preparationist sermons, in which each step can be logically anticipated . . . Cotton's circular, repetitive structure refuses anticipation, relies on a remembered affection, a recalled experience of grace" (116).

I share Knight's sense that Cotton's repetition is strategic. However, I find it less hypnotic or stasis engendering than structurally unifying. Cotton's repetition of this verse provides a structural backbone for his sermon, allowing him to incorporate an enormous amount of collated material while at the same time emphasizing his central argument. Moreover, Cotton subtly varies his repetitions to create a building argument, rather than a static one, suggesting to his listeners that the argument is intrinsic to the text itself. In the first part of this sermon, Cotton repeats the phrase *"that beleeve on the name of the Son of God."* First, he uses the phrase to set the parameters of his discussion: "Now, at this time, we shall treat of the first part of this conclusion, which is an expression that *John* here makes, or a description of the persons here spoken to; to them that *beleeve on the name of the Son of God*" (177). He repeats the verse midway through the discussion of his first doctrine; "looke at all *Iohns* writings," he writes, "and they are all written to them that *beleeve on the name of the Son of God*" (178). He paraphrases the text on the next page, noting that "you read in the words of the Text, to them that did beleeve" (179). He quotes the text again in his reasons, noting that "were it not for some beleevers among them, whom God had respect unto, none of all the Apostles would have vouchsafed to have written any one Epistle to any unbeleever of any Town or Assembly, none of them all writes to any, but to such as *beleeve on the name of the son of God*" (180).

In his uses, Cotton quotes from a slightly different section of the verse. Again, he asserts that the epistle is aimed only at believers, but he includes the subject and object of the original verse, subtly encouraging his listeners to personalize his message: "so then, marvaile not that the Holy Ghost saith these things, *I write unto you that beleeve*; to Beleevers only was this written" (186). Later in the uses, Cotton repeats the verse, again including the personal pronouns: "the principall thing the Apostle aymes at is this; *I write unto you that beleeve on the name of the Son of God*" (188). No longer is this purely theoretical; Cotton is no longer discussing "such as beleeve" or "them that beleeve," but "you that beleeve," encouraging those present to internalize the preceding theoretical discussion, as is appropriate to the uses section of his sermon (*CTF*, 186, 180, 177, 178).

In the final section of his sermon, Cotton considers a second doctrine: *"Such as doe beleeve on the name of the Lord Jesus Christ, by these Epistles of* John, *may know that they have everlasting life"* (189). Here he quotes from the next part of the verse, which reads "that ye may know that ye have eternall life" (177). As in the previous section, Cotton slightly varies his quotations from the verse as he develops his explication. In his first use, Cotton applies the verse more generally, and somewhat hypothetically: "If *John* did write these Epistles for this end, *that we may know we have eternall life,* then sure we may know it, else *Iohn* failes of his end" (190). The pronoun is plural, and the quotation fits into a logical proposition.

Cotton's next use of the quotation similarly casts it within a theoretical construction:

> A man may beleeve a thing, and upon good ground he may looke for salvation there, and waite for it, and desire that he may be more assured of it, but to *know that thou hast eternall life;* and the certainty of it, that God hath sealed it up to thy soule and conscience, of which thou needest doubt no more, this is a far more greater blessing then to beleeve in Christ, though by beleeving we have eternall life. (191)

Although Cotton uses the pronoun "thou" within the quotation, the first part of the quotation is omitted, leaving it somewhat abstract. He does not say that "thou mayst know that thou hast eternall life," but merely that "to know that thou hast eternall life" is better than to "beleeve" it. In theory, knowledge is better than mere belief.

But in the final sentence of the sermon, Cotton inserts the quotation into an exhortation, personalizing it fully. "[T]herefore," he instructs, "be diligent and conversant in reading these Epistles, and as you would search for treasure, so be diligent and laborious herein, *that you may know that you have eternall life"* (192). Here, the quotation is fully applied to the audience: *you* that listen here may know that *you* have eternal life. Once again, Cotton links reading with listening to the preached word. Cotton's repetition of the verse thus unifies his sermon both thematically and aurally, creating a shifting refrain that marks transitions in his argument. And once again, that argument connects regenerate reading with faith and confidence. Those who have faith, and only those who have faith, must read "diligent[ly] and laborious[ly]" to find comfort in the biblical text.

## CONSEQUENCES OF THOROUGHNESS

Many of Cotton's auditors apparently found his sermons greatly comforting, valuing their subtle artistry and esteeming Cotton's ability to make them hear "the Lord Jesus Christ himself speaking in [their] . . . heart[s]."[28] But the admiration that Cotton inspired in his own day has puzzled modern readers, who have found his sermons unappealing compared to the preaching of his colleagues. Teresa Toulouse suggests that "[l]istening to Cotton's scrupulously logical exegetical method and his careful opening of every facet of a text could hardly have been as exciting as listening to Thomas Hooker . . . exhort, threaten, or cajole them within the 'uses,'" and Alfred Habegger suspects that Cotton's sermons failed to "sustain the emotional power" that Hooker's did.[29] Both Toulouse and Habegger find intellectual interest and appeal in Cotton's sermons, despite their hesitation, but Babette Levy can only hope, at best, that something has been lost in transmission that would otherwise explain Cotton's popularity. Most of Cotton's printed sermons, she explains, "were taken down in shorthand while they were being delivered and afterwards submitted to Cotton for his correction. This means of transcription perhaps eliminated many of his illustrations and figures of speech, and Cotton may have considered it vanity to reintroduce them into the printed versions."[30] Perhaps recognizing that the process of transmission does not sufficiently differentiate Cotton from his contemporaries to account for the stylistic differences between them, however, Levy suggests another explanation as well: "Then again, he may well have been one of those great preachers whose evangelistic appeal is more dependent on the force of their living personality than their contemporaries realize" (141). This explanation is, of course, at odds with Wilson's description of Cotton as effaced from his own preaching, but in Levy's opinion, the surviving texts of Cotton's sermons fail to explain his original popularity.

These critics attribute the failures of Cotton's sermons—their lack of emotional power—to the extremely close attention that Cotton pays to the biblical text, and to his commitment to unfolding the biblical text fully. Habegger contrasts Cotton with Thomas Hooker, who used texts selectively to support and enliven his arguments about the preparatory process. Cotton, he notes, "scrupulously opens the entire text, frequently the entire chapter, and extracts as many doctrines as are necessary to comprehend 'the sence of the whole Scripture,' even if this exhaustive procedure destroys the unity of the sermon."[31] Habegger finds that Cotton's commitment to preaching comprehensively forced him to sacrifice unity, artistry, and argumentative force.

Though Cotton's preaching does sometimes seem digressive, his comprehensiveness does not merely allow him to cover large portions of the biblical text. It also further effaces Cotton's personal presence from the sermon, creating the impression that he is driven by the text, rather than by his own argument. Even when Cotton's thoroughness seems to verge on the self-indulgent, as if he himself has gotten caught up in the argument he is making and finds himself unable to stop, the accumulation of examples is generally quite pointed. Once again, the twelfth sermon of *Christ the Fountaine of Life* serves as a useful example. Here, Cotton supplies numerous examples to demonstrate that the first epistle of John was written only to believers. First, he suggests that his audience look at the text of the epistle (178). Then, he refers them to John's second epistle (178). Then to his third (178). One suspects that by this point Cotton's auditors have been convinced, but for Cotton, this is not sufficient. He instructs them to "looke at all *Iohn's* writings," and then, even more: "And in very deed looke at all the Epistles of all the rest of the Apostles, and they are all written to *Beleevers*" (178). By citing such extensive prooftexts, Cotton asserts the authority of his argument, and also extends it. He emphasizes that his reading is neither personal nor idiosyncratic, nor is it unique to a single epistle of John. Rather, he contends that it is true of all of John's writings and the epistles of all the apostles. Moreover, it is not a reading that only he can see; he suggests that congregants reviewing the Bible on their own will see his interpretation borne out by the broader canon of the Scriptures. Here, then, thoroughness serves to buttress Cotton's argument, suggesting the inevitability of his interpretation.

Moreover, an exploration of Cotton's nonsermonic writings reveals that, even in his most digressive sermons, he held his proclivity for greater thoroughness in check. Cotton's *Briefe Exposition With Practicall Observations Upon the Whole Book of Ecclesiastes*, a commentary on Ecclesiastes that is not presented in the form of sermons, shows the sort of exegesis he undertook when not preaching, but rather presenting a verse-by-verse exegesis of a full book.[32] In this text, Cotton places less emphasis on ministerial transparency; indeed, he emphasizes the difference between a minister's "use of spiritual gifts requisite in a Prophet or Preacher, to the exercise of his ministery" and bare "reading," "which even a School-boy may perform, that never attained any spirituall gift at all" (10). In the *Briefe Exposition*, Cotton demonstrates both his training and his gifts.

Cotton opens the *Briefe Exposition* by examining the rhetorical techniques used to characterize "vanity." He notes that "The condition of all things, by the Adjunct of *vanity, all is vanity*" and then explains that "this vanity is amplified by many ornaments of Rhetorique" (2). Cotton proceeds to enumerate and define these ornaments. He begins:

1. An Hyperbole, *vanity* it selfe, for vaine.
2. *Polyptoton, vanity of vanities.*
3. *Epizeuxis*, the like sound continued in the same sentence, *vanity of vanities.*
4. *Anadiplosis*, (the same sound repeated in the end of one sentence and the beginning of the other) *vanity of vanities, vanity* &c.
5. *Epanalepsis* (the same sound repeated in the beginning of the sentence, and in the end, *vanity* &c. all is vanity. (2–3)

And so Cotton proceeds, through Epistrophe, Epanodos, Numerus Oratorius, Climax, and Paranomasia (3). Such thoroughness, accompanied by attention to technical details like "the Feminine gender" of the word "Koheleth," induces Emerson to remark that this "kind of commentary does not strike the reader as morally edifying."[33] In fact, Emerson dismisses the text as "not one of Cotton's more important books . . . not memorable for its prose or for its thoughts," and lacking "even . . . much of that quality which makes some of Cotton's writing interesting, a peculiar habit of thought which is fascinating in its fantasticality" (95).

For readers steeped in the biblical text, the *Briefe Exposition* may well have been "fascinating." Despite his lament that those who had "left all to enjoy the Gospel" were now "ready to leave the Gospel," Cotton clearly expected quite a lot of his lay readers (1). Certainly, an audience familiar with seventeenth-century encyclopedism might not have found Cotton's enumeration of rhetorical ornaments overwhelming. Moreover, Cotton's encyclopedic account of the ornaments contained in a single verse demonstrated that all things—even all rhetorical ornaments—were contained in the text of scripture. Beyond this, however, Cotton seems to have been indulging in a moment of virtuosic exegesis: how many rhetorical ornaments could he find in this single phrase? The colony's star exegete was showing his skills to those who read his commentaries rather than simply listening to him preach. Putting his ordinary mode of self-effacement aside, Cotton's catalog of ornaments stands as an exegete's version of the child's "Look Ma! No hands!" And this flourish of erudition and thoroughness testifies to the restraint that Cotton exercised more typically, as he consciously effaced himself and his expertise in preaching to the mixed groups of congregants in his churches.

Of course, it might still be argued that Cotton's commitment to thoroughness skated dangerously close to compromising the aesthetic value and coherence of his sermons. Collation, combined with full attention to the circumstances of the place propounded, sometimes risked overwhelming his listeners. But unlike those who dismiss the attractions of Cotton's sermons as inexplicable, Cotton's seventeenth-century auditors on balance seem not to have felt overwhelmed. Instead, admiration for Cotton's subtle artistry made him a star in his own day. Though his method increased the risk of failure, it also allowed for tremendous triumphs of scriptural artistry.

## DILIGENT HEARERS

The perils of Cotton's method extend beyond the risk of aesthetic or argumentative failure. In ways that would unsettle the Massachusetts Bay Colony, Cotton's preaching made the techniques of exegesis available to his auditors. And because he encouraged them to read on their own, to "search for treasure" as they "diligent[ly]" studied the scriptures, those auditors sometimes found themselves in interpretive difficulty (CTF, 192).

Along with his contemporaries, Cotton demonstrated many of the methods of exegesis to his congregants, encouraging them to try their own Spirit-assisted openings of scripture. Because Cotton's readings seemed so clearly text driven, they presented his congregants with guides to exegesis, incomplete and difficult to follow as those guides might have been. In addition, Cotton was sometimes explicit about the steps he took to arrive at an interpretation. In preaching on Revelation, for example, he admitted that in one passage, "the words are somewhat dark, and there is much variety in the Interpretation of them."[34] Consequently, he explained, he would "open" the text "by comparing of this, and other Scriptures together" (2).

Having demonstrated these techniques, Cotton urged his congregants to read the Bible with seriousness and diligence:

> if by reading these Epistles you might beleeve, and be humbled & comforted, and your joy might be full in reading, then truly you should not rest, till by reading you finde some measure of faith strengthened in you, to an holy feare of God, in whose presence you stand, and whose word you take in hand, and finde your hearts take comfort from what you doe read, since they were writen for your sakes that beleeve, and for your sakes onely if you shall be negligent to read them, shall you not take this blessed Ordinance of God in vaine? and therefore read them, and read them diligently, and profitably, for the blessed ends for which God hath written them, that you may finde the blessed fruites of them. (CTF, 189)

Cotton limited his encouragement to those who believed, as the text could only strengthen faith that had already been divinely supplied. Nevertheless, individual congregants were clearly exhorted to study the biblical texts and apply them to themselves. Nor did Cotton caution them to restrict their attention to texts on which he had preached; instead, he urged them to extend their study, as in his suggestion that they "looke at all the Epistles of all . . . of the Apostles" (*CTF*, 178).

Moreover, Cotton encouraged his auditors not only to read on their own, but also to evaluate their ministers' readings. In *Christ the Fountaine of Life*, for example, Cotton repeatedly encouraged his English congregants to verify their ministers' teachings by comparing them with their own biblical reading. When he referred them to the "Epistles of all . . . the Apostles," it was to verify the accuracy of his interpretation (*CTF*, 178).

More broadly, Cotton invited his congregants to apply their own understanding of the biblical text to preached interpretations they heard in the churches, to "examine the things that . . . [they] have heard" (200). Indeed, he exhorted, "goe home and consider whether the things that have been taught were true or no: whether agreeable to the holy Scriptures or no; for a Preacher speaks not the expresse words of the Scripture, but comments and explications of the Scriptures, and therefore examine whether that which is delivered be agreeable to the Scriptures which are alleged for to prove the doctrine" (200). Cotton emphasized that the minister's transparency to the motions of the Spirit might be limited. Though ministers strove to offer their congregants minimally mediated divine communication, they were nevertheless human interpreters. They hoped that the "comments and explications" that they offered to illuminate the text had themselves been illuminated by the assistance of the Holy Spirit: "preaching the Word and the Interpretation of the Word, are of God, but the phrase and Method is of men, yet so of men, as they have commandement and warrant from God, to preach and interpret the Word: and not in what phrase and Method pleases themselves: nor in such words as mans wisdome teacheth but which the Holy Ghost teacheth, I *Cor.* 2.13."[35] They hoped for divine illumination, but Christians had to distinguish the divine message from the human medium, "the Word and the Interpretation of the Word" from human "phrase and Method."[36]

Under the best of circumstances, the minister would preach with the assistance of the Spirit. And in those circumstances, his congregants should find no conflicts between the preached word and their own readings of the Scriptures. Even in England, Cotton predicted that private examinations of the ministers' interpretations would be "of special use to helpe forward the faith of such as do beleeve, yea, (and which is more) it may bring on men to beleeve, which it may be never did beleeve before, mightily stirred before, but beleeved not, til they goe home and searched the Scriptures, seeing that which is spoken to be fully agreeable to the word of God, they have been brought on wonderfully to beleeve" (*CTF*, 201). Private scripture reading,

Cotton anticipated, would confirm the exegesis preached by the minister, and help to confirm and strengthen the faith of the believing amateur exegete.

In New England, of course, this proved not to be the case. Anne Hutchinson, evaluating the preaching of the local ministers, found the preaching of some more to her liking (and more to her conscience) than the preaching of others, and, if the charges alleged at her trial before the Boston court are to be believed, she publicly expressed her perceptions.[37] Believing that she had the authority of her Teacher behind her, indeed that she was following his instructions, Hutchinson debated interpretation with the colony's ministers and magistrates. Many of them blamed Cotton for the disturbance. To some degree, they were correct. Cotton's preaching both taught Hutchinson the techniques of exegesis and encouraged her to apply those techniques to evaluate the sermons she heard. Little wonder that Hutchinson, intelligent and well educated, found Cotton's preaching exciting and absorbing. Having followed him to New England, she discovered that Cotton's soteriology differed from that taught by Thomas Shepard and Thomas Hooker, that some of their views in fact resembled approaches he had criticized sharply in his English sermons. And noticing these differences, Hutchinson believed that she was following Cotton's advice when she pointed them out, even at her court and church trials.

But the difficulties resulting from Cotton's approach and Hutchinson's response to it were part of a larger problem, one built into the Puritan system of exegesis. Cotton's sermons, holding more closely to straightforward exegesis, exposed tensions within the system most dramatically. His sermons seemed to unfold naturally and inevitably, thus dramatizing the Reformed notion of preaching as an activity of the Spirit working through the minister. In reality, the appearance of inevitability was an illusion, hiding artistry and argumentative strategy. The gap between the surface appearance of Cotton's sermons and their actual nature existed, on some level, in all Reformed preaching. But it was most dramatic in Cotton's sermons, and perhaps as a result, it was Cotton who stood at the center of the Antinomian Controversy. Nevertheless, Shepard and Hooker each negotiated the same tensions that Cotton did, though they did so in different ways. For the complicated nature of Bible reading, exegesis, and preaching was not limited to the preaching of John Cotton, but instead grew out of the entire tradition of Reformed exegesis through Perkins and back to Calvin and Luther, shaping the crises of biblical authority that troubled New England well before the Antinomian Controversy and that were far from resolved by the expulsion and excommunication of Anne Hutchinson.

## CHAPTER 3

# THOMAS SHEPARD: GOD'S WORD
# AND GOD'S WORDS

Like John Cotton, Thomas Shepard (1605–49) hoped that
when he preached, his congregants would hear not him,
but Christ.[1] He lamented those occasions when the Word was
"wonderfully ineffectual to the souls of many men," who heard
"Latimer speak, but not God speaking."[2] But as he strove to
help his congregants hear God speaking in his own sermons,
Shepard used strategies quite different from Cotton's, crafting his sermons as collages of biblical language. Indeed, the
frequency with which Shepard quoted short phrases and full
verses from the biblical text was exceptional even among the
"notable text-[men]" of early New England.[3] Throughout his
preached and later published sermons, Shepard used biblical
quotations, both marked and unmarked, not merely as prooftexts or examples, but as the basic building blocks of his language. Shepard saw such biblical language as offering more
than knowledge and understanding of God. He believed that
the Holy Spirit could choose to inhabit the Word, so that scriptural language offered the possibility of intimate, even mystical, closeness with God. Seeking such closeness for himself
and for his congregants, Shepard took the possibilities of collation to the point of Barthesian "plenitude," crafting sentence
after sentence from biblical verses and verse fragments.[4]

In a typical passage from the sermon series *The Sound Believer*, for example, Shepard incorporated the language of six
different biblical verses into two sentences, interweaving his
own vivid threats with equally vivid biblical ones:

O, reckon now you have yet time to call them to mind, which it may be shall
not continue long; it is the Lord's complaint (Jer. viii. 6) of a wicked generation, "that he could hear no man say, What have I done?" "Winnow yourselves," (as the word is, Zeph. ii. 1,) "O people not worthy to be beloved." I
pronounce unto you from the eternal God, that ere long the Lord will search
out Jerusalem with candles; he will come with a sword in his hand to search
for all secure sinners, in city and country, unless you awaken; he will make
inquisition for blood, for oaths, for whoremongers, which grow to be common; for all secret sins that we are frozen up in.[5]

Besides the marked quotations from Jeremiah and Zephaniah, Shepard inserts
other biblical phrases without indicating his quotations. From Deuteronomy
30:1, he borrows the phrase "call them to mind"; from Zephaniah 1:12, he
takes the phrase "will search out Jerusalem with candles." The "sword in his
hand" of the same sentence comes from 1 Chronicles 21:16, and the "inquisition for blood" is made by the Lord in Psalm 9:12.

Because this passage is fairly typical, Shepard's modern readers have
sometimes associated him with heavy-handed biblical quotation and stulti-
fying reliance on prooftext. If Puritan biblicism in general has been viewed as
restrictive, smothering any creative impulses that New England Puritans
might have had, Shepard presents a particularly difficult case, since other
ministers drew on the biblical text with more evident artistry.[6] John Cotton
crafted elaborate patterns of quotation and exegesis in which a single verse
opened outward into multiple verses, with individual verses returning as
refrains to create a sense of symmetry and balance. Thomas Hooker used
biblical texts to create dramatic dialogues moving through his sermons. But
Shepard's quotations sometimes seem simply excessive, self-indulgent, and
distracting rather than purposeful and focused.

In the passage from *The Sound Believer*, for example, some of the quotations are quite pointed, while others actually seem to pull against his argument. Shepard substitutes his own translations of passages from Jeremiah and Zephaniah for published Bible translations. For example, he uses the
word "winnow" where "gather" appears in both the Authorized and Geneva
translations of Zephaniah 2:1, emphasizing his desire to purify the visible
church. In Shepard's mind, the gathered church is (or should be) equivalent
to the winnowed out church; the emphasis is on separation from the unfit
rather than on coming together as a holy body.[7] Thus Shepard's translation
reinforces his point.

Similarly, some of the biblical phrases that Shepard weaves into this passage are thematically tied to his topic. The phrase from Zephaniah, for example,
is taken from a passage describing God's promised punishment of those who

do not believe.[8] The "sword" of 1 Chronicles 21:16 is drawn against Israel as a punishment for David's disobedience, but its ravages are cut short by God's mercy.[9] These phrases carry with them thematic echoes of the biblical passages that Shepard cites more fully, thus invoking other biblical contexts that tell of God's punishments for the wicked, and driving home his point.

The quotations from Deuteronomy and Psalms, however, are slightly more complex in their interaction with Shepard's argument. In the text from Deuteronomy, the blessing and the curse between which Israel must choose should be "called to mind."[10] The exhortation is prospective—to think about this choice, and return to God—rather than retrospective, as in Shepard's call to reflect on one's sins. The quotation from Psalms, too, is wrenched slightly out of context. Psalm 9 promises the humbled and oppressed that God will punish the wicked; the "inquisition for blood" is celebrated, rather than feared, as in Shepard's appropriation of the text.[11] For Shepard, however, the attraction of biblical language per se takes precedence over concerns about competing contexts. Even at the cost of investing his text with associations that pull against the direction of his argument, Shepard chooses to fill the passage with biblical echoes. As a result, the echoes that enrich the text complicate it as well, tempting us to think that Shepard has simply run amok with his biblical quotations.

## GOD'S WORD AND THE JOY OF PRESENCE

Shepard's obsessive biblical quotation has roots in his sense that scripture and its language offered possibilities of intimacy with the divine. Shepard saw the elect—the "sound believers" and "sincere converts" of his sermon series—as specially beloved by God. He represented would-be converts as virgins awaiting the arrival of the bridegroom, and suggested that they might find God through the biblical text. Shepard explained that God's "words have an everlasting excellency and efficacy in them, and goodness in them, the sweetest token of his love" (*IH*, 371). Indeed, he urged his congregants to "look upon the whole word rightly dispensed as the Bridegroom's voice," and find that "truly his words are sweet" (*IH*, 372).

Shepard envisioned intimate communion between the Christian and God through God's "sweet" words, and minimized the minister's role in achieving that intimacy (*IH*, 372). Though the possibility of connection came with the preached word—the word "rightly dispensed"—Shepard chose not to mention the minister who "dispensed" it. In fact, in his sermon *Of Ineffectual Hearing the Word*, Shepard mentions the minister only as an example of the human voice heard during "ineffectual hearing" of the word; when communion through language does not occur, the Christian hears "a sound of words," "the word spoken," and "Latimer speak," without hearing "God speaking" (*IH*, 367). Consciousness of the minister might intrude on the intimacy between Christian and God, but only in the absence of the ideal communion for which Shepard strove.

For Shepard, real communion through the language of scripture was especially vital, since the relationship between God and the Christian could reach its consummation only in heaven; as Jonathan Mitchell noted in his preface to *The Parable of the Ten Virgins*, Shepard believed "this present life . . . to be preparation time," preparation for the soul's ultimate union with God.[12] Meanwhile, the biblical word provided the avenue for the highest degree of union that could be experienced on earth: "I can not come to God now; the most I can have of God now is in his word. If it be happiness in heaven to close with God in Christ, truly then it is a man's happiness to close with God in his word on earth" (*IH*, 382). Shepard saw the biblical word as a source of closeness with the divine, allowing the Christian both to be close to God and to close with Him as much as was possible in the earthly realm. And with that closeness came "a marvelous deal of assurance of God's love, and sense of mercy and joy in the Holy Ghost," and "peace" (*IH*, 374).

Nor was this an illusory closeness; the divine presence in the Word was real and strong, almost physical in Shepard's imagery: "This blessed word and voice of God, every tittle of it cost the blood of Christ; written all the lines of it in the blood of Christ. O, make much of it, and it will make much of you; it will comfort you, and strengthen you, and revive you" (*IH*, 382–83). To Shepard, the preached word of God was simultaneously a real sound to be heard and a real written transcript made in blood, carrying with it both the awesome power of God's voice and the mystical associations of Christ's blood.

Shepard did not suggest that this power was universally experienced by all who read the Bible and heard it preached. Like Cotton, he emphasized the Word's possibilities for regenerate readers, for those who were reading with the assistance of the Spirit. Beyond distinguishing between unregenerate and regenerate readers, however, Shepard distinguished as well between "God's external or outward word" and "God's internal word and voice" (*IH*, 365). The former is the bare text itself, "containing letters and syllables," or "God's external voice" (*IH*, 365). It is indeed "God's word, . . . full of glory," but it "only speaks to the ear": those who hear only the external word hear "the word spoken, but only man speaking it" (*IH*, 365). "God's internal word and voice," on the other hand, "secretly speaks to the heart, even by the external word" (*IH*, 365). Not everyone who heard the external voice of God—the human voice reading the "letters and syllables" of the biblical text—would hear God speaking to the heart.

Even those who sometimes heard this internal voice might not always hear it: "the Lord is in his word at one time, the word goes alone at another time; as in Elijah, the Lord was not in the whirlwind, but he spake in the still voice, and hence there he was to Elijah" (*IH*, 367). But when it was audible, those who heard this "internal word" effectually experienced a special intimacy with God; in Shepard's view, the Word was actually inhabited by the divine, and was less a conduit for divine communication than a repository for divine presence. God was *in* the Word, when God chose to be there, just as in the story of Elijah God chooses to be present *in* the "still voice" rather than in the whirlwind.

Shepard had an almost mystical sense of the Word's power. When it was efficacious, that is, when God was present in the Word, Shepard believed that it could have "marvelous" effects: "all the words that run by and pass by the souls of God's people, they do leave a marvelous virtue, to make the souls of God's people like watered gardens, and to increase in grace" (*IH*, 377–78). This "marvelous virtue" could be a "secret virtue," hidden and undetectable until it bore fruit in "a flourishing Christian," without conscious recognition at the time (*IH*, 377–78).[13] Reason, too, was subordinate to God's real presence in the Word: "Reason can see and discourse about words and propositions, and behold things by report, and to deduct one thing from another; but the Spirit makes a man see the things themselves, really wrapped up in those words" (*SB*, 127). Bypassing the conscious mind, the Word and that which is "really wrapped up in" it may travel directly to the heart to produce conviction that is not merely "notional," but "real" and "intuitive" (*SB*, 127).

In his willingness to bypass the mind in the salvific action of the Word, Shepard demonstrates his tendency to set "mystical passion above and against the claims of discursive reason."[14] Nevertheless, as Michael McGiffert notes, the Puritans were hardly "foes of rationality."[15] Shepard's vision of mystical experience operated within the constraints of the Word and of language; virtue might be "secret," but it was nevertheless governed by the operation of God's voice through the biblical text. Anne Hutchinson's examination before the General Court tested the limits of Shepard's comfort with hearing God's voice in the biblical text; nevertheless, Shepard did not speak out against Hutchinson's "immediate revelations," which in fact closely resembled the kind of textual intimacy with the divine that he continued to celebrate in his own preaching, even after the Antinomian Controversy.[16] Shepard's sermons proclaimed his gratitude for the gift of divine presence in and through the Word, for "if thou hast thus heard particularly, and though but little light, life, and peace, yet it is of eternal efficacy, and all to draw thee to Christ"; consequently, he urged, "then bless the Lord: 'for blessed are your ears that hear'" (*IH*, 372). This was a remarkable blessing, Shepard argued, drawing on biblical language of distinction to emphasize the gift that had been granted to

God's chosen ones: "and I say as Moses said, (Deut. iv. 32,) 'Ask, if ever people heard God speaking and live.' The apostle (Heb. xii. 24) makes it a greater matter to come to hear God on Mount Sion, and yet live."[17] And Shepard enthused for himself, "Blessed be God, I live" (*IH*, 373). The biblical text afforded Shepard contact with God's presence, and he rejoiced in that presence as in a continued revelation.

## PREACHING AND PRESENCE

Rejoicing in this gift, Shepard attempted to share it with his congregants. In his sermons, he both celebrated the power of the Word and strove to exploit its spiritual possibilities by using as much biblical language as he could, and by encouraging his congregants to do the same. If the words of the biblical text served as vessels of God's presence, Shepard reasoned, they were to be treasured and used whenever possible, especially on occasions when closeness to God was at issue.

Consequently, Shepard saw biblical language as the appropriate language of preaching. For the goal of preaching was not that the auditors hear the minister, but rather that they hear God through the preaching (*IH*, 367). Ministers must "Preach convincing truth and gospel truth, fetched from heaven" (*IH*, 380). And "How," Shepard asked, "would you have the Lord Jesus by his Spirit to convince men? Must it not be by his word?" (*SB*, 131) Linking the Word and the words that compose it, Shepard built his own prose around biblical quotation whenever he could, simultaneously facilitating more direct transmission of God's voice to his audience and celebrating the joy of that transmission. Whether he wove fragments of quotations into his own sentences, as in his exhortation to "then know God spared not the angels that sinned, and how wilt thou escape, unless the Lord die for thee," incorporating the language of 2 Peter 2:4 into his prose, or whether he used longer sections of biblical material, Shepard was committed to speaking divine language and placing it before his congregants (*SB*, 135). He hoped that God would choose to inhabit that language and create an intimate and efficacious connection with his people, and he reveled in the language of the biblical text because it carried the possibility of that joyous intimacy. In his joy in biblical language, Shepard exemplifies Roland Barthes's account of "heterology by plenitude," a profusion of signifiers by which "the author (the reader) seems to say to them: *I love you all* (words, phrases, sentences, adjectives, discontinuities: pell-mell: signs and mirages of objects which they represent)."[18] Perhaps more than any of his contemporaries, Shepard loved the words and phrases of the biblical text, and expected his reader or listener to share that love.

Shepard's sermons often contain complicated chains of quotation in which he plays with competing contexts to add interest and richness to his preaching. He builds on biblical passages in ways that overturn his audience's expectations, exploiting the contrast between the original contexts of the quotations and the passages into which he inserts them. In *The Sound Believer*, for example, Shepard uses a description of God's treatment of the reprobate to emphasize the glory of the saints:

> What then shall we think, on the contrary, of the glory of the saints,
> wherein the Lord shall set forth his power in glorifying them, as he doth
> the glory of his power in punishing others? and therefore (2 Thess. i. 9) the
> punishment of the wicked is expressed by separation of them "from the
> glory of the Lord's power;" because that in the glory of the saints the Lord
> will (as I may so say) make them as glorious as by his power, ruled by wis-
> dom, he is able to make them. (273)[19]

While the meaning Shepard derives from the verse is not contradicted by the biblical passage itself, it is almost precisely the opposite of the verse's literal meaning. The text promises punishment for the reprobate; from this Shepard derives a promise of glory for the saint, associating the verse not with threat, but with reassurance. Moreover, in the succeeding verse, God is "glorified in his saints," whereas Shepard looks forward to the saints being glorified by God.[20]

Shepard's inversions of these verses are complicated by the fact that the biblical passages themselves yoke together contradictory impulses of glory and destruction, forcing a confrontation with God's destructive power. Shepard exploits this confrontation, winding the tension one turn tighter by yoking punishment and glory to reward as well. By setting the initial context of the verse and the sermonic context into opposition, Shepard uses the pleasure that Barthes locates at such "collisions" simultaneously to enhance his audience's understanding of the original verse and to call attention to his own virtuosity.[21]

Shepard similarly plays with competing contexts and competing expectations when he quotes from Psalm 22 elsewhere in *The Sound Believer*:

> A man accounts it a matter of nothing to tread upon a worm, wherein here
> is nothing seen worthy either to be loved or feared; and hence a man's heart
> is not affected with it. Before the Spirit of conviction comes, God is more
> vile in man's eye than any worm. As Christ said in another case of himself
> (Ps. xxii.,) "I am a worm, and no man," so may the Lord complain, I am viler
> in such a one's eyes than any worm, and no God; and hence a man makes it a

matter of nothing to tread upon the glorious majesty of God, and hence is
not affected with it. (129)

Here, Shepard manipulates the quotation from Psalm 22:6, engaging a variety of contexts beyond the "literal" meaning of the verse.[22] Before introducing the quotation, he first sets up the image of a worm trodden underfoot. In light of Shepard's fascination with divine punishment, this image leads Shepard's auditor/reader to expect a prediction that God will crush the human sinner.

Instead, however, Shepard inverts the image, using it to describe the distorted—and paradoxical—relationship that sinners have with God. He introduces the quotation from Psalms as spoken by Christ, although the text is "A Psalm of David" glossed by the Geneva editors as a plea *to* Christ. In Shepard's construction, the divine speaker proclaims "I am a worm, and no man," rendered lowly, argues Shepard, in the mind of the true worm—the sinning man (129). In elaborating upon this image, Shepard repeats the language and rhythms of the biblical verse, having God remark that he is "viler in such a one's eyes than any worm, and no God" (129). By using—and modifying—the biblical phrasing, Shepard heightens the impact of his image, and thus emphasizes the perversity of the sinner's attitude. Here, as elsewhere, the success of Shepard's image depends on his willingness to invert biblical images, and on the dislocation produced by this inversion. And the triumph that he achieves is twofold—both aesthetic and doctrinal.

Beyond his delight in piling up biblical quotations, in playfully inverting the biblical text, and in the serious results of such play, Shepard often incorporates brief biblical phrases more simply, using biblical language in place of his own words. Sometimes he marks these inclusions as quotations; elsewhere, he expects his audience to recognize his sources without further prompting. Shepard takes particular pleasure in the sounds of biblical words, especially as those sounds relate to his own language. In *The Saint's Jewel*, for example, Shepard uses a biblical text to rhyme his own phrase. He exhorts his audience: "Comfort thyself, Christ is thine. 'I am my beloved's, and my beloved is mine.'"[23] The quotation from Canticles 6:3 testifies to the possibility of comfort; Shepard follows the quotation by advising his audience that "if, therefore, there be enough in Christ's merits," it is proper to "hold up thy head and take comfort to thyself" (289).

Beyond the theological comfort that the Song of Songs itself offers—the attractive idea that the church is beloved by God—Shepard seems here to delight in the rhyming of the biblical language with his own exhortation. On a theological level, the rhyme reinforces the harmony between Shepard's pastoral point and the biblical prooftext, thus validating his invitation to draw comfort. Shepard also takes pleasure on a more straightforwardly aesthetic level, however. The quotation rhyming Shepard's language evinces his satisfaction, not only with the beauty of the biblical words, but with his own ability to manipulate them deftly.

Elsewhere, Shepard shows a similar enjoyment of word sounds, and particularly of rhyme. Just as he cites certain biblical books more frequently than others for their compatibility with his theological approach, certain biblical passages recur frequently, at least in part because Shepard seems to have liked the way they sound.[24] John T. Frederick argues that Shepard composed his sermons "for the ear of the hearer rather than for the eye of a reader," and Charles E. Hambrick-Stowe notes that Shepard often "repeated similar sounds both at the end of successive lines . . . and within lines."[25] Shepard showed a particular predilection for biblical phrases that themselves repeat sounds. He was fond, for example, of the phrase "kick against the pricks," which appears twice in Acts.[26] In one twenty-five-page section of *The Sound Believer*, Shepard uses this phrase three separate times. "O you that walk on in the madness of your minds now, in all manner of sin," he promises, "if ever the Lord do good to you, you shall account your ways madness and folly, and cry out, O Lord, what have I done in kicking thus long against the pricks?" (123). A few pages later, he refers more directly to the biblical text: "When Paul saw Jesus speaking, 'Why persecutest thou me?' (Acts ix.,) he falls down astonished, and dares not kick against the pricks any longer" (134). And still later, he explains, "the Lord therefore lets in this fear to make them know they be but men, and that as proud, and stout, and great as they are, yet that they are not above God, and that it is vain to kick against the pricks, and go on as they have done; for if they do, he will not endure it long" (147). Certainly, the phrase describes a struggle that is very real for Shepard; he often catches himself "kicking against the pricks," and this explains in part the verses' appeal for him. But Shepard also seems to find the sound of the words appealing—they satisfy his aesthetic sense, and his attraction to rhyme. Here, as throughout his sermons, Shepard's quotations mark not merely his interest in particular theological points, but delight in the possibility of virtuosic biblical play. And this delight energizes Shepard's commitment to including biblical words and phrases in his own preached sermons. His joy in God's presence is enriched by his joy in biblical language and in his own.

## Extravagant Quotation and the Cycles of Anxiety

While Shepard's extravagant quotation often seems joyful, loving, and occasionally self-consciously virtuosic, at other times it seems frenetic and even anxious. At numerous points in his sermons, Shepard uses quotation from the biblical text to cover hesitation. In *The Sound Believer*, for example, biblical quotations multiply remarkably when Shepard tries to convey the glory of something he has never seen, but hopes fervently (and anxiously) to see some day. "Consider the glory of the place," Shepard exhorts:

> the Jews did and do dream still of an earthly kingdom, at the coming of their Messiah; the Lord dasheth those dreams, and tells them "his kingdom is not of this world," and that he "went away to prepare a place for them, that where he is, they might be," (John xiv. 2, 3,) and "be with him to see his glory." (John xvii. 23, 24.) The place shall be the third heaven, called our father's house, built by his own hand with most exquisite wisdom, fit for so great a God to appear in his glory (John xiv. 2, 3) to all his dear children; called also a "kingdom." (Matt. xxv. 31,) "Come, ye blessed, inherit the kingdom prepared for you," which is the top of all the worldly excellency, called also "an inheritance," (1 Pet. i. 3,) which the holy apostle infinitely blesseth God for . . . . (268)[27]

Here, Shepard splices together numerous citations, quoting from them rather freely. His appeal to biblical language seems almost frenetic, suggesting not only a desire to use the divine language available to him, but also a reluctance to use his own more fallible words. Shepard's inability to describe the heavenly kingdom heightens his awareness of his current alienation from the divine, even as the text that he appropriates exalts the possibility of future union. In the face of this anxiety, Shepard turns to language that is biblically sanctioned, splicing together descriptions and even seemingly indisputable phrases like "dear children," as well as potentially controversial terms such as "inheritance." Moreover, Shepard's need to appropriate this biblical language is pressing enough that he is willing to bend quotations slightly, changing, for example, the tense of his quotation from the second and third verses of John 14 and marking it as a quotation nonetheless.[28]

Shepard's anxiety about that which he does not know, as well as about that which he cannot feel, shapes his use of biblical language. And Shepard's theological position is particularly anxious, even for a Puritan of his generation. In *The Saint's Jewel*, Shepard describes the Christian as "at board in the world," rather than at home; throughout his earthly life, Shepard's Christian is uneasy (291). In heaven, Christians "are subjects in their own country," while they are "strangers for a time here on earth" (*PTV*, 18). Despite his alienation from the world, however, Shepard finds himself (and the typical Christian) often even more alienated from God.

Shepard's *Autobiography* describes a spiritual pilgrimage that moves not in a straight line, but in a sine wave of spiritual highs and lows. Rather than proceeding smoothly through the stages of conversion, Shepard repeatedly finds himself falling back. Sometimes he feels God's presence intimately, and even believes that God acts "miraculously" on his behalf, but at other times he feels just as strongly that he has fallen away—or that perhaps he never experienced a true conversion after all—and he sorrows in his profound alienation from God.[29]

Shepard's account is full of false starts. He describes a potentially promising moment early in his Cambridge years, but then reports backsliding: "when I was at Cambridge I heard old Doctor Chaderton, the Master of the College, when I came, and the first year I was there to hear him upon a Sacrament day my heart was much affected, but I did break loose from the Lord again" (42). Then, he reports, "half a year after I heard Mr. Dickinson common-place in the chapel upon those words—I will not destroy it for ten's sake (Genesis 19)—and then again was much affected, but I shook this off also and fell from God to loose and lewd company, to lust and pride and gaming and bowling and drinking" (42–43).[30] Although Shepard reports that "the Lord left [him] not," giving him further contact with the godly to help him, later in the same paragraph he finds himself "fearfully left of God" (43).

Throughout his *Autobiography*, Shepard moves between experiences of intimacy with the divine—occasions when God responds to prayers over various predicaments, "hear[ing] and bless[ing]" Shepard and his family, saving them from earthly perils—and times of "affliction," when Shepard believes that he is being punished for his sins (56–57). Even after his conversion, and after serving for several years as a minister, Shepard often finds himself "low sunk in spirit," partially due to his external circumstances and partially because his "sins [are] upon" him (54). As he makes his first attempt to travel to New England, Shepard is troubled by his "weak faith, want of fear, pride, carnal content, immoderate love of creatures," and judges himself unworthy because of his "unmortified, dark, formal, hypocritical heart" (63).

For Shepard, the process of conversion is an anxious one, for any setback throws into question the validity of any positive evidences found earlier. But this anxiety itself becomes a form of evidence—evidence (perhaps) that God has acted to initiate the process that begins with conviction. Even if the moment of God's action cannot be pinpointed, Shepard admits the possibility that God has touched the soul:

> Do not think there is no compunction or sense of sin wrought in the soul
> because you can not so clearly discern and feel it, nor the time of the
> working and first beginning of it. I have known many that have come with

complaints—they were never humbled, they never felt it so, nor yet could
tell the time when it was so; yet there hath been; and many times they have
seen it, by the help of others' spectacles, and blessed God for it. (*SB*, 189)

In such cases, concern about *not* feeling God's action can in fact testify to its
having taken place, and the minister's role is to provide "spectacles" with which
the Christian can discern the heretofore undetectable change.

Anxiety thus becomes a possible source of assurance, as McGiffert emphasizes: "the sound believer could measure his assurance by his anxiety: the
less assured he felt, the more assurance he actually had."[31] Inevitably, however, this assurance cycles back into anxiety. McGiffert explains: "[H]ow could
an aspiring saint, hoping beyond hope, come to believe himself saved without
feeling great joy and relief? If he did not, his case was very doubtful. And how
could these feelings be prevented from dissolving into something very like
complacency or even pride? And how could a proud complacent soul be
saved?" (25). This consequence was especially pronounced for Shepard, who
had a tremendous fear of hypocrisy, and who repeatedly cautioned his audience to "Take heed of defiling secretly the church of God" (*PTV*, 19). Even
in the midst of encouraging the would-be saint, Shepard finds the danger of
hypocrisy creeping into his argument: "Many a soul," he notes, "may think
the Lord hath left it, nay, smitten it with a hard heart, and so make his moan
of it; yet the lord hath wrought real softness, under self-hardness" (*SB*, 189).
This is a fitting argument in a section that seeks to hearten the would-be saint
who has yet to feel God's intervention. But, as if unable to stop himself, Shepard continues: "as many times in reprobates there is felt softness when there
is real hardness" (*SB*, 189). And so the encouragement that Shepard tries to
offer collapses in a worry of unreadable signs and perpetual uncertainty.

Not surprisingly, then, the would-be saint who follows Shepard's program experiences cycles of assurance and anxiety, much like those described
in Shepard's *Autobiography*. For Shepard, as McGiffert astutely observes,
"sainthood . . . was . . . rather a settled process than a settled condition";
Shepard's "mature piety cyclically reenacted in abbreviated form . . . [the]
initial trauma" of Shepard's "original conversion."[32]

Even at the most joyous points in this cycle of anxiety and assurance,
Shepard asserts, even for the true convert, what Phyllis Jones and Nicholas
Jones call "the essential incompleteness of any stage in the process of salvation. The preparation of the sinner is succeeded by that of the saint; the tem-
poral communion a saint enjoys with Jesus Christ during life on earth, by an
everlasting communion during life in heaven."[33] Under the best of circumstances, then, earthly union with the divine is incomplete.[34]

Shepard, however, rarely finds himself in the best of spiritual circum-

stances, and often seems hard put to imagine his audience in those circumstances as well. More often he describes periods of worry and dejection, in
which he is troubled by a sense of alienation from God. Upon his wife's death,
for example, Shepard laments, "the Lord seemed to withdraw his tender care
for me and mine which he graciously manifested by my dear wife."[35] Shepard grieves not only for the loss of his wife and for the spiritual gifts she
brought to him, however; he fears that her death reflects divine abandonment, for God "refused to hear prayer when I did think he would have hearkened and let me see his beauty in the land of the living in restoring her
to health again" (72).[36] On other occasions, in his journal, Shepard records
a similar sense of separation from the divine: as a result of sin, his soul is
marred with "darkness, death, distance from God and God from [him]."[37]

The language of separation appears often in his sermons as well. Shepard
identifies with the story of Saul, who is anointed by God and later finds God's
presence withdrawn as a result of his disobedience. In *The Parable of the Ten
Virgins,* Shepard describes the "loss of God" as "the greatest loss; for it is the
utmost and last plague upon the damned in hell": "My comforts, my friends,
means, heaven is gone; but if God were mine, I would be comforted. No, God
is gone; hence, no sorrow for any loss so much as for this. Saul, (1 Sam. xxvii.
15,) 'God is departed from me.' Hence sore distressed" (33–34). Nor, Shepard
emphasizes, is this sense of abandonment the experience only of those who
are "damned in hell" (33). In fact, it may be more painful for those, like Saul,
who have experienced both God's presence and its withdrawal: "Nay, the Lord
Jesus, when the Father departed for a time, and he knew he would return and
visit him, cried out, 'My God, why hast thou forsaken me?'" (34).[38]

Shepard's invocation of Saul seems more personal in *Of Ineffectual Hearing the Word,* in which he describes the predicament of the Christian from
whom God has withdrawn:

When a man looks for love and speech, and he doth not speak at those times
he is not wont to speak, one may take it as no sign of anger; but when the
Lord shall speak usually, and then he speaks not, this is a sad sign. (1 Sam.
xxviii. 6. 15.) He cries out of this, "He answers me not by Urim nor dreams,"
nor thee by the gospel nor law, neither where he useth to answer. If this
anger were to come, it were some comfort; but when it is now upon thee,
even that very sermon and word whereby he speaks to others, but not a
word to thee. (368)[39]

The pain of having felt God's presence and then feeling only God's silence
seems especially real to Shepard, whose *Autobiography* and journal record
swings between miraculous divine interventions and divine silences. When

God speaks "not a word" to him, Shepard fears that he, like Saul, has been cast off by God.

This pain, of course, has its consolation. Identification with the sufferings of Jesus may help to counter the would-be saint's sense of alienation from the divine. Moreover, if Jesus himself could feel abandoned, then feeling alienated from God is not an incontrovertible sign of reprobation. But in Shepard's soteriology, any sign that is not incontrovertible carries with it great uncertainty, setting off still further cycles of anxiety and assurance.

Shepard, however, finds an antidote to alienation from God in the biblical word. Although Shepard feels that "We are far from God, and therefore we can not hear him," he encourages his listeners to "Draw near to God in the word, by looking on it as God speaking to" them (*IH*, 381). When Shepard must struggle to feel God's presence, his manipulation of biblical language "help[s] to restore the sense of God's presence through discourse."[40] If Shepard cannot feel God's actual presence, he can approach it through divine language, and can hope that God will choose to inhabit the Word as Shepard invokes it.

Thus biblical language, for Shepard, works against anxiety. When God seems absent from him, or when he finds himself on shaky ground theologically, he invokes God's presence by appropriating language that is guaranteed to be true, language that draws him closer to God. For example, in *The Sound Believer*, Shepard uses his skills at collation to paste together quotations describing the glory of the soul: "Consider the glory of the soul: now we know but in part and see but in part; now we have joy at sometimes, and then eclipses befall us on a sudden; but then 'the Lord shall be our everlasting light,' (Is. lx. 19;) then we shall 'see God face to face.' (1 John iii. 1, 2.)" (270).[41] For Shepard, biblical language fills in the gaps in his vision; what he can now "see but in part" he hopes someday to see in full. He can describe his current state—alternating periods of "joy" and "eclipse[d]" joy. But his own words seem inadequate to describe the joy that he hopes will come to him later, a joy that Shepard has not yet experienced and a joy for which human language itself may be inadequate. And so he turns to divine language to describe this other condition. What he cannot describe with confidence, the words of Isaiah and Genesis can. And when Shepard feels that even the earthly possibilities of joy are unfulfilled for him, the divine presence that he experiences in these texts of promise stands in for the presence that seems "eclipsed" in his own soul, drawing him closer to it.

Moreover, Shepard saw language itself as bound up in the process of salvation. He envisioned his converts not only reading the Bible in new ways, but also using its language themselves, for biblical language was the language appropriate to the experience of salvation. The would-be convert must learn proper speech: "our Saviour (Jude 15) will one day convince the wicked of all their hard speeches against him, which will chiefly be done by manifesting the evil of such ways, and taking away all those colors and defenses men have made for their language" (126).[42] Replacing the "colors" and rhetorical devices that hide sin, biblical language is the proper medium for expressing divine activity in the human soul and the awareness of this divine presence.

And so Shepard envisioned souls who become aware of God speaking in the phrases of the biblical text. If "the Lord do[es] good" to those who "walk on in the madness of [their] minds," they will "account [their] ways madness and folly, and cry out," expressing their remorse in the language of Acts, "O Lord, what have I done kicking thus long against the pricks?" (123). And similarly, "when the Spirit hath thus convinced, now a man begins to see his madness and folly in times past," and marks his new closeness to God by imitating the language of Jesus on the cross, "saying, I know not what I did" (128).[43] In his preaching, Shepard demonstrated to his congregants how they could make biblical language their own, speaking its words and thus achieving intimacy with Christ.

As Shepard lived through the cycles of assurance and anxiety in his spiritual life, he turned to the language of the biblical text both to express his joy and to assuage his sense of alienation from God. When he felt confident of his salvation, he loved the text for the divine presence that inhabited it. When he feared that he was doomed, he clung to the text as his only contact with the divine. And when his assurance returned, he felt even more love and gratitude toward the words that had sustained him in his alienation from God. Through the various phases of Shepard's spiritual cycles, he incorporated biblical language into his own prose, reveling in its artistry and using it to support his own. Above all, he hoped, by speaking in divine language, to bring the divine presence into the sermons he preached and published, and into the lives of his audience.

## CHAPTER 4

# Applying the Word Home:
# Thomas Hooker's Affective
# Reading and Preaching

In his *Magnalia Christi Americana*, Cotton Mather offers an anecdote to demonstrate the remarkable power of Thomas Hooker's preaching. During Hooker's English ministry, a "profane person, designing therein only an ungodly diversion and merriment, said unto his companions, 'Come, let us go hear what that bawling Hooker will say to us.'"[1] Although he and his companions went to Hooker's lecture at Chelmsford "with an intention to make sport," Mather reports:

> The man had not been long in the church, before the *quick and powerful word* of God, in the mouth of his faithful Hooker, pierced the soul of him; he came out with an awakened and distressed soul, and by the further blessing of God upon Mr. Hooker's ministry, he arrived unto a true *conversion;* for which cause he would not afterwards leave that blessed ministery, but went a *thousand leagues* to attend it and enjoy it. (1:337)

Hooker's contemporaries echoed the assessment of this "profane person." John Cotton, writing in a preface to Hooker's *A Survey of the Summe of Church Discipline*, praised him for his "powerfull" preaching, despite what Perry Miller calls "rivalry and even enmity" that had existed between the two men.[2] That rivalry may account for the somewhat backhanded compliment that precedes Cotton's assessment:

*Paul* in the Pulpit, *Hooker* could not reach,
Yet did He Christ in Spirit so lively Preach:
That living Hearers thought He did inherit
A double Portion of *Pauls* lively spirit.[3]

And John Winthrop, the eminent governor of Massachusetts Bay, marked Hooker's death by noting in his journal that "the fruit of [Hooker's] labours in bothe Englandes shall preserve an honourable ∧& happye∧ remembrance of him for ever."[4] Moreover, Winthrop asserted that "for pietye, prudence, wisdome, zeale, learninge, & what els might make him serviceable in the place & tyme he liued in," Hooker "might be compared with men of greatest note" (690–91).[5]

Although most modern readers of Hooker's sermons respond with considerably less enthusiasm than his contemporaries, they acknowledge Hooker's reputation as "a particularly *affective* preacher," and often find Hooker more readable, more accessible, and even more likable than his ministerial colleagues in New England.[6] Hooker's enduring appeal is on some level surprising; after all, his sermons emphasize the early steps in the preparatory process, demanding contrition, humiliation, and "a true sight of sinne."[7] On the other hand, Hooker's sermons are, by modern standards, the most obviously artful of the early New England pulpit; they contain moments of drama, and even moments of humor.[8] Moreover, of the ministers in New England's first generation, Hooker was the most concerned with audience response, and the most skilled at manipulating that response. Indeed, as he "opened" the text to his congregants, Hooker specialized in applying God's word to his auditors, and demanded in turn that they as readers actively and emotionally engage the text.

To encourage such engagement, Hooker manipulated the text carefully and artfully. He emphasized the personal application of the Bible to the reader or auditor, and his interpretive strategies broke down boundaries among author, reader, interpreter, and text. Like his colleagues, Hooker drew on the interpretive tools and guidelines stressed by Perkins and Bernard, but rather than "pour[ing] his sermons into a mould which had been prepared by" Perkins and Bernard, Hooker applied them fluidly and flexibly.[9] Often, he "opened" texts by manipulating the interaction between collation and the circumstances of the place propounded. By exploiting the various contexts activated by his biblical quotations, Hooker forced his listeners to identify powerfully with the biblical figures he invoked and to develop a sense of personal interaction with the biblical text. Hooker also treated the text itself as fluid, sometimes blurring the boundaries between the written text and the Word as he understood it. Bending the text to his own pastoral purposes, he created sermons that, in the words of Cotton Mather, had a "rare mixture of *pleasure* and *profit*," and which were "exceedingly frequented," both during his English ministry at Chelmsford and in New England (*Magnalia*, 1:335).[10]

## AFFECTIVE PREACHING AND PARTICULAR APPLICATION

Hooker's sermons were so effective, Mather explains, in part because "his *preaching* was notably set off with a *liveliness* extraordinary" (*Magnalia*, 1:337). Mather praises Hooker for the "nimbl[eness]" and "fluency" with which he suggested and moved between "distinct *images* of things," as "the true *zeal* of *religion* [gave] *fire* to his discourses" (1:337). Indeed, Hooker's sermons are full of shifts and dislocations. He played with the dislocations produced by his collations, shifting from biblical image to biblical image, from biblical image to natural image, and from biblical personage to contemporary listener. As Mather reports, these shifts dazzled and delighted his audience.

Hooker, however, was not interested in merely dazzling his audience. Rather, he believed in the power of the preached word to produce a personal response in each listener: "There was never any convicting Ministry," argued Hooker in one of his best-known sermon series, "nor any man that did in plainenesse apply the word home, but their people would be reformed by it, or else their consciences would be troubled, and desperately provoked to oppose God and his ordinances, that they may be plagued by it" (*SP*, 64). Hooker stressed the particular and personal application of the biblical text to the individual listener. Building on the biblical image, he described effective preaching as an attack that overcomes the listener's defenses: "The word of God is like a sword; the explanation of the text is like a drawing out of this sword, and the flourishing of it, and so long it never hits: But when a man strikes a full blow at a man, it either wounds or puts him to his fence: So the application of the Word is like the striking with the sword, it will worke one way or other, if a man can fence the blow, so it is: but if not, it wounds" (64).[11] Hooker recognized that even the most skillful minister had limits—"awaken[ing] the heart" was God's sole prerogative, "beyond [the minister's] power" (64). But a minister who preached to his listeners without pushing for emotional identification with the biblical promise was merely playing with the sword of the Spirit, showing off his flourishes at the expense of his congregants' spiritual welfare. In Hooker's case, the sword was apparently brandished to great effect, for Mather records that Hooker "had a most excellent faculty at the applications of his doctrine; and he would therein so touch the *consciences* of his auditors, that a judicious person would say of him, 'He was the best at an use that ever he heard'" (*Magnalia*, 1:335).

This was Hooker's sense of his role; he aspired, in Mather's words, to touch "the *consciences* of his auditors" (*Magnalia*, 1:335). The congregation should be dazzled not with the minister's skill, but with deeper spiritual realities, by the impact of the Word:

> When there is that wisedome and knowledge revealed to the soule so powerfully, that it prevailes with the heart, and it gives way thereto, so that all the replies and pleas of the soule be taken away, and the soule falls under the stroke of the word, not quarrelling, but yeelding it selfe, that the word may worke upon it, and withall there is a restlesse amazement put into the heart of the creature, and a kinde of dazeling the eye, so that the soule is not content now before it see the worst of his sinne that is revealed, and then it lies under the power of that truth which is made knowne. (*SP*, 26–27)

Hooker believed that this dazzling was best accomplished by particular application, which he consequently defined as the minister's particular concern. This was the *"place and duty of a Minister,"* his "special charge"; each minister bore a grave responsibility for his congregation's spiritual welfare, those "under his guidance and of whose safety he must give an account."[12] Hooker urged that the minister "therefore should have a particular care to foresee, and so to prevent the particular and special evils, which he perceives to blemish the Christian course, and endanger the spiritual comforts of [those] people; and this wil not be done unless a man single out the persons and set home their sins in special" (*AR 9–10, 195*).

Hooker's emphasis was on reaching the individual sinner with his applications, "to hit the humor of the heart of a sinner, to make a receipt on purpose to meet with the particular distemper such as wil worke upon" whatever sins that sinner may have (195). For this practice, he cited biblical precedent: "and so the Lord to the Prophet *Ezek.* 16.2. *Cause the house of Israel to know their abominations*" (195).[13] Part swordsman, part physician, Hooker's ideal minister fulfilled the role of biblical prophet, addressing himself to the hearts of his listeners, and applying the Word "home."

## INTERACTION WITH THE WORD

Hooker's understanding of the minister's role, and of the need to create emotional identification with the biblical promise, reflected his overall approach to the Bible. Taking seriously "the severe command that the Apostle gave his Scholar *Timothy, I charge thee before God, and the Lord Iesus Christ, who shall judge the quick and the dead, preach the word, be instant in season, and out of season, reprove, rebuke,"* Hooker applied it to the minister's task, adding his own emphasis: "(as if he had said) the stubborne hearts of men need this specially, *reprooving,* and therefore doing this, this is the maine thing that God requires, and the maine end for which the Word serves" (*SP,* 69). In Hooker's view, the biblical text's main function was to be a source of reproof, a way of pressing people into the regenerative process by producing a true sight of sin. Though only God could plant the seed of grace which would enable a sinner to see his sin clearly, and allow him then to experience contrition and humiliation, Hooker saw preaching as a means by which God opened the sinner's eyes, and the biblical text as the minister's primary tool.

Though Hooker was tremendously respectful of the text's power as a spiritual sword, he emphasized the text not in and of itself, but for its potential impact on its reader.[14] Nevertheless, as Thomas Goodwyn and Philip Nye, publishers of *The Application of Redemption,* explained in their preface, Hooker "had been trained up from his Youth, in the Experience and Tryal of Gods Dispensations and Workings this way; and vers'd in digging into the Mines and Veins of Holy Scriptures, to find how they agreed with his own Experiments."[15] Hooker's emphasis was experimental—evaluating and interpreting the Scriptures in accordance with his experiences as a Christian and as a minister. Moreover, his approach was affective, privileging the heart over the understanding as the proper locus of interaction with the biblical text. Hooker explained that "hee that thinks himselfe the wisest in understanding . . . knowes little or nothing of which he should and ought to know: But imagine men had knowledge of the Word, that is not the maine end of preaching to instruct men: but to worke upon their hearts" (*SP,* 70). Hooker disdained mere biblical knowledge divorced from its affective power.

That disdain extended to displays of linguistic virtuosity, for which Hooker had little use: "What doth it profit a man to scrape up a ltttle *[sic]* Greek and Latine together, and to leave the sense of the Scripture undiscovered and the conscience no whit touched, nor the heart stirred? He that knowes any thing, though he were but an ordinary schoole-boy, that had but any skill in the tongues, if he could not doe it, hee should be scourged by my consent" (*SP,* 59–60). One who had such knowledge and failed to apply it was contemptible in Hooker's eyes, not because his knowledge itself was insignificant, but rather because it was precious. Knowledge for its own sake wasted the gift of God's word, a gift which had so much power to do good to the minister's congregants.

In fact, ministers who showed off their linguistic skill could hinder their congregants' spiritual growth. Hooker explained "why a company of Gentlemen, Yeomen, and poore women, that are scarcely able to know their A.B.C. . . . have a Minister to speake Latine, Greeke, and Hebrew, and to use the Fathers, when it is certaine they know nothing at all" (*SP,* 66). The reason was far more grievous in his eyes than some sort of misplaced respect for learning: "The reason is, because all this stings not, they may sit and sleepe in their sinnes, and goe to hell hood-winckt, never awakened, and that is the reason they will welcome such to their houses, and say, Oh he is an excellent man, I would give any thing I might live under his Ministery" (66). Echoing Perkins's objections to ostentatious displays of learning, Hooker argued that the minister who used Latin, Greek, and Hebrew decreased the impact of the Word on his listener by increasing the distance between the text and the listener.[16]

Hooker's project was instead to decrease that distance in order to maximize the emotional impact of the biblical text. This emphasis affected Hooker's approach to the Bible—both his instructions about proper biblical reading and the ways in which he used the biblical text in his preaching. In *The Poor Doubting Christian Drawn Unto Christ*, his "earliest published sermonic text," Hooker laid out rules for the Christian reader of Scripture.[17] These rules, in keeping with Hooker's practical approach to the text, explicitly related scripture reading to a particular purpose; they were "[Four] Rules to Direct a Christian How to Use the Word of God for the Evidence of His Assurance" (168). Hooker proposed an approach to scripture reading which was reader-centered and affect-centered, rooted in his understanding of faculty psychology and soteriology.[18] His instructions were concerned with the proper orientation of the reader, with the reader's attitude, and with the reader's reaction to the text, rather than with particular properties of the text itself.

In his instructions to the doubting Christian, Hooker emphasizes "uses": "First, that we may so use the word of God as we ought. As thou must in the conditions that concern thy soul repair to the world, so thou must consider thine own uprightness, and what work of grace is in thy soul, that will answer the Word and testify that the work of grace is true. Be sure to take thy soul at the best" (168).[19] Hooker advises his reader to seek assurance by engaging in a dialogue with the text, examining his or her soul to find "grace . . . that will answer the Word" (168). Comparing the promises to a staff, which one cannot grasp with the back of one's hand, Hooker exhorts his reader: "turn thou the right side of thy soul to the promise, and then thou mayest take it" (169). Just as Hooker's soteriology emphasized necessary human responses to divine grace, his instructions here relate not to the staff itself, but to the hand reaching out to it.[20] The doubting Christian is instructed to scrutinize not the text so much as herself, so that she can receive its promises. The difficulty lies not in reading the text, but in reading one's own soul.

The remaining rules advise similar strategies. Hooker urges his reader, "Secondly, labor to have thy conscience settled and established in that truth which now out of the Word thou hast gotten, to bear witness to the work of grace in thee" (169). The truth has already been "gotten" "out of the Word," and the Christian's proper focus is now on herself, specifically on her conscience and on personal manifestations of grace. In his third rule, Hooker directs the reader's attention to her own heart, exhorting the Poor Doubting Christian to "strive mightily to have our hearts overpowered with the evidence which reason and conscience makes good to us, that so we may quietly receive it and calmly welcome it, and yield and subject our hearts to that truth" (171).

In the final rule, the Christian is advised to "maintain the good word which thy heart hath submitted to, and keep it as the best treasure under heaven" (174). Here, Hooker does direct the Christian's attention back to the text, calling on the reader to "Hear nothing but out of the word of God against that comfort and evidence of the Word which thou hast been persuaded of by the Word" (174). While the reading process requires the Christian to extract the truth from the text and then apply it in self-examination, and while the predetermined goal of this is "comfort," the text nonetheless remains the arbiter of doubts: "If Satan or carnal reason have anything to say against thee, let them bring Scripture, and then yield to it; but without the Word hear nothing" (174). Hooker maintains the authoritative status of the text, even as his approach emphasizes the reader's interaction with that text.

Nevertheless, Hooker's approach to biblical reading contrasts sharply with the parallel discussions in William Perkins's *Arte of Prophecying*. Unlike Hooker, Perkins focuses significant attention on the text itself. While he is certainly concerned with the applied text, most of his instructions concern the proper methods for deriving meaning and for proper understanding of the text. One might suggest that Hooker's lay audience determines his less scholarly emphasis. But his instructions seem firmly oriented toward the reader even when compared to those in Lewis Bayly's lay-directed *The Practise of Pietie*.[21] Like Hooker, Bayly is concerned with scripture reading's practical benefits, exhorting his readers to apply the Bible to their own lives, "eyther to confirme thy *faith*, or to encrease thy *Repentance*" (313). Nevertheless, he places greater emphasis on the meaning of the text unapplied, and on the integrity of the text itself. Bayly advises a schedule of readings enabling the Christian to read the Bible through over the course of the year "in *order*," which "will helpe thee the better to understand both the *History* and *scope* of the holy *Scripture*" (315). Though Hooker never objects to reading through the Bible each year, he expresses less concern about the Christian's knowledge of scriptural history than about the potential impact of various segments of that history on the Christian's spiritual life.

In his preaching, Hooker exploited a number of techniques to heighten the impact of the preached word (and the read biblical word) on his audience. He strove, above all, to personalize the biblical account, encouraging his au-

dience to internalize the biblical text. In *The Application of Redemption . . .
The Ninth and Tenth Books,* Hooker explains that preaching "General Truths
generally do[es] little good":

> That which is spoken to all, is spoken to none at al. No man heeds more
> than needs he must to such things he hath little heart unto, or takes little
> delight in. An Inditement or Attachment without a name, read, published,
> and proclaimed in the face of the Worlds, no man is either troubled at it, or
> reclaimed by it; but when the name is recorded, and the man challenged, it
> makes him bethink himself how to get a Surety, or pay the debt, or prevent
> the danger. So is it with a general reproof, no man will own it, and therefore
> no man reforms by it, or is forced to seek out. (196)

Although Hooker believed in pointing out the particular sins of the individual sinner, the names he named in his sermons were not those of his congregants, but those of biblical figures. His scriptural art involved various techniques by which he led his audience to identify with the biblical text, and with
its personages, both saints and sinners.[22] In Hooker's ideal scenario, the soul
that "falls under the stroke of the word" recognizes himself in the sinners
that the minister describes: "The Minister saith, God hates such and such a
sinner; and the Lord hates me too, saith the soule, for I am guilty of that
sinne" (*SP*, 26–27). The minister, with a full range of sins available as material for preaching, relies on a certain amount of chance if he is to hit on the
particular sins of an individual—and of course, divine assistance, "if now the
Lord be pleased to worke mightily" (27). Then, it often happens that "at last
the Minister meetes with his corruptions, as though he were in his bosome,
and he answereth all his cavills; and takes away all his objections" (27). The
results are happy ones indeed: "With that the soule begins to be amazed to
thinke that God should meete with him in this manner," and recognizes his
need for God's mercy and his status as "the most miserable sinner that ever
was borne" (27). Under such circumstances, a "sinner" attending "unto the
ordinary means" of the word preached may achieve a true sight of sin, an important step in the preparatory process as Hooker understood it (27). Identification can be powerful, Hooker suggests, with the assistance of God
"work[ing] mightily" through the means.

John Collins testified to the effectiveness of Hooker's strategy. On hearing Hooker preach on "First Romans 18," Collins reported: "I thought he certainly knew what a sinner I had been what covenants I had broke and seeing
I had held the truth in unrighteousness I thought I was as good as in hell already one that had so grievously abused the light there would be no other
portion for me."[23] To attach "a name" to his "Inditements" without actually

singling out particular members of his congregation, Hooker manipulated his audience's identification with biblical figures, personalizing those figures and setting up dialogues between individual sinners and the biblical text.

## IDENTIFICATION AND DISLOCATION

To develop his audience's identification with biblical figures, Hooker often manipulated the dislocations produced by collation. Using stories of biblical figures, Hooker quoted from the texts in ways that played consciously with the multiple contexts within which his quotations functioned. In both *The Sovles Preparation for Christ* and *The Application of Redemption*, for example, Hooker uses the story of Jonah's stormy passage to dramatize the need for particular calling. "Overly discourses that men be great sinners, and the like," he explains, "are like the confused noise that was in the ship when *Ionah* was *a sleepe* in it" (*SP*, 63).[24] This

> confused noise . . . never troubled [Jonah], till at last the Master came and said, *Arise, O Sleeper, and call upon thy God;* And, as a father obserues, they came about him, and euery man had a blow at him, and then hee did awake: So because of generall reproofes of sinne, and termes a far off, men come to Church, and sit and sleepe, and are not touched nor troubled at all. But when particular application commeth home to the heart, and a Minister saith; This is thy drunkennesse, and thy adulterie and prophanenesse, and this will brake thy necke one day. . . . Then men begin to looke about them. (63–64)

This passage is typical of Hooker's biblical intertextuality in several ways. First, he uses a biblical example to emphasize the importance of particular application—a much favored theme. Second, Hooker uses this example to render a spiritual problem concrete and almost physical: one can sleep through general applications, just as one can sleep through a general hubbub, but someone trying to wake up a particular sleeper is much harder to ignore. Moreover, Hooker reinforces the translation of the spiritual to the physical (or even biological) by moving beyond the biblical realm to the world of everyday England—Jonah sleeping through the storm is not only the sleeping soul, but the Chelmsford parishioner sleeping through the sermon. The biblical words of the shipmaster apply on all levels, to each of the "sleepers" envisioned: *"Arise, O Sleeper, and call upon thy God,"* indeed, whichever of these three you may be.[25]

Aside from the multiple identifications for the sleeper suggested in this passage, Hooker exploits the additional complexities invoked by the figure of Jonah. Hooker's sermons reveal a particular investment in prophetic examples, even more so when the prophets themselves play ambivalent roles. Jonah the sleeping sinner shuts out the storm of God's wrath, and thus models the sleeping sinner repressing the minister's call to recognize his sin. But as Hooker's audiences would certainly recognize, the sleeping Jonah is also a sleeping prophet, having fled God's call to admonish the people of Nineveh. Jonah's explanation of his flight—his confidence that particular application will be powerful enough to bring about the repentance of the people of Nineveh—and the eventual repentance of the Ninevites confirm the importance of particular application once again.

Moreover, the sinning biblical prophet emphasizes the possibility of multiple or confusing identities; just as the prophet can sin by fleeing God's word, the sinners within the congregation are potentially prophets. Hooker was especially interested in biblical examples that testify to the fluidity of these roles—sinners can sometimes teach well, and prophets can sin. So the Christian operating in a preparationist system can expect to be confused sometimes about who he is, about whether he is a sinner or a saint.

Finally, Jonah appealed to Hooker because he models both bad and good listening, topics of particular interest to Hooker, whose affect- and, finally, effect-centered approach to reading paralleled a similar approach to the related act of listening to sermons. Just as a reader must strive to make his reading affect his soul, Hooker contended that the sermon hearer must make an effort to be affected by the sermon preached to him. As Bush explains, "Hooker was consistently working to develop a receptive audience, he was helping them to see that their own receptive attitude as listeners was itself a sign of their election."[26] Consequently, Hooker devoted much sermonic attention to good and bad hearers, citing "many 'listeneres' in both the Old and New Testaments as representatives of the type of the good hearer."[27]

Often, the listeners invoked by Hooker required his auditors to make elaborate shifts in identification. In *The Sovles Preparation*, Ahab appears as a complex example of a bad listener influenced in spite of himself by the power of particular application. Quoting extensively from the text of 1 Kings 21, Hooker relates Ahab's confrontation with Elijah: "When *Ahab* had slaine *Naboth*, the *Prophet Elias* came to him, and sayes, *In the place where dogges licke the blood of* Naboth, *shall dogges licke thy blood: Ahab* said, *Hast thou found mee out, O my enemy? And he said, I have found thee out, because thou hast sould thy selfe to worke* nickednesse [sic] *in the sight of the Lord;* and the text saith, *When he heard this, hee put on sackcloth and went softly*" (*SP*, 61). Ahab's response to Elijah's prophecy anchors Hooker's argument: "This was the power of a particular reproofe, though he were a miserable wicked man" (61–62). Hooker proceeds to cite other scriptural precedents, concluding with another near-quotation, "And this is the rule in generall, as the Apostle saith, *Reproove them sharply that they may be sound in the faith*" (62).

Ahab serves as an example not only of the efficacy of particular application, but also of proper listening. Even this "miserable wicked man," Hooker emphasizes, accepts reproof and reacts accordingly. How much more so, then, must good Christians living under a sound ministry? Hooker thus asks his audience simultaneously to identify with and to distance themselves from the figure of Ahab. They must know, as Ahab did, that they have been "found out," and "put on sackcloth and [go] softly," if not literally, then at least figuratively (61). On the other hand, the impetus to emulate Ahab's response to particular application stems in part from a need to separate from him—to avoid being "a miserable wicked man" (62). Of course, all are miserable, and all are wicked, but once again the Christian is asked to acknowledge the depth and intractability of his sin even as he determines to work to overcome it.[28]

Hooker further complicates this identification by returning to Ahab a few pages later. Once again, he exhorts his congregants to recognize the Ahab in themselves, and to reject him. Those who wish to live under the less-piercing ministry of the scholar who injects Latin and Greek into his sermons show their kinship to Ahab: "it is just *Ahabs* old humour, hee could sute seasonably with *foure hundred false Prophets,* and if there had been five thousand more, they should all have been accepted of him: but when *Iehosaphat* said, Is there never another *Prophet* of the Lord: Oh yes (saith *Ahab*) *there is one Michaiah but I hate him, hee never spake good to mee:* that is, hee never soothes me up" (66). Having already recognized the dimensions of Ahab within themselves—those to be rejected and those to be emulated—the congregation is now asked to assimilate further (perhaps familiar) identifications. Ahab has already heard a prophecy of condemnation, both in the biblical narrative and in Hooker's own, and is now the sinner who would avoid hearing such prophecy at all costs. He thus models not only resistance to effective preaching, but also the complexities of backsliding. Here, Ahab is the bad listener, but complicated by our knowledge that he *can* listen well, that he is capable of some level of repentance. Hooker demands that his audience hear Ahab's language as their own, and then reject it, rejecting as well his resistance to the divine will.

The manipulation of Ahab in this sermon engages the psychological predicament of a Christian working within a preparationist soteriology. Hooker addresses his congregants, asking them to be good listeners. But in explaining good listening to them, he presses them to identify with bad listeners. Similarly, in the preparatory process that Hooker espoused, recognizing the depth of one's sin was a necessary step, but one could paradoxically take comfort in sincere feelings of self-disgust. This seems to have been a rather precarious position; Hooker in fact devoted attention in *The Application of Redemption* to the problem of identifying sound contrition, and to the challenge of separating God-given feelings of self-disgust from more ordinary human ones.[29] At the same time, Hooker exploited the tentativeness of this position through shifting identifications with biblical saints and sinners, throwing his audience off balance by surprising them with the multiple directions in which he expected them to identify. These identifications thus became a powerful tool Hooker used to render his audience receptive, both to his message and to the promises of the biblical word.

## IN DIALOGUE WITH THE WORD

In exploiting identifications with biblical characters, Hooker exploited as well the language of the biblical text, placing his audience in dialogue with it. He incorporated biblical language into his own prose, drawing from it both the aesthetic pleasures that came from audience recognition of quotation and the sanction of the biblical text. Hooker drew heavily on passages that exhort or plead, and showed a marked predilection for the books of Job, Psalms, Isaiah, Jeremiah, and Matthew. As in the examples discussed above, Hooker skillfully exploited the multiple layers of meaning that he derived from the various contexts in which he situated the quoted text—the biblical context, the spiritual context, and often the quotidian context as well. Also, Hooker most often identified speakers and addressees by name, as he does in the passages drawn from Jonah, Samuel, and Kings. Consistent with his theory of particular application, Hooker thus personalized and humanized both the biblical figures and the message of the biblical language.

Hooker often used the language of the prophets and apostles to exhort the congregation, turning their voices to address his assembled audience. In *The Sovles Preparation*, for example, he paraphrases Acts 7:51, pulling his congregation into biblical roles and appropriating prophetic authority for himself:

> I tell you that there is never an creature that lives in any such sinfull course, but hee is a fighter against God, and hee resists the Lord as really as one man doth another: And as *Stephen* saith, *You stiffe-necked and uncircumcised in heart, you have resisted against the holy Ghost:* You must not think that you resist men onely, no (poore creatures) you resist the Spirit, and so ayme at the Almighty in opposing the means of grace. (*SP*, 17–18)[30]

As is often the case in this sermon series, prophetic authority is identified with ministerial authority. Hooker emphasizes the seriousness of resisting the minister, and thereby resisting the means of grace; in doing so, one resists not "men onely," but "the Spirit, . . . the Almighty" himself (17–18).

Hooker allowed not only prophets and apostles, but God himself, to address the congregation directly through biblical inclusions in the sermon text. Emphasizing the prophetic quality of preaching, Hooker quotes God in his discussion: "First, know this, that there is a time that god will not shew mercy, *Behold*, saith God, *I gave her a time of repentance, but she repented not; therefore I will cast her upon the bed of sicknesse:* as our Saviour saith to *Ierusalem, Oh that thou hadst knowne in this thy day, the things belonging to thy peace; but now they are hid from thine eyes*" (50–51). Here, Hooker splices together multiple verses. The first quotation, for example, though marked marginally "Revel.2.21.22," in fact splices those verses together with Psalm 41:3.[31] Hooker thus appropriates divine authority for a human patching together—a human interpretation—of God's word. The immediate effect, however, is to make God speak as a character in Hooker's sermon, emphasizing his presence and his communication with the congregation.

Hooker further emphasizes communication with the divine when he sets up dialogue between the Christian (usually doubting or sinning) and the biblical text. Crafting dialogues out of biblical verses allows Hooker to stress the responsibilities of the human participant in the process of salvation; the Christian interrogates both the text and himself, and often receives answers of comfort. In Book 10 of *The Application of Redemption,* for example, Hooker draws on Isaiah 55:7–9 to emphasize the magnitude of God's mercy.[32] He describes the "largeness" of "Mercy" that is available from an "Infinite" God, "and therefore infinitely exceeds all our wants, and can supply them, all our weaknesses and infirmities, and therefore can forgive them, and remove them as he will, as though they had never been" (22). Without interrupting his sentence, Hooker moves from his own description of God's mercy to the biblical one: "*Isa. 55.7. Let the wicked forsake his way, and the unrighteous man his thoughts, and return unto the Lord, for he will abundantly pardon, and to our God, for he will have mercy*" (22).

Hooker envisions a dialogue between the sinner and the text, imagining a sinner unable to trust this offer of mercy, and interrupting the text with his objections: "But the discouraged sinner might happily reply, It is mercy tendered, yet I in the time of my folly have trampled under my feet, and therefore with what face could I beg mercy, or upon what ground could I think ever to receive it?" (22) The text, of course, has an answer for this: "He answers, *For my thoughts are not your thoughts, nor your waies my waies; for as the*

*Heavens are higher than the Earth, so are my thoughts than your thoughts"*
(22). Hooker elaborates upon this answer, explaining that "there is no proportion, no comparison, the earth is not of a valuable consideration to the
heavens, but like a Centre in the Circumference, it is as though it were not"
(22). But the answer itself is provided by the biblical text.

Often, Hooker extends the dialogue between sinner and text so that the
biblical text speaks both parts: *"Let him make speed* (saith the wicked) *that
wee may see it, and let the counsell of the most high draw nigh, that we may
know it. . . .* To which I answer; It is desperate ignorance, and marvailous
Atheisme of heart, whereby the devil labours to keepe men in sin; the *Lord
knowes thy thoughts long before"* (*SP,* 47). Here, again, Hooker allows one
biblical paraphrase to answer another.[33]

Hooker found ample material for such dialogues in the Bible's cast of negative exemplars—multitudes of sinners who could be quoted in their errors,
scoffings, and objections. But surprisingly, Hooker sometimes wrenched texts
from saintlier mouths and placed them in the mouths of sinners, radically altering the implications of texts from their original contexts. In describing the
ways "that the soule useth to put by the word, and to prevent the danger threatened," Hooker in fact inverts biblical words of comfort (*SP,* 46). In 1 Timothy
1:15, Paul declares, "This *is* a faithful saying, and worthy of all acceptation, that
Christ Jesus came into the world to save sinners; of whom I am chief." Hooker,
however, rejects a similar declaration from a contemporary sinner. "Some will
say," explains Hooker, "God may give me repentance, Christ came into the
world to *save sinners* and why may he not save mee? I answere, Is that all? is
it come to this? And who knowes but that God may damne thee too?" (*SP,* 50)

For Hooker's audience, this twist would present a surprise—an instance
of intertextuality in which the original context of the text collided with what
Roland Barthes might call the "plagiarizing edge" of Hooker's sermon.[34] Nor
is this merely a rhetorical flourish. The dislocation invites scrutiny of the biblical text, and calls attention to the difference between the biblical frame and
the sermon frame of this statement. The biblical speaker reveals that he has
a "true sight of sin." The reprobate of *The Sovles Preparation,* on the other
hand, knows that he is a sinner, but hasn't yet recognized the magnitude of
his sin. He is appropriating the promises prematurely and presumptuously.
The ordeal of Joanna Drake, the woman Hooker successfully counseled for
despair, had taught him how painfully the biblical text could be misread and
misapplied.[35] Here, Hooker's own inversion of the biblical text warns against
such misuse by emphasizing the gap between his sermon and the original
"circumstances of the place propounded."

At the same time, Hooker's placement of an explicitly biblical justification
in the reprobate's mouth is typical of his manipulation of biblical dialogue.

Hooker reveled in such inversions, and often exploited them skillfully. A particularly effective example is found in a discussion of David and Nathan early in *The Sovles Preparation*, in which Hooker manipulates both shifting identifications and biblical dialogue. David as the psalmist-prophet was a favorite figure of Hooker's. In this instance, however, Hooker brings David forth as the sinner who has arranged Uriah's death out of lust for Bathsheba, asking the congregation to identify with David as a sinner in need of particular application:

> you shall obserue the same in *David* so long as *Nathan* spake of sinne in generall, he conceived of it truly, and confessed the vilenesse of it, and the heart of this good King did rage against the man, saying, it is the *Sonne of death:* but as soone as the Prophet had said, *thou art the man,* though he never saw his sinne kindly before, yet now his heart yeelded, and hee began to see himself and his sinne in the naturall colours of it. So the Apostle *Iohn* saith; *hee that hateth his brother is a man-slayer, and you know no man-slayer hath eternall life abiding in him.* (25)

Hooker asks his audience to identify with David, not merely as a sinner, but as a sinner who is especially blind to his own sin, and thus needs particular application. Moreover, the David presented in this example is David at his most vicious—David as adulterer and murderer—and the quotation from 1 John 3:15 testifies to the seriousness of David's sin. At the same time, though, David is the prophet, king, and psalmist. His role as exemplar of sin combined with his role as exemplar of devotion and repentance again emphasizes the confusion and doubleness of the preparatory process.

But Hooker takes this doubleness even further, collapsing the boundaries between text and reader-listener. He demands that his audience simultaneously step into the biblical dialogue, and take the dialogue into themselves. The next paragraph of *The Sovles Preparation* begins with the exhortation, "Then play thou the part of *Nathan* and say, *I am the man*" (25). Here, using the dramatic language that Alan D. Hodder finds common in Puritan sermons, Hooker emphasizes the multiple roles that the would-be convert must play.[36] He asks his listener to speak all parts in this biblical story, to be not only David the sinner and David the exemplar of repentance, but also Nathan the prophet. Hooker suggests that his listener appropriate Nathan's exhortation, internalizing the biblical language. Here, the appropriation and rewriting of the biblical language is disruptive and dislocating to the listener, who is confronted with the complexity of his role in a salvific process in which only God's actions are efficacious, but in which the human participant nevertheless bears multiple responsibilities.

What Mather calls "nimbl[eness]," then, and what Shuffelton calls the "logical intricacy" and "intellectual and emotional density" of Hooker's preaching are due in part to the skill with which Hooker forced his audience to assimilate such multilayered and shifting identifications.[37] Hooker's fondness for engaging biblical texts in dialogue with one another, and with doubting or sinning Christians, reflected his approach to biblical reading. For Hooker, the importance of the biblical word lay in how it was read, understood, and most of all felt, by the Christian audience. The dialogues that Hooker constructed, and the exhortations that he appropriated, emphasized the need for intense interaction between text and reader, and thus between God and Christian.

## PROOFTEXTS AND ILLUSTRATIONS

Despite this emphasis, Hooker did not neglect the intellectual possibilities of the sermon. He strove most of all for conviction; nevertheless, he sought as well to convince and to explain. Consequently, Hooker also used the Bible as a source of prooftexts, authorizing and clarifying various points of argument. In doing so, he often explicitly invoked divine authority, as for example in asserting: "It is not I that say so, but our *Saviour* himselfe, *By thy words thou shalt be justified; and by thy words thou shalt be condemned*" (*SP*, 41). Hooker's stake in appropriating divine authority is especially strong here, as he quotes from Matthew 12:37 in response to scoffers who do not listen to those who "presse men to the inward worke of the soule" (41).[38]

Many of Hooker's biblical quotations, on the other hand, invoked divine authority for the minister more subtly. Often, he simply piled quotation on quotation, authorizing his arguments even as he dazzled and delighted his audience with shifting contexts and biblical passages. Early in *The Sovles Preparation*, Hooker uses five texts in a single paragraph to support the doctrine that "there must be a true sight of sinne before the soule can be broken" (10–11). First, he draws on the initial text of the sermon, Acts 2:37, noting that "the text saith, they did first *heare*, and then apprehend the evill that was done by them" (11).[39] Then Hooker begins to pile on biblical elaborations, explicitly noting the multiple texts:

> and thus they were brought to a saving remorse for their sinnes: *Ezek.36.31.* the text saith, *Then shall you remember your owne evill wayes and your doings that were not good, and shall loath your selves for your abominations.* First, they shall remember their workes, and then loath themselves; it is the course that *Ephraim* takes in *Ieremiah, After I was instructed, I smote upon my thigh; and after I was turned, I repented, I was ashamed and confounded, because I did beare the reproach of my youth.*[40]

Interestingly, Hooker inverts the order of events in this verse. In Jeremiah 31:19, repentance precedes instruction: "Surely after that I was turned, I repented; and after that I was instructed, I smote upon *my* thigh: I was ashamed, yea, even confounded, because I did bear the reproach of my youth." While this may be an instance of parallelism rather than an assertion of chronological sequence, it seems significant that Hooker places instruction before repentance, emphasizing and legitimating the preparatory process.

Hooker continues with an invocation of Job 36:8–10: "And it is Gods course which he takes with his, as in *Iob. When the Lord had once gotten the people into fetters, hee shewed them their wickednesse, and makes their eares open to discipline*" (11). Here, Hooker is paraphrasing rather than quoting, staying close to the language of the biblical text but selecting from it.[41] Finally, Hooker returns to Jeremiah, using the prophetic text as a jumping-off point for his own set of illustrations:

> And in an other place the Prophet sheweth the ground and reason why the people repented not, they understood not the ground and reason of their sinne, *For no man saith, what have I done?* As a horse rusheth into the bat-taile and feareth nothing: so a wicked man continues in a sinfull course, never considering what he hath done; the drunkard doth not say, how have I abused Gods creatures? and the despiser of Gods Ordinances doth not say, how have I rejected the Lord Iesus Christ? And therefore no wonder though he be not affected with that hee doth. (11)

Here, Hooker incorporates the end of the biblical quotation into his discussion. The text from Jeremiah reads: "I hearkened and heard, *but* they spake not aright: no man repented him of his wickedness, saying, What have I done? every one turned to his course, as the horse rusheth into the battle."[42] Characteristically, Hooker turns the verse outward, toward his audience, using the prophetic comparison to a horse rushing into battle as a transition to the world of seventeenth-century England. By reassigning the referent of this descriptive clause, Hooker sets up a transition from this quotation-dense section with its biblical focus to a more discursive explanation of "this true sight of sinne" that is relatively bare of biblical elaboration and that focuses on the experience of his audience.[43]

Elsewhere, Hooker used prooftexts to support his marshaling of specific terms and, by extension, to validate his own definitions of them. In book 3 of *The Application of Redemption*, he takes as his text the end of Luke 1:17: "To make ready a People prepared for the Lord."[44] Hooker draws several doctrines from this text, the second of which is that *"The Soul must be fitted for Christ before it can receive Him, or Salvation by Him"* (144). In explaining this doctrine, he takes particular care to marshal texts that justify his use of the term "preparation," generally capitalizing the word "Prepare" wherever it appears. He quotes from Malachi, "Thus was it Prophesied, *Mal.3.1. Behold, I will send my Messenger, and he shall Prepare the way before me,* and the Lord whom yee seek will suddenly come into the Temple" (144).[45] Then he appeals to Luke: "Thus was it accomplished by the Baptist, to whom the Word of the Lord came, and he came Preaching in the Wilderness about Jordan, saying, The voyce of one crying in the Wilderness, *Prepare yee the way of the Lord, and make his paths streight, Luke, 3.4*" (144). And slightly later, he appeals to the same verse in Isaiah which John the Baptist quotes above, saying, "As the Prophet *Isaiah* says, *Prepare yee the way of the Lord:* As though he had said, *Repenting is Preparing*" (144).[46] Here Hooker elaborates, bending the passage slightly to stress not only the legitimacy of preparation as a spiritual concept, but also his own interpretation of that concept.

Hooker only infrequently used prooftexts to elaborate on single words. More often, he used biblical passages to legitimate and render comprehensible subtle spiritual points. Hooker was concerned, for example, with the problem of assurance that preoccupied Massachusetts Bay in the mid-1630s. Faced with congregants who lacked confidence that they had been saved and who questioned how one could be granted grace and yet not know it, Hooker responded by drawing on the story of Jacob, in a discussion that appears in different versions in several of Hooker's sermon series.[47] He addresses the problem that "Christ is come, but thou perceivest it not" by reminding his auditors that "When *Iacob* awaked out of his sleepe, *Surely* (said hee) *the Lord is in this place, and I perceived it not:* And so the Lord is in thy soule, and thou perceivest him not."[48] As in Hooker's quotation from Jonah in *The Sovles Preparation*, the quotation is used to explain a difficult spiritual concept by placing it in human terms, mediated by the biblical text. Jacob's awakening here is somewhat less prosaic, of course, than is Jonah's; his discovery comes after a dream-vision.[49] But the concept to be explained is less prosaic as well; really listening to the minister is somewhat less mysterious than coming to know the work of God in one's soul. Hooker's use of the biblical text simultaneously heightens his listener's identification with biblical figures and renders difficult theological concepts more accessible.

## WRESTING THE TEXT TO HONOR GOD'S NAME

As Hooker strove to break down boundaries between his auditors and God's word, his commitment to affective preaching led him to treat the text itself as quite fluid. As he drew on the biblical text, he sometimes privileged his sense

of the divine author's intent over the precise language of individual translations, presenting idiosyncratic near-quotations as biblical language. Interestingly, however, in *The Sovles Preparation* Hooker condemned "carnall ministers" who twist texts (68).[50] Such men, he lamented, "though they have no
reason in the text, no ground in the Word to warrant them; though they cannot condemn a poor Christian upon good grounds, yet they will invent new
wayes, and wrest the *Text* to dishonour Gods name, and then in all bitterness
they can, vent themselves against faithfull Christians, and conscionable Ministers" (68). In keeping with Hooker's practical approach to the biblical text,
his objection to this text-twisting was result-oriented. Hooker objected to
texts twisted "to dishonour Gods name," so that "the hands of the wicked
are strengthened, and the hearts of Gods people are much daunted; and the
Gospell of Iesus Christ prevailes not in the hearts of such as it is preached
unto" (68). He was less concerned with misreading per se than with the purpose for which the text was misread and the results this misreading produced.

This is evident from Hooker's own use of the biblical text. Alfred Habegger demonstrates Hooker's reworking of the sermon structure advocated by
William Perkins, notably his subordination of the biblical text to the *ordo
salutis* as the primary structural principle of the sermon.[51] Habegger explains
that "Hooker often considers only as much of the text as coincides with what
he already has in mind," citing as an example the first sermon in *The Application of Redemption*, in which Hooker declares that he "will pass all the
other Specials in the Verse, and point at that Particular which will suit our
proceeding, and may afford ground to the following Discourse."[52] Hooker suggests that this practice will result in closer allegiance to divine truth: "that we
may go no further than we see the Pillar of Fire, the Lord in his Truth to go
before us" (*AR 9–10, 2*).

In fact, though, the biblical "Pillar of Fire" leads Hooker farther than he
would go, and he chooses to "fasten then upon the last words only, as those
that fit our Intendment" (2).[53] This is not an unusual practice for Hooker; he
repeatedly considers only a limited portion of a verse, according to his "Intendment." For example, in book 3 of *The Application of Redemption* and in
*The Soules Implantation into the Naturall Olive*, where Hooker takes as his
text Luke 1:17, he focuses so exclusively on the end of the verse that he does
not even quote the first three-quarters of it. He includes only *"To make ready
a people prepared by the Lord."*[54]

Habegger argues that Hooker's willingness to select only parts of verses
is consistently shaped by his commitment to elucidating the preparatory
process. "Hooker's sermons," he explains, "although they follow the conven-
tional sequence of text, doctrine, and application, do not elaborate doctrine
and application from the text but from a scheme of the stages of prepara-

tion."[55] Hooker's biblical flexibility moves well beyond structural issues, however, allowing him to play freely with more than the guidelines of Perkins's sermon form. In fact, Hooker's commitment to structuring his preaching according to the *ordo salutis* is only part of the issue. More significant is his sense that the biblical text may be less than all-sufficient to produce the proper affective response. In *The unbeleevers preparing for Christ*, Hooker notes that "The Scripture never enough expresseth the love that is betweene sinne and the soule."[56] Charles Lloyd Cohen cites this passage to demonstrate the depth of Hooker's commitment to preaching the preparatory process, but remains silent about the rather surprising way in which Hooker expresses that importance.[57] Certainly, Hooker is speaking hyperbolically; nevertheless, even in hyperbole the sufficiency of scripture is not to be slighted. As Perkins declares, "The sufficiencie is that, whereby the word of God is so compleate, that nothing may be either put to it, or taken from it, which appertaineth to the proper end thereof" (*Arte*, 731–32).

Hooker's sense of the text's insufficiency is, of course, heavily qualified; in fact, he supports his claim by a series of appeals to the text itself. Hooker demonstrates that "the Scripture never enough expresseth the love that is betweene sinne and the soule" by citing texts to illustrate the degree to which the soul is bound to sin.[58] For Hooker, the biblical text was neither limiting nor all-enclosing; rather, it represented a wealth of possibilities, a palette of stories, characters, and language with which the minister could, and indeed must, work.

The fluidity of seventeenth-century biblical translations afforded Hooker opportunities to bend the text to his purposes. His published sermons suggest a greater looseness with fixed translations than those of either John Cotton or Thomas Shepard. Though some of this looseness may be explained by failures of memory and problems of transmission, in other instances Hooker's manipulation (and altering) of scriptural language seems more conscious, and more purposeful.[59] Often, his explanations of cited texts almost suggest alternate versions of those texts. For example, Hooker frequently uses the phrase "as if hee had said" to introduce explanatory material. Generally, he uses this locution to add emphasis, to introduce a paraphrase of and an elaboration upon biblical words. He explains, for example, that

> the soule that is truly convicted of sinne yeelds it selfe, and saith I have sinned; *Oh what shall I doe unto thee thou Preseruer of men*, saith *Iob*? as if hee had said, lord, I have no plea at all to make, nor no argument to alledge, for my selfe, I onely yeeld up the bucklers, I cannot say so bad of my selfe as I am, I have sinned, and done foolishly in thy sight. Thus it is with a heart truly convicted, and thoroughly informed of the vilenesse of sinne. (*SP*, 29)[60]

Here, Hooker expands on the quotation from Job, shaping the emphasis slightly to fit his purposes, but in ways that seem consistent with the biblical text itself.

Similarly, Hooker expands on a paraphrase of Revelations 3:18: "marke what the Lord saith to his Church, I counsell thee to buy of me *eye-salve:* Shee thought all her compters to bee good gold, and all her appearances to bee good Religion: but the Lord bids her buy of him *eye-salve;* As if hee had said, you see not your sinnes, and therefore goe to God, and beseech him that dwells in endlesse light, to let in some light into your soules" (*SP*, 36). Although Hooker alters the biblical passage slightly, his extension of the text is essentially consistent with the thrust of the text itself.[61]

Elsewhere, though, the elaborations that follow the "as if hee said" locution bend the text to support Hooker's theological emphases. For example, Hooker exhorts the congregation to "Marke the severe command that the Apostle gave his Scholar *Timothy*" in 2 Timothy 4:1–2: "*I charge thee before God, and the Lord Iesus christ, who shall judge the quick and the dead, preach the word, be instant in season, and out of season, reprove, rebuke*" (*SP*, 69). As this passage supports Hooker's understanding of the minister's role, it is hardly surprising that he invokes it. But Hooker seems to find Paul's statement insufficiently emphatic, for he embellishes it: "(as if he had said) the stubborne hearts of men need this specially, *reprooving*, and therefore doing this, this is the maine thing that God requires, and the maine end for which the Word serves" (*SP*, 69). While nothing in the passage from Timothy contradicts this statement, Hooker elevates the minister's duty of reproof beyond the level prescribed by Paul. He uses the locution "as if he had said" to attach his own interpretation to the biblical verse, associating his reading with Paul's intention, and marking it as divine mandate rather than as his own understanding of the minister's role.

Hooker makes similar moves in *The Application of Redemption*. In book 3, he quotes from Isaiah: "As the Prophet *Isaiah* says, *Prepare yee the way of the Lord.*"[62] Again, he attaches his own interpretation with a variation on the "as if he had said" locution, adding "As though he had said, *Repenting is Preparing*" (144). Here, again, Hooker's interpretation is not inconsistent with the biblical text, which does seem to associate preparation and repentance. Nevertheless, his construction suggests a greater level of textual support for his position than might be obvious to one reading for the "literal" meaning. Moreover, the typography used emphasizes the degree to which this locution blurs the lines between the biblical text and the text as Hooker reads it; like the biblical quotation itself, Hooker's proposed paraphrase is set in italics. Hooker uses this locution, then, to appropriate biblical authority, to emphasize what the text *means*, rather than what it *says*. And he seems confident in his ability to tell the difference.

In other instances, Hooker embellishes the biblical text without acknowledging that he is making such changes. In book 10 of *The Application of Redemption*, for example, he tells the story of Barabas. In order to heighten the drama of the telling, Hooker merges accounts from Matthew and Luke, and embellishes the combined account with his own emphasis. Hooker asks his audience to "attend the Text" to see "the most loathsom Hellhounds that ever the Sun saw, or the Earth bore," to "hear these hideous blasphemies, they belch out against the Son of God" (*AR 9–10*, 26).

In Hooker's version, however, the "Hellhounds" seem more wicked—or at least more enthusiastic in their wickedness—than they do in "the Text." As Hooker tells the story, "they cried, *away with him, away with him; not him, but* Barrabas; they chuse a Murderer rather than a Saviour" (26). The source for Hooker's quotation is marked in the margin as Matthew 27:21, but the text in Matthew is rather barer: "The governor answered and said unto them, Whether of the twain will ye that I release unto you? They said, Barabbas." The vehement dismissal of Jesus, as Hooker reports it, is borrowed from the account in Luke, where the crowd responds "Away with this *man*."[63] Even in Luke, however, the rejection of Jesus is pronounced only once. Hooker's addition heightens the drama of the moment, painting a more vivid picture of a frenzied mob. Of course, this revision of the biblical text seems quite unthreatening. It is possible, as well, that Hooker did not intend to pass this off as a biblical quotation—that the biblical annotation in the margin and the use of italics are the products of an obsessive but careless editor. But Hooker does exhort his audience to "attend the Text," and the text that he provides is a composite—of Luke, of Matthew, and of Hooker himself.

At other points, this kind of emendation has more significant theological implications. Throughout *The Sovles Preparation*, Hooker extends the text of Acts 2:37, which reads: "Now when they heard *this*, they were pricked in their heart, and said unto Peter and to the rest of the apostles, Men *and* brethren, what shall we do?" Hooker repeatedly appends the words "to be saved" to the end of the verse, placing a preparationist emphasis on the biblical text (*SP*, 1, 206).[64] It is, moreover, a preparationist emphasis with a somewhat worksy slant. Hooker's twisting of the verse gives some support to those among his contemporaries who found preparationist soteriology excessively concerned with efficacious human action; after all, the question is "what shall we doe *to be saved*" (1, 206). Hooker's revision of the biblical verse finds biblical—and thus divine—sanction for this soteriology, making it seem that there is biblical precedent for human activity that can lead to salvation.[65]

Occasionally, Hooker's scriptural looseness seems even more extreme—

and even more pointed. On rare instances, Hooker seems to fabricate verses altogether. In *The Sovles Preparation*, one such fabricated verse emphatically marks ministerial authority, linking ministerial and Mosaic authority:

> I must confesse that the consideration of these passages sometime makes the soule of a poore Minister shake within him; and were it in my power as it is not, the first worke that I would doe, should be to humble and break the hearts of all such vile wretches; but all that I can or will doe, is this, that which the holy man *Moses* spake, and hee spake it with a marvailous caution; you that never came to the height of this horrible contempt, *take heed that there be not any among you that saith, It shall goe well with me whatsoever the Minister saith.* (44)

The words Hooker attributes to "the holy *Moses*," however, do not appear in the biblical text. In placing words in Moses' mouth, Hooker makes a doubly appropriative gesture. He identifies himself with Moses, thus appropriating Moses' authority as leader of the people. At the same time, he lays claim to Moses' status as a biblical author, by asserting his own right to compose texts and declare them "biblical."

Hooker's appropriation of this text simultaneously unsettles and re-inscribes the authority of the biblical text. On one hand, Hooker's appropriation of biblical authority for his own language destabilizes the biblical text, and decreases the distance between the divine author and the human one. On the other hand, this appropriation is rooted in and dependent upon the assumption that the biblical text (and its divine author) are ultimately authoritative. Moreover, Hooker's textual practice both emerges from and supports his understanding of the minister's role, breaking down boundaries between the divine text and its human reader or auditor even as it encourages the congregation to find biblical sanction for ministerial authority. And in Hooker's view, this authority is necessary for effective application of the Word—even if occasionally "the Word" is not explicitly stated in the biblical text.[66]

Thus, for Hooker, the biblical text and its authority proved far from constraining. Though he maintained his allegiance to the authority of the text, and though his approach to biblical reading was rooted in Reformed doctrine, he applied that approach flexibly. In his sermons, he sometimes manipulated the biblical text in ways that mainstream Reformed preaching manuals did not recommend, and exploited the contradictions that troubled Reformed exegesis.[67] In part because of his flexibility, Hooker's sermons were tremendously popular, and brought conviction, comfort, and entertainment to many of his congregants and readers. Hooker respected the power of the biblical word as a source of spiritual sustenance and valued its richness as a palette of literary reference. His flexibility as a reader allowed him to hone and wield the "Sword of the Spirit" with singular strength and dexterity, and made him tremendously successful at applying the word "home."

Though Hooker's biblical manipulations were particularly flexible, he joined Cotton and Shepard in applying the apparently straightforward methods of Puritan exegesis in idiosyncratic ways which suited his particular understanding of the conversion process and of the minister's role in it. As each minister negotiated the complexities of Reformed exegesis, he produced sermons that reflected not only his soteriology and his aesthetic preferences, but also his approach to Bible reading. These sermons presented a range of interpretive strategies to the eagerly listening laity, immersing them in the theoretical perplexities of Reformed exegesis. As they joined their ministers in wrestling with the biblical text, they found in it sources of comfort and creativity, but also sites of contention and conflict.

## CHAPTER 5

# "Goe Home and Consider": Lay Responses to the Preached Text

Though Puritan theories of preaching and exegesis had their most direct impact on the clergy, lay readers were implicated in them as well. Part of the Protestant heritage, after all, was belief in the importance of biblical accessibility to the laity. The role of the biblical text in the lay reader's life extended beyond his or her faith. The Bible was a primary text of instruction, the book in which many New Englanders learned to read. They were taught to be active readers not only of the Bible itself, but of the biblical text as presented in their ministers' sermons, on which they were expected to take notes for later discussion, either within the household or in groups of other Christians. The techniques ministers used to interpret the Bible were thus carefully studied by the laity, who adopted these practices themselves. Moreover, as texts by New England's Puritan laity reveal, the ministers' practices shaped not only the laity's reading strategies, but also their writing practices. The diverse biblical practices of the ministers demonstrated to the laity the flexible possibilities of Puritan scripturalism, and they adapted those possibilities to their own purposes. For lay writers as well as for Puritan ministers, the assumptions and techniques of Puritan exegesis shaped the aesthetics of their prose and poetry.

## LITERACY AND THE BIBLE

The Bible was closely bound up not only with the laity's most sophisticated
reading practices, but with the barest beginnings of literacy. Historians of literacy and reading in early America have demonstrated that literacy in early
New England was closely linked to scripture reading. Defining literacy as
"the skill of reading English," David D. Hall describes a New England population almost universally literate.[1] Though Kenneth Lockridge has described
mid-seventeenth-century New England as "a society little more than half-
literate," evolving by the end of the eighteenth century to "a society of nearly
universal male literacy," Hall rejects Lockridge's estimate as too conservative,
emphasizing the limitations of signature studies.[2] In any case, Lockridge asserts that the literacy rate in first-generation New England was very high
compared with that in most European countries: "England was at this time
one of the most literate nations in the world," and "the rate of male literacy
among the arrivals in New England was nearly double the base rate prevailing in England" (45–46). Lockridge notes that most explanations for this
phenomenon cite "the Protestant impulse. Protestants were convinced that
access to the Word would free men from superstition, and it seems that the
gathered groups of devotees responded by providing for the education of
their young" (46).

   In revising upward Lockridge's literacy estimates, Hall cites a 1642 Massachusetts law that "voiced the expectation that children, servants, and apprentices should acquire the 'ability to read & understand the principles of
religion & the capitall lawes of this country.'"[3] Hall cautions that "the effects
of these laws must not be exaggerated," for colonial schooling was varied in
quality, and only in New Haven did laws mandate "that children learn to write
or that they attend school for any period of time" (120). Yet he asserts that
"the colonists were able to sustain a distinctively high rate of reading and writing literacy, far higher than in the seventeenth-century Chesapeake and in
most parts of England" (120). Estimates of male signature literacy range from
50 percent to 90 percent, and Hall suggests that "[b]ecause reading was taught
prior to writing, we may safely conclude that the ability to read exceeded the
ability to write by a considerable margin" (120).[4] Whether New Englanders
could sign their names or not, Hall asserts, "they were comfortable with the
language of their Bibles," and "enjoyed privileged access to the Bible."[5]

   This "access" was linked to New England pedagogical practices. Hall suggests that "most people in New England learned to read as children," with
mothers serving "as the key instructors," supplemented by institutions like
apprenticeship and dame schools.[6] Most important, "[l]iteracy emerged from

a process of instruction that began with hearing others read aloud and with memorizing certain texts," especially passages from the Bible and catechism.[7] Children memorized these texts even before they could fully understand them, and as a result eventually "commanded a surprising repertory of ideas and images."[8] The ministers' incorporation of numerous scriptural verses into their sermons reinforced the textual literacy (and the textual orthodoxy) of the population, even for adults no longer actively engaged in childhood learning by repetition and memorization. Moreover, the auditors' recognition of biblical references was validating, affirming their status as scripturally literate Christians.[9] The biblical text shaped not only New Englanders' experiences as readers, but also the vocabulary of images and phrases of New England's writers. In the words of Theodore Dwight Bozeman, the Bible "exercised a virtually tyrannical claim upon imagination and belief."[10]

This tyranny, however, was mitigated by the practices that shaped Puritan encounters with the biblical text. Hall observes that the prominence of the Bible in schooling imposed limits on intellectual freedom: the uses of literacy "were determined—'channeled' is perhaps a better word—by an interpretive community."[11] But the practices of this interpretive community tended toward fluidity, rather than toward determination or channeling. For members of the Puritan laity learned their interpretive practices from the ministers, and were expected to engage in active reading not only of the biblical text, but of the sermons in which their ministers "opened" that text as well.

## "Apply All That Thou Readest"

Though John Cotton and his colleagues emphasized the importance of the preached word, they also shared a Reformed emphasis on lay scripture reading. Lewis Bayly's *The Practise of Pietie*, which was extremely popular in early New England, explained how Christians could read the Bible through over the course of a year by reading three chapters a day (morning, noon, and night) and six on the last day of the year.[12] Bayly prescribed active and engaged reading. He urged the Christian reader to read a chapter, "then Meditate a while with thy selfe how many *excellent things* thou canst remember out of it" (310–11). Particular attention should be paid to "good counsels and exhortations to *good workes,* and to *holy life*" and, conversely, to "threatnings of *iudgements* against such and such a *sinne:* and what fearefull *example* of Gods punishment or vengeance vpon such and such *sinners*" (311). The reader should then consider "what blessings G O D *promiseth to patience, chastity, mercy, almes-deedes, zeale* in his seruice, *charity, faith,* and *trust* in

God, and such like Christian vertues," "what gracious *deliuerance* G O D hath wrought, and what speciall *blessings* hee hath bestowed upon them who were his true and zealous *seruants*" (311–12).

In *The Practise of Pietie*, Bayly's readers found reinforcement for their ministers' instructions to read the text and apply it to their own lives. After exploring the text's promises and threats, the Christian reader must "apply these things to thine owne heart" (312). Just as Thomas Shepard suggested that the preached text might offer opportunities for intimacy with the divine, Bayly suggested that such possibilities lay in the read text as well. Urging a personal and engaged encounter with the text, he cautioned: "reade not these Chapters as matters of *historicall* discourse: but as if they were so many *Letters* or *Epistles* sent downe from God out of *Heauen* vnto thee: for *whatsoeuer is written, is written for our learning. Rom. 15. 4*" (312). Bayly suggested that the heavenly source of these communications did not render them remote and inaccessible; instead, he exhorted his reader to feel God's intimate presence, reading the Bible "with that *reuerence*, as if G O D himselfe *stood* by, and *spake* these vvords vnto thee, to excite thee to those *vertues*, to diswade thee from those *vices*" (312). Bayly's course of reading was purposive— "eyther to confirme thy *Faith*, or to encrease thy *Repentance*"—and active, requiring the engagement of both mind and will (313).

Such active reading was extended to the ministers' preaching as well. As William Ames explained in his *Medulla theologica*, or *The Marrow of Theology*, "The receiving of the word consists of two parts: attention of mind and intention of will."[13] Attention of mind required more than mere careful listening. Many churchgoers took notes during their ministers' sermons, so that they would be able to study them later.[14] Notetaking was encouraged, and was in fact used by some as an index of spiritual progress. Thomas Shepard, for example, treated notetaking itself as a spiritual challenge and subject of prayer:

> But I was studious because I was ambitious of learning and being a scholar, and hence when I could not take notes of the sermon I remember I was troubled at it and prayed the Lord earnestly that he would help me to note sermons. And I see cause of wondering at the Lord's providence therein, for as soon as ever I had prayed (after my best fashion) then for it, I presently the next Sabbath was able to take notes who the precedent Sabbath could do nothing at all that way.[15]

While Shepard may have been more scrupulous than some, that he took notes of sermons did not make him unique. On the contrary, in his discussion of the Puritan conventicle, Patrick Collinson explains that "the main function of the domestic meetings of early protestant generations . . . was repetition: that is, repetition of sermons."[16] Such repetition, Collinson explains, "was akin to the process of catechizing, in that sermons having been reduced in summary form to their 'heads' (it seems to have been a rare gift to memorise an entire sermon, verbatim) were by repetition impressed, perhaps permanently, on the minds of the hearers" (241).

Puritan ministers expected their auditors to take notes on their sermons or to memorize them, and these practices helped to shape Puritan sermon structure. In his *Medulla theologica*, William Ames stressed the importance of preserving the sermon structure described by Perkins in *The Arte of Prophecying*. His argument was a practical one: the sequence of doctrine, reasons, and uses aided memory and facilitated later discussion of sermons by the auditors. "Those who invert and confuse these parts," he argued, "make it difficult for their hearers to remember and stand in the way of their edification. Their hearers cannot commit the chief heads of the sermon to memory so that they may afterwards repeat it privately in their families; and when this cannot be done, the greatest part of the fruit, which would otherwise be made available to the church of God through sermons, is lost."[17] In Ames's account, listening to a sermon was not a passive activity; rather, the discussion that followed was an integral part of preaching's efficacy.

Nor did Ames expect such discussions to be entirely deferential. For in addition to encouraging lay discussion of sermons within families, Ames's text described several kinds of faulty preaching, criticizing them quite harshly. He suggested, for example, that "Ministers impose upon their hearers and altogether forget themselves when they propound a certain text in the beginning as the start of the sermon and then speak many things about or simply by occasion of the text but for the most part draw nothing out of the text itself" (191). He condemned preachers who failed to apply their doctrines immediately in uses. Since "the chief purpose of the sermon . . . is the edification of the hearers," he argued, "They sin, therefore, who stick to the naked finding and explanation of the truth, neglecting the use and practice in which religion and blessedness consist. Such preachers edify the conscience little or not at all" (192). Moreover, he condemned as sinful those "who do care little about what they say provided it may appear they may have thought about and spoken many things" (193). "They do this frequently," he lamented, "forcing many things out of the text which are not in it and often borrowing for it from other places, bringing anything out of everything" (193). "The result," he suggested, was dire: "the ruin rather than the edification of the hearers, especially among the untutored" (193).

Aimed at ministers, such strong language would be unsurprising. But Ames's audience was the learned laity, rather than the clergy. As John D. Eusden explains, "Ames wrote his *Marrow* not as a scholarly treatise but as a useful compendium for laymen and students."[18] Though it was read by ministers—both Thomas Hooker and Increase Mather recommended it to other ministers—*The Marrow of Theology* was "originally offered . . . as a series of lectures to the sons of Leyden merchants between 1620 and 1622" (1). Published in its first Latin edition in 1623, Ames's *Medulla theologica* was assigned to undergraduates "as part of basic instruction in divinity" at Emmanuel College, Leyden, Harvard, and Yale.[19]

Thus when John Cotton exhorted his Lincolnshire congregants to "goe home and consider whether the things that have been taught were true or no: whether agreeable to the holy Scriptures or no," he was addressing a laity at least some of whom had been primed to criticize vigorously, rather than deferentially.[20] And indeed, Cotton himself did not encourage deference; in encouraging the laity to evaluate their ministers' preaching, he explained that "a Preacher speaks not the express words of the Scripture, but comments and explications of the Scriptures, and therefore examine whether that which is delivered be agreeable to the Scriptures which are alleged for to prove the doctrine" (200). Though Cotton issued this invitation more emphatically than some of his colleagues, his expectation was not unusual among Puritan ministers.

Of course, such invitations were hardly welcomed by ecclesiastical authorities. Perhaps because discussions of sermons were not always deferential, authorities in England often frowned upon or even banned private meetings of Christians, branding them "conventicles" and associating them with heresy.[21] Though New England's ministers agreed on the usefulness of private meetings, they came to see some such meetings (especially those held in Anne Hutchinson's home) as threats, in part because those present read the ministers' sermons actively and critically. Nevertheless, the General Courts of Massachusetts and Connecticut protected "private meetings for edification in Religion amongst christians of all sorts of people so it be without just offence."[22] While reserving the right to restrict schismatical meetings, New England's civil leadership maintained the general legitimacy of lay meetings, and the clergy continued to acknowledge their importance.

## READING AND CONVERSION

While lay readers sometimes challenged ministerial authority, more often they followed the ministers' guidance to find instruction and spiritual comfort in their Bibles. As the ministers proclaimed the spiritual efficacy of the biblical text, their congregants associated reading with the conversion process.

Puritan personal narratives are replete with examples in which individuals report spiritual progress in the course of reading their Bibles, from the orthodox conversion narratives of Thomas Shepard's congregants to Anne Hutchinson's more provocative declaration during her court trial.[23] Such narratives offer a window into the laity's responses to their ministers' exhortations.

In relating their spiritual experiences, Shepard's congregants often cite reading and preaching as formative events. Their conversion narratives emphasize the impact of biblical texts read privately and preached publicly, often describing a back-and-forth interaction between private reading and public preaching. Mary Angier Sparrowhawk begins her narrative by citing the impact of the "powerful ministry of Mr. Rogers of Dedham," under which she "had often stirrings" (168–69). Later, however, she reports that "she found her heart more hard and [in]sensible": "Every sermon made her worse, and [she] sat like a block under all means" (169). Despite her frustration over her spiritual state, Sparrowhawk reports that she "durst not neglect any public means," describing several of the sermons which she continued to attend (169–70). Yet, she laments, she "thought it was in vain to use any more means and began to neglect Lord in private" (170).

Following the guidance of some sermons, Sparrowhawk sought help in scripture. Her narrative describes a series of scriptures that offered her "encouragements" (170). She cites Hosea, Isaiah, and Matthew, quoting multiple verses from these books as well as eight others. The impact of biblical passages and sermons blends together for her: "hearing what an enmity there was in the will against God, she saw it so clearly from Matthew 23—you would not. There she saw that, and this did lie sad upon her and thought, did I think I could take Christ on any terms? And yet had a will to resist him. And being in that sermon exhorted to go to him, to plead with God to subdue her will, which she did, yet saw her rebellion still exceedingly" (170). Sliding from preached scripture to read scripture, Sparrowhawk takes direction from sermons and finds comfort in biblical texts that are "brought to" her (171). When "a question [was] made whether she had closed with the person of Christ," Sparrowhawk "saw if she had not, yet she saw the fault was in her" (170). "And then," her narrative continues, "that place—fury is not in me, let him take hold of my strength—and she saw that strength was Christ" (171). This scripture, she reports, allowed her to see the promise, and the need to "take hold" of it (171). "That other scripture—he had laid salvation on Christ" leads her to believe that "she closed" with Christ (171). When asked "how know whether united to Christ," she responds by "mentioning a scripture" (171). Following more doubt—and more scripture reading—she finally finds comfort in the seventh chapter of John, and comes to believe that "the Lord called her to himself" (172).

Sparrowhawk's spiritual journey begins with sermons, but moves back and forth between public and private reading. Once she believes in her own regenerate state, Sparrowhawk testifies to the impact of the text both by describing it and by appropriating biblical language. In *The Sound Believer*, Shepard had pressed his congregants to make biblical language their own, explaining that converts would turn to scriptural language to describe their experience.[24] Sparrowhawk's narrative and others in Shepard's notebook reveal the degree to which Shepard's congregants heeded this exhortation. As Sparrowhawk traces her spiritual progress, her narrative is increasingly punctuated with biblical language. While the first page of her narrative includes no biblical references, its final two pages relate Sparrowhawk's experience using nearly thirty biblical references and quotations.

Patricia Caldwell notes that "the outburst of these citations [occurs] only after the central step of her 'unwilling' migration . . . to New England. It is as if she steps out of the ship directly into a Bible world; and indeed, a comparison of scriptural use in conversion narratives suggests that this is so, for it shows that in New England there is a dependence on, and an emotional and imaginative involvement with, the Bible that are not matched among most of the English converts."[25] For the converted Sparrowhawk, God's words offer the appropriate language for relating her experience. Describing Elizabeth White's conversion narrative, Caldwell places it within a "Puritan tradition of scripturalism" to which Sparrowhawk belongs as well: "Describing an extremely personal and potentially dramatic event, [White] transmutes it into the reenactment of a biblical truth with, in effect, the Word as her midwife."[26] This new birth, however, does not produce a new subjectivity. Rather, the convert learns to subordinate his or her subjectivity to the text, the minister, and most of all the Holy Spirit. And when this occurs, as Shepard prescribes, biblical language and the convert's language are one and the same.[27]

This subordinated subjectivity is revealed as well in the hybrid mode of narration in many of these accounts, including Sparrowhawk's. Perhaps because Shepard's attention was divided between questioning these converts and recording their narratives, his accounts alternate between first- and third-person narration, producing confusing narratives in which the identities of congregant and minister are blurred. A particularly extreme example is found in Shepard's account of John Sill's conversion narrative. Here, as elsewhere, Shepard begins the narrative in the third person, telling us, for example, that "He was brought up in an ignorant place" (155). But as he does in other narratives, Shepard alternates between the first and third person with effects sufficiently confusing that the editor of the *Confessions* has seen fit to clarify the pronoun references:

The word had not yet efficacy upon him and teaching of the branch, John 15:5 and Revelation 22:17—take water of life freely. After sermons were done, some asked how I liked. I spake very freely, but next day, I having conference with some, I wished them to take heed upon what grounds they believed what I [Shepard] had taught. And my heart was against him [Shepard], so diverse people came to him [Sill] to hear the notes. And so he read over the notes, and reading them over to them the Lord let him see there was more in them than I [Sill] apprehended. And so [at] night in prayer, he was convinced of the sin in being set against him [Shepard]. And from something that he [Shepard] taught next day and before he was put to a plunge and so to question what was formerly done. (157–58)

While such pronominal confusion can be explained by the challenge of rapid-fire notetaking, it is tempting to read it as suggestive as well of the fluidity built into the Puritan sense of the regenerate reader's subjectivity. If, as Perkins and Bernard had prescribed, both preacher and reader were connected by the interpretive agency of the Holy Spirit, if the preacher was ideally transparent to the motions of the Spirit "opening" the text and the reader dead to the world and alive only to the interpreting Spirit, then Shepard's fluid movement between pronouns seems not only unsurprising, but even appropriate. In these narratives, the voices of Shepard's congregants blend with the biblical texts they cite and with the voice of the minister who examines them and records their narratives, just as the convert's subjectivity was subordinated to the biblical text and to the Holy Spirit.

## BIBLICAL PROSE

Though the conversion narratives of Shepard's congregants reveal individual subjectivity subordinated to biblical language, other instances of Puritan scripturalism present more complex negotiations between human authors and biblical texts. For Puritan scripturalism was not confined to sermons and conversion narratives, or even to explicitly theological texts. Rather, it filtered outward into other kinds of writing. Puritan writers drew on the memorized repertory of biblical ideas and texts described by Hall, as well as on continued active engagement with their Bible and the textual modes fostered by Puritan theories of exegesis and preaching. The interpretive strategy of collation was particularly influential, fostering elaborate patterns of quotation and allusion in a wide range of texts. Puritan biblical appropriations were not simply reflections of authors' piety, nor were they always self-effacing. They often reflected authors' appropriations of biblical language to their own purposes, drawing on the Bible's expressive power in a scripturally immersed society, and exploiting the aesthetic possibilities of biblical quotation as well.

Such possibilities could be turned to such personal purposes as complimenting a friend or colleague. Joseph Caryl's address "To the Reader" of John Cotton's *A Treatise of the Covenant of Grace* provides a fairly typical example. Caryl writes that "The Works of this Reverend Author (now with God) have already praised him in the gate," offering Cotton a subtle but multilayered compliment.[28] Caryl takes his language from the concluding verse of Proverbs, which sums up the description of the "virtuous woman" with the words "let her own works praise her in the gates."[29] Puritan writers used this phrase quite commonly to praise their pious coreligionists, but Caryl's application of it is particularly apt. He builds on both the biblical text and Cotton's own biblical propensities, turning the language of spiritual marriage of which Cotton is so fond back toward Cotton. The traditional reading of this passage sees the virtuous woman as a maturer version of the Canticles bride; in the christological reading, the church is both blushing bride and faithful and industrious wife. In saying that Cotton's works have praised him "in the gates," Caryl casts him as the virtuous bride of Christ, thus a fitting (and authoritative) instructor in the workings of the covenant.

The gracefulness of this subtle compliment is not simply metaphorical; it works by quotation and recognition, and by summoning forth the echoes and associations of the brief quotation from the biblical text. The "layering of significance," to use Roland Barthes's expression, "captivates" the reader who is aware of the multiple implications of Caryl's compliment.[30] These implications, of course, are not merely aesthetic; they also reinforce Cotton's authority as a representative of the true church. But this identification is not straightforwardly typological. While Cotton becomes the counterpart of the biblical "virtuous woman," the identification is implied only. Moreover, the implied identification does not suggest that Cotton fulfills any proverbial prophecy; he is not a latter-day manifestation of the proverbial "virtuous woman," but merely shares her virtues.

Caryl's subtle effort would have been appreciated by Puritan audiences, who valued their ministers' abilities to manipulate biblical texts. But such ability was not restricted to the clergy. The writings of the Puritan laity demonstrate the rich expressive possibilities lay writers found in biblical appropriation. In *Of Plymouth Plantation*, William Bradford demonstrates the intertextual facility achieved by laymen immersed in the biblical text, as well as the potentially unsettling consequences of that facility. After describing the arrival at Cape Cod, Bradford asks: "May not and ought not the children of these fathers rightly say: 'Our fathers were Englishmen which came over this great ocean, and were ready to perish in this wilderness; but they cried unto the Lord, and He heard their voice and looked on their adversity,' etc."[31] Bradford marks this as a quotation, adding the footnote "Deuteronomy xxvi.5, 7" (63). The Deuteronomic text, of course, mentions not "Englishmen which came over this great ocean," but a "Syrian ready to perish" who "went down to Egypt" (Deut. 26:5). By revising this text to insert himself into the biblical role, and by marking his revised text as a biblical quotation, Bradford unsettles the authority and integrity of the biblical text. If the text's authority stems from its divine author, then stepping into authorial status appropriates some of that authority. Moreover, by revising the text without indicating that he has done so, Bradford places an alternate text into circulation, one that competes with the original for scriptural status. Whose text, one might ask, is this? Is it Bradford's, to appropriate and revise as he will, or is it God's?

But Bradford's "quotation" simultaneously reinscribes the same authority that it unsettles. He does not expect his revision to go unnoticed; his intended reader knows as well as Bradford that the Deuteronomic reference is to a "Syrian," and not to an "Englishman." His substitution testifies not to a desire to supplant the biblical text with his own history, but rather to an impulse to link his own history typologically to the biblical one.[32] This gesture reflects his confidence that the biblical text will remain the single authoritative text even in future generations. And while he might be disappointed with the biblical knowledge of modern readers, even we recognize his substitution. So even as Bradford's manipulation of the biblical text unsettles it, it testifies at the same time to the stability of the Bible's authoritative status.

Anne Bradstreet often used scriptural quotations in similar ways. In her "As Weary Pilgrim," biblical quotation is both expressive and unsettling. Critics have debated whether the poem marks Bradstreet's ultimate accommodation with the surrender of the body to death, or whether it dramatizes a continuing struggle with the problem of weaned affections.[33] In the poem's first line, the speaker compares herself to a pilgrim who is "now at rest," and proceeds to describe a cessation of physical torments.[34] But Bradstreet's speaker also asks God to "make her ready," suggesting that she is not yet prepared to leave the earthly world behind. She further indicates her unreadiness by appropriating the language of Canticles 2:10 and 2:13 to close the poem: "Then come, dear Bridegroom, come away" (l. 44). In the biblical text, the bridegroom calls the bride away. Bradstreet's appropriation reverses this call, perhaps suggesting a fantasy of union with Christ without surrender of the world if the divine "dear Bridegroom" would come away from the heavens to join her on earth.[35] At the same time, the speaker's use of Canticles language marks her intense desire for union with Christ. In addition, it reflects her allegiance to the Bible as linguistically and religiously normative, and as a source of poetic inspiration.

Beyond testifying to the fluid but enduring authority of the biblical text, these writers' substitutions also serve aesthetic purposes, giving pleasure to readers attuned to the biblical references. That pleasure is illuminated by Barthes's identification of "the cohabitation of languages *working side by side*" as the source of textual "bliss," and "the text of pleasure" as "a sanctioned Babel."[36] He locates pleasure in "breaks" or "collisions" between these different languages or "codes," and in the interactions along the "two edges [that] are created: an obedient, conformist, plagiarizing edge (the language is to be copied in its canonical state, as it has been established by schooling, good usage, literature, culture), and *another* edge, mobile, blank (ready to assume any contours), which is never anything but the site of its effect: the place where the death of language is glimpsed" (6). These edges are very much present in Puritan writing—where the canonical biblical text meets the appropriating force of a William Bradford or a Thomas Hooker—and the reader-listener derives pleasure from perceiving "the seam" that results (7). Barthes explains this pleasure in terms of "heterology by plenitude," an abundance of signifiers by which "the author (the reader) seems to say to them: *I love you all* (words, phrases, sentences, adjectives, discontinuities: pell-mell: signs and mirages of objects which they represent)" (8). This sense of loving fullness, indeed of almost overwhelming overabundance, is characteristic of many Puritan texts. Thomas Shepard's nearly obsessive propensity for incorporating multiple quotations, for example, reflects not only a pious desire to use sanctioned language, but also a real love for what he perceives as the divine word, aesthetic pleasure in its language, and a desire to incorporate as much of that language as possible into his own text as an expression of his love and gratitude.[37]

Barthes also compares intertextual pleasure to "the children's game of topping hands" (12). As in the game, he argues, "the excitement comes not from a processive haste but from a kind of vertical din (the verticality of language and of its destruction); it is at the moment when each (different) hand skips over the next (and not one *after* the other) that the hole, the gap, is created and carries off the subject of the game—the subject of the text" (12). Barthes's notion of "vertical din" is appropriate to New England texts that pile up quotations one after the other, a practice that endured into the eighteenth century. Thomas Prince, for example, celebrated the taking of Louisbourg in a long collage of biblical quotations, in a paragraph marked by quotation marks along its left margin:

When the Tydings came of surrendring the City, "we were like Them that
dream: Our Mouth was fill'd with Laughter, and our Tongue with singing:
Even the Heathen said, *The* LORD *hath done great Things for them;* and
We—*The* LORD *hath done great Things for us, whereof we are glad.* Not
unto us, O LORD, not unto us, but unto thy Name give Glory: Our GOD hath
done whatsoever he pleased: The LORD hath been mindful of us: And we
will bless the LORD, from this Time forth & for ever."[38]

Piling up quotation on quotation, Prince used biblical language of praise to
indicate his own exuberance.

Barthes's account of intertextual manipulations is particularly useful
because it calls attention to textual pleasure. For Puritan congregations certainly took pleasure in the preaching of their ministers. Surely more than
piety underlay the enthusiasm for sermons that John Winthrop described
in his journal as damaging and potentially hazardous.[39] Sermons were both
frequent and long, and New England Puritans often traveled to neighboring
communities to hear visiting preachers. Winthrop's description of a 1639 lecture by Thomas Hooker testifies to the attention span of the community on
such occasions:

> Mr. Hooker being to preach at Cambridge, the governour and many others
> went to hear him, (though the governour did very seldom go from his own
> congregation upon the Lord's day). He preached in the afternoon, and hav-
> ing gone on, with much strength of voice and intention of spirit, about a
> quarter of an hour, he was at a stand, and told the people, that God had de-
> prived him both of his strength and matter, etc., and so went forth, and
> about half an hour after returned again, and went on to very good purpose
> about two hours. (*Journal,* 297)

Aside from the length of the lecture itself (nearly three hours, including the
break), the incident is striking for the eagerness to hear Hooker that kept congregants patiently awaiting Hooker's apparently unpromised return for half
an hour. The explanation that such enthusiasm came only from wildly aroused
religious passions is inadequate. Moreover, it seems to exaggerate the differences between contemporary readers and seventeenth-century Puritans. My
sense is that these eager auditors must have liked, even enjoyed, their ministers' sermons, must have found them aesthetically satisfying, in some ways
that are not entirely alien to the emphatically non-Puritan response of to-
day's Puritanists.

My assessments of Puritan sermons and of early New England religious controversy are grounded in the assumption that aesthetic pleasure was part of the reading experience of New England Puritans, and thus draw on Barthes's analysis. Nevertheless, Barthes's account has limitations for the discussion of Puritan texts. Most significantly, his consideration of the erotics of textual pleasure seems differently pitched than the pleasure produced by Puritan biblical quotation: "The pleasure of the text is like that untenable, impossible, purely *novelistic* instant so relished by Sade's libertine when he manages to be hanged and then to cut the rope at the very moment of his orgasm, his bliss."[40] It is not that Puritanism and sexuality are inevitably opposed; Puritan writers were in fact deeply invested in the language of Canticles, of the parable of the ten virgins, and of the wedding feast. But the subtle pleasure of these texts is hardly the orgasmic "bliss" that Barthes privileges.

On the other hand, Puritan texts do not fit neatly into the category of "the text of pleasure" which Barthes opposes to the "text of bliss" (14). In Barthes's formulation, the "text of pleasure" is "the text that contents, fills, grants euphoria; the text that comes from culture and does not break with it, is linked to a *comfortable* practice of reading" (14). But the aesthetic of Puritan quotation is not always "comfortable," even for its author. Often, in fact, the Puritan text comes closer to Barthes's "text of bliss": "the text that imposes a state of loss, the text that discomforts (perhaps to the point of a certain boredom), unsettles the reader's historical, cultural, psychological assumptions, the consistency of his tastes, values, memories, brings to a crisis his relation with language" (14). Puritan texts often combine pleasure with discomfort and unsettlement, exposing tensions in the authors' relationships with biblical and/or divine language even as they revel in those relationships.

Captain John Mason's account of the 1637 Puritan attack on Mystic demonstrates this dynamic. Having described the burning of a Pequot village and its inhabitants, Mason declares triumphantly, "And thus when the LORD turned the Captivity of his people, and turned the Wheel upon their Enemies; we were like Men in a Dream; then was our Mouth filled with Laughter, and our Tongues with Singing; thus we may say the LORD hath done great Things for us among the Heathen, whereof we are glad. Praise ye the LORD!"[41] Here, Mason is paraphrasing the first three verses of Psalm 126: "When the LORD turned again the captivity of Zion, we were like them that dream. Then was our mouth filled with laughter, and our tongue with singing: then said they among the heathen, The LORD hath done great things for them. The LORD hath done great things for us; *whereof* we are glad" (Ps. 126:1–3).

Mason's appropriation of Psalm 126 is pointed and complex. The biblical text speaks of the joy of the return from exile. By appropriating that joy, Mason suggests that the conquest of America is a divinely orchestrated reclamation, identifying the Puritans as returning exiles, rather than as conquerors.[42] The inserted reference to the "Wheel" emphasizes God's agency, absolving the colonists of responsibility for the destruction. Blending the language of Proverbs and the vision of Ezekiel, Mason associates the flames of Puritan arson with the flames of the divine chariot, and also with the actions of a "wise king."[43]

Yet there may be a degree of anxiety provoking this assertion of divine activity. For in the penultimate sentence of this paragraph, Mason inverts the biblical text, asserting that "we may say the LORD hath done great Things for us among the Heathen, whereof we are glad" (22). In the biblical text, it is the "heathen" who are to notice and remark on God's beneficence to His people: "then said they among the heathen, The LORD hath done great things for them" (Ps. 126:2). In the history that Mason describes, however, few "among the Heathen" remain alive to comment; the potential for glorifying God "among the Heathen" has been severely compromised in the attempt to glorify God by destroying them completely. The slippage between the biblical text and its appropriation here demonstrates both the way that quotation can unsettle the author's text, and Mason's need to unsettle the biblical text in order to make his own text coherent and heroic.[44]

Bradford, Bradstreet, Prince, and Mason testify to the pervasiveness and complexity of biblical intertextuality among the laity. The foundation of such writing was established, as Hall explains, by the methods of early education, while ongoing lessons in the techniques of reading, interpretation, and writing were presented in the ministers' sermons, which often explained Puritan theories of exegesis even as they modeled them. The prose and poetry that emerged reflected both spiritual and aesthetic possibilities of Puritan interactions with the biblical text. At the same time, they demonstrated that applications of Puritan biblical theory—by ministers and by laymen—could have unsettling implications. In early New England, Puritan scripturalism had disruptive consequences not only on the printed page, but in the church and courtroom as well. For Puritan scriptural practices played important roles in the controversies that plagued New England's first generations. As the community struggled through conflicts with Roger Williams, the Antinomian Controversy, and the Halfway Controversy, the laity's reading practices and interpretive skills were often at issue. In each case, ministers found that lay readers had learned their lessons too well, applying their biblical skills with confidence and conviction.

## CHAPTER 6

# "Mist and Fog": Roger Williams and the Problem of Interpretation

A s New England churches filled with listeners eager for the
sermons of Thomas Hooker, Thomas Shepard, and John
Cotton, the founders of the Massachusetts colony hoped that
they would not only hear the Word preached, but also govern their lives according to it. Freed from the constraints imposed by the English church, they expected to build a scripturally ordered commonwealth. But Puritan theories of reading
and exegesis complicated that endeavor. Drawing on Reformed
theories of Spirit-illumined reading, New England's Puritan
migrants anticipated that their biblical society would be rooted
in interpretive consensus, that their holy community reading
"in the Spirit" would agree on what God's will was. To their
dismay, they found the enterprise disappointingly difficult.
Having hoped "to walke together in all [God's] waies," Massachusetts Bay's Puritan settlers found all too often that
they disagreed on what the Bible demanded of them, and that
their hoped for unity erupted instead into dissent and controversy.[1] First indications that something serious was amiss
came as the colony confronted the persistent dissent of Roger
Williams. That dissent—and its spread to include the laity—
suggested that all would not proceed smoothly in this scriptural community. And Williams took some pains to tell his interlocutors that their premises were faulty: contrary to their
expectations that scriptural perfection and the assistance of
the Holy Spirit would lead to interpretive consensus, he in-

sisted that there could be no interpretive stability in the earthly realm, even in this would-be holy commonwealth.

## RICHARD HOOKER AND ACCUSATIONS OF LITERALISM

The premises that Williams challenged had long separated the Puritans from their Conformist counterparts. English Conformists—those who maintained their allegiance to the English Church—held "that scripture leaves men free to work out any polity which suits their circumstances, so long as they do nothing contrary to the general precepts of the Bible."[2] They did not discount the importance of scripture. In fact, Richard Hooker (1554–1600), who attempted to codify the basic doctrines of the English church in his *Lawes of Ecclesiasticall Politie* (1593), acknowledged that the Bible communicates all "things absolutely unto all men's salvation necessarie, eyther to be held or denied, eyther to be done or avoyded. For which cause Saint Augustine acknoweledgeth, that they are not onely set downe, but also plainely set downe in Scripture: so that he which heareth or readeth may without any great difficultie understand."[3] These things so "necessarie" to salvation were set down clearly—"plainely"—so that any Christian could understand them. Less basic doctrine, on the other hand, things "more obscure, more intricate and hard to be judged of," might not be as clear to the average Christian. Rather, such matters should be left to interpretive professionals—to those whom "God hath appointed . . . to spende their whole time principally in the studie of things divine, to the end that in these more doubtfull cases, their understanding might be a light to direct others" (preface, 3.2.13).

Such professional skill was necessary, in Hooker's view, because these more obscure things were not necessarily spelled out in the biblical text. Rather, he maintained that "God hath left sundry kindes of lawes unto men, and by all those lawes the actions of men are in some sort directed" (2.1.2.145). Included in this category were the adiaphora—things neither expressly commanded nor expressly forbidden in the biblical text. Hooker argued "that it sufficeth if such actions be framed according to the lawe of reason" (2.1.2.145). In making this argument, however, he did not reject scriptural authority. Rather, he insisted that "the lawe of reason" was itself encoded in the biblical text: "the generall axiomes, rules, and principles of which law being so frequent in holy scripture, there is no let but in that regard, even out of scripture such duties may be deduced by some kind of consequence (as by long circuit of deduction it may be that even all truth out of anie truth may be concluded)" (2.1.2.145). If the logical processes by which a practice was devised were consistent with scriptural logic, Hooker argued, that practice could be not only allowed, but even mandated by the Church. Moreover, this method of determining right-ful practice was not merely permissible; it was necessary to create a smoothly functioning church polity in the face of biblical instructions that were some-times less than clear.

Puritan exegetes, of course, did not eschew the use of logic and reason in the interpretive process.[4] Nor did Hooker accuse them of completely reject-ing reason in their exegesis. Instead, he objected to their insistence on the in-sufficiency of logic unsupported by specific textual evidence. He "dissent[ed]" from their insistence that man was "bound . . . to deduce all his actions out of scripture," so that "if eyther the place be to him unknowne, whereon they may be concluded, or the reference unto that place not presently considered of," they would argue that "the action shall in that respect be condemned as unlawfull" (2.1.2.145). In doing so, accused Hooker, Puritans were letting their "desire to enlarge the necessarie use of the word of God" lead them to an "error," "enlarging it further then . . . soundnes of truth will beare" (2.1.2.145). Essentially, he accused them of being overly literal and insufficiently flexible in drawing practices from the biblical text.

In fact, Puritan exegesis was far less literal than its rhetoric declared; "lit-eral" meaning allowed for a range of approaches and for a good deal of syllo-gistic reasoning.[5] Hooker's portrayal of Puritan insistence that every cere-mony be scripturally specified was exaggerated as well.[6] Puritans did not deny, in Thomas Cartwright's words, that "certain things are left to the order of the church, because they are of that nature which are varied by times, places, per-sons, and other circumstances, and so could not at once be set down and es-tablished forever."[7] Nevertheless, Puritan exegetes did insist that reasoning on theological and ecclesiastical matters be more firmly rooted in the biblical text than did the more flexible—and perhaps more rationalist—Conformists. As John S. Coolidge explains, Puritans and Conformists "approach[ed] the question of the relationship between reason and scripture with the same log-ical and epistemological assumptions but with different preoccupations. For the Puritan, obedience to God's word must be something more than a rational adjustment of man's behaviour to God's truth, although undoubtedly it is that. He insists on trying to hear God's voice of command in all his thoughts and cannot feel that he is obeying God if it is 'shut out'."[8] This preoccupation, warned Hooker, was dangerous, tending "to overthrowe such orders, lawes, and constitutions in the Church, as depending thereupon if they should there-fore be taken away, would peradventure leave neither face nor memory of Church to continue long in the world" (Laws 2.7.1.175). And, noted Hooker, this was especially dangerous in troubled times, "the world especially being such as it now is" (2.7.1.175).

Indeed, Hooker suggested, it tended to unsettle human authority altogether. And it tended as well to make the unlearned overly confident in their own exegesis:

> it hath alreadie made thousands so headstrong even in grosse and palpable errors, that a man whose capacitie will scarce serve him to utter five wordes in a sensible manner blusheth not in any doubt concerning matter of scripture to think his own bare *Yea*, as good as the *Nay* of all the wise, grave, and learned judgements that are in the whole world. Which insolency must be represt, or it will be the verie bane of Christian religion. (2.7.7.183)

Puritan insistence that doctrine be spelled out clearly and literally in the biblical text, Hooker argued, led the laity to respect their own exegetical abilities too highly. Conversely, and perhaps more troubling to Hooker, they ceased to accord proper deference to their ministers' biblical learning. His sense that the laity might be dangerously stirred up was echoed in the 1622 *Directions* to preachers issued by James I. In the third article of the *Directions*, preachers under the rank of bishop or dean were forbidden from preaching on "the deep points of predestination, election, reprobation, or of the universality, efficacy, resistibility or irresistibility, of God's grace," topics "fitter for the schools and universities, than for simple auditories."[9] Moving well beyond Richard Bernard's exhortation to avoid controversial topics, the *Directions* extended the category of topics inappropriate for an unschooled and "headstrong" laity to include the basic substance of much Puritan preaching.

Hooker suggested not only that Puritans' overly literal approach to scripture would produce a "headstrong" laity, but also that it would generate interpretive controversy that would be resolved only by granting some interpretive authority to expert exegetes, whom he called "men of judgement" (2.7.6.183). This, argued Hooker, was the lesson of Christian history. In repeated controversies, he noted, appeals to scripture had failed to resolve disputes: "In that auncient strife which was betweene the Catholique fathers and Arrians, Donatistes, and others of like perverse and frowarde disposition, as long as to fathers or Councells alleaged on the one side, the like by the contrarie side were opposed, impossible it was that ever the question should by this meane growe unto anie issue or ende" (2.7.6.183).

In such disputes, both sides had accepted the authority of the biblical text and both had remained confident that scripture held the answers: "The scripture they both believed, the scripture they knewe could not give sentence on both sides, by scripture the controversie betweene them was such as might be determined" (2.7.6.183). And yet, noted Hooker, the controversies persisted, and the various parties were unable to convince one another of the truth of their respective positions. If the biblical text could resolve their disputes, he asked, why did the disputants persist: "In this case what madnes was it with such kindes of proofes to nourish their contention, when there were such effectual meanes to end all controversie that was betweene them?" (2.7.6.183) But they were not madmen, in Hooker's view; rather scripture itself had proved insufficient for the resolution of their controversies. These disputes thus suggested that human authority could not be dismissed: "Hereby therefore it doth not as yet appeare, that an argument of authoritie of man affirmatively is in matters divine nothing woorth" (2.7.6.183). In Hooker's view, human interpretive authority had proved decisive in past interpretive controversies, and there was no reason to believe that the will of God would be sufficiently more clear in his day to make such human interpretive authority unnecessary.[10]

In New England, Hooker's warnings would prove prescient indeed. Eventually, the laity of saints, persuaded by Reformed exegetical rhetoric, felt sufficiently empowered to challenge the interpretations of their own ministers. And the ministers themselves often found it difficult to resolve their own scriptural debates.

## BEST-LAID PLANS

Hooker's arguments, however, failed to convince his Puritan opponents, who persisted in their desire for reform.[11] They maintained that the biblical text provided a working plan for the construction of a society that would allow a pure church to flourish, one that would recapture the purity of the apostolic church.[12] Moreover, they found that the English church was failing to live up to the apostolic model, and that their attempts to reshape the church from within met with tremendous resistance. Ultimately, many members of the nonconformist clergy found themselves forced to choose among conformity, martyrdom, and flight, and chose to set sail for New England. They were accompanied in significant numbers by their congregants, some of whom, like Anne Hutchinson, found the departure of their ministers "a great trouble," and took comfort in the words of Isaiah, who promised that "thine eyes shall see thy teachers."[13]

In New England, Puritan migrants expected to build a scriptural church and a scriptural society. As late as 1636, when several challenges had already arisen for Bostonians who hoped to enact God's "waies" in New England, John Cotton maintained that "when a commonwealth hath liberty to mould his owne frame (*scripturae plenitudinem adoro*) I conceyve the scripture hath given full direction for the right ordering of the same, and that, in such sort as may best mainteyne the *euxia* of the church."[14] In framing the laws of the commonwealth, magistrates would consider the biblical text carefully. Certainly they would not legislate adiaphora. But, as the ministers explained in *A Model of Church and Civil Power,*

> Magistrates upon due and diligent search what is the counsell and will of
> God in his Word concerning the right ordering of the Church, may and
> ought to publish and declare, establish and ratifie such Lawes and Ordi-
> nances as Christ hath appointed in his Word for the well ordering of Church
> affaires, both for the gathering of the Church, and the right admistration
> *[sic]* of all the Ordinances of God amongst them in such a manner as the
> Lord hath appointed to edification.[15]

Free from the constraints imposed by the crown and the English church, Puritan migrants expected their magistrates to order the new society such that
the church could flourish and the populace could apply the biblical text to
their everyday lives. As Edward Davidson explains, "The colony had been
given the Word restored in all its clarity and purity just as it had been com-
pleted by the Apostles," as well as "a ministry capable of teaching and preaching the truth contained in the Word in ways rarely opened to the children
of men."[16] Early expectations of success were high indeed. In John Cotton's
words, "the Order of the Churches and of the Commonwealth was so settled,
by common Consent, that it brought to his mind, the New Heaven and New
Earth, wherein dwells Righteousness."[17]

Early settlers' optimism about the possibility of establishing a scripturally
governed community is reflected in the simplicity of their early church covenants. The covenanting members of the Salem church, for example, promised in 1629 simply: "We Covenant with the Lord and one with an other; and
doe bynd our selves in the presence of God, to walke together in all his waies,
according as he is pleased to reveale himselfe unto us in his Blessed word of
truth."[18] They were confident, at least at the outset, that this would be fairly
straightforward. After all, God's "waies" were clearly revealed "in his Blessed
word" for all to read and understand.

Similarly confident, the first church of Boston made a similarly simple
covenant:

> In the Name of our Lord Jesus Christ, & in Obedience to His holy will
> & Divine Ordinaunce.
> Wee whose names are herevnder written, being by His most wise, &
> good Providence brought together into this part of America in the Bay of
> Masachusetts, & desirous to vnite our selves into one Congregation, or
> Church, vnder the Lord Jesus Christ our Head, in such sort as becometh all
> those whom He hath Redeemed, & Sanctifyed to Himselfe, do hereby

solemnely, and religiously (as in His most holy Proesence) Promisse, & bind o'selves, to walke in all our wayes according to the Rule of the Gospell, & in all sincere Conformity to His holy Ordinaunces, & in mutuall love, & respect each to other, so neere as God shall give vs grace.[19]

They acknowledged that they might not achieve perfection, for that would be impossible in this earthly realm. Nevertheless, they expected consensus. "Conformity" in the church would no longer require spiritual compromise, as it had in England; rather, it would result from "sincere" assent (131). And they expected that God would give them "grace" to walk quite "neere" to his will indeed, following "the Rule of the Gospell" (131).

While the New England ministers hoped to build a biblically directed commonwealth, they knew that God's word would require some interpretation. They did not, however, anticipate intractable interpretive controversy. Puritan theories of Bible reading acknowledged that scripture could be read incorrectly. But drawing on earlier reformers, they usually assumed that incorrect reading was an activity of the unregenerate—a conscious twisting or perversion, rather than a conscientious disagreement. John Calvin, for example, described those who "corrupt the meaning of Scripture" in arguing for the acceptability of images in worship, and suggested that they "abrogate all trust in themselves either by treating Scripture so childishly or by rending it so impiously and foully."[20]

Like Calvin, William Perkins conceived interpretive conflict as a consequence of heresy. For example, he emphasized "that collections ought to be right and sound, that is to say, derived from the genuine and proper meaning of the Scripture."[21] "[O]therwise," he warned, "we shall draw any doctrine from any place," citing as an example Proverbs 8:22, from which "the Arians collect very wickedly" to show "that the *Son* was created" (751). For Perkins, then, misinterpretation was identified with heresy, and with willful, even wicked, misreading.

John Cotton, too, associated misreading, heresy, and willfulness: "the Word of God is so cleare, that after once or twice Admonition, the Heretick cannot but be convinced in his owne Conscience"; the heretic persists in his error because he is "wilfully obstinate, . . . not through want of light, or weaknesse of knowledge, but through strength of will."[22] It was expected that there would be those who misread willfully, "impiously" perverting scripture. But they would not be found among the godly, and, it was to be hoped, not among the members of the holy commonwealth being founded in New England. Rather, as Larzer Ziff points out, "the religious pretext" of the New England Puritans considered an audience of those sharing in the Holy Spirit.[23]

The Holy Spirit, Reformed exegetes argued, would assist the readings of the regenerate.[24] For this reason, they expected any interpretive problems that arose to be resolvable. Perkins described the consequences of spiritual illumination for readings hindered by difficulties, citing Augustine as an exemplar of proper reading.[25] Because his text was faulty, Augustine had to make great efforts to "wittily gather" doctrine (751). Despite this serious obstacle, Augustine succeeded in his reading because, unlike the Arians, he accommodated his reading to the illumination of the Spirit. In a community of saints, early New Englanders expected that this would be the rule, and that even misreadings would be cleared up when the erring readers had their errors explained to them.

In *The Faithfvll Shepheard*, Richard Bernard suggested that ministers study past controversies, drawing from church fathers "onely as farre as they agree with Scriptures in matters of saluation," and not adopting their errors.[26] "When they differ," he suggested, "consider them as men, reuerence them and receiue them in the truth: but be tied to none in their errors" (41). Instead, "If it be possible, reconcile and cure the iarre, to make them agree" (41). Like apparent discrepancies in the biblical text, controversy offered a challenge for interpreters: to resolve the controversy by reconciling the positions into agreement. This was the approach that would be repeatedly taken in New England's early years.

Sometimes, New Englanders found, this model worked. In November of 1631, for example, the Watertown congregation experienced some conflict concerning a certain Richard Brown, one of the church elders.[27] Brown, who had a history of separatist views, had also published an opinion "that the Churches of Rome were true churches" (*Journal*, 54). In July, John Winthrop reports, "the matter was debated before manye of bothe Congregations, & by the approbation of all the Assembly except 3: was concluded <as> an errour" (54). In November, however, with Brown "persistinge in his opinion of the truthe of the Rom[ish] Churche, & maintayninge other errours withall, & beinge a man of a very violente spirit, the Court wrote a Lettre to the Congregation directed to the Pastor & brethren, to advise them to take into Consideration whither mr Brown were fit to be continued their elder or not" (60). Some dispute ensued; according to Winthrop, "The said Congregation . . . [was] muche devided aboute their elder" (61). They appealed to the governor, who traveled to Watertown with the deputy governor and Increase Nowell, and presented several modes in which those assembled might proceed to resolve the conflict: "1: as the magistrates (their assistance beinge desired) 2: as members of a neighbor Congregation: 3 vpon the Answer which we received of our Lettre, which did no waye satisfy vs. but the pastor mr Ph: desired vs to sitt with them as members of a neighbor Congregation onely whereto the Governor &c. consented" (61). Thus far, at least in Winthrop's account, the community was working well. Certainly the dispute was troubling, but they were at least able to reach consensus about how to approach the problem, despite the complexities raised by different congregations and by the involvement of civil authorities in church matters.

The proceedings themselves were even more encouraging. One side in the dispute presented their grievance: "that they could not communicate with their elder being guilty of errours bothe in Iudgment & Conversation" (61). The discussion that followed proved productive, and moved the disputants toward consensus: "after muche debate of these thinges, at lengthe they were reconciled, & agreed to seeke God in a daye of humiliation, & so to have a solemn vniting, each partye promisinge to referre what had been amisse, &c: & the Pastor gave thankes to God & the Assembly broke vp" (61). Interestingly, Winthrop omits details about precisely what reforms were agreed upon by "each partye." In his narrative, as in mine, the process of resolving the dispute and the fact that the dispute could be resolved into reconciliation and unity seem more significant than the actual elements of the agreement.[28] Certainly, the incident boded well for the way in which New Englanders expected to deal with conflicts in their midst.


## ROGER WILLIAMS AND EARLY DISSENT

One of New England's most prominent biblical interpreters, however, proved surprisingly steadfast in his "misreadings," and much more persistent in the controversies that he generated. Though Roger Williams was initially welcomed to Massachusetts, preceded by a reputation for eloquence and learning, his disruption of the colony began almost immediately upon his arrival.[29] In 1631, he declined the office of teacher in the Boston church, refusing to minister to a church that had not formally separated itself from the Church of England (notwithstanding the de facto separation established by the migration to New England).[30]

After spending some time at separatist Plymouth, Williams apparently found even the colonists there to be insufficiently separatist for his beliefs. Specifically, he objected that colonists who visited England and attended church there were not rebuked by the Plymouth congregation.[31] After leaving Plymouth in 1633, Williams became an assistant to Samuel Skelton, pastor of the Salem church, who shared Williams's separatist views.[32] There, Perry Miller reports, "he rapidly put himself in opposition to the regime of the colony by declaring that the royal charter gave no valid title to the land, denying that a magistrate could tender an oath of civil obedience to the unregenerate, continuing to insist that the churches profess separation, and asserting that the civil authorities should not punish breaches of the first four Commandments."[33] The disruptive nature of these positions was exacerbated by Williams's growing popularity in the Salem church, which was experiencing a revival, and by the fact that Williams composed treatises attempting to persuade his colleagues of his opinions.[34] In December of 1633, Williams sent the governor and assistants of the Bay colony a treatise disputing "their right to the landes they possessed" (*Journal*, 107). On consultation with the colony's ministers, the assistants concluded that the treatise was sufficiently offensive to warrant censure.[35] Williams avoided censure by writing to the governor and council "verye submissively: professing his intent to have been onely to have written for ∧the private∧ satisfaction of the Governor &c: of Plim: without any purpose to have stirred any further in it, if the Governor heere had not required a Copye of him. withall offering his booke, or any parte of it to be burnt &c:" (*Journal*, 107–8). Moreover, Williams "appeared privatly" at the next meeting of the court, "and gave satisfaction of his intention [———] his loialty" (108).[36] "[S]o," concludes Winthrop, "it was left & nothing doone in it" (108).

But Williams's disruption of the Massachusetts Bay community continued, confronting both clergy and laity with the problem of dissent over biblical interpretation. Williams's dissent spread to the laity as well, as troubled church members disputed their perplexities with their ministers. During his Salem ministry, Williams mandated that women wear veils to church.[37] Shortly thereafter, some members of the Boston church suggested that it should follow Salem's model. On March 7, 1634, Winthrop reports that "At the Lecture at Boston a Question was propounded about vayles" (*Journal*, 111). In response, "mr <u>Cotton</u> concluded that where (by the Custom of the place) they were not a signe of the womens subiection, they were not comanded by the Apostle" (*Journal*, 111).

Cotton's biblical interpretation did not stand unchallenged. And the objection came from a layman, albeit one with a reputation for being headstrong and somewhat impatient: "mr Endecott opposed, & did maintaine it by the general Argumentes brought by the Apostle" (111).[38] Just as significant as the willingness of the laity to debate scriptural interpretation with the colony's foremost minister was the reluctance of the clergy to assert their own interpretive authority. Instead, the question was left unresolved: Winthrop records that "after some debate, the Governor, perceivinge it to growe to some earnestnesse interposed & so it brake off" (111).

Even in this seemingly simple and straightforward case, the godly community in Boston found it impossible to reach consensus about what scripture required of them. Instead, consideration of the proper way of walking according to the "Rule of the Gospel" had provoked strife and unresolved debate, as well as the contentious laity that Richard Hooker had predicted.[39] While Winthrop grants the incident only brief mention, it must have been a disappointing moment indeed. Certainly it augured ill for the prospects of a scriptural community.

Meanwhile, Williams continued to declare publicly positions that were deemed dangerous by the Boston ministers.[40] Repeatedly, he was called to account for his positions. At some points, he apologized and agreed to retract his statements, while on other occasions he forcefully debated his position and held his ground. In the summer of 1635, Williams "beinge sicke & not able to speake wrote to his churche a protestation," refusing to communicate with the other churches of the bay (*Journal*, 153). Moreover, he refused to communicate with his own church unless they, too, separated fully from the other Massachusetts churches (153). This proved the last straw for the colony's magistrates and ministers, and Williams was called before the General Court once more in October of 1635 (158). Thomas Hooker was appointed to debate with him, but unlike the dissenters envisioned by earlier reformers, Williams proved steadfast in his errors (158). Consequently, the court banished him from the colony, with "all the ministers save one approvinge the sentence" (158). Williams was allowed a six-week grace period, and, in consideration of the season and of Williams's ill health, "an extension [of that grace period] until the spring if he refrained from publicizing his views."[41]

At the same time, Winthrop reports, Williams's church at Salem "had him vnder question allso for the same cause" (158). When Williams returned to Salem during the grace period allowed him before leaving the colony, he "refused Communion with his owne Churche" (158). The Salem church "openly disclaimed his errours," though Winthrop reports that many in Salem found Williams's arguments persuasive: "He had so far prevayled at Salem as <dive> ∧many∧ there (especially of devoute women) did imbrace his opinions, & separated from the Churches, for this cause that some of their members goeinge into England did heare the ministers there, & when they came home, the Churches heere held comunion with them" (158, 164). Despite their expectations of walking "together in all [God's] waies," church and community found themselves plagued by division.

Nor did Williams seem particularly interested in healing the strife. Winthrop reports that "notwithstandinge <his> the Iniunction layd vpon him (vpon the libertye granted him to staye till the Springe) not to goe about to drawe others to his opinions," Williams continued to preach privately to his followers "even of suche pointes as he had been Censured for," and planned a plantation on Narragansett Bay as well (163). After his activities were reported to the governor and assistants, they decided in January to send him back to England. When Williams refused to return to Boston, Captain John

Underhill was sent to Salem "to apprehende him & carrye him aborde the shippe" (163). Williams, however, eluded Underhill, fleeing Salem for the Narragansett Bay three days ahead of Underhill's arrival.[42]

Anne G. Myles suggests that "[w]hen Williams gave his ultimatum to the Salem church, he must have expected some kind of church censure, but the civil sentence of banishment and the severity of its enforcement after he defied the conditions for extending the deadline seem to have come as a surprise" (141). If she is correct in her assessment, Williams's surprise must have paralleled the surprise of ministers and magistrates at having to deal with such an intractable problem so soon in their enterprise. Though Williams later complained of the cruelty of banishment in the "howling Wildernesse in Frost and Snow," one suspects that many in Salem were relieved to see him go.[43] And if his punishment was severe, even cruel, it did reflect the seriousness of the disruption that Williams presented not only to Salem, but to his colleagues' understanding of the New England project.

## Sources of Debate

The difficulties that Williams raised in Massachusetts were wide ranging, and had complex causes and effects. They touched church polity, civil governance, the status of the charter, and relations with Native Americans. But many of these differences stemmed from issues of theology and scriptural interpretation. It was in these arenas that Williams may have generated his most profound disruption, for he called into question his colleagues' theories of reading and interpretation, challenging the basic premises of the scriptural commonwealth.[44]

For Williams, the prospect of a scriptural commonwealth was overshadowed by the profound spiritual limitations of this world, as was the ability of even a regenerate human interpeter. In his view, even the most pious Christian was bound to earthly, physical, and bodily existence, and consequently was limited in purity, in perception, and in contact with the divine. As Jesper Rosenmeier explains, Williams's understanding of Christ's incarnation and crucifixion differed significantly from that of the Boston ministers: "Williams interpreted Christ's incarnation as the historical moment when God had changed the nature of his kingdom radically."[45] For Williams, "the suffering body on the cross was the mirror which clearly revealed that the nature of Christian life until the millennium was implacable opposition between Christ and the world," and separation between "spiritual virtues" and "the life of the body."[46]

Williams's emphasis on earthly limitations, rather than on earthly possibilities, shaped his interpretive practices. It was reflected, for example, in his approach to typology, which challenged the vision of New England that his colleagues shared. Many New England divines believed in a typological system in which Old Testament types were fulfilled not merely by New Testament antitypes, but by antitypes in history as well.[47] So, for example, New England could be a new Israel, fulfilling some of the promise of ancient Israel as described in the biblical text. This conferred not only privilege, but also obligation: living up to that promise demanded rigorous adherence to the model of society that biblical Israel offered, and the fates of disobedient biblical figures promised that the failure to fulfill divine commandments would be disastrous.

Joining the tradition of scholars who have considered Williams's typology, Rosenmeier offers a useful account of Williams's position. He explains that the fundamental break that Williams perceived "between the two dispensations of grace" precluded a historically oriented typology.[48] Instead, Williams insisted that Old Testament types were fulfilled *only* by New Testament antitypes, and that such antitypes were spiritual rather than historical.[49] Particularly misguided, in Williams's view, were attempts to make modern nations or even national churches antitypes for biblical Israel. He insisted that "the *Pattern* of the *National Church* of *Israel,* was a *None-such,* unimitable by any *Civil State,* in all or any of the *Nations* of the *World* beside."[50] No modern nation could fulfill the pattern of ancient Israel, or even be a pale imitation.[51] In fact, Williams asserted, the very concept of a national antitype for the biblical nation was misguided. Rather, "There is no holy Land or *City* of the *Lord,* or *King* of *Sion,* &c. but the *Church* of *Jesus Christ,* and the King thereof, according to 1 *Pet.* 2. 9" (*BT,* 158/281). The antitype of Old Testament Israel was the church as a spiritual entity. What Williams called the "*shadowish* and *figurative* state" of the national church in biblical Israel had "vanished at the appearing of the *Body* and *substance,* the *Sun* of *Righteousnesse,* who set up another *Kingdome* or *Church* (Heb. 12)" (111/209–10). Failure to recognize this, he charged, "wakens *Moses* from his unknown Grave, and denies *Jesus* to have seene the earth" (118/221).

If the model of biblical Israel could not apply to New England's church government, scriptural accounts of Israelite law could not be the basis for New England polity. As Edmund Morgan explains, Williams "denied that those laws which had been given to Moses should be . . . enforced [in New England] with the same rigor that the Israelites had practiced."[52] Indeed, Morgan argues, "[t]o Williams, the holy covenant that Winthrop claimed for Massachusetts was an unholy delusion" (103). If it was a delusion, it was a widespread one, shared by Christians from Constantine forward, and Williams acknowledged that many of the deluded were well intentioned if misguided, showing "heavenly *affection,* rare *devotion,* wonderfull care and *diligence,*" and "propounding to themselves the best *patternes* of the *Kings* of *Judah, David, Salomon,*

*Asa, Jehosaphat, Josiah, Hezekiah"* (*BT*, 212/369). But, lamented Williams, because

> the *light* of their *eye* of *conscience,* and the *consciences* also of their *Teach-*
> *ers* [had] been darkened, . . . they lost the *path,* and *themselves,* in perswad-
> ing *themselves* to be the *parallels* and *antitypes* to those *figurative* and *typi-*
> *call* Princes: whence they conceived themselves bound to make their *Cities,*
> *Kingdomes, Empires* new holy lands of *Canaan,* and themselves *Gov-*
> *ernours* and *Judges* in *spirituall* causes, compelling all *consciences* to *Christ,*
> and persecuting the contrary with fire and sword. (*BT*, 323/369)

Blinded by the darkness that Williams perceived as afflicting the eyes of human interpreters, these leaders clung to a misguided typology. And this misguided typology, Williams suggested, led to government interference in spiritual matters, and to persecution of dissenters—serious matters indeed.

## THE GARDEN AND THE WILDERNESS

In rejecting the historical typology of his ministerial colleagues, Williams did
not deny that the Bible offered important guidance for the new colony. While
he insisted that New England could not be a new Israel, he nevertheless maintained that biblical precepts ought to shape the community and the churches.
But in order to apply those precepts appropriately, Williams argued that it
was important for New Englanders to understand the nature of the world
they inhabited and their place within it. Williams's perception of the world as
a profoundly disordered and chaotic place shaped his understanding of the
need for toleration, separation of church and state, and separation from the
English church.

For Williams, these positions were linked, and were rooted in interpretive
issues that set him apart from many of his New England colleagues. Like his
understanding of typology, Williams's sense of the proper application of biblical models to New England was shaped by his understanding of existence in
the wake of the incarnation and crucifixion. Emphasizing the opposition between the Christian and the world throughout his debates with Cotton and
the other elders, Williams relied on the biblical text to delineate the parameters of earthly existence and of appropriate roles for earthly church and state.
Instead of focusing on descriptions of biblical Israel, however, Williams drew
heavily on New Testament passages that highlight distinctions between the
true church and everything outside of it. For Williams, such passages offered
more appropriate guidance both because they did not require misguided ty-

pological gestures and because they rested in the post-incarnation revelation of the New Testament.[53] Williams's readings were varied and often seemed not entirely consistent; he was, however, consistent in insisting firmly and emphatically that both the civil state and the earthly institution of the visible church be clearly recognized for what they were: institutions of this world, and thus imperfect ones. As such, they must be emphatically distinguished from the perfection described in scriptural passages concerning God's garden. Williams's sense that his interlocutors failed to understand this relationship shaped his debate with them.

For Williams, the world that had endured Christ's crucifixion was fundamentally a wilderness, and he was especially drawn to passages that describe this wilderness and contrast it with the garden of God's church. He was drawn as well to passages that speak of fields, suggesting to Williams that portions of this wilderness could be marked off as areas of potential growth in need of careful cultivation. To Williams, such areas represented the civil state and the earthbound church, in which individuals under certain circumstances might be cultivated in preparation for the harvest that would come in God's—not man's—good time. Images of gardens were reserved for the true and invisible church, and Williams reminded his opponents that they needed to be more attentive to the distinction between field and garden. For when he spoke of the "Garden of the Church," he reminded his readers that "the promise of Christs presence, *Matth.* 28. cannot properly and immediately belong to the *Church* constituted and gathered, but to such *Ministers* or *Messengers* of *Christ Jesus,* whom he is pleased to employ to gather and constitute the *Church* by *converting* and *baptizing*" (*BT,* 235/405–6). Even in New England, despite the endeavors of the ministers, "a true *Church* of God" was not to be found (25/73).[54]

Williams repeatedly accused his colleagues of misunderstanding the biblical metaphors of wilderness, field, and garden, and consequently of conflating these in their church and civil governments: "it will appear that in spirituall things they make the *Garden* and the *Wildernesse* (as often I have intimated) I say the *Garden* and the *Wildernesse,* the *Church* and the *World* are all one" (*BT,* 126/233). The image of the wilderness seems to have had particular resonance for Williams after his banishment and flight into the New England winter, but he found the confusion of church and world similarly serious. In fact, he suggested that the intermingling of church and state, specifically in requiring that magistrates be chosen from among church members, was "to turne the *World* upside down, to turne the *World* out of the *World,* to pluck up the *roots* and *foundations* of all *common societie* in the *World?* To turne the *Garden* and *Paradice* of the *Church* and *Saints* into the *Field* of the *Civill State* of the *World,* and to reduce the *World* to the first *chaos* or *confusion*" (241/415). Not only did Williams's opponents mistake themselves for the new Israel; they also failed to see where they stood. Consequently, he contended, they misapplied the biblical text, conflating categories of world, wilderness, field, and garden and reducing the entire civil structure to chaos.

Williams was particularly concerned with such conflation when scriptural images of field, garden, and wilderness were used to justify the persecution of dissenters. As he lamented in *The Bloudy Tenent of Persecution*, "when ever a *toleration* of others *Religion* and *Conscience* is pleaded for, such as are (I hope in truth) *zealous* for *God*, readily produce plenty of *Scriptures* written to the *Church*, both before and since *Christs* comming, all commanding and pressing the putting forth of the *uncleane*, the cutting off the *obstinate*, the purging out the *Leaven*, rejecting of *Hereticks*" (39/94–95). Often, such scriptural justifications focused around images of the field and the garden. In Williams's formulation, his opponents argued that "because *briars, thornes, and thistles* may not be in the *Garden* of the *Church*, therefore they must all bee pluckt up out of the *Wildernesse*" (39/95). In other words, because the biblical text excludes weeds (in the form of false Christians, heretics, and the like) from the garden of the church invisible, Williams's opponents seemed to believe that they must pluck out those weeds even outside the heavenly church, in whatever earthly wilderness they might happen to find themselves.

At the center of this debate lies the parable of the wheat and the tares, found in the thirteenth chapter of Matthew. In this parable, Jesus compares "the kingdom of heaven" to "a man which sowed good seed in his field" (Matt. 13:24). But the field fares badly: "But while men slept, his enemy came and sowed tares among the wheat, and went his way. But when the blade was sprung up, and brought forth fruit, then appeared the tares also" (Matt. 13:25–26). For both Williams and Cotton, this was the condition of the church—full of tares, along with the good wheat. As both wrestled with the appropriate course of action to address that condition, they found the remainder of the parable particularly instructive:[55]

> So the servants of the householder came and said unto him, Sir, didst not thou sow good seed in thy field? from whence then hath it tares? He said unto them, An enemy hath done this. The servants said unto him, Wilt thou then that we go and gather them up? But he said, Nay; lest while ye gather up the tares, ye root up also the wheat with them. Let both grow together until the harvest: and in the time of harvest I will say to the reapers, Gather ye together first the tares, and bind them in bundles to burn them: but gather the wheat into my barn. (Matt. 13:27–30)

Though both Cotton and Williams believed that the end of the parable addressed their concerns, each found a different answer in it. For Williams, this parable justified toleration. In fact, he began *The Bloudy Tenent of Persecution* with an excerpt from an older tract in which this parable is discussed, *Scriptures and Reasons written long since by a Witnesse of Jesus Christ, close Prisoner in Newgate, against Persecution in cause of Conscience*.[56] In advocating toleration, the author of this tract uses the parable to demonstrate that "*Christ* commandeth that the *Tares* and *Wheat* (which some understand are those that walke in the *Truth*, and those that walke in *Lies*) should be *let alone* in the *World*, and not *plucked* up untill the *Harvest*, which is the end of the *World, Matth.* 13. 30. 38. &c." (1/29). Williams endorsed this reading of the parable, and used it to anchor his own insistence on toleration.

Cotton, however, understood the parable very differently, and in the course of their debates, Williams and Cotton spent hundreds of pages arguing over the differences in their readings. Replying to *Scriptures and Reasons*, Cotton asserted instead that "*Tares* are not *Briars* and *Thornes*, but partly *Hypocrites*, like unto the *Godly*, but indeed *Carnall*, as the *Tares* are like to *Wheat*, but are not *Wheat*."[57] His emphasis was on the apparent similarity of tares and wheat: "Or partly such Corrupt *Doctrines* or *Practices* as are indeed unsound, but yet such as come very neere the Truth, (as *Tares* doe to the *Wheat*) and so neere, that Good men may be taken with them, and so the Persons in whom they grow, cannot be rooted out, but good will be rooted up with them. And in such a case *Christ* calleth for *Toleration*, not for *penall prosecution*, according to the 3. Conclusion" (8/43). When doctrines or practices are difficult to distinguish from truth, one must tolerate them because of the risk of uprooting the good. Cotton's emphasis on the indistinguishability of the wheat and the tares, however, suggested that Christ's call for toleration does not apply in egregious cases. In support of his reading, Cotton also cited John Calvin and Theodore Beza, both of whom seemed to agree with Cotton's interpretation (14/52).

In *The Bloudy Tenent of Persecution*, Williams raised several objections to this reading. Finding even the endorsement of such estimable authorities as Calvin and Beza insufficient, he accused Cotton of bringing "no evidence or demonstration of the Spirit . . . to prove such an interpretation, nor Arguments from the place it selfe or the Scriptures of truth to confirme it; but a bare Affirmation that these Tares must signifie persons, or doctrines and practices" (41/98). Claiming the scriptural high ground, Williams framed his own argument in explicitly scriptural terms. In asserting that the resemblance of the wheat and the tares was not at issue in the parable, he first offered specific arguments based on the language of the text:

First, the Originall word ζιζάνια, signifying all those *Weeds* which spring up with the *Corne*, as *Cockle, Darnell, Tares*, &c. seemes to imply such a

kinde of people as commonly and generally are knowne to bee manifestly
diferent from, and opposite to the true *worshippers* of *God,* here called the
*children* of the *Kingdom;* as these *weeds, tares, cockle, darnell,* &c. are commonly and presently knowne by every *husbandman* to differ from *wheat,*
and to be opposite, and contrary, and hurtfull unto it. (42–43/101)

Both the language of the parable, contended Williams, and basic principles of
agriculture supported his reading—tares are noticeably different from wheat,
and thus may represent those whose dissent is blatant rather than subtle.

Moving beyond the details of the text's language, Williams then directed
his interlocutors' attention to the circumstances of the place propounded, the
specific context of the parable. He noted that in the text, distinguishing the
wheat and the tares is not an issue: "The *Parable* holds forth no such thing,
that the likenesse of the *tares* should deceive the servants to cause them to
suppose for a time that they were good *wheat,* but that as soone as ever
the *tares* appeared, ver. 26. the *servants* came to the *housholder* about them,
ver. 27. the Scripture holds forth no such time wherein they doubted or suspected what they were" (43/102). The tares are recognized as soon as they appear, so identification is not the problem. Consequently, Williams contended,
the tares cannot be mere hypocrites or subtle differences of doctrine, and the
parable does not mean that only such differences are to be tolerated. Rather,
the tares in fact represent even "many thousands who love not the *Lord Iesus
Christ,* and yet are and must be permitted in the World or Civill State, although they have no right to enter into the gates of *Jerusalem* the *Church* of
God" (39/94). Denying the distinction between those who reject fundamental points of doctrine and those who are to be tolerated for subtle dissent,
Williams insisted that even fundamental differences of belief are not to be
persecuted in the earthly church (20/64). This is Christ's will, argued Williams,
and a practical matter as well, for although one can often distinguish the tares
quite easily, it remains difficult to uproot them without causing harm to the
good Christian wheat nearby.

Though Williams argued that tares can be readily distinguished from
wheat, he did suggest that issues of differentiation were relevant in another
way. While there is no problem distinguishing between tares and wheat, it is
difficult to know whether tares will remain tares: "he that is a *Briar,* that is, a
*Jew,* a *Turke,* a *Pagan,* an *Antichristian* to day, may be (when the Word of the
*Lord* runs freely) a member of *Jesus Christ* to morrow cut out of the wilde
*Olive,* and planted into the true" (39/94–95). Noting another practical objection, Williams called attention to one of the pastoral difficulties of Puritan soteriology: in a system that insists that grace is divine activity unmerited by
human behavior, the vilest individual may tomorrow be granted grace and

become "a member of *Jesus Christ*" (39/94–95). Even those who insisted that salvation usually proceeded by certain steps were loath to deny that it could occur without such steps; God, after all, remained omnipotent and could do as He pleased. So one could not with confidence separate the definitively unregenerate from those who had not *yet* experienced God's grace.

One caveat is necessary here: though many accounts of Williams proceed from his advocacy of toleration to render him an attractive, indeed a "liberal" political figure, his approach had a darker side as well. For his claim that the "tares" should be left alone until God can deal with them was not meant to imply that they would be tolerated by God. Indeed, Williams devoted considerable interpretive energy to the ultimate fate of the tares within the parable: "he gives to His owne *good seed* this *consolation*, that those heavenly *Reapers* the *Angells* in the *harvest* or end of the *World*, will take an order and course with them, to wit, they shall binde them into *bundles*, and cast them into the *everlasting burnings*, and to make the cup of their consolation run over: He addes vers. 4. Then, then at that time shall the *Righteous* shine as the *Sun* in the *Kingdome* of their *Father*" (45/106). He did not deny that it is galling to the righteous to endure the presence of the wicked, and he suggested that the ultimate fate of the wicked offers consolation. Though it does not fit well into his popular image as the father of religious liberty, Williams took comfort and even perhaps joy in his faith that the wicked would be burned up by the angels, while the righteous "shine as the sun."

This position, though, epitomizes the complexities of Williams's approach to toleration. He had neither affection nor even patience for the wicked; he simply found the problem of their presence intractable. This world struck him as uncomfortably heterogeneous. Although in spiritual terms "they that are truly *Christs* (that is, annointed truly with the Spirit of *Christ*)" are "as far as the *Heavens* are from the *Earth*" from "those who love not the *Lord Iesus Christ*," the practical reality that confronts Christ's people on earth presents a challenge: "*Gods* people (in their *persons*) are *His*, most deare and precious: yet in respect of the *Christian Worship* they are mingled amongst the *Babylonians*, from whence they are called to come out, not *locally* (as some have said) for that belonged to a materiall and locall *Babell*, (and, literall *Babell* and *Jerusalem* have now no difference, John 4. 21.) but *spiritually* and mystically to come out from her sins and *Abominations*" (39/94, 21/65–66). Mingled among the Babylonians, Christ's people are commanded to separate themselves, to "come out" of Babel. But this separation, in Williams's reading, cannot be a physical or "literal" one.[58] Drawing on a New Testament precedent to collapse historical distinctions between Babel and Jerusalem, Williams emphasized instead a spiritual separation, one that leaves Christians physically intermixed with the Babylonians: in his view, it is impossible for the righteous to escape proximity and physical intermingling with the ungodly.

In fact, Williams emphasized that the conditions of this world are such that it is impossible for the godly to escape even some kinds of mixing within themselves. He asserted, for example, that "*Gods* people in their persons, *Heart-waking, (Cant. 5. 2.)* In the life of *personall grace*, will yet be found fast asleep in respect of *publike Christian Worship*" (21/65). In noticing this admixture within the regenerate, Williams was not of course unusual; most Puritans believed that the regenerate heart's presence in a corrupt earthly body imposed some temporary limits on the transformation accomplished by God's grace. But for Williams, the mixed state of individuals and of the community seems to have been particularly disturbing, a signal of something profoundly wrong with earthly existence.

Such mixing was not only an unhappy indicator of the world's corrupt state; in Williams's view, it also threatened more serious consequences. For in the apostolic moment, separation rather than mixing was the rule: "the Church of the Jews under the Old Testament in the type, and the *Church* of the Christians under the New Testament in the Antitype, were both separate from the world."[59] Williams cited biblical examples of separation, beginning with God's selection of Abraham and his seed and culminating in Paul's exhortation in First Corinthians: "And therefore saith *Paul* expressly, 1 *Cor.* 5. 10. we must goe out of the world, in case we may not company in civill converse with Idolaters, &c." (BT, 52/116, 183–84/323–24). For Williams, this was an important model, suggesting a need for "a separation of holy from unholy, penitent from impenitent, godly from ungodly, &c."[60]

But to Williams's dismay, many of those separations seemed to have collapsed, and with dramatic results. Though the apostolic church was appropriately "separate from the world," Williams lamented "that when they have opened a gap in the hedge or wall of Separation between the Garden of the Church and the Wildernes of the world, God hath ever broke down the wall it selfe, removed the Candlestick, &c. and made his Garden a Wildernesse, as at this day."[61] Breaking down separations between the church and the world raised the risk that God would break down the separations even further, making even "his Garden a Wildernesse," as Williams perceived the case to be in his own day.

To repair such damage, separation must be restored, as much as possible in the earthly realm and then in its full form in the heavenly realm: "And that therefore if he will ever please to restore his Garden and Paradice again, it must of necessitie be walled in peculiarly unto himselfe from the world, and that all that shall be saved out of the world are to be transplanted out of the Wildernes of the world, and added unto his Church or Garden" (45/108/392).

Williams believed firmly in biblical promises of ultimate separation; God would accomplish what man could not. Meanwhile, however, Williams did not advocate patient acceptance of the world's mixed state. Rather, he argued that Christians should be particularly careful to separate those people and institutions that they could, minimizing the mixing as much as possible.

For Williams, then, it was vital to keep state and church separate. He cited scriptural justification for "a two-fold state, a *Civill state* and a *Spirituall*" (*BT,* 71/147). The existence of these two parts of the state, however, required clear separation between them. There would be "*Civill officers* and *spirituall, civill weapons* and *spirituall weapons, civill vengeance* and *punishment,* and a *spirituall vengeance* and *punishment,*" and the categories were not to be confused: "although the *Spirit* speaks not here expresly of *Civill Magistrates* and their *civill weapons,* yet these States being of different Natures and Considerations, as far differing as *Spirit* from *Flesh,* I first observe, that *Civill weapons* are most improper and unfitting in matters of the *Spirituall state* and *kingdome,* though in the *Civill state* most proper and sutable" (71/147). Maintaining this proper separation was as fundamental as the distinction between the flesh and the spirit.

In practice, this meant that the two aspects of the community should operate in very different ways. Civil offenses should be punished by magistrates with their "civill weapons," and in defining such offenses Williams hardly favored permissiveness. Indeed, he argued that offenses "against the good and peace of their Civil state" should be punished by the magistrates, "and therefore neither *disobedience* to *parents* or *magistrates,* nor *murther* nor *quarrelling, uncleannesse* nor *lasciviousnesse, stealing* nor *extortion,* neither ought of that kinde ought to be let alone, either in lesser or greater *families, townes, cities, kingdomes,* Rom. 13. but seasonably to be supprest, as may best conduce to the *publike safety*" (47/108–9). Moreover, he emphasized that the tares could not be "offenders against the *civill state* and Common welfare, whose dealing is not suspended unto the comming of the *Angels,* but [is committed] unto Men, who (although they know not the Lord *Jesus Christ,* yet) are lawfull *Governours* and *Rulers* in *Civill things*" (47–48/110). Offenders against the civil state were not to be tolerated, insisted Williams, citing scriptural precedents: "*Moses* for a while held his peace against the *sedition* of *Korah, Dathan,* and *Abiram. David* for a season tolerated *Shimei, Joab, Adonijah;* but till the *Harvest* or end of the World, the *Lord* never intended that any but these *spirituall* and *mysticall Tares* should be so permitted" (48/110).

Spiritual problems, on the other hand, should be dealt with by the church, and in these cases as well Williams did not maintain a permissive stance. In his argument with Cotton over the parable of the tares, for example, he listed

among his reasons that the tares could not be mere hypocrites his sense that
"when they are discovered and seen to be *Tares* opposite to the good fruit of
the good seed, [they] are not to be let alone to the *Angels* at Harvest or end of
the world, but purged out by the *Governours* of the *Church,* and the whole
*Church* of *Christ"* (47/110). In other words, the anti-Christian tares in the
parable were to be let alone, but hypocrites within the church were not.

Though Williams called for civil and church discipline, he was adamant
that the authorities and tools appropriate to each not be confused. Civil offenses must be punished by the magistrates, who could choose to use the
physical sword. But in spiritual matters, the magistrates ought to have no authority. And when church authorities mete out discipline, it should be with
the sword of the spirit. Again, Williams cited apostolic precedent, invoking
the example of Titus's admonitions to offenders. These admonitions, emphasized Williams, "were not *civill* or *corporall* punishments on mens *persons* or
*purses,* which the *Courts* of Men may lawfully inflict upon *Malefactors"*;
rather "they were the *reprehensions, convictions, exhortations,* and *perswa-
sions* of the Word of the *Eternall God,* charged home to the *Conscience,* in the
name and presence of the *Lord Jesus,* in the middest of the *Church"* (36/90).
When such admonitions fail, drastic measures are justified: "in the last place
followes *rejection"* (BT 36/90). But this, too, is not a physical punishment,

> not a *cutting off* by *heading, hanging, burning,* &c. or an *expelling* of the
> *Country* and *Coasts:* neither [of] which (no nor any lesser *civill punishment*)
> *Titus* nor the Church at *Crete* had any power to exercise. But it was that
> dreadfull cutting off from that visible *Head* and *Body, Christ Jesus* and his
> *Church;* that *purging* out of the *old leaven* from the *lumpe* of the *Saints;* the
> putting away of the *evill* and wicked person from the holy *Land* and *Common-
> wealth* of *Gods Israel,* 1 Cor. 5. where it is observable, that the same word
> used by *Moses* for putting a malefactor to *death* in typicall *Israel,* by *sword,
> stoning,* &c. Deut. 13. 5. is here used by *Paul* for the *spirituall killing* or *cut-
> ting off* by *Excommunication,* 1 Cor. 5. 13. Put away that evill person, &c.
> (36/90–91)

The biblical language is the same for physical and spiritual punishment, but
Williams emphasized the importance of reading the scriptures with a proper
understanding of their spiritual significance.

Alas, he found in practice that those who called themselves Christians
misread those texts, confusing the spiritual and the material, the spirit and
the flesh. He charged that such misreading caused them to "fling away the
*spirituall sword and spirituall artillery* (in *spirituall* and *religious* causes) and

rather trust for the suppressing of each others *God, Conscience,* and *Religion* (as they suppose) to an *arme* of *flesh,* and *sword* of *steele*" (18/61). In doing so, he argued, they participated in "that *old dreame* of *Jew* and *Gentile,* that the *Crowne* of *Jesus* will consist of outward *materiall gold,* and his *sword* be made of *iron* or *steele,* executing judgement in his *Church* and *Kingdome* by *corporall punishment*" (35/89). And this, lamented Williams, was "the overturning and rooting up the very *foundation* and *roots* of all true *Christianity,* and absolutely denying the *Lord Jesus* the Great *Anointed* to be yet come in the Flesh" (35–36/89). Again, Williams suggested that mistaking the spiritual for the material was to deny the materiality of the incarnation.[62]

This, he lamented, had happened in Massachusetts, citing his own banishment to demonstrate that church and state had been unduly conflated. On the one hand, he contended, this could not be truly called a civil banishment, as Cotton seemed to claim; spiritual matters were involved, he insisted, and besides, it was an uncivil act: "why should he call a civill sentence from the civill State, within a few weeks execution in so sharp a time of *New Englands* cold."[63] On the other hand, Williams's banishment was not a strictly spiritual matter, as he had been banished from the colony, rather than simply excommunicated. Indeed, suggested Williams, accepting a spiritual component to his banishment would force acknowledgment that New England church and civil government were inextricably intertwined: "Why should he call this a banishment from the Churches, except he silently confesse, that the frame or constitution of their Churches is but implicitly National (which yet they professe against) for otherwise why was I not yet permitted to live in the world, or Common-weale, except for this reason, that the Common-weale and Church is yet but one, and hee that is banished from the one, must necessarily bee banished from the other also."[64]

The accusation that New England's gathered churches were in fact national churches was a serious one, especially for ministers who were so wary of episcopacy that they initially resisted the convening of synods. Williams also pressed his colleagues hard on questions of separation from the English church. Again, given that the state of the world was mixed, with all sorts of necessary separations broken down, Williams emphasized the particular importance of maintaining whatever separations could be maintained. And he found the New England position particularly strange. For he emphasized the degree to which New England church polity seemed to be separatist in fact: "what is that which Mr. *Cotton* and so many hundreths fearing God in New England walk in, but a way of separation? Of what matter doe they professe to constitute their Churches, but of true godly persons? In what form doe they cast this matter, but by a *voluntary uniting,* or *adding* of such godly persons, whom they carefully examine, and cause to make a *publike confession of sinne,* and *profession* of their *knowledge,* and *grace* in Christ?" (46/109/393) Why were New Englanders so resistant to separation when they seemed to be practicing it themselves?

On the other hand, "If Mr. *Cotton* maintaine the true *Church* of *Christ* to consist of the true *matter* of *holy persons* call'd out from the World; and the true *forme* of *Union* in a *Church-covenant;* And that also neither *Nationall, Provinciall,* nor *Diocesan* Churches are of *Christs institution,*" Williams asked how he could be so inconsistent as *not* to separate from the corrupt English church:

> And however his own *Soule,* and the soules of many others (precious to God) are perswaded to separate from *nationall, Provinciall,* and *Diocesan Churches,* and to assemble into particular *Churches:* yet since there are no *Parish Churches* in England, but what are made up of the *Parish* bounds within such and such a compasse of *houses;* and that such *Churches* have beene and are in constant dependence on, and subordination to the *Nationall Church:* how can the *New-English particular Churches* joyne with the *Old English Parish Churches* in so many *Ordinances* of *Word, Prayer, Singing, Contribution, &c.* but they must needs confesse, that as yet their soules are farre from the *knowledge* of the *foundation* of a true *Christian Church,* whose matter must not only be living stones, but also separated from the *rubbish* of *Antichristian confusions* and *desolations.* (BT, 21–22/66–67)

In the extremeness of his rhetoric, and ultimately of his position, Williams in effect answered his own question. Though the mainstream New England divines seemed more separatist than they acknowledged, their position was significantly more moderate than that of Williams and his separatist colleagues.

This made it easier for Cotton to distance himself theoretically from Williams's separatist position.[65] But the degree to which such theoretical distinctions discomfited those who had set up a church structure that was separate from the Church of England in fact, if not in theory, was demonstrated by the shakiness of Cotton's response to Williams on this point.[66] Accusing Williams of "wrest[ing]" the scriptures, he contended that it was not necessary for every member of a New England church to renounce and regret his former membership in an English parish church; in an uncomfortable choice of metaphor, he denied "that it is necessary to the admission of members that every one should be convinced of the sinfulnesse of every sipping of the Whores cup, for every sipping of a drunkards cup is not sinfull."[67] Cotton suggested that only drunken sipping was sinful, but the language of "Whores cup" and "drunkards cup" works against his otherwise reasonable argument, suggesting some discomfort with it even on Cotton's part. It may not be sinful to drink from a "Whores cup" or a "drunkards cup," but it certainly is not the ideal activity of the godly. Here, Cotton's rhetoric dramatizes the difficulties of a system that rested on so many subtle distinctions.

Faced with such a system, and faced with the inherent mixing and messiness of earthly existence, Williams advocated as much separation as was humanly possible—and this was a very serious limitation. Given the gross imperfections of this world, he sought to contain the chaos and disorder as much as he could. Though he recognized that in earthly terms this appeared to be a losing battle, Williams was confident that ultimately God would restore order, punishing sinners and rewarding His saints. And meanwhile, the church must be kept as far from contamination as possible. Certainly the New England institutional structure was unacceptable, for in giving magistrates some power over the church, the Massachusetts leaders were placing the church under human, rather than divine, control: "And if this be not to pull *God* and *Christ*, and *Spirit* out of *Heaven*, and subject them unto *naturall*, sinfull, inconstant men, and so consequently to *Sathan* himselfe, by whom all *peoples* naturally are guided, let *Heaven* and *Earth* judge" (*BT*, 137/250). His New England colleagues, Williams charged, had mistaken the wilderness that they inhabited for God's garden, and had misunderstood their own roles as tillers of the field. Faced with the corrupt and chaotic world, they had increased the chaos, mist, and darkness, rather than diminishing it.

## CLARITY AND CONFLICT

Beyond his specific objections to New England church and state governance, and beyond his broader objections to the typological practices of his ministerial colleagues and their understanding of the world they inhabited, Williams raised concerns that challenged his colleagues' basic interpretive assumptions. Again drawing on his sense of the profound spiritual limitations faced by Christians in this world, he suggested that the very process of interpretation on which the other ministers relied was unworkable. Challenging their expectations of consensus, Williams emphasized the long history of dissent and conflict within the Christian world. He insisted that "*Gods people* by their preaching, disputing, &c. Have beene (though not the cause) yet accidentally the occasion of great contentions and divisions, yea tumults and uproares in Townes and Cities where they have lived and come, and yet neither their Doctrine nor themselves *Arrogant* nor *Impetuous,* however so charged" (*BT,* 28/77). Good Christians often generated nasty controversies, though Williams insisted that this was through no fault of their own.

On the contrary, Williams claimed that conflict was in fact the apostolic model, quoting in justification Jesus's proclamation in Luke: "Suppose ye that I am come to give peace on earth? I tell you nay, but rather division for from hence forth shall there be five in one house divided, three against two, and two against three, the father shall be divided against the sonne, and the sonne against the father, &c."[68] Williams emphasized that such division was the norm, noting that "upon the occasion of the Apostles preaching, the King-dome and Worship of God in Christ, were most commonly uproares and tu-mults, where ever they came: For instance, those strange and monstrous up-roares at *Iconium,* at *Ephesus,* at *Jerusalem, Acts* 14.4. *Acts* 19. 29. 40. *Acts* 21. *vers.* 30. 31" (28/78). In Williams's view, a genuine apostle or prophet was bound to trouble a community.[69]

Nor, emphasized Williams, was this problem limited to the apostolic mo-ment. Rather, he reminded his readers that dissent and dispute had been the rule throughout history, and noted that ministers in Old and New England were even then disputing the question of toleration (*BT,* 114/215).[70] He an-ticipated a response—confidence that mutual conversation will produce con-sensus: "Yea, but they say, they doubt not if they were there but they should agree; for, say they, either you will come to us, or you may shew us light to come to you, for we are but weak men, and dreame not of *perfection* in this life" (115/216). However, Williams cautioned, experience suggested that con-sensus would be at best elusive:

> Alas, who knowes not what lamentable *differences* have beene betweene the same *Ministers* of the *Church of England,* some conforming, others leaving their *livings, friends, country, life,* rather than conforme; when others againe (of whose personall *godlinesse* it is not questioned) have succeeded by *con-formity* into such forsaken (so called) *Livings?* How great the present *differ-ences* even amongst them that feare *God,* concerning *Faith, Justification,* and the evidence of it? concerning *Repentance* and *godly sorrow,* as also and mainly concerning the *Church,* the *Matter, Forme, Administrations* and *Government* of it? (115/217)

Past differences had been intractable enough to bring New Englanders across the Atlantic, and to separate them from their colleagues who chose to remain behind. Even the godly disagreed among themselves, Williams pointed out, highlighting issues that divided the Boston elders and reminding New Eng-landers how elusive they were finding consensus to be.[71]

Moreover, he suggested that this failure of consensus should be no surprise: "Let none now thinke," he cautioned, "that the passage to *New England* by Sea, or the nature of the *Countrey* can doe what onely the Key of *David* can doe, to wit, open and shut the Consciences of men" (115/217). Puncturing New England hopes of exceptionalism, Williams asserted that no country could be the New Israel that the ministers hoped to build in New England—at least before the Second Coming.

Instead, in Williams's view, Massachusetts was emphatically a new *England*, sharing some of old England's worst faults. The main difference was that the Puritan migrants had switched sides. Now that Cotton and his compatriots were in power, they had changed their approach to persecution of dissenters:

> When Mr. Cotton and others have formerly been under *hatches*, what sad and true complaints have they abundantly powred forth against *persecution*? How have they opened that heavenly Scripture, *Cant.* 4. 8. Where *Christ Jesus* calls his tender *Wife* and Spouse from the fellowship with *persecutors* in their *dens* of *Lions*, and mountaines of *Leopards*?
>
> But comming to the Helme (as he speaks of the *Papists*) how, both by *preaching, writing, Printing, practice,* doe they themselves (I hope in their persons *Lambes*) unnaturally and partially expresse toward others, the cruell nature of such *Lions* and *Leopards*? (108/205)

In this passage, Williams made several rather serious charges. First, he accused his persecutors of having changed their minds about the legitimacy of persecuting dissenters simply because they themselves were no longer being persecuted.[72] Second, he insinuated that in their new role of persecutors, they resembled the dreaded papists, a harsh charge in this enthusiastically Protestant age. Third, he accused his interlocutors of having shifted their reading of scriptural passages to support their new position, implying some less than ideal scriptural flexibility at best, and at worst fundamental scriptural dishonesty.[73]

In contrast, Williams suggested that the consistent pattern of dispute and difference running through Christian history presented yet another argument against the persecution of dissenters. Certainty and confidence could not justify persecution: "Nor shall their confidence in their being in the *truth* (which they judge the *Papists* and others are not in) no nor the *Truth* it selfe priviledge them to *persecute* others, and to exempt themselves from persecution" (108/205). In Williams's view, certainty and confidence themselves were suspect. He argued that the prevalence of controversy required some doubt or, at the very least, humility and restraint: "Againe, since there is so much controversie in the World, where the name of *Christ* is taken up, concerning the true *Church*, the *Ministrie* and *Worship*, and who are those that truly feare *God*; I aske who shall judge in this case, who be those that feare God?" (114/214) Indeed, it might be difficult, if not impossible, to be sure who was correct. Similarly, where *A Model of Church and Civil Power* asserted that the magistrates should diligently search the scriptures to determine God's will, and then "publish and declare, establish and ratifie such Lawes and Ordinances as Christ hath appointed in his Word for the well ordering of Church affaires," Williams asked, "who shall sit here fit to Judge, whether the Magistrate command any other Substance or Ceremonie but what is Christs?" (145/261, 146/263). Williams denied that even "due and diligent" searching would result in a clear consensus about what was commanded and what was merely an indifferent thing.

This was a great part of the problem. While the New England interpretive establishment assumed biblical clarity, Williams found the experience of interpretive difficulty compelling and theoretically significant. Christians in this world, he argued, faced serious interpretive limits; Satan could raise "palpably grosse and thicke . . . mist and fog" around the scriptures, leading people into woeful and even bloody misinterpretations (32/84). Nor would discussion necessarily clear up misunderstanding; indeed, Williams emphatically asserted "how hard it is to be undeceived, especially in *Spirituals*" (154/275). Persecution, then, would not help dissenters to see clearly; it would merely harden them in their heresy or drive them to hypocrisy out of fear (154/275).

The language of the exchanges between Williams and Cotton reveals how loaded this issue was. For Williams, all earthly attempts to read the text were necessarily fumbles in fog and darkness. Williams was relatively untroubled by the fumbles themselves. He showed relative confidence in the strength of his own biblical interpretations, and insisted on the importance of allowing all Christians to read (and by implication misread) for themselves. Otherwise, he suggested in his address to the reader of *The Bloudy Tenent of Persecution*, the basic premises of the Reformation were threatened: "In vaine have *English Parliaments* permitted *English Bibles* in the poorest *English* houses, and the simplest man or woman to search the Scriptures, if yet against their soules perswasion from the Scripture, they should be forced (as if they lived in *Spaine* or *Rome* it selfe without the sight of a *Bible*) to beleeve as the Church beleeves" (13).

While Williams seemed untroubled by the potential misreadings of the "simplest" and the "poorest," he described the consequences of Cotton's misreadings in dramatic and bloody language. His emphasis was not on Cotton's misreading itself, but on the actions and abuses that flowed from it. At one point, for example, he accused Cotton of "darkening that [Psa. 101:8], and other lightsome Scriptures with such direfull clouds of bloud" (158/282).[74] By using the biblical text to justify persecution, Williams insisted, Cotton and his colleagues produced violent and even bloody abuses, metaphorically sullying the scripture with the blood of the persecuted.[75]

Similarly, he accused Cotton of responding to the prisoner's letter in bloody writing and actions:

> The *Answer* (though I hope out of milkie pure intentions) is returned in *bloud: bloudy* & slaughterous *conclusions; bloudy* to the *souls* of all men, forc'd to the *Religion* and *Worship* which every civil State or Common-weale agrees on, and compells all subjects to in a dissembled *uniformitie.*
>
> Bloudy to the *bodies,* first of the holy *witnesses* of *Christ Jesus,* who tes-tifie against such invented worships.
>
> Secondly, of the *Nations* and Peoples slaughtering each other for their severall respective Religions and Consciences. (19/62)

Again, Williams emphasized the bloody consequences of misreading, both spiritually and physically. The central misreading of the *"bloody tenent"* it-self—the justification of persecution for cause of conscience—was so called because of its consequences, because it was "so directly contradicting the spirit and minde and practice of the Prince of Peace; so deeply guilty of the blood of soules compelled and forced to Hypocrisie in a spirituall and soule rape; so deeply guilty of the blood of the Soules under the Altar, persecuted in all ages for the cause of Conscience, and so destructive to the civill peace and welfare of all Kingdomes, Countries, and Commonwealths" (116/219). Bloodiness was not inherent to the misreading itself, but rather stemmed from the bloodshed, both literal and figurative, produced by that misreading.

Conversely, Cotton treated misreading itself as violence. His own reading of a disputed passage, he explained, "tendeth toward edification," while Williams's reading tended "to dissipation and destruction of the Church, and of them that wrest blood in stead of milke from the breasts of holy Scripture."[76] In Cotton's metaphor, misreading itself was a bloody act, making the biblical text itself bleed.

Significantly, neither Williams nor Cotton disputed the authority of the biblical text. Despite his sense of the difficulties that the text presents, Williams insisted that "The Scriptures or writings of truth are those heav-enly righteous scales, wherin all our contraversies must be tried, and that blessed Starre that leads all those soules to Jesus that seek him."[77] Each ac-cused the other of being unscriptural, and of misreading and misapplying the biblical text. They differed, however, in their understanding of misreading.

For Williams, misreading was a necessary consequence of the human reader's position in the corrupt earthly realm, and the only way to limit the damage was to minimize human involvement in spiritual matters, leaving issues of spiritual discipline to Christ. For Cotton, misreading represented the avoidable intrusion of the human will into a spirit-assisted process, the conscious activity of a heretic, at least when the reader persisted despite communal correction. So the case seemed to be with Roger Williams.

## PLANS REVISED

After Williams's departure, the communities of Massachusetts were forced to reevaluate their initial expectations. The controversy had dealt a particularly severe blow to the Salem church, demonstrating to them that their early hopes had been excessively optimistic. Faced with the failure of their community to "walke together in all [God's] waies," they found it necessary to revise and expand their original church covenant.[78] In 1636, they prepared a new covenant, noting sadly that they did so "having found by sad experience how dangerous it is to sitt loose to the Covenant wee make with our God: and how apt wee are to wander into by pathes, even to the looseing of our first aimes in entring into Church fellowship."[79] As they renewed their original promise to "walke together in all [God's] waies, according as he is pleased to reveale himselfe unto us in his Blessed word of truth," they chose as well to specify more clearly what that entailed (117).

They chose, indeed, to "more explicitly in the name and feare of God, profess and protest to walke as followeth through the power and grace of our Lord Jesus," specifying nine articles of faith and behavior, several of which emphasized communal solidarity and submission to communal authority (117). For example, they promised "to walke with our brethren and sisters in this Congregation with all watchfullnes and tendernes, avoyding all jelousies, suspitions, backbyteings, censurings, provoakings, secrete risings of spirite against them; but in all offences to follow the rule of the Lord Jesus, and to beare and forbeare, give and forgive as he hath taught us" (117). Apparently, the biblical revelation needed clarification, even in a community of saints, and the saints needed to be reminded particularly of their stake in consensus and communal peace. While Williston Walker emphasizes the "sense of contrition for disagreement and ill-feeling that finds expression in this enlarged and particularized pledge of fellowship," Philip F. Gura advances a somewhat darker view, noting that Hugh Peter, who had been called as Salem's minister in December of 1636, used the new covenant as an opportunity for consolidation by excommunicating those who would not subscribe to it.[80] In any case, those who remained hoped that, with Williams gone, this reaffirmation would resolve their remaining difficulties.

The ministers of Massachusetts, too, hoped that Williams's departure would allow them to recover from the interpretive challenges that had so shaken the colony. Of course, his departure did not entirely free them of his disruptive ideas; Williams continued a polemical correspondence with Cotton for many years, and also maintained contact with other Massachusetts Bay settlers, even proving useful to the colony in negotiations with the Narragansetts. Meanwhile, he continued to refine his positions, in some cases shifting between extremes; in 1639, Winthrop reported in his *Journal* that "having, a little before, refused communion with all, save his own wife, now he would preach to and pray with all comers" (*Journal*, 300).

Following Williams's departure, Cotton found it necessary to engage in a lengthy correspondence with him, betraying his lingering anxiety about the questions Williams raised, about the questions raised by the entire controversy, and about Williams's representation of New England to an English audience, especially amid the upheavals of the 1640s and 1650s. Throughout this correspondence, Cotton insisted on scriptural clarity—at least in regard to fundamentals.[81] And he insisted, too, on the continued applicability of biblical law, distinguishing between the ceremonial and judicial laws.[82] Thus he reaffirmed the basic principles of the biblical commonwealth.

Even as Cotton continued to debate specific questions with Williams, he turned his attention to the theoretical problem of Williams's dissent as dissent. With his exile, Williams had been effectively removed from the physically constituted interpretive community of Massachusetts Bay, and was thus no longer a dissenting voice *within* the community. As their correspondence continued, with Williams maintaining his dissent and stirring up trouble for the colony on both sides of the Atlantic, this seems to have struck Cotton as insufficient. For Cotton eventually read Williams out of the interpretive community of regenerate readers as well, insinuating in *The Bloudy Tenent, Washed and made white in the blood of the Lambe* that Williams was among "those whose hearts are not stayed and steered by the Spirit of Truth" (38–39). Whether his misreadings were simply misguided or actually wicked, they were clearly *not* Spirit-assisted readings. So perhaps there was hope that his exile would allow the scriptural community to flourish, without unsettling further its theoretical foundations.

Alas, it did not. Disruption continued in Salem in the wake of Williams's departure, and things quickly went from bad to worse for the colony as a whole, as the Antinomian Controversy unfolded, touching not only unruly laypeople but the illustrious Cotton as well.[83] Throughout, participants affirmed their allegiance to biblical authority. And with each affirmation, each unresolved point of debate, it became increasingly clear that New England would not be the New Israel for which its founders had hoped. Instead, it would be the site of conflict and contention that Roger Williams had anticipated.

## CHAPTER 7

# "ALL THE STRIFE AMONGST US":
# CONSENSUS, READING, AND REVELATION
# IN THE ANTINOMIAN CONTROVERSY

With Roger Williams exiled, leaders of Massachusetts Bay hoped, in Thomas Weld's words, that they "had prettily well outgrowne [their] wildernes troubles in [their] first plantings in New England," and set about returning to the task of building a scriptural commonwealth.[1] To this end, John Cotton was asked "by the general court, with some other ministers, to assist some of the magistrates in compiling a body of fundamental laws."[2] In October 1636, Cotton presented the General Court with "a model of Moses his judicials, compiled in an exact method, which were taken into further consideration till the next general court" (*Journal*, 195). But further controversy was already brewing, and in the next few years much of the community's energy would be devoted to the problem of the Antinomian dissent.

These events—known to many of their interpreters as the Antinomian Controversy—have generated huge amounts of interpretive energy, from their own day to ours. Scholars have viewed the events through a variety of lenses, including those of economics, politics, gender, and theology.[3] But the events of the controversy turned as well on Puritan theories of preaching, reading, revelation, and interpretive consensus. The controversy was fed by tensions and complexities encoded in these theories, and in turn raised troubling questions about their implications. As ministers and the laity read the Bible, they struggled not only with specific interpretive questions about the process of salvation, but also with questions about the reading process itself. What kinds of reading were acceptable, and what kinds were not? Who would properly interpret the biblical text, and in what circumstances would such interpretation take place? How would other readers relate to the texts' interpreters, both ministers and lay leaders such as Anne Hutchinson? How could the community deal with disputed readings, and what did the persistence of such disputes suggest about the nature of interpretive authority?

Moreover, many of the basic issues of interpretation over which New Englanders struggled were questions not only about what biblical texts instructed on doctrinal issues, but also about how other kinds of evidence would be read. In debating the relationship between justification (the imputation of Christ's righteousness to the elect individual) and sanctification (the process by which that individual, enabled by grace, becomes increasingly obedient to God's will), participants were considering the degree to which a would-be saint's behavior could serve as evidence of his or her spiritual state, in effect considering whether behavior could be added to the range of other testimonies on which a Christian might draw. And in their debates about the indwelling of the Spirit and the nature of revelation, participants spent a good deal of time sorting out the relationship among God's word as revealed in the Bible, God's word as preached, the legitimate assistance of the Holy Spirit to a Christian reader of the Bible, and the possibility of genuine revelations separate from the biblical text.

As they wrestled with these questions, New England's ministers discovered that they disagreed among themselves on many important issues, unsettling their ideas of what their community would become and challenging their expectation of interpretive consensus. Once again, they encountered tremendous difficulties as they attempted to resolve their disagreements, and the involvement of the laity in their debates once more exacerbated their struggles over the nature of human interpretive authority.

## THEOLOGICAL RUMBLINGS

Despite hopes that the colony's troubles had ended with Williams's exile, in the spring of 1636 the ministers of the Bay colony were troubled by strange opinions circulating in the churches, especially in the Boston church, where John Cotton was the teacher. In his account of these opinions, John Winthrop suggested that the Antinomian heresy centered on "two dangerous errors . . . [from which] grew many branches": "That the person of the Holy Ghost dwells in a justified person" and "That no sanctification can help to evidence to us our justification" (*Journal*, 193). Though the issues debated and discussed were many, Winthrop's analysis offers a useful organizing principle. The first "error" that he describes involves the nature of the spiritual change produced by conversion. Puritan salvation centered around justification, the imputation of Christ's righteousness to the convert. Along with this change in status, Puritans believed that the convert would experience sanctification, a transformation of the convert's heart, will, and ability to obey God. But some Bostonians were articulating a more radical position—that conversion involved not merely a change in the convert, but the actual indwelling and continued presence of the Holy Spirit: "the person of the Holy Ghost dwells in a justified person," potentially transforming his or her every act (193).

Belief in the presence of the Holy Spirit in the soul of the justified person had consequences for approaches to the authority of biblical law. By definition, the basic heresy of antinomianism is the rejection of that law, on the grounds that the authority of the indwelling Spirit supersedes any previous law. Orthodox authorities feared that belief in the indwelling Spirit would undermine morality, as a person might deny responsibility for his or her actions by insisting that they were the actions of the Holy Spirit within.

The presence of the Holy Spirit would theoretically affect the saint's relationship not only to the law, but to scripture as a whole. The lively voice of the Spirit might prove more compelling to the saint than God's voice in the biblical text, and reports that some of the Antinomians had claimed to have "immediate revelations" from God, unmediated by biblical text or by ministerial preaching, troubled Massachusetts Bay elders and magistrates alike. Massachusetts leaders interpreted these local radicals through the lens of European antinomians (both English and continental), insisting that the relatively tame beliefs of Boston's so-called antinomians would, in Stephen Foster's words, "presumably lead in time to sanctified libertinism, generally in the form of some sort of community of both women and property, and just possibly also to Münster-like slaughter of the uninitiated in the name of extra-scriptural revelation."[4]

The second error Winthrop identified—"That no sanctification can help to evidence to us our justification"—involved the issue of assurance, which David D. Hall has called "the central issue in the controversy."[5] Given the predestinarian system in which New England Puritans believed they operated, how were they to assess their spiritual status? How could a Christian know whether he was among the elect? Certainly, as the sermons of their ministers revealed, most Puritans believed that specific kinds of experiences would ordinarily accompany the process of conversion. But in many cases, as in that of Thomas Shepard, anxiety and doubt remained. Most of the ministers, including Shepard and John Wilson, pastor of the Boston church, suggested that a Christian who doubted his or her status might look for evidence in his or her behavior. A would-be saint might be reassured if he or she seemed to be undergoing the process of sanctification: freed from corruption and morally renewed by God, the saint or convert was enabled by his or her faith to obey God's will more completely. Texts of the period—both journals and conversion narratives—reveal individuals focusing intense attention on their spiritual lives, assessing the implications even of small spiritual triumphs, such as taking notes at sermons more effectively.[6]

Hall suggests that questions about the legitimacy of this approach may have been particularly compelling in the mid-1630s. The early 1630s had been a time of intense religious revival; in September of 1633 John Cotton was admitted to the Boston church, and in the next six months, sixty-three more members joined the church. By 1636, however, the revival was over, and the attendant religious exuberance had waned; in fact, Hall describes a "spiritual depression of 1635–1636."[7] Spiritual anxieties were high, and for some of the anxious, sanctification could provide comforting reassurance of their spiritual state. But the later 1630s also brought boatloads "of refugees from what was increasingly the Church of England as by William Laud established," raising "the sectarian temperature of the Bay Colony."[8] These new arrivals brought with them "expectations created in the heat of resistance to the Laudian regime," and "had little patience with either moderation or hesitancy."[9] And, as Foster explains, "on the whole their new militancy had a sympathetic reception from the expatriates who had left England at an earlier date" (657). Thus, those in the Boston church who objected to Shepard's and Wilson's positions were often ill inclined to moderate their objections. Instead, they asserted firmly "That no sanctification can help to evidence to us our justification," as taking sanctification as evidence of justification would imply a reliance on human rather than divine activity (*Journal*, 193). In fact, the more extreme among the dissenters suggested, using sanctification as evidence of justification would constitute "going aside to a covenant of works," a grievous and dangerous sin.[10] And, if rumors were accurate, they accused ministers who invited their congregants to take such comfort of preaching a covenant of works.

## DISPUTES AMONG THE CLERGY

Prominent among the dissenters were Anne Hutchinson (1591–1643), Henry Vane (1613–62), and John Wheelwright (1592?–1679). Hutchinson, who had come to Boston in 1634 with her husband William Hutchinson, was holding meetings in her house at which sermons were discussed. Her popularity soon grew, with as many as sixty people attending some meetings. Moreover, as

Richard S. Dunn and Laetitia Yeandle note, the meetings held at the Hutchinson house "rivaled in influence the clerical conferences of ministers and elders."[11] Wheelwright, Hutchinson's brother-in-law, was a minister who had been silenced in England and had joined his relatives in Massachusetts. Vane, most prominent and powerful of the three, was the colony's governor, in Winthrop's report "a wise and godly gentleman" who nevertheless "went so far beyond the rest [of the dissenters], as to maintain a personal union with the Holy Ghost" (*Journal*, 200).

Concerned community leaders, both ministers and magistrates, saw Hutchinson, Vane, and Wheelwright as the most important dissenters. Winthrop, for example, suggested that Hutchinson had "brought over with her" the "dangerous errors" that had become so popular (*Journal*, 193). In October of 1636, "the other ministers in the bay" met privately with Hutchinson and Wheelwright in Cotton's presence, "to the end that they might know the certainty of these things; that if need were, they might write to the church of Boston about them, to prevent (if it were possible) the dangers, which seemed hereby to hang over that and the rest of the churches" (194). Though they saw Hutchinson and Wheelwright as the center of the problem, the ministers suspected as well that John Cotton was somehow responsible for the opinions that were flourishing in his congregation, that whether intentionally or unintentionally, he was encouraging his congregants to adopt radical positions, and perhaps even held them himself. And so several of the Bay Colony's ministers began a series of exchanges with Cotton, in which they attempted to clarify points of theological difference and to reassure themselves of their agreement with one another.[12] Both Thomas Shepard and Peter Bulkeley wrote to Cotton, exploring issues on which Cotton's preaching seemed to suggest disagreement.

That such disagreements be resolved was urgent not only because of the local disturbances in the Bay, but because of the theoretical problems posed by disagreements themselves. Leaders of the Bay Colony expected consensus; indeed, expectations of interpretive consensus enabled by the Holy Spirit were high enough that church polity rested on assumptions of unanimity.[13] Reformed exegetical theory had anticipated those who would "impiously and foully" pervert scripture, and Roger Williams had proved to be an intractable troublemaker with radical ideas, among them his insistence that his opponents' vision of consensus was a dangerous delusion.[14] But with his banishment, he had been excluded from the community of the saints, the community of those reading together in the Spirit. Thus it was all the more disconcerting to find a controversy swirling around John Cotton. Certainly, thought the clergy of Massachusetts Bay, Cotton was one of the saints, neither impious nor foul, and not, they had thought, particularly radical.[15] Moreover, he was noted for his great skill in biblical studies. John Norton later praised Cotton's remarkable "dexterity" with scripture, and Cotton Mather lamented "how vast a treasure of *learning* was laid in the grave" on Cotton's death, praising him as "a most *universal* scholar, and a *living system* of the liberal arts, and a *walking library.*"[16] In his theology, Mather continued, "*there* 'twas that he had his greatest *extraordinariness*, and most of all, his *Textual Divinity*" (*Magnalia*, 1:274).

In this dispute, then, the disputants believed each other to be not vile heretics, but rather members of a community of saints who were interpreting in the Spirit. Consequently, they consistently attempted to minimize their differences. Shepard, for example, professed that his purpose was "to cut off all seeming differences and jarrs," acknowledging only the *appearance* of disagreement, and not its reality.[17] In a process related to the strategies that these Reformed exegetes used to resolve apparent contradictions in the biblical text, participants in this discussion hoped that they would discover that their seeming differences were illusory.[18] In a letter to Cotton, for example, Shepard asserted confidently, "I do beleeve we shall not differ when things are hereby ripened for we are desirous and glad to learne" (29). And in his reply, Cotton shared Shepard's emphasis on consensus: "As for differences, and jarres, it is my unfeigned desire to avoide them with all men especially with Brethren: but I doe not know, I assure you, any difference, much lesse jarres, betweene me, and any of my Brethren, in our Publique ministry, or other wise, to any offence."[19] Throughout the controversy, many participants made similar declarations.

But if all were interpreting in the Spirit, they believed, they ought to agree; they could not accept the possibility that competing doctrines might be derived by legitimate and Spirit-guided exegesis. Each side therefore challenged the exegesis of the other, confident that they could isolate and determine the single proper meaning of the disputed texts. In one exchange, the elders wrote to Cotton:

> As for your argument from the publican, We cannot reach whereto it tendeth. For, the Scripture saith not, [1.] That the Publican saw himself justified at all. Nor [2] That our Saviour gave him rather the sight of his sinful corruption than of his Sanctification. Nor [3] Can any more be concluded thence in our apprehensions, but this, viz. That a man without sight of his Sanctification may be justified.[20]

The other elders disputed both Cotton's understanding of the biblical text and the consequences he drew from it. In response, Cotton objected that they were misreading both the text and his argument, and remained unpersuaded of their position.[21] He accused them of misreading elsewhere as well. In considering the elders' thirteenth question, for example, he noted: "The places you quote out of John do neither speak of our first knowledg of Christ and our fellowship with him, nor of our knowledg by faith of our Interest in him"; in other words, Cotton accused, the other elders were applying the tools of exegesis improperly.[22]

It is significant not only that Cotton and the elders disagreed doctrinally, but also that appeals to scripture once again failed to resolve their conflicts. They had not anticipated such conflicts as they planned their community, nor did they have room in their theories of exegesis to account for legitimate differences of opinion about scripture-derived doctrine. And Cotton and the elders seemed unable to reach consensus, even after numerous lengthy exchanges. Apparently, despite declarations of consensus and agreement, there *were* significant differences of opinion at stake.

As the controversy wore on, mutual professions of love, affection, and respect grew more than a little strained.[23] Having responded to letters from both Bulkeley and Shepard, Cotton was presented in December with a list of points "wherein [the other elders] suspected Mr. Cotton did differ from him, and pressed him to a direct answer, affirmative or negative, to every one; which he had promised, and taken time for" (*Journal*, 203). By this point, Cotton's patience shows signs of having been seriously taxed. In his reply to these questions, Cotton's professions of love and mutual affection do not quite mask his hostility and anger. For example, the opening of Cotton's reply to the elders' sixteen questions, while overtly polite, has nasty undertones:

> For an Answer unto your (Interrogatories, shall I call them?) or Questions. Though I might without Sinne referre you (as our Saviour did the *High-Priest* when his Doctrine was questioned) to what *I* have ever taught and spoken openly to the world, as having in secret said nothing else, *Iohn* 18.20.21. Yet because you are much more deare and precious to me, than the *High-Priest* was to him; and because *Love* thinkes no Evill, and *Truth* feareth not the *Light:* I have (by the helpe of Christ) sent you (according to your Desire) a plaine and short Answer to each particular.[24]

That Cotton felt persecuted is evident in his identification with Christ, and in his identification of the other elders with the High Priest. Even his protestations of love and affection are muted here; certainly, it is not saying much to assert that the elders are "much more deare and precious" to him than the High Priest was to Christ. Moreover, his comment that "*Love* thinkes no Evill, and *Truth* feareth not the *Light*" seems to imply precisely the opposite: that Cotton presumed neither his interlocutors' good intentions, nor their allegiance to truth and light. In the following round of exchange, Cotton expressed his hope that "it [would] be no offence to" the elders if he "borrow[ed] light from Calvin," subtly if a bit snidely impugning their Calvinist credentials.[25] Thus the shared hope for ministerial consensus was being dramatically challenged.

## CRISIS AMONG THE LAITY

The elusiveness of consensus was rendered all the more alarming by the state of the laity. This theological debate was not simply a disagreement among ministers, carried on behind closed doors. Not only had lay opinions aroused ministerial concerns in the first place; lay people also involved themselves in the disputes, taking sides in the ministers' conflicts. Manuscripts of exchanges among the ministers circulated quite widely, even before their eventual publication in print.[26] Members of the laity, both dissenting and orthodox, were attempting to sort through issues even as their ministers debated one another, and dangerously radical opinions were circulating.[27] The controversy continued to grow increasingly heated and increasingly public, and along with doctrinal concerns, individual ministers and individual occasions of preaching often occupied center stage. In October of 1636, members of the Boston church attempted to have John Wheelwright appointed as a second teacher, thus shifting the balance of power in the church away from Wilson and toward Cotton and his allies. In this instance, the community managed to proceed without full-fledged explosion, at least in the short term. Winthrop objected to Wheelwright's appointment on doctrinal grounds (as well as out of loyalty to his friend John Wilson), and Cotton conceded that "though he thought reverendly of [Wheelwright's] godliness and abilities, so as he could be content to live under such a ministry; yet, seeing he was apt to raise doubtful disputations, he could not consent to choose him to that place" (*Journal*, 195–96).[28] The church capitulated as well, and Wheelwright was called to a new church being gathered at Mount Wollaston instead.

But discussion of the matter did not end there. "Divers of the brethren took offence" at Winthrop's speech against Wheelwright, because he had spoken publicly rather than privately of Wheelwright, because he had spoken with apparent bitterness, and because he had allegedly misrepresented Wheelwright's positions (*Journal*, 196). Following further discussion in the congregation, the matter was dropped a bit uneasily. Winthrop suggested that because disputed terms such as "person of the Holy Ghost" and "real union" were human rather than scriptural, they should be "forborn," and cut off discussion by asserting "that he did not intend to dispute the matter" (*Journal*,

197). His account betrays some anxiety about the reception of this approach by the congregation, for he notes that "How this was taken in the congregation, did not appear, for no man spake to it" (*Journal*, 197). The holy community seemed uneasy, at the very least.

In the wake of this incident, Winthrop wrote to Cotton, and also sent two "papers" to Thomas Shepard, in which he attempted to clarify the theological issues occupying the community and calm the contention that divided it.[29] In the first, which Shepard called Winthrop's "Declaration," Winthrop asserted that "a man is justifyed by fayth, and not before he beleeueth" (326). In the second, which Shepard called a "Pacification," Winthrop attempted "to quiet and still those tumults, which [his] wisdom may forsee [would] arise in the Churches concerning Justification by fayth, as its conceiued by some, and contradicted by others" (326–27). But Shepard's reaction reveals the difficulty of lay–clerical relations in this period. Winthrop, as an educated layman, clearly felt qualified to take these issues on; after all, his ministers had quite consistently encouraged him to read the Bible for himself. Yet in Shepard's view, even Winthrop, the educated and empowered reader, lacked both sufficient sophistication (theoretically unnecessary in this emphatically Protestant reading system) to sort through these doctrines and the "arte" of expressing them appropriately, despite his obvious skills as a writer. While Shepard praised Winthrop's motivation, he advised him delicately to consider "whether it will be most safe for yow to enter into the conflict with your pen (though the Lord hath made yow very able and fit for it) or if yow doe, whether then so largely" (327). He expressed concern that "a subtill adversary" might "take aduantages at woords" (327).

Shepard's concern was rooted in his doubts about the orthodoxy of Winthrop's theological statements. Very gently, after emphasizing that he wrote "not with a spirit to contradict, or to dispute it with yow," Shepard nevertheless expressed "an humble desire that yow would be pleased to haue a few second thoughts of some passages, of which some seeme to me to be doubtfull and some others to swerue from the truth" (327). In its discussion of the justice of justification, for example, Shepard cautioned that Winthrop's text "[bore] a colour of Arminianism" (328). Later, Shepard suggested that Winthrop's fourth conclusion about faith "seeme[d] to crosse the whole current of scripture, which without manifest wresting cannot be gainsaid" (332). Overall, though he saw in the "Pacification" "the sweetness of [Winthrop's] spirit inclining and deuising for peace and truth if possible," Shepard's letter suggested that even the best of allies among the laity had difficulty negotiating between orthodoxy and dangerous "wresting" of the Scriptures, that even they might verge on dreaded heresies (329).[30]

Meanwhile, individual churches found themselves suspected by members of other churches. Late in 1636, members of the Boston church met with members of the Newtown (later Cambridge) church to clarify their differences, a conference that Dunn and Yeandle characterize as "unsuccessful" and that prompted the Boston church members to compose a document denying that they held most of the positions with which they had been charged.[31] Moreover, they contended that even in the wake of the conference, they had been misrepresented in a fashion that was neither "brotherly" nor "Christianly."[32]

As tensions escalated, public debates over ministerial leadership grew increasingly contentious. Winthrop reports that Boston church members attended and disrupted sermons of other ministers, and "did make much disturbance by public questions, and objections to their doctrines, which did any way disagree from their opinions" (*Journal*, 209). Bostonians also voiced criticisms of the ministry. Lumber merchant Stephen Greensmith, for example, was reportedly "affirming that all the [ministers] (except Mr Cotton, Mr Wheelright, & hee thought Mr Hooker) did teach a covenant of works."[33]

Nor were lay people the only ones publicly critical of the ministers; quite frequently, ministers found that their colleagues held them up to criticism as well. At a December session of the General Court, John Wilson made "a very sad speech of the condition of our churches, and the inevitable danger of separation, if these differences and alienations among brethren were not speedily remedied" (*Journal*, 203). Embattled in his own church, Wilson "laid the blame upon these new opinions risen up amongst us," a proposition with which "all the magistrates, except the governour [Vane] and two others [William Coddington and Richard Dummer], did confirm, and all the ministers but two [Cotton and Wheelright]" (*Journal*, 204, 204 n. 51).

On this occasion, discussion turned to the sermon Cotton had preached that morning, and subtle questions were raised about Cotton's position on sanctification. Cotton, emphasizing his common ground with his colleagues, had said that "evident sanctification was an evidence of justification," that "true desires of sanctification was found to be sanctification," and even that "if a man were laid so flat upon the ground, as he could see no desires, etc., but only, as a bruised reed, did wait at the feet of Christ, yet here was a matter of comfort for this, as found to be true" (*Journal*, 204). Such statements seemed cautiously conciliatory; Cotton seemed to be acknowledging that a Christian lacking confidence in his justification could take comfort in "evident sanctification," and even in his desire for it. When questioned, however, Cotton again qualified his claims, denying that "any of these, or evident sanctification, could be evidence to a man without a concurrent sight of his justification" (*Journal*, 204). Sanctification could only serve as evidence of justification if justification could also be established independently. Otherwise, one could not distinguish between sanctified obedience and ordinary good works.

At this point in the controversy, however, it was Wilson who was on the defensive. His speech "was taken very ill by Mr. Cotton and others of the same church," who "went to admonish" him (*Journal*, 204). Wilson defended himself, claiming that he had been called to the court and "exhorted to deliver [his mind] freely and faithfully, both for discovering the danger and the means to help" (*Journal*, 204). Moreover, he claimed, he had not named names; rather he had spoken "only in general, and such as were under a common fame," and "professed he did not mean Boston church, nor the members thereof, more than others" (*Journal*, 204). Unconvinced by this explanation, the Boston church called him to answer publicly for his behavior, in an occasion that Winthrop describes as marred by "much bitterness and reproaches" (*Journal*, 204). Church members and Cotton both condemned Wilson's actions, with the laity "eager to proceed to present censure" (*Journal*, 205). Cotton, however, "with much wisdom and moderation . . . staid them from it," citing as a reason the lack of unanimity, and instead offering Wilson a "grave exhortation" (*Journal*, 205). Wilson's sermon the following day was better received, even by Vane, though the incident did not fully blow over; rather Winthrop wrote to Cotton defending Wilson. Cotton responded, reaffirming his sense of Wilson's offense. Winthrop answered these charges, but sent his letter to the Boston church's two ruling elders, Thomas Oliver and Thomas Leverett, rather than to Cotton himself. Tensions between Wilson and Cotton remained high.

Wilson and Cotton were not the only ministers whose preaching proved controversial, of course. In January, a general fast was called in response to misfortunes and afflictions both local and international, ranging from the states of churches in Germany and England to threats from the Indians and "the dissensions in our churches" (*Journal*, 207–8). As a gesture of conciliation, John Wheelwright was invited to preach. His sermon proved incendiary rather than conciliatory, full of images of battle and combat. Though he urged his listeners to "keepe the unity of the spiritt in the bond of peace," he nevertheless polarized the debate further.[34] Sharing Roger Williams's language of disruption, Wheelwright suggested that "It is impossible to hold out the truth of God with externall peace and quietnes" (166). He identified with the persecuted Jesus, and urged his supporters to "prepare for a spirituall combate": "and therefore wheresoever we live," he urged, "if we would have the Lord Jesus Christ to be aboundantly present with us, we must all of us prepare for battell and come out against the enimyes of the Lord, and if we do not strive, those under a covenant of works will prevaile" (153, 158). Moreover, his words sometimes seemed to suggest physical battles as well as spiritual ones, as when he urged his supporters to be "willing to lay downe [their] lives, and . . . overcome by so doing," citing as his model Samson, who "slew more at his death, then in his life, and so we may prevaile more by our deathes, then by our lives" (166). Such calls alarmed other leaders of the community, who took Wheelwright to be identifying those who "maintain sanctification as an evidence of justification, etc" with "antichrists," and feared that when he "stirred up the people against them with much bitterness and vehemency," they might follow the lead of the biblical exemplars he had cited and draw real, rather than merely spiritual, weapons.[35] Using an image in which the biblical text itself becomes a weapon, Winthop feared that the opposition party might turn to physical violence, "like him who when he could not by any sentence in the Bible confute an Heretick, could make use of the whole booke to break his head" (*Short Story*, 293–94). Though Winthrop's image cast his own party uncomfortably in the role of the unconfuted "Heretick," it also suggested that Wheelwright's followers lacked biblical authority for their views. Unresolved contention over the meaning of the biblical text left both sides in a precarious state; under those circumstances, Winthrop warned, contention might be provoked by sermons such as Wheelwright's into full-fledged rebellion.[36]

Moreover, as the laity involved themselves in ministerial disputes, the colony's leaders grew concerned about New England's image abroad. Winthrop reports that "The differences in the said points of religion increased more and more, and the ministers of both sides (there being only Mr. Cotton of one party) did publicly declare their judgments in some of them, as all men's mouths were full of them" (*Journal*, 208). Such "full" mouths seemed dangerous, especially as a ship prepared to set sail for England in early February.[37] Both Cotton and Wilson attempted to minimize the conflict, and to cast it in a positive light. Cotton suggested to the ship's passengers that they explain events to their English counterparts by saying "that all the strife amongst us was about magnifying the grace of God; one party seeking to advance the grace of God within us, and the other seeking to advance the grace of God towards us, (meaning by the one justification, and by the other sanctification;) and so bade them tell them that, if there were any among them that would strive for grace, they should come hither" (*Journal*, 208).[38]

Wilson, too, encouraged the travelers to minimize the conflict. Speaking after Cotton, he "declared, that he knew none of the elders or brethren in the churches, but did labor to advance the free grace of God in justification, so far as the word of God required; and spake also about the doctrine of sanctification, and the use and necessity, etc., of it" (*Journal*, 208). Wilson's attempt at conciliation was skillful enough that "no man could tell (except some few, who knew the bottom of the matter) where any difference was" (208). But those who could tell, including "those of Mr. Cotton's party," were offended, rather than reconciled (*Journal*, 208). Even as participants attempted to minimize the divisions, then, they only provoked further dissent; in Winthrop's words, "Thus every occasion increased the contention, and caused great alienation of minds" (208).

## THE COURT TAKES ACTION

At its March 1637 meeting, the General Court turned its attention to the unhappy state of affairs in the colony. Though the magistrates themselves were divided in their opinions of these matters, they shared a sense that a communal crisis was at hand, and thus managed to take several steps they hoped would restore the peace of the colony. First, they vindicated Wilson for his speech at the previous court session, though without bringing charges against his critics (*Journal*, 209). They also clarified the relationship between the court and the church, establishing with the agreement of the ministers that "no member of the court" would be questioned by the church for speeches made to the court, without the court's consent (209). Moreover, they established that the General Court might proceed against "heresies or errors of any church members as are manifest and dangerous to the state" without awaiting the church's action (209–10).

This cleared the way for the court to proceed against Wheelwright, who was convicted of sedition and contempt on the basis of his sermon. A group led by Vane offered a "protestation," which the court rejected "because it wholly justified Mr. Wheelwright, and condemned the proceedings of the court," and the Boston church also offered a petition on Wheelwright's behalf (211).[39] Meanwhile, the magistrates entertained the possibility of silencing Wheelwright, as they had tried to do with Williams. When the ministers were consulted, however, they responded that "they were not clear in that point," perhaps because it seemed uncomfortably close to the inquisitorial ecclesiastical courts that they had feared in England (211). Instead, they suggested that Wheelwright be "commended to the church of Boston to take care of him, etc. . . . and enjoined to appear at the next court" for sentencing (211).[40]

The court took other measures as well. It disciplined Stephen Greensmith for his criticism of the ministers, fining him and requiring him "to acknowledge his fault in every church" (*Journal*, 210).[41] It concluded "that Mr Wheelright was guilty of contempt & sedition."[42] The magistrates agreed to hold the May Court of Elections at Newtown (now Cambridge), though Vane refused to put the matter to a vote.[43] Finally, faced with the incendiary state of the community and acknowledging that preaching itself had become disruptive, the ministers took the drastic step of "put[ting] off all lectures for three weeks, that they might bring things to some issue" (*Journal*, 206).

As spring warmed into summer, the political aspects of the controversy heated up as well. The Boston church—members and ministers—absented themselves from the ordination of the elders of the Concord church, and were perceived by their opponents as boycotting the event to show disapproval of those ordained.[44] The May Court of Elections was politically tumultuous, with fierce debate about the order of events (specifically, whether a petition on Wheelwright's behalf should be considered before or after the elections, a significant issue given Vane's strong support for Wheelwright). Those present voted to hold the election first, and ousted Vane, as well as magistrates William Coddington and Richard Dummer, Bostonians prominent in the Antinomian party (*Journal*, 214–15).[45]

The election of John Winthrop as governor, Thomas Dudley as deputy governor, and John Endecott to the standing council marked a move toward the consolidation of orthodoxy. The ministers, alarmed at the threat of "tumult," also moved carefully toward reconciliation. While ministers and laymen were circulating "divers writings"—treatises, tractates, and remonstrances— among the ministers there were signs of rapprochement.[46] A group of ministers had written a reply to Wheelwright's sermon, and Cotton responded to their reply, representing "the differences in a very narrow scantling" (*Journal*, 216). On the day of the May elections, Shepard preached a sermon minimizing differences among the parties:

> Mr. Shepherd, preaching at the day of the election, brought them yet nearer, so as, except men of good understanding, and such as knew the bottom of the tenents of those of the other party, few could see where the difference was; and indeed it seemed so small, as (if men's affections had not been formerly alienated, when the differences were formerly stated as fundamental) they might easily have come to reconciliation. (*Journal*, 216)

Though they still differed on some important questions regarding assurance, the ministers had reached at least a semblance of consensus about the fundamental relationship between justification and sanctification.[47]

The court took other measures to defuse the situation as well. Notably, at the May Court of Elections, the magistrates attempted to stem the continuing influx of militant English refugees, requiring that all new immigrants to the colony and visitors staying more than three weeks be approved by a member of the council or by two other magistrates.[48] Despite such efforts, tensions mounted over the course of the summer. There was petty squabbling around the transfer of power from Vane to Winthrop, with those who had served as sergeants-at-arms to Vane refusing to accompany Winthrop (*Journal*, 219– 20). Several Bostonians refused to join an expedition against the Pequots, in part because Wilson was serving as one of the party's chaplains.[49] Pro-

tests were lodged against the court's decision to hold elections before considering the petition in support of Wheelwright, as well as against the court
order barring unapproved immigrants or long-term guests.[50] In addition to
the general protests against these measures, individual cases aroused ran-
cor. Winthrop reports, for example, that Hutchinson's brother-in-law and
other friends of Wheelwright arrived from England, whom "the governour
thought not fit to allow, as others, to sit down among us, without some trial
of them" (226). Winthrop's effort to act moderately—"to save others from
the danger of the law in receiving of them, he allowed them for four months"—
received a disappointing reception: "This was taken very ill by those of the
other party, and many hot speeches given forth about it, and about their removal, etc." (226). Protestations and "hot speeches" increasingly seemed to
be the order of the day.

## Ministerial Response

Faced with these events, the ministers prepared for an August synod to figure
out how to address the controversy. In advance of the synod, they assessed the
state of the laity—and of each other—and prepared to present a more united
front. First, they tried to clarify what exactly they were opposing. As Cotton
explained, "The thing attended to, for preparation to the synod, was the gathering up of all the corrupt and offensive opinions that were scattered up and
down the country, and to commend them to public disquisition in the synod:
that howsoever, the authors of them were loath to own them publicly, yet at
least, they might see them publicly tried, confuted, and condemned."[51]

In addition to assessing the state of their congregants, the ministers addressed the divisions among themselves. They did so in private, attempting
to resolve their differences away from the contentiousness of their congregations, and they attended to personal tensions as well as theological ones. "At
their private meetings," Winthrop reports, "some reconciliation was made
between Mr. Cotton and Mr. Wheelwright and Mr. Wilson," with Wilson
"professing, that, by his speech in the court, he did not intend the doctrine of
Mr. Cotton or Mr. Wheelwright delivered in the public congregation, but
some opinions, (naming three or four,) which were privately carried in Boston
and other parts of the country" (Journal, 230). Cotton seems to have accepted
this apology of sorts, for Winthrop noted both a "sudden change" in Cotton's
reception of Wilson's claims, and the unanimity of the elders' agreement that
the rest of Wilson's speech was "inoffensive" (230).

Next the ministers turned to their doctrinal differences. Here again Cotton was the focus of attention, as the elders attempted "to gather out of [his]

sermons to the people, and [his] conferences (in word and writing) with the elders, all such opinions of [his] as were conceived by some, to be erroneous" (*Way Cleared*, 226). "Having gathered them together," Cotton explains, the other elders set out "to inquire in a brotherly conference with me, how far I would own them, or how I did understand them, that so the true state of the questions in difference might appear" (226). Cotton's description suggests optimism about the potential for resolution; when "the true state of the questions in difference" was understood, participants hoped that differences would be minimal. Moreover, Cotton's account emphasizes the connection between privacy and brotherliness, and the importance of calming personal tensions: "and withal, if there were any aguish distemper, or disaffection grown in any of our spirits amongst ourselves, it might be healed in a private brotherly way, and mutual satisfaction given and taken on all hands" (*Way Cleared*, 226).[52] Though this conference could not resolve all disagreement, the ministers made great progress, managing to reduce their differences to five points.

Having gathered their information and contained their own disagreement, the ministers attempted to calm the strife among their congregants and prepare them for the synod. They instituted a "solemn fast kept in all the churches" as a "day of humiliation" (*Way Cleared*, 225; *Journal*, 230). In Boston, Cotton announced to the congregation that Wilson had not meant to criticize either Cotton's doctrine or Wheelwright's, and John Davenport preached a sermon calling for unity. Preaching on 1 Corinthians 1:10, "Now I beseech you, brethren, by the name of our Lord Jesus Christ, that ye all speak the same thing, and *that* there be no divisions among you; but *that* ye be perfectly joined together in the same mind and in the same judgment," Davenport emphasized the need for consensus.[53] Along the way, Winthrop notes, he "fully set forth the nature and danger of divisions, and the disorders which were among us, etc.," and "clearly discovered his judgment against the new opinions and bitter practices which were sprung up here" (230).

On August 30, 1637, the synod began. First, teaching elders of Massachusetts Bay and Connecticut churches gathered at Newtown. After an opening prayer by Shepard, the list of errors which the ministers had assembled was read, followed by a list of "unwholesome expressions" and "the scriptures abused."[54] Thomas Hooker and Peter Bulkeley served as moderators for the discussion over the next several days, during which assembled elders agreed to condemn all of the errors, with most agreeing as well to sign a document to that effect (*Journal*, 232). Even differences that remained between the other ministers and Cotton were cleared up after discussion and clarification, though three points of difference remained between Wheelwright and the rest of the clergy (*Journal*, 233).[55] Apparently, ministerial hopes that all differences would be cleared up through open discussion were being fulfilled.

One disturbance, however, marred this occasion of conciliation. Members of the Boston church protested, once again, that their theological positions were being misrepresented, and that the long list of errors generated by the ministers exaggerated their radicalness. Some non-Bostonians agreed, suggesting that such an extensive list of errors presented "a reproach laid upon the country without cause" (*Journal*, 232). Stephen Foster notes that their complaint may have had merit, and that the list of errors may have reflected preconceptions of antinomianism based on British and continental sectarians as much as or more than local radical beliefs.[56] In any case, the Bostonians demanded that the elders name names, or demonstrate through witnesses that these opinions were actually held. The elders responded that they had produced ample evidence, and moreover that "this assembly had not to do with persons, but doctrines only" (*Journal*, 232–33). Some Bostonians persisted in their rejection, and when threatened with civil action for refusing to "forbear speech unseasonably," several left the synod "and came no more" (233).

On the last day of the synod, the assembled elders dealt with questions of policy. They agreed that small meetings of women "to pray and edify one another" were acceptable, but laid groundwork for prosecution of Anne Hutchinson by ruling that "such a set assembly, (as was then the practice at Boston,) where sixty or more did meet every week, and one woman (in a prophetical way, by resolving questions of doctrine, and expounding scripture) took upon her the whole exercise, was agreed to be disorderly, and without rule" (*Journal*, 234). They also discouraged questioning of the ministers after sermons, though they did not expressly forbid the practice. Instead, they called for greater deference to the ministers and greater oversight by the elders, and condemned questions that were overtly combative, rather than instructive (234). They determined that a person who refused to attend church proceedings against him could be censured in absentia, and ruled that a member should not leave a church over differences that were not "fundamental" (234).

Having agreed on these points as well, those assembled congratulated themselves on their successful resolution of their differences and on their unity. "[S]eeing the Lord had been so graciously present in this assembly, that matters had been carried on so peaceably, and concluded so comfortably in all love," Winthrop proposed that such meetings be held annually, "or, at least, the next year, to settle what yet remained to be agreed" (*Journal*, 235). Differences were now things that "remained to be agreed," rather than painful divisions, and Winthrop's proposal was received positively, though it was not formally adopted. Finally, John Davenport preached a closing sermon in which he "laid down the occasions of difference among Christians, etc., and declared the effect and fruit of the assembly, and, with much wisdom and sound argument, persuaded to unity, etc." (*Journal*, 235).[57] Once again, the community had been chastened by the difficulty of resolving their doctrinal disputes, but Winthrop reported "great hope" that unity had been restored—"that the late general assembly would have had some good effect in pacifying the troubles and dissensions about matters of religion," and that they would be able to live up to their early expectations (239).

## WHEELWRIGHT AND HIS SUPPORTERS

While the ministers and elders had reached consensus, however, more than loose ends remained. Wheelwright had been convicted of sedition and contempt but had not yet been banished, in hopes that he would be reconciled with his colleagues. Although much distance between Wheelwright and his colleagues had been closed, he had not joined them fully in their agreement, and he continued to preach (*Short Story*, 248). Problems remained among the laity as well. Though Vane had returned to England, Anne Hutchinson continued to hold meetings in her home, and many members of the Boston church remained heretical at worst and disaffected and angry at best. Indeed, Winthrop lamented, they were "as busy in nourishing contentions . . . as before" (*Journal*, 239). Despite Cotton's public agreement with his clerical brethren, "the leaders in those erroneous wayes would not give in, but stood still to maintain their new light, which they had boasted of, and that the difference was still as wide as before, *viz.* as great as between heaven and hell" (*Short Story*, 248).

Seeing the case as "desperate," but encouraged by the ministers' consensus, the General Court then moved against the dissenters, finding in the Boston church's petition on Wheelwright's behalf "a fair opportunity" for discipline (*Short Story*, 248; *Journal*, 239). Hoping that Wheelwright had been given enough time "to come to the knowledge of his offence," the court summoned him and asked him "how his mind stood, whether he would acknowledge his offence, or abide the sentence of the Court" (*Short Story*, 252). Once again, they hoped to avoid conflict and confrontation. But Wheelwright would have none of it. He insisted "that hee had committed no sedition nor contempt, hee had delivered nothing but the truth of Christ, and for the application of his doctrin it was by others, and not by him, &c." (*Short Story*, 252).

In response, the court, in a move made repeatedly during these controversies, emphasized that they were not prosecuting him for his doctrine. That would, of course, have been uncomfortably close to the religious courts that they had so dreaded in England. In this case, though, their claim was complicated by the fact that their defendant was a minister and his offense a sermon, one which civil authorities found particularly objectionable. In attempting to justify their prosecution, the court drew on the subtleties of sermon form, revealing in the process the extent to which congregations were invested in theories of preaching. Defining "doctrine" in its narrow and technical sense, the magistrates claimed that "they had not censured his doctrine, but left it as it was" (Short Story, 252).[58] Instead, they insisted, they objected to

> his application, by which he laid the Magistrates, and the Ministers, and most of the people of God in these Churches, under a Covenant of works, and thereupon declared them to bee enemies to Christ, and Antichrists, and such enemies as Herod and Pilate, and the Scribes and Pharisees, &c. per-swading the people to look at them, and deale with them as such, and that hee described them so, as all men might know who hee meant, as well as if he had named the parties. (Short Story, 252–53)

Exploiting the requirements of sermon form articulated by William Perkins, the court treated the application portion of Wheelwright's sermon as political behavior, rather than as belief. Rejecting Wheelwright's claim that "the application of his doctrin" was not "by him," they blamed Wheelwright's applications for the colony's unrest, suggesting that events had "declared it to tend to sedition" (Short Story, 253).

But just as the structures of the Puritan sermon were less rigid than the coda to The Arte of Prophecying might suggest, this definition of Wheelwright's offense was uncomfortably subtle. In Winthrop's account of the trial, the distinction between doctrine and applications blurred: "for whereas before hee broached his opinions, there was a peaceable and comely order in all affaires in the Churches, and civill state, &c. now the difference which hee hath raised amongst men, by a false distinction of a Covenant of grace and a Covenant of works; whereby one party is looked at as friends to Christ, and the other as his enemies, &c. All things are turned upside down amongst us" (Short Story, 253). Here, Winthrop located the problem in Wheelwright's doctrine itself—a "false distinction of a Covenant of grace"—and not merely in his applications of this doctrine to his opponents.

In their accusation, the magistrates also suggested that Wheelwright was responsible for the community's divisions. Now that the other ministers had successfully negotiated many of the issues that had divided them, the magistrates identified Wheelwright as the source of all problems. In a move that they had made in the cases of both Williams and Vane, and that they would later make in Hutchinson's case as well, they insisted that before he had promulgated his opinions, "there was a peaceable and comely order in all affaires in the Churches, and civill state, &c." (Short Story, 253).[59] Blaming isolated individuals was far easier than acknowledging the nearly disastrous failure of their interpretive process, and Wheelwright made this easier by refusing to acknowledge his wrongdoing. Indeed, he resisted his opponents' attempts "to convince him and to reduce him into the right way," refusing even to read a defense of court proceedings against him (*Short Story*, 254–55). He insisted instead that he had not caused the colony's problems, or, at least, that such problems had developed "by accident" (*Short Story*, 256). Moreover, echoing Williams, he emphasized that this was to be expected, that such disruptions were "usuall in preaching of the Gospell" and that "it was not his Sermon that was the cause of them, but the Lord Jesus Christ" (256). Such claims hardly disposed the court to leniency. Following further discussion, the court, noting Wheelwright's previous offenses, as well as his "obstinately maintaining and justifying his said errours and offences" and his refusal to depart voluntarily, banished and disenfranchised Wheelwright, citing a verse from Matthew to justify its verdict (*Short Story*, 256).[60]

Having dealt with Wheelwright directly, the court turned its attention to his supporters. They began with Bostonians who had signed the petition on Wheelwright's behalf, including John Coggeshall, William Aspinwall, and William Coddington.[61] Dealing first with Aspinwall, who was later reported to have framed the petition, the court noted that "his hand was to the Petition, he had justified Master *Wheelwright* his Sermon, and had condemned the Court, and therefore what could he say, why the Court should not proceede to sentence?" (*Short Story*, 261, 259). Wheelwright's supporters were prosecuted for these acts, as well as for civil disturbances and contentious behavior. Coggeshall, for example, had not signed the petition, but had written a remonstrance or protestation, and had further made "menacing speeches" (*Short Story*, 257–58). He was charged with "seditious libell," and found a "great part of the Court" inclined to banish him (258–59). He narrowly escaped banishment, however, because the court found his "speech and behaviour" at this session "more modest and submisse, than formerly they had beene," and Coggeshall was instead disenfranchised and admonished that further disturbances of the "publike peace" might lead to further censure and exile (258–59). Each of the Wheelwright supporters whose examination is described in the *Short Story* cited scripture to justify his actions, and each challenged his prosecutors to justify their own in the same way. Other Wheelwright supporters were variously banished, disarmed, and disenfranchised, with the most repentant and submissive generally receiving the lightest punishments.[62]

Apparently, the members of the court were not eager to banish the troublemakers, preferring instead to be reconciled to them. Consequently, complaints about the law requiring approval of immigrants were treated seriously. Members of the court had prepared a reply to reproaches of the court on this subject, but had not published it, in "expectation that the late As

sembly would have had some good effect, in clearing the points in controversie, and reconciling the minds of the adverse party" (*Short Story*, 251). When
it became clear that this would not suffice, "it was thought fit the whole proceedings about the law should bee brought forth, and accordingly the next
day, the Declaration, the Answer, and the Reply were all brought to the Court,
and there openly read" (251). Once again, this attempt to build consensus
seemed successful, for the discussion "gave such satisfaction to those which
were present as no man ought to object, and some that were of the adverse
party, and had taken offence at the Law, did openly acknowledge themselves
fully satisfyed" (251).

Other problems proved less tractable. Most troublesome among Wheelwright's supporters addressed by the court was militia leader Captain John
Underhill (1597?–1672), whose case played into deep anxieties underlying
the controversy. Like his colleagues, Underhill challenged the magistrates to
justify their proceedings scripturally, engaging the court in debate over the
biblical figure of Joab (*Short Story*, 276). But Underhill went further than did
other Hutchinsonians, highlighting both of the errors that Winthrop cited as
fundamental. First, he identified the political action of the petition with immediate revelation. In language that foreshadowed his eventual conversion to
Quakerism, Underhill claimed that the petition was conceived when a group
of Wheelwright supporters who attended Wheelwright's trial for sedition
"were sore grieved at it, and suddenly rushing out of the Court, a strange
motion came into all their mindes, so as they said (in a manner all together)
Come let us petition" (277). Underhill identified this "motion" as a genuine
revelation, and affirmed that "from that time . . . [forward], his conscience
which then led him to it, [would] not suffer him to retract it" (277). Underhill's claim was alarming indeed. He was claiming a revelation totally separate from the biblical text, as well as from ministerial authority. Moreover, it
was a revelation that moved its recipients to seditious and disruptive behavior, and that led them to view such behavior as a matter of faith and conscience. Underhill's military background, and his claims of the "liberty which
all States do allow to *Military* Officers," made this all the more alarming:
what if he had responded to Wheelwright's rhetoric and this "strange motion" by engaging his opponents in an all-out civil war? (277) Little wonder that the court "tooke notice how these ungrounded revelations began to
work, and what dangerous consequences were like to follow them, when so
many persons upon such a sudden motion had not scruple to enterprize such
a seditious action, nor can bee brought by any light of reason or Scripture, to
see their error" (*Short Story*, 277). What better proof of the dangers of immediate revelations did they need?

Because they "pitied him much," the General Court disenfranchised Un-

derhill and removed him from office, but did not banish him (277). Underhill's subsequent behavior seemed to confirm fears of antinomianism's danger on several fronts. First, he was admonished for sexual improprieties, which
he excused by explaining that "the woman was in great trouble of mind, and
sore temptations, and that he resorted to her to comfort her; and that when
the door was found locked upon them, they were in private prayer together"
(*Journal*, 264). The following September, he was questioned for trying to se-
duce a woman on shipboard, where he claimed that "the Spirit set home an
absolute promise of free grace with such assurance and joy, as he never since
doubted of his good estate, neither should he, though he should fall into sin"
(*Journal*, 263). In fact, this woman explained, he had boasted of his adulter-
ous affair with another woman, and had insisted that "she never came to be
driven from her own righteousness," though he "enjoy[ed] her three or four
times a day."[63] Moreover, like others in his party, he had insisted to her that
"he held nothing but what Mr. Cotten held."[64] Underhill, then, embodied all
of the spectres which antinomianism threatened—revelation independent of
scripture and of ministerial authority, civil disorder, armed rebellion, and
sexual license. The court responded by banishing him (*Journal*, 263).[65]

## THE CASE OF ANNE HUTCHINSON

Though Underhill seems in many ways to have been the most alarming of the
Antinomians, it was of course Anne Hutchinson who received the most attention, both in her own day and in ours. Recently, historians such as Michael P.
Winship and David D. Hall have suggested that it is a mistake to follow the
lead of Hutchinson's contemporaries, and give her "the leading role" in the
controversy.[66] Nevertheless, Hutchinson has been a source of fascination to
the controversy's chroniclers. Even Hall, very shortly after his cautionary comment on the relative roles of Hutchinson and John Cotton, suggests that "[t]he
story of what occurred during those months must begin with a woman" (4–
5). Her appeal to modern historians has several explanations: she is appealing
because she was a woman, because interesting and detailed accounts of her
survive, because those documents reveal a lively mind and voice, and because
they show Hutchinson's contemporaries reacting to her in complex and interesting ways.

Their reaction to Hutchinson will be the focus of the remainder of this
chapter. Hutchinson receives heavy attention here not because she was the
most important figure in the Antinomian Controversy, but because her contemporaries often identified her as such, and because their interpretations of
Hutchinson reveal a great deal about their understanding of the crisis. Even

after Cotton, Wheelwright, and Wheelwright's other supporters had been questioned and disciplined, deputy governor Thomas Dudley blamed Hutchinson for the colony's troubles: "About three years ago," he noted, "we were all in peace. Mrs. Hutchinson from the time she came hath made a disturbance, and some that came over with her in the ship did inform me what she was as soon as she landed."[67] Hutchinson, asserted Dudley, "hath been the cause of what is fallen out" (318). Though it seemed that they had already addressed other causes of the controversy, Dudley asserted at this late date that by dealing with Hutchinson, the court would "take away the foundation and the building will fall" (318). Richard Brown, a deputy from Watertown, suggested that Hutchinson's errors were "the foundation of all mischief and of all those bastardly things which have been overthrowing by that great meeting. They have all come out from this cursed fountain" ("Examination," 344). Winthrop advised the court that they should determine how to proceed, "looking at her as the principal cause of all our trouble," and identified her as "the root of all these troubles" ("Examination," 344; *Short Story*, 265). And at Hutchinson's church trial, John Wilson identified Hutchinson as a *"dayngerus Instrument of the Divell* raysed up by Sathan amongst us to rayse up Divissions and Contentions and to take away harts and affections one from another. Wheras befor thear was much Love and Union and sweet agreement amongst us before she came, yet since all Union and Love hath bine broken and thear hath bine Censurings and Judgings and Condemnings one of another."[68]

Of course, such statements of sweeping blame did not make Hutchinson unique in these proceedings; as I have already noted, other individuals were blamed for the community's difficulties in nearly the same words.[69] Such claims suggest eagerness to assign blame to an individual, thus identifying the problem as personal rather than systemic, and it is thus unsurprising that such charges were lodged against several participants in these events. But against Hutchinson, the charges seem to have stuck more securely, and it is worth considering why that might be. Many scholars have seen Hutchinson's sex as the primary factor, and most certainly it was significant. Winthrop included in his opening charges that Hutchinson had "maintained a meeting and an assembly in [her] house that hath been condemned by the general assembly as a thing not tolerable nor comely in the sight of God nor fitting for [her] sex" ("Examination," 312). When he later found himself out-argued, he cut off discussion, saying "We do not mean to discourse with those of your sex" ("Examination," 314). And at Hutchinson's church trial, Hugh Peter linked Hutchinson's gender, her lay status, and her political status in oft-quoted lines: "I would commend this to your Consideration that you have stept out of your place, *you have rather bine a Husband than a Wife and a preacher than a Hearer; and a Magistrate than a Subject.* And soe you have thought to carry all Thinges in Church and Commonwealth, as you would and have not bine humbled for this" ("Report," 282–83). Such comments validate the approaches of scholars who have focused on Hutchinson's sex.[70]

Claims about the importance of class issues in the controversy, and in the singling out of Anne Hutchinson, are also supported by the documents of the controversy.[71] Winthrop's report of the case of Salem's Mary Oliver suggests how important Hutchinson's status was to perceptions of her role. He notes that Oliver was "(for ability of speech, and appearance of zeal and devotion) far before Mrs. Hutchinson, and so the fitter instrument to have done hurt, but that she was poor and had little acquaintance" (*Journal*, 275). Clearly, Hutchinson's contemporaries saw her social prominence as a significant aspect of Hutchinson's disruptive power.

While these factors were certainly important, they do not fully explain the nature of Hutchinson's disruption, nor can they answer all of the questions raised by the documents of her court and church trials. At her court trial, most of the accusations made against Hutchinson were dropped without resolution. Hutchinson out-argued Winthrop when he accused her of participating in the faction that supported Wheelwright; she noted that she had not in fact signed the petition, and rejected his claim that counseling those who had constituted a breach of the Fifth Commandment ("Examination," 313–14).[72] She deftly parried objections to the meetings she held in her home, provoking Thomas Dudley to change the subject in frustration ("Examination," 314–17). Even the charge that Hutchinson had traduced the ministers by accusing them of preaching a covenant of works became mired in debates about what had actually been said. At her church trial, Hutchinson either recanted or denied holding almost all of the errors of which she was accused. These factors have led some interpreters to conclude that she was made the scapegoat in this controversy—blamed for the errors of Cotton, Wheelwright, Vane, and others, and for the overall disruption that resulted.

Though Hutchinson's threat was exacerbated by the context in which she operated, and her activities were interpreted in light of her relationships to Cotton, Wheelwright, Vane, and those who have often been called the Hutchinsonian party, she was not merely an innocent scapegoat for the errors of less vulnerable individuals such as Cotton. Rather, Hutchinson's claims must be read in the context of the broader controversy and assessed in light of the interpretive issues that troubled the Massachusetts churches. Her activities, while clearly not responsible for the colony's difficulties, highlighted the interpretive crisis and the ways in which it was shaped by Puritan theories of reading, preaching, and interpretation. Most dramatically, Hutchinson's claims about immediate revelation exposed the potential dangers of Puritan theories of exegesis. In the meetings held in her home, Hutchinson criticized widely held views on the relationship between sanctification and assurance. In doing so, she challenged both the ministers' authority and their understandings of their role. Moreover, by highlighting divisions among the ministers, Hutchinson unsettled the consensus that they were trying so desperately to maintain.

## "The Voice of His Own Spirit to My Soul"

The turning point of Hutchinson's court trial came when she claimed that she had enjoyed "immediate revelations" of God's will, apparently shocking even those who already identified her as the source of the community's problems ("Examination," 337). Winthrop suggested that this claim showed "the ground of all the disturbances to be by revelations" ("Examination," 341). He rejected revelations lacking ministerial validation: "for we receive no such made out of the ministry of the word and so one scripture after another, but all this while there is no use of the ministry of the word nor of any clear call of God by his word" ("Examination," 341). Winthrop was particularly alarmed that "the ground work of her revelations is the immediate revelation of the spirit and not by the ministry of the word," and worried that such revelations would prove contagious: "that is the means by which she hath very much abused the country that they shall look for revelations and are not bound to the ministry of the word, but God will teach them by immediate revelations and this hath been the ground of all these tumults and troubles, and I would that those were all cut off from us that trouble us, for this is the thing that hath been the root of all the mischief" ("Examination," 341–42).

Moreover, Winthrop emphasized, Hutchinson's readings, unsupported by ministerial authority, were likely to be wrong: "Ey it is the most desperate enthusiasm in the world, for nothing but a word comes to her mind and then an application is made which is nothing to the purpose, and this is her revelations when it is impossible but that the word and spirit should speak the same thing" ("Examination," 342). Though his assessment seemed somewhat overexcited, the court concurred, saying "We all consent with you" (342). Having been plagued by division, they could agree at least that revelations apart from "the ministry of the word" were dangerous. Hutchinson's claim alarmed the elders, and seemed to seal her fate: having heard these claims, two ministers who had been reluctant to swear that Hutchinson had accused them of preaching a covenant of works were convinced to take oaths to that effect.

Yet the revelations to which Hutchinson confessed were for the most part strikingly biblical, and in fact seemed only subtly different from the norms of Bible reading that the Massachusetts Bay clergy advocated. Hutchinson used the word "revelation" to describe God's "opening" the text to her, and "bring[ing a] . . . scripture out of the Hebrews" to address her questions about the legitimacy of the English church ("Examination," 336). What she called the "voice of [God's] own spirit to [her] soul" spoke in the language of the ninth chapter of Hebrews, and Hutchinson referred to other biblical texts to explain and justify her experience ("Examination," 336–37).[73] Hutchinson turned to the biblical text in her perplexities—as she had been instructed to do by the preaching of the ministers—and felt the agency of the Spirit enabling her reading. This she called "immediate revelation," though the line between it and the spiritually illumined reading described by Calvin as "the inward testimony of the holy Ghost speaking in the Scriptures" is rather fine.[74]

Marilyn J. Westerkamp suggests that Hutchinson's claim to immediate revelations was problematic primarily because of her gender, which rendered the challenge of "discounting any spiritual experience that suggested extraordinary revelation" both more "acute and, suddenly, easy to solve, for patriarchal ideology, unable to tolerate the power of a female mystic, provided several avenues of attack."[75] While Hutchinson's gender certainly exacerbated the threat she presented, Underhill's case suggests that it was not the sole problem. Moreover, Hutchinson's claims about scriptural revelations were interpreted in light of Underhill's even more alarming claims that his seditious acts had been inspired by an immediate revelation—and an unscriptural one, at that.

Hutchinson's approach was far less radical, and she may very well have learned it from John Cotton, the minister she most admired. In his exchanges with the other elders, Cotton had insisted that "the word of God it self hath no power in itself or from it self to encrease faith or the assurance of faith, but as the Spirit of God revealeth and applyeth Gods free grace in it."[76] Though holy, the text alone could not foster faith without God's revelation of free grace "in it" (126). Consequently, in sermons probably preached in 1636, Cotton had exhorted the Boston Church "not to be afraid of the word *Revelation.*"[77] Certainly, he had cautioned them "not to look for any *revelation* out of the Word; for the Spirit comes in the mouth of the *Word,* and the Word in the mouth of the Spirit"; he had also urged suspicion of "all *Revelations* in which the Word of God is silent" (179). Revelations must always be linked to scripture, he noted, "for the Spirit of God will speak *Scripture* to you: when he comes, he will not bring a *new Gospel,* and *new Revelations;* but he alwaies speaks in the Word of the Gospel of Jesus Christ, which is given unto us: therefore if any Spirit shall speak, and not according to the *Word,* it is but a *delusion:* rest not therefore in any *assurance,* nor *revelation,* unless thou hast a *word* for it" (179). Despite such caveats, Cotton had urged individual Christians to take the lively presence of the Spirit very personally: "Now the Word of God, though it be a Divine testimony in regard of the truths taught in it, and in regard that God delivered them; yet the application of them (as was said before) is not of Divine force, as a divine testimony unless the Spirit breathe in them, and apply them to me."[78] In his preaching, he had expressed this idea in language quite similar to Hutchinson's own, asserting that God "communicate[s] sundry of his counsels" to the saint, acquainting him "with his secret purpose about a people."[79] In Cotton's account, hearing the voice of the Spirit in the words of the scriptures was not only permissible; it was a necessary part of efficacious reading.

Thomas Shepard had earlier expressed suspicions of such claims, cautioning Cotton that heretical Familists often affirmed their allegiance to the biblical text even as they claimed disturbing revelations.[80] Consequently, Shepard warned, professed allegiance to scripture was not a reliable test of orthodoxy; Cotton should not assume "that the Familists doe not care for woord or ordinances but only the spirits motion," and therefore naively trust that his followers were not Familists.[81] Shepard knew from his own experience that the situation was far more complex: "I have bin with many of them and hence have met with many of there bookes; and I doe know thus much of them, that scarce any people honour woord and ordinances more, for they will professe that there they meet with the Spirit and there superlative raptures" (28). In Shepard's view, Cotton's emphasis on the relationship of word and Spirit might breed dangerous and destructive errors; Shepard feared that "under this colour of advancing woord together with the spirit, [Cotton might] meet in time with some such members (though I know none nor judge any) as may doe your people and ministry hurt, before you know it" (28–29). Such, perhaps, was Hutchinson.

Admittedly, even for Shepard, the line was quite fine. Later, when the Antinomian Controversy was safely behind him, Shepard suggested in his sermon *Of Ineffectual Hearing the Word* that Christians who read the biblical text and hear it preached should hope to hear not only "God's external or outward word" but also his "internal word and voice," experiencing a mystical and revelatory intimacy with God through the medium of biblical language.[82] However, faced with the danger and disruption of the controversy, Shepard was inclined to be both cautious and slightly suspicious. Perhaps significantly, though, in the portion of Hutchinson's examination during which immediate revelations were discussed, Shepard remained curiously silent, as did many of his ministerial colleagues. Perhaps he recognized that Hutchinson's revelations sounded closer to his own view than to the "superlative raptures" about which he had warned Cotton.

Cotton, however, did not remain silent during this part of the examination, nor did he repudiate Hutchinson's revelations. Instead, he acknowledged the potential validity of her assertions, insisting that revelations "dispensed . . . in a word of God and according to a word of God" were both possible and positive:

> and though the word revelation be rare in common speech and we make it uncouth in our ordinary expressions, yet notwithstanding, being understood in the scripture sense I think they are not only lawful but such as christians may receive and God bear witness to it in his word, and usually he doth express it in the ministry of the word and doth accompany it by his spirit, or else it is in the reading of the word in some chapter or verse and whenever it comes it comes flying upon the wings of the spirit. ("Examination," 340–41)

Cotton thus approved in theory a model of Bible reading in which the Holy Spirit's presence was powerfully felt by the individual reader. At the same time, he clearly had some concerns about Hutchinson's revelations. When William Bartholomew reported that Hutchinson had been "very inquisitive after revelations" in England, claiming to have had them and approving of Thomas Hooker's prediction that England would be destroyed, Cotton was eager to establish that Bartholomew had not told him of these concerns (339). And the *Short Story* reports that talk of revelations prompted Cotton to preach "diverse sermons" against "such revelations as *Abraham* had to kill his Son, and as *Paul* had in the ship" (278).

The specific content of Hutchinson's revelations complicated the matter, and demonstrated the risks of a model of scripture reading that emphasized the role of the Holy Spirit. Left alone with her Bible (even with its glosses) and with the Holy Spirit, Hutchinson interpreted the text in a way that put her at odds with her community.[83] On the basis of a text from Daniel, Hutchinson concluded that God would deliver her from affliction: "this place in Daniel was brought unto me and did shew me that though I should meet with affliction yet I am the same God that delivered Daniel out of the lion's den, I will also deliver thee" ("Examination," 337–38). Though Hutchinson's application of the text troubled some of the elders, her approach closely resembled the model of particular application of the biblical text advocated by Thomas Hooker, who insisted that his listeners hear the Scriptures speaking directly and personally to them, and that they apply the Scriptures to their own experiences.[84] Moreover, John Cotton acknowledged that Hutchinson might be right; at least, he refused to "bear witness against" the possibility "that she may have some special providence of God to help her" ("Examination," 341).

Even Hutchinson's threat to the court that "if [they went] on in this course [they would] bring a curse upon [themselves] and [their] posterity" bore enough resemblance to Hooker's preaching to make those present uncomfortable (338). When William Bartholomew remembered that Hutchinson had approved of Hooker's prediction that England would be destroyed, John Eliot suggested that Hutchinson's attribution was faulty (339). He was, however, in error; Hutchinson's approving comments clearly refer to Hooker's sermon *The Danger of Desertion*, in which he proclaims: "What if I should tell you what God told me yesternight that he would destroy England and lay it waste? What say you to this, my beloved? It is my message, by meditation in God's word, that he bid me do to you, and he expects an answer from you. I do my message as God commanded me."[85] Both in content and in form, Hooker's prophecy here sounds remarkably like the threats Hutchinson made against the General Court. What distinguished Hutchinson's threat from Hooker's was its target. Taught to interpret her text by an embattled ministry, Hutchinson turned these practices against her teachers when she found herself embattled in the new world. That Hutchinson's warning resembled Hooker's earlier prophecy only made her words more alarming, emphasizing the unanticipated uses that the laity could make of the ministers' teachings.

To some extent, Hutchinson may have suffered, as Cotton did, from the more radical applications of her followers. Certainly, the "immediate revelations" that Hutchinson described were less radical than the "strange motion" to write a petition described by Underhill (*Short Story*, 277). Though, as Foster explains, "Underhill's peculiarities antedated any contact with Mrs. Hutchinson," Hutchinson's accusers saw the two figures as closely linked.[86] Her claims were alarming not only because they radicalized Cotton's doctrine, but also because Hutchinson's accusers had reason to fear radicalized versions of her teachings as well.[87] Certainly, the various positions of Cotton, Hutchinson, and Underhill suggested what a slippery slope an orthodox theory of Spirit-assisted reading could generate. That such errors could be traced through Cotton and Hooker to Calvin himself made them more alarming, rather than less.

## Traducing the Ministers

Hutchinson's claims also highlighted tensions in Puritan theories of lay–ministerial interaction. Many of Hutchinson's interpreters have viewed her as an anticlerical figure, and there is some evidence to suggest that she was perceived as such in her own day. Edward Johnson, for example, suggested that the Antinomians' claims of revelations, and their emphasis on the distinction "betweene the Word of God, and the Spirit of God," "was onely devised to weaken the Word of the Lord in the mouth of his Ministers."[88] In place of ministerial authority, Johnson suspected, the Antinomians hoped "to put both ignorant and unlettered Men and Women, in a posture of Preaching to a multitude, that they might be praised for their able Tongue" (127). In his account, Hutchinson's followers had taken Protestant claims about access to the biblical word to an extreme position. Drawing on their ministers' emphasis on prophecy over "arte," Johnson's Hutchinsonians privileged lay preaching over ministerial preaching:

> Come along with me, sayes one of them, i'le bring you to a Woman that
> Preaches better Gospell than any of your black-coates that have been at the
> Ninneversity, a Woman of another kinde of spirit, who hath had many Rev-
> elations of things to come, and for my part, saith hee, I had rather hear such
> a one that speakes from the meere motion of the spirit, without any study at
> all, then any of your learned Scollers, although they may be fuller of Scrip-
> ture (I) [ay] and admit they may speake by the helpe of the spirit, yet the
> other goes beyond them.[89]

Taking the ministers at their word, some of Hutchinson's followers rejected even their ministers' carefully concealed art in favor of more spontaneous lay preaching.

At Hutchinson's trials before court and church, her accusers stressed this strain of anticlericalism. Winthrop, for example, charged that many of Hutchinson's followers were "flown off from magistrates and ministers since they have come to you," and emphasized that her revelations were dangerous because they were "not by the ministry of the word" ("Examination," 316, 341). Even Cotton, who upheld the possible legitimacy of Hutchinson's revelations at her court examination, reported in *The Way of Congregational Churches Cleared* that he had shared with Hutchinson his concerns about her "spiritual estate," among them "That her faith was not begotten nor (by her relation) scarce at any time strengthened, by public ministry, but by private meditations or revelations only" (240). Coupled with this concern was his sense that Hutchinson had come "to disesteem generally the elders of the churches" (240).

At her church trial, however, Hutchinson insisted that she did *"not allow the slightinge of Ministers nor of the Scriptures* nor any Thinge that is set up by God" ("Report," 377). And indeed there is evidence to complicate views of Hutchinson as anticlerical. Had she been a man, one suspects, she would have been a minister herself. Denied that opportunity, she was instead a minister's daughter and committed church member with strong ideas about proper preaching. At least some of Hutchinson's disruption lay not in hostility to ministers, but in profound allegiance to particular ministers, and in the ways such allegiances emphasized the human activity that Puritan theories of preaching downplayed. At her examination, Hutchinson asserted that her migration to New England was inspired by Cotton's departure. "When our teacher came to New-England it was a great trouble unto me," she explained; once Cotton had left and John Wheelwright had been silenced, "there was none left that I was able to hear, and I could not be at rest but I must come hither" ("Examination," 337). Such comments hardly suggest a lack of reliance on the ministry.[90]

In fact, the intensity of Hutchinson's commitment to Cotton made both Cotton himself and others uncomfortable. Robert Baillie insinuated that "Mrs. Hutcheson [sic] did visite M. Cotton in his house much oftener then by any other of his whole flock was wont to be done," a charge that Cotton firmly denied:

> Mistress Hutchinson seldom resorted to me: and when she did, she did seldom or never enter into any private speech between the former governor and myself. And when she did come to me, it was seldom, or never (that I can tell of) that she tarried long. I rather think she was loath to resort much to me, or to confer long to me, lest she might seem to learn somewhat from me. And withal I know (by good proof) she was very careful to prevent any jeolousy in me, that she should harbor any private opinions, differing from the course of my public ministry. Which she could not well have avoided, if she had kept almost every day so private and long discourse with me.[91]

Cotton here seems to have been placed in an uncomfortable position; having rebuked Hutchinson for her inadequate reliance on ministerial authority, he nevertheless needed to emphasize that she relied less on him than people suspected. Such suspicions persisted, however, and later accounts sometimes represented the purported intimacy between Hutchinson and Cotton as a sexual one.[92] Thus Hutchinson's reliance on particular preachers, and the intensity of her loyalties, while hardly unusual, had potentially troubling implications.

During the controversy itself, Hutchinson's alleged comparisons between Cotton and the other ministers received considerable attention. Her alleged comments highlighted ministerial division, especially the differences between the elders and John Cotton that they had worked so very hard to smooth over. Hutchinson insisted at various points that "she held nothinge but what Mr. Cotten held" ("Report," 381). By emphasizing the connections between her positions and Cotton's, she accentuated doctrinal differences among the ministers. Moreover, Cotton's refusal to reject Hutchinson's doctrinal claims, including the revelations that so clearly horrified many of his colleagues, emphasized that their divisions had not been fully healed by the

series of conferences and synods that they had been holding. As Richard Col-
licut, a deputy from Dorchester, lamented, "It is a great burden to us that we
differ from Mr. Cotton and that he should justify these revelations" ("Examination," 343). Hutchinson's conduct made that burden inescapable.

In evaluating the ministers' preaching, Hutchinson was, of course, heark-
ening to Cotton's advice. In England, Puritan parishioners had been encouraged to read scripture independently, aided by glosses in their Bibles, and
had even been urged to evaluate their ministers' preaching in accordance
with their own reading. In old Boston, for example, Cotton had urged his parishioners (among them, perhaps, Hutchinson herself) to "goe home" from
church "and consider whether the things that have been taught were true or
no; whether agreeable to the holy Scriptures or no" (*CTF*, 200). English Puritan divines, themselves part of an embattled minority, had encouraged their
parishioners to test ministerial authority according to their own biblical
lights. In New England, however, the ministers of the Bay did not expect to
find themselves the objects of their congregants' critical scrutiny.

Furthermore, Hutchinson was accused of impugning not only the ministers' doctrine, but also their ability to preach it. According to Hugh Peter,
Hutchinson had told him that "there was a wide and broad difference between our brother Mr. Cotton and our selves" ("Examination," 320). Given
the exchanges that had been taking place between Cotton and the other elders, this should hardly have been surprising; Cotton had in fact used very
similar language in his own correspondence with the other ministers. In his
*Rejoynder*, for example, Cotton had responded with very strong words to his
colleagues' willingness "to encourage those Christians who gather the evidence of their safe estate from the work of Christ in them, before any former
evidence of their justification by the seal of the Spirit":

> I must profess, though a child might lead me (and much more the least of
> you) according to God; yet herein I dare not hearken to you my self, nor
> persuade our brethren thereunto: For I know not how to excuse it from go-
> ing in a way of the Covenant of Works, first to see a work before the seal
> and witness of the Spirit (and so he must needs see it only by enlightned
> Conscience) and then to see a promise made to that work; and then from
> both to gather a faith of my justified estate: Such a faith is not a work of
> Gods almighty power begotten by the divine testimony and operation of the
> Spirit of God, (for it is before it) but hammered it is and engendred out of
> the concurse of three creatures, 1st. from the work or fruit of our own Spirit
> then from the letter of the word (which without the power of the Spirit of
> God is not able to beget faith) and then from the help of an enlightned Con-

science reasoning and concluding from both. The danger whereof is evident, and will also by Gods help further appear in the sequele. (85)

Cotton himself had thus suggested that his colleagues were encouraging their congregants to go in a covenant of works. If Hutchinson accused the other ministers of preaching a covenant of works, then, she was not making an accusation that they had not heard before, nor one that Cotton himself had not made. Hutchinson, however, emphasized the laity's awareness of differences among the ministers, and the local disturbances that emerged from that awareness made it all the more alarming—and all the more offensive to those who had been criticized.

Ministerial comments recorded in the documents of the court and church trials suggest that the Bay clergy were offended indeed. Clinging to ideas of ministerial transparency to divine truth, several participants insisted that they were concerned not about themselves, but about true doctrine. Weld, for example, insisted that "for ourselves we cared not but for the precious doctrine we held forth we could not but grieve to hear that so blasphemed," while Winthrop answered Hutchinson's objection that the ministers ought not be witnesses in their own cause by asserting that "It is not their cause but the cause of the whole country" ("Examination," 321, 327).[93] Nevertheless, despite claims that the controversy was theological rather than personal, the ministers seem to have taken Hutchinson's criticisms of their preaching ability very personally. Peter asserted that Hutchinson said that Cotton preached "the covenant of grace" while he and the other ministers preached "the covenant of works," that they were "not able ministers of the new testament and [knew] no more than the apostles did before the resurrection of Christ" ("Examination," 320). Moreover, George Phillips added that Hutchinson, "Being asked of particulars . . . did instance in Mr. Shephard that he did not preach a covenant of grace clearly, and she instanced our brother Weld" (322). When he asked her about his own preaching, she answered that she could not comment, having "never heard" him preach (322). Though debate ensued about the details of what had been said, clearly discussions of local preaching had taken a very personal turn. Illusions of transparency to the illumination of the Spirit could not be maintained when lay people like Hutchinson paid so much attention to individual variations in style and substance, and when ministers took that attention so personally. And certainly, it was hard for ministers not to take personally congregants' walking out of their sermons. Hutchinson thus challenged the ministers' understandings of their roles, of their relationships to one another, and of their relationships to the laity. Had they criticized Hutchinson for her partisanship, the clergy would have emphasized the differences that persisted among themselves. By instead representing her as anticlerical, the ministers constituted themselves as a unified body standing against Hutchinson. By disciplining her, they could thus neatly resolve the crisis, a solution all the more attractive given their relatively minimal anxiety about anticlericalism more generally.[94]

## THE PROBLEM OF BIBLICAL AUTHORITY

Though treating Anne Hutchinson as anticlerical helped to minimize tensions that divided the ministers, other implications of her dissent were less easily contained. Hutchinson's examination and trial emphasized what the community had already started to learn in other cases—that attempts to use the biblical text as a guide were more complicated than they had expected, and that the hoped-for model of interpretive discussion leading to consensus would often fail them. Throughout the controversy, individual participants asserted their allegiance to the biblical text and attempted to impose biblical standards on the debate. In November of 1636, for example, parties to a debate about "personal union with the Holy Ghost" agreed that "the word person might be forborn, being a term of human invention, and tending to doubtful disputation in this case" (*Journal*, 200–1). Throughout her examination and her trial, Hutchinson demanded biblical proof from her accusers, and skillfully debated interpretations of the prooftexts they produced. When Winthrop charged her with violating the commandment to "honour thy father and thy mother," Hutchinson showed that she had learned the ministers' techniques of exegesis well by calling his attention to the passage's context. Because the biblical text "saith in the Lord," she argued, parents were to be honored only when they demanded righteous action ("Examination," 313).[95] Later, she introduced texts herself, finding justification for holding meetings in her home because "there lyes a clear rule in Titus, that the elder women should instruct the younger" ("Examination," 315). Despite debate over whether rules to receive students trumped rules to turn them away, both parties agreed that the standard must be scriptural ("Examination," 315). But Hutchinson debated interpretation with enough skill that she often put the elders at a loss, leaving them to change the subject in frustration when they found themselves out-argued. Here, then, a skilled member of the laity, believing herself to be reading in the Spirit, had reached different conclusions from her elders, and, as she had been taught by her ministers, gave ground only when she found their scriptural justification convincing.[96]

More broadly, Hutchinson's activities challenged ideals of communal unity and consensus, particularly ideas of ministerial consensus. Throughout the controversy, participants struggled against painful recognitions of their differences to insist that they agreed. At several points in his *Journal,* for example, Winthrop seems to hope that the controversy is about to be resolved and minimizes differences among the disputants.[97] Even after several court sessions dealing with the controversy, and after several of the Hutchinsonians had been disciplined, some participants seemed eager to deny the severity of the crisis. At Hutchinson's trial before the General Court, for example, several participants were reluctant to acknowledge that a controversy was in progress. When Hutchinson called for the ministers who had testified against her to take oaths that she had accused them of preaching a covenant of works, Richard Brown, the deputy from Watertown who had himself been at the center of religious debate a few years earlier, objected anxiously that "an oath is of a high nature, and it is not to be taken but in a controversy" ("Examination," 328). Even when John Endecott offered the narrowest definition of a controversy, in which individuals take oaths to opposite positions, Brown was reluctant to define the community's difficulties as a controversy.

Instead of a controversy, in which both sides advocated fixed positions, many participants in the debates called for "free and open" discussion, hoping that they would be able to convince one another (*Journal,* 203). Dudley, for example, urged participants to be "free and open" early in the debates, when the court called the elders "to advise with them about discovering and pacifying the differences among the churches in point of opinion" (*Journal,* 202). But quite early in the controversy, the difficulties of "free and open" discussion became clear: it was soon apparent that such openness could produce bad feeling or worse. When Wilson was rebuked for his early speech about the churches' condition, he defended himself by saying that "he was called by the court about the same matter with the rest of the elders, and exhorted to deliver their minds freely and faithfully" (204). Nevertheless, many had been offended by his comments. Hutchinson made similar claims at both her court and church trials. At the former, she emphasized that the ministers whom she was accused of criticizing had pressed her to explain her understanding of the "difference between them and Mr. Cotton . . . as fully and as plainly" as she would have them speak to her, that they had "come for plain dealing and telling [her their] hearts" ("Examination," 325). Peter confirmed this in his testimony, acknowledging that they had asked her "to clear herself and deal plainly" (320). And Thomas Leverett noted that "Mr. Peters did with much vehemency and intreaty urge her to tell what difference there was between Mr. Cotton and them" (333).

Similarly, at Hutchinson's church trial, she complained that elders had misrepresented themselves as pursuing honest discussion, coming to her "in private to desire Satisfaction in some points, . . . profess[ing] in the sight of

God that they did not come to Intrap nor insnare me" ("Report," 352).[98] And
yet, she lamented, "without speaking to [her] and expressinge any Unsatis-
faction," they had brought her statements "publickly unto the Church before
they had privately dealt with" her (352–53). As the accusations surfaced in
lists at her church trial, Hutchinson seemed gradually to realize that those
earlier meetings had not been candid discussions of theology designed to help
clear up her perplexities, but attempts to pin down her heresies. Even then,
she did not acknowledge that what was expected of her was humble repentance, and continued to debate and discuss points of doctrine. Hutchinson's
willingness to believe that the elders had come to "inquire for Light" suggests
the persistence of her hopes for the New England interpretive community
(353). Her mounting frustration and sense of betrayal as the trial proceeded,
and the sense of defeat that can be read into her silence in the latter part of
the trial, reveal the disappointment of those expectations.

Participants worried not only about misrepresentations, but also about
misunderstandings. As they wrestled with the meanings of the biblical text,
they also expressed concerns about interpreting each other's words. Early
in the controversy, Shepard pressed Cotton to answer his queries "by way of
wrighting rather than speech," hoping that this would produce greater clarity.[99] Cotton, too, expressed concern about the ways in which his words were
being interpreted:

> But by this I discern, whence it cometh to pass, that I am thought to speak
> so obscurely; for if men that hear me, do instead of my words take up words
> of their own, and carry them to infer other conclusions than I aime at; I do
> not wonder if they cannot well understand, how that which I speak at one
> time, and that which they take me to speak at another can agree together.
> Words uttered in the Pulpit are transient, and may more easily be mistaken
> and forgotten, when I see even words written and extant, and abiding extant
> and obvious to the sight are so much mistaken and by mistake turned up-
> side down.[100]

Citing a difficulty that has long frustrated scholars of the controversy—the
difficulty of ascertaining what the participants actually said—Cotton noted
the particular challenge of "transient" preaching, sermons preached from
notes and discussed from notes taken by congregants, whose comprehension
and notetaking skill varied widely. Even with the best of intentions, Cotton
feared, members of this community were misinterpreting one another—
especially him.

Others complained of this as well. Members of the Boston church, as I
have noted above, lamented that they had been accused of holding opinions

more radical than those they in fact held. Hutchinson complained that the elders had misinterpreted her words, and she seemed as well to misinterpret the nature of their exchanges. Though Winthrop complained that "It is well discerned to the court that Mrs. Hutchinson can tell when to speak and when to hold her tongue," the documents of the controversy belie his claim ("Examination," 319). Hutchinson, hardly cagey or cautious, appeared eager to explain herself, her beliefs, and her actions, even when it seemed against her interests to do so. Far from politic, throughout her examination and through much of her church trial, Hutchinson debated forcefully and stood her ground, at points venting her frustration by exercising her quick wit and sharp tongue at the elders' expense. At one point, for example, pressed into a dispute about the biblical justification for teaching women, Hutchinson responded angrily, "Do you think it not lawful for me to teach women and why do you call me to teach the court?" ("Examination," 315). Even as her frustration with the proceedings mounted, however, she seemed remarkably slow to recognize the nature of the dialogue in which she was participating, reluctant to relinquish a vision of interpretive community in which those who disagreed discussed their concerns and perplexities openly, helping each other to understand the Scriptures and the workings of the Spirit. At her church trial, even when it seems clear to a modern reader that Hutchinson's fate had been all but sealed, she nevertheless continued to discuss doctrinal details seriously, allowing herself to be persuaded of some points and holding steadfastly to others. And she claimed in her own defense that many of the positions of which she stood accused reflected not firmly held positions but perplexities with which she struggled. "I did not hould divers of these Things I am accused of," she protested, "but did only ask a Question Ecclesiastes 3.18–21" ("Report," 354). Like James F. Maclear, I am inclined to credit this assertion.[101]

If Hutchinson placed too much confidence in a system of "free and open" discussion, she was not alone in hoping that it would persist. Throughout the controversy, Hutchinson's interlocutors betrayed anxiety about imposing limits on discussion. They found themselves faced with critics on both sides—from figures like Williams, who saw them as adopting English models of persecution, to more conservative critics who feared that New England was becoming a hotbed of heresy. They seem to have felt it necessary to assert repeatedly that they were not inquisitors, and that the civil state was *not* punishing its citizens for their beliefs, but rather for their actions. Hugh Peter, for example, emphasized at Hutchinson's examination his "desire that [the elders] not be thought to come as informers against the gentlewoman" ("Examination," 319). Winthrop felt impelled to defend himself before the Boston church, asserting that those who had been "sent away" were "so divided from the rest of the country in their judgment and practice, as it could not stand with the public peace, that they should continue amongst [them]" (*Journal*, 243–44). Even Thomas Hooker, who urged Winthrop to take "secret," "sud-dayne," and "resolute" action, suggested that he "attend nothing for ground of determination, but that which will cary an undeniable evidence to an impartiall iudge."[102] Though they were not nurturing heresy, the elders and magistrates were eager to emphasize, neither had they become the persecuting religious authorities from whom so many had fled.

As they dealt with Hutchinson's case, the ministers and magistrates struggled to address her disruption without entirely abandoning a model of open discussion. While Hutchinson's examination and church trial seem to many modern readers strikingly predetermined, we might allow ourselves to be surprised by the seriousness with which the magistrates, ministers, and elders argued with Hutchinson, even after her banishment had been pronounced. Rather than dismiss her and her ideas, they wrestled with them quite seriously. Hutchinson's fate may have been a foregone conclusion, but the surviving accounts suggest that these were nevertheless occasions of serious debate and discussion.[103]

Certainly, the elders were increasingly aware of the dangers of open discussion, and of open questioning of the ministers. When Hutchinson claimed at her church trial that she had merely raised questions, rather than affirming errors of which she had been accused, Thomas Shepard emphasized that "the vilest Errors that ever was brought into the Church was brought by way of Questions 42.7" ("Report," 354). Cotton elaborated upon this point, suggesting to Hutchinson that people who "hear of [such questions] will conclude them possitively and thay will thinke: suer thear is some thinge in it if Mrs. Hutchinson makes a Question of it, if those that have greate parts of Wisdome and Understandinge and if such eminent Christians make a Question of them, Thear is somethinge that needs further Serch and Inquirie about them" (373).

Yet despite their heightened awareness of the dangers of questions, the elders did not choose to ban them entirely. Rather, they urged that they be limited, deciding at the August 1637 synod that "Though a private member might ask a question publicly, after sermon, for information; yet this ought to be very wisely and sparingly done, and that with leave of the elders: but questions of reference, (then in use,) whereby the doctrines delivered were reproved, and the elders reproached, and that with bitterness, etc., was utterly condemned" (*Journal*, 234). In limiting these questions, the elders did not suggest that lay people should inevitably bow to ministerial opinion; rather, they attempted to impose standards of civility and deference for questioners, containing such discussions without banning them altogether.

Even at Hutchinson's church trial, when a chastened Boston church voted to excommunicate her, ministers did not press deference as far as one might have expected. During the trial, the elders debated Hutchinson seriously, inquiring into the details of her beliefs and asking if she was "clear" on various issues ("Report," 362). Indeed, so thoroughly did they discuss her doctrinal perplexities that John Eliot complained that it was "very dayngerous to dispute this Question so longe in this Congregation" (363). Even after his statement, Zechariah Symmes and Winthrop offered further arguments, apparently hoping to resolve the differences that divided Hutchinson from the community. Ultimately, of course, they found her to hold "Opinions that cannot be borne," and that "shake the very foundation of our fayth and tends to the Overthrough of all Religion," and on this basis Wilson called the congregation to vote on whether Hutchinson erred (364).

Cotton's admonition of Hutchinson was remarkable for its openness to lay evaluation of ministerial doctrine.[104] In the admonition, Cotton reaffirmed the need for women of the congregation to evaluate things they heard (in this case, from Hutchinson) by biblical standards. "Looke to your selves," he advised, "and . . . take heed that you receave nothinge for Truth which hath not the stamp of the Word of God from it" ("Report," 370). Though Cotton meant them to question Hutchinson's teachings, he acknowledged that they had received some "good" from her (370). When he might have urged reliance on ministerial authority, he instead encouraged them to evaluate the teachings on their own.[105]

Moreover, although Cotton admonished Hutchinson for her heresies, he did not pronounce her excommunication. Hutchinson interrupted Cotton's admonition with the claim that she *did not hould any of thease Thinges before* [her] *Imprisonment* ("Report," 372). Because the elders perceived this as a "Lye," Cotton suggested that Hutchinson be disciplined for this "poynt of fact or practise" (386). It would thus be Wilson, the pastor, who pronounced Hutchinson's excommunication. This fact has drawn a great deal of scholarly attention, with some scholars reading it as Cotton's attempt to avoid condemning Hutchinson for errors that lay all too close to his own positions. Some see him as abandoning his pupil out of fear that she would drag him down, while others have argued that Cotton was genuinely distressed by the radical turns that Hutchinson's theology had taken, and by her insistence at the same time that "she held nothinge but what Mr. Cotten held" (381).[106] In any case, later historians and Cotton's contemporaries alike have attributed his behavior to political opportunism rather than principle. For example, with more than a modicum of hostility, Thomas Shepard in 1639 recorded his suspicions that "Mr. Cotton repents not, but is hid only."[107]

In truth, Cotton was not the only leader relieved that Hutchinson was excommunicated for practice, rather than for doctrine. Questions of practice were

attractively clear cut, and again, they suggested an individual and even isolated act, rather than a systemic problem. Moreover, the congregational affirmation of an excommunication pronounced by Wilson reaffirmed the unity
of the Boston church and its support for *both* of its ministers.[108] Finally, an excommunication on practical rather than doctrinal grounds preserved the model
of free and open discussion once again. Certainly, the victors were eager to affirm this model in the aftermath of the controversy, emphasizing, for example,
that they had given their opponents "free leave, with all lenity and patience, to
lay downe what they could say for their Orations," that they had allowed "all
the Opinionists to come in, and take liberty of speech (only due order observed) as much as any of our selves had, and as freely" (*Short Story*, 212–13).

## Divine Deliverance

In addition to affirming their openness and the integrity of the process that
they had followed, the controversy's victors also drew comfort from Hutchinson's fate. They found evidence of her error in her gynecological problems,
which they saw as "monstrous births" (*Short Story*, 214). In his preface to
the *Short Story*, Thomas Weld exhorted his reader to "see how the wisdom of
God fitted this judgement to her sinne every way, for looke as she had vented
misshapen opinions, so she must bring forth deformed monsters; and as about
30. Opinions in number, so many monsters; and as those were publike, and
not in a corner mentioned, so this is now come to be knowne and famous all
over these Churches, and a great part of the world" (214–15). God's judgment
confirmed their own, allowing Weld to emphasize the results of Hutchinson's
rejection of an appropriate wifely role: having vented monstrous opinions
rather than confining herself to appropriate womanly activities, she was now
producing monstrous biological offspring as well.[109]

Nor was this the only validation they found in Hutchinson's later experiences. In the winter of 1640, a delegation from the Boston church traveled to
Rhode Island to meet with the exiles, to remind those still under church membership of their obligations to the church and to check on Hutchinson and on
others who had been disciplined.[110] Hutchinson remained intractable, refusing to "acknowledg [the Boston church] any church of Christs," and leading
Cotton to suggest that she might merit even "the greate Censure of Anathama
Marinatha."[111]

And finally, of course, Weld reported Hutchinson's death at the hands of
Indians, who "slew her and all her family, her daughter, and her daughters
husband, and all their children, save one that escaped" (*Short Story*, 218). The
unusualness of the attack inspired Weld to read it providentially: "I never

heard that the Indians in those parts did ever before this, commit the like out-
rage upon any one family, or families, and therefore Gods hand is the more
apparently seene herein, to pick out this wofull woman, to make her and those
belonging to her, an unheard of heavie example of their cruelty above al others" (218). Weld's emphasis on the attack represents his final blow against
Hutchinson, a strong refutation of her claims that God would deliver her and
punish the colony. Instead, God had not only *not* delivered her, but had in fact
singled her out for providential punishment. For Weld, then, the attack represented not only God's judgment against Hutchinson, but also His gracious
act to the community at Massachusetts Bay; Weld observed in biblical language that "Thus the Lord heard our groanes to heaven, and freed us from
this great and sore affliction, which first was small like *Elias* cloud, but after
Spread the heavens, and hath (through great mercy) given the Churches rest
from this disturbance ever since, that we know none that lifts up his head to
disturbe our sweet peace in any of the Churches of Christ amongst us, blessed
for ever be his name" (218). Once more, the formulation was repeated: with
Hutchinson gone, the community would proceed in peace.

Yet anxieties persisted. In the wake of the Antinomian Controversy, the
victors were anxious to emphasize that they had not become persecutors, that
they had punished offenses of practice rather than those of doctrine (*Short
Story*, 266, 285). They were eager to show as well that this controversy had
been imported rather than homegrown. Hutchinson was not a product of a
dangerous local environment; rather, she "had learned her skil in *England*,"
and on board ship during her crossing had expressed opinions so objectionable that the Boston church had initially been reluctant to admit her (*Short
Story*, 263). They sought to demonstrate as well that these were problems generated by individuals, rather than difficulties symptomatic of systemic problems. Specifically, as the title of Cotton's account suggests, they were eager to
"clear" the "way of Congregational churches," to demonstrate (especially to
English Protestants) that Congregationalism had not generated these problems, but that it had handled them appropriately and successfully. In Cotton's
words, "our Independency (as it is called) doth no more breed, nor nourish,
nor tolerate errors, or heresies, than Presbyterian discipline doth. And if there
should a defect arise in any church, there is the like remedy in the vigilancy
of other churches, and finally, obstinacy in all evils of notorious offense,
whether in judgment or practice, meeteth at length with the same or like
censure, in either government" (*Way Cleared*, 292). Like Weld, Cotton was
eager to affirm that "upon our clear understanding of one another's minds
and judgments, and upon the due proceeding of our church against convinced notorious errors and scandals, we have ever since (by the grace of
Christ) much amiable and comfortable communion together in all brotherly

kindness" (233–34). Consensus had been restored, they insisted, and all could return to the project of building their scriptural commonwealth.

Had anything changed, then? Certainly many were eager to affirm the restored unity and health of the Bay colony and its churches. James F. Cooper Jr. has suggested that the Bay clergy were not even moved to consolidate their authority in the wake of these events.[112] But something seems to have changed subtly. Some participants remained suspicious of one another. Thomas Shepard, for example, suspected that Cotton was "hid only," and felt compelled to preach on sanctification for four years in the wake of the controversy.[113] The accounts of the controversy produced by Winthrop, Weld, Cotton, and others suggest as well that anxieties had not been laid to rest. And as the colony's ministers returned to the task of drawing up a body of scriptural laws, the committee appointed to the project by the General Court would be headed by John Winthrop, and would not include the colony's foremost biblical scholar, John Cotton (*Journal*, 249, 249 n. 1). These facts, and subsequent events, suggest that the ground had shifted subtly, that approaches to scriptural authority and ministerial authority were being refined in light of the chastening experiences of the 1630s.

# INTERPRETIVE EXPERTISE AND
# QUESTIONS OF BAPTISM

As the Antinomian Controversy drew to a close, several participants expressed the hope that the Massachusetts Bay community would return to normal. Scholars have debated the extent to which this occurred, with some insisting that the controversy reshaped theological orthodoxy and local institutions and others countering that the changes produced by the controversy were less significant.[1] What is clear, however, is that the controversy produced an important shift in interpretive modes. Without renouncing their biblical allegiance or even formally clamping down on lay interpretation (indeed, while insisting that the laity continue to examine the ministers' claims in accordance with their own readings of scripture), the ministers nonetheless began to place greater emphasis on human mediation and interpretive authority than they had before. Faced with a laity that was often eager to hold themselves and their ministers to a stricter and simpler scriptural standard, in these later discussions the ministers placed much less emphasis on their own transparency in the interaction between congregant, text, and the divine Author/Interpreter. Instead, texts dealing with debates over baptism (both anti-Baptist tracts and the documents of the Halfway Covenant controversy) reveal the ministers placing more emphasis on the "arte" of exegesis and preaching, and locating their authority in their own interpretive expertise.

## EARLY INDICATIONS

Even in some of the later writings of the first generation, some ministers were presenting their own expertise in subtly different ways. John Cotton, for instance, had earlier emphasized his transparency to the text and the Spirit even as he revealed some of his technical learning, for example in his enumeration of rhetorical ornaments used to elaborate on vanity in his *Briefe Exposition With Practical Observations Upon the Whole Booke of Ecclesiastes.*[2] When Anabaptist ideas troubled the colony in the 1640s, however, Cotton's response showed a greater willingness to emphasize his own expertise. In 1647, he published a defense of infant baptism, couched in the form of a dialogue between Silvester, the erring church member who has been led astray, and Silvanus, the wiser and more orthodox friend.[3] Silvester has been persuaded by Baptist tracts that baptism "wanteth a word both of Commandment and Example from the Scripture" (3). Having accepted Puritan assumptions about proper ordinances and the importance of the text's "literal" meaning, he thus suspects that infant baptism is consequently unlawful (3). Nevertheless, he insists, he remains open to Cotton's arguments.

Cotton objects to what he deems Silvester's overly literalist position as "a Tempting of God, even limiting of the Holy one of *Israel*, to put upon him to deliver his will onely by Commandment or Example, or not at all; As if God might not deliver his will, by promise or threatning, by Proportion, or deduction, by Consequence, as well as by expresse Commandment or Example" (4). Sounding remarkably like Richard Hooker in his rebuke of Puritan literalism, Silvanus suggests that Silvester is demanding too much from the text. He attempts to clarify what he means by drawing on the parallel case of women's participation in the Lord's Supper—an ordinance not under debate. "What Commandment or Example," asks Cotton, "is their for women to partake of the Lords Supper? yet the Proportion of the Lords Supper with Passeover, and Deduction from such Scriptures as put the will and Ordinance of Christ, That women able to examine and judge themselves should partake of the Lords Supper, as well as the men" (4). Indeed, Cotton insists that "Whatsoever is drawn out of the Scripture by just consequence and deduction, is as well the word of God, as that which is an expresse Commandment or Example in Scripture" (4). And later, Cotton asserts that "if one Proposition in a Syllogisme be found in the Word of God, and the other Proposition be found certaine and evident by sense or reason, the conclusion is a conclusion of faith" (167).

Though Cotton here sounds uncomfortably close to the language of Richard Hooker's *Lawes of Ecclesiasticall Politie*, this similarity is somewhat deceptive. Cotton has neither embraced Hooker's position on adiaphorism nor altered his exegetical method. He bases most of his argument on scriptural passages, attempting to demonstrate that "the Baptisme of children is not without a Commandment, and word of Institution from Scripture," although he also considers the consequences of Anabaptism at some length (4).

Nevertheless, it remains significant that one of New England's foremost exegetes found it necessary to chide church members for believing too naively in the literal meaning of the text and for an overly literal understanding of scriptural ordinances. Moreover, he found it necessary to suggest to them that the process of deriving God's will from the Scriptures was more complex than they might have thought. Assertions of scriptural clarity and accessibility have given way to claims about methodology and skill, as Silvanus warns Silvester that proper testing of ordinances by scriptural standards requires an understanding of "Proportion, or deduction, by Consequence" and of syllogisms, in addition to the ability to understand what was communicated "by expresse Commandment or Example" (4, 167). Larzer Ziff blames Cotton's difficulties in this debate on "his opponents' lack of university training and their consequent maddening insistence upon a literal reading of the scriptures."[4] In fact, it was not their lack of university education itself that was to blame, but rather that lack coupled with the education that they had received from their ministers. Having been told that they did not need a university education to read the scriptures, having been exhorted to read them and to find them clear, it is not surprising that the laity expected to find clarity and literal meaning in their biblical texts. Faced once again with the difficulties that these expectations could generate—and indeed the persuasiveness with which Silvester argues throughout the text testifies to Cotton's awareness of how well the New England laity had learned the lessons of Reformed preaching—Cotton found it necessary to emphasize that understanding the Scriptures was not so simple, that expertise and interpretive sophistication were necessary.

## "WORKMEN THAT NEED NOT TO BE ASHAMED"

Cotton was not alone in increasingly emphasizing the need for learning and expertise. On the day following commencement in 1655, Harvard College president Charles Chauncy delivered a sermon praising *Gods Mercy Shewed to his People in Giving Them a Faithful* Ministry *and Schooles of* Learning *for the Continual Supplyes Thereof,* which was later published in expanded form.[5] Taking as his text Amos 2:11, "And I raysed up of your Sonns for Prophets, and of your Young men for Nazarits, is it not so O ye children of Israel, saith the LORD?" Chauncy explored the balance between "prophecying" and "arte" that William Perkins had described in his *Arte of Prophecying*, and chose to emphasize the "arte" (1).

In the book of Amos, Chauncy found two kinds of prophets. In *"Amos. 7. 14. 15. Amos saith I was not a Prophet nor the son of a Prophet, but I was an heardsman, and a gatherer of sycamore fruit"* (4). Chauncy explains, "that is, *I was not trayned up in any of the schooles of the Prophets, but I had another calling, untill the Lord was pleased to advance me to the office and dignity of a Prophet, & vers. 15. He took me as I followed the flock and said Prophecy to my people Israel"* (4). Distinguishing between schooled and unschooled prophets, Chauncy insisted that "both such as had there education in the schooles of the Prophets and such as were called immediatly, and extraordinarily inspired, God was the rayser up of them both" (4–5). He asserted that the power of prophecy came from God, and not from learning itself, but that God employed learning for his people's edification: "for humane instruction is not sufficient to make any man to be a Prophet: yes and no less power of God and grace is requisite to raise up your Sonns to be Prophets whatsoever their educatiõ is, thẽ where he doth inspire others immediately & extraordinarily, therefore where extraordinary meanes is wanting, the goodness of God in blessing ordinary means must not be forgotten" (5).

In distinguishing between learned and unlearned prophets, Chauncy asserted that both were found in Amos's day. Now, however, "those extraordinary Prophets are wanting," making "much more need of schools now" (33). Asserting that the age of extraordinary and unlearned prophecy had passed, Chauncy emphasized the value of a trained preaching ministry. Though not "extraordinary" in a technical sense, such prophets were, of course, extraordinary in their own way.[6] Though their gifts might seem less dramatic, Chauncy noted, "it is a mighty change that young men that are addicted to their pleasures & lusts, that now they should be so changed as to preach Christ, & to favor heavenly things, and to be set apart by God" (5). Indeed, Chauncy explained, they are "persons that have more of God in them then other men" (11). He emphasized that the gift of prophecy came from God, and was not a product of human learning: "it is neither your own study or parts, nor the teaching and instruction of others, that can possibly rayse you up out of that dunghill wherein you ly, to this degree to be true *Prophets* of the Lord, but is the Lord himself that must put underneath you his everlasting armes to rayse you up" (23–24). He thus advised would-be ministers "to be much in prayer unto the Lord: dayly and duely to draw neer unto the Lord, to beg of him the spirit of wisdome and *revelation*, and a blessing upon, and assistance in [their] studyes" (24).

At the same time, Chauncy emphasized the value of the Harvard curriculum and the learned ministry. "I could wish as Moses," Chauncy explained, "*that all Gods people were Prophets:* But you shall find it here, as in other trades, that there is a great difference between those that have been bound apprentices to a trade and others that are handy, & have gotten a little skill by the observation of others, this latter will serve to patch or bungle, but wise men will rather choose to deal with those that have been trained up in such a course" (30). Treating the ministry as a skilled trade, Chauncy insisted that the preaching of trained ministers would be superior to that of the untrained: "Thus from persons educated in good literature we may rather expect that they should be *workmen that need not to be ashamed &c* as Paul speaks to Tim: *Isay* 50.4 they that have had *an ear to hear as the learned,* and the Lord hath given them *the tongue of the learned,* are most likely [to] . . . *speak a word in due season to him that is weary &c*" (30). While the ability to hear and to speak came from God, Chauncy represented the minister as a "workman" whose God-given gifts of prophecy would be enhanced by the study of "good literature" and other disciplines, and who would thus be more skilled at reaching his congregants.

Chauncy emphasized that human learning was a gift from God as well: "the Lord works with, & blesseth this means, for the laying up of provision, & making of supplys for the work of the ministry; and the Lord here reckons it up as the chiefest of all blessings mentioned" (33). He also cited scriptural grounds for "Schools of learning," and proposed that one of the uses of his text "was To teach us, that Schools of learning are approved and appointed of God, and of great importance for the benefit of Gods people" (33). In doing so, he was not simply congratulating the young Harvard graduates on their good fortune and on the value of their studies. Chauncy was responding to criticism of the ministry and of the Harvard curriculum by which ministers trained: "Some goes so far as to account these blessings to be curses, so as to say, that our ministryes are antichristian, and schools of learning popish, and the seminaryes of wickedness, & loosness in the Country" (16).[7] Such critics, he argued, showed their "contempt of the word of God and his Ordinances, and listening to lying books & pamphlets, that are brought over into the country, whereby multitudes are poysoned amongst us" (19).

Chauncy addressed himself specifically to "Mr. Dell in his answer to Mr. S. Simpson," who had preached and published a consideration of "humane learning."[8] Chauncy considered two definitions of "humane learning." First, he defended the study of pagan authors as scriptural, noting that "we find in Scriptures, some testimonies out of humane writers, . . . which the Spirit of God would not have alledged, if their writings had been utterly unlawfull to read" (35). He argued that such writings contained truth and that they also "attested many Scripture historyes," confirming scriptural accounts with external evidence (36).

Chauncy considered a second definition of "humane learning" as well: "all those Arts that are commonly taught in Universities, as *Physicks, Ethicks, Politicks, Oeconomicks, Rhetorick, Astronomy, &c:* or also for the learned tongues of *Latine, Greek, and Hebrew &c:*" (39). These, Chauncy defended even more strongly: "I will be bold to affirm, that these in the true sense and right meaning thereof are Theologicall & Scripture learning, and are not to be accounted of as humane learning" (37). For he found all of these disciplines in the Scriptures themselves (37–38). Dell himself, noted Chauncy, encouraged the teaching of many of these arts widely, not only at Oxford and Cambridge (39–40).

Perhaps more important, affirmed Chauncy, was the usefulness of these arts for the illumination of scripture. Like Perkins and Richard Bernard before him, he insisted that learning was necessary for proper exegesis. Chauncy considered Dell's argument that

> *there is no necessity of Schools or Universityes, or any humane learning to teach men Divinity, or to make able preachers of the Gospell: the teaching of the Spirit of God alone is sufficient: which Mr. Dell proves by the examples of our Saviour Christ & his Apostles, seeing Christ himself had only the unction of the Spirit. Isay 61. 1–4. Luke 4. Mat: 13. 54,55. Besides when he would send forth preachers to all the world, he chose Fishermen, Publican, Tent makers, plain men, and of ordinary employment in the world, and only put his Spirit upon them Acts 2. 17.* (40)

Chauncy turned this objection on its head, suggesting that a parallel between the apostles enabled by "the miraculous and extraordinary gifts of the Spirit" and "other ministers in after times, that have no such extraordinary gifts" was "ridiculous," just as it would be ridiculous to suggest that "if Aholiab and Bezalel were filled with the Spirit of God in wisdom, and in knowledg, and all manner of workmanship, to devise cunning works, (as they were *Exod.* 31. 3,4.) then no man need to be an apprentice to learn any Mechanicall trade, seeing the teaching of the Spirit is sufficient for any cunning work" (41). Again comparing preaching with other crafts, Chauncy asserted that ordinary preachers needed more human training than their biblical counterparts. Chauncy insisted as well that "the Lord Jesus and his Apostles" were not unlearned, but rather were "learned, and beyond that which is attainable by ordinary teaching" (42). For they had "the gifts of tongus the gifts of miracles, of discerning of Spirits, yea the gifts of wisdom & knowledg, (The Pasteurs and Teachers gifts) mentioned 1 Cor: 12 and also 1 Cor: 14" (42). Endowed with miraculous and extraordinary spiritual gifts, they were far different from ordinary ministers of Chauncy's day.

Rather than suggesting that ministers in his own day needed nothing beyond the illumination of the Spirit, Chauncy suggested that such illumination was not in itself sufficient to "make an able minister" (43). "Gods ministers," argued Chauncy, needed a range of skills specified in the Bible: they
*must rightly divide the word of trueth 2 Tim: 2.15. must be apt to teach.*
1 Tim: 3.2. *must be able by sound doctrine, both to exhort, to convince the*
*gainsayers: They must have the tongue of the learned, that they may not be*
*as those unlearned ones that wrest the Scriptures to their own & others*
*perdition. 2. Pet. 3.16"* (43). The unlearned might "wrest" the scriptures dangerously, and a minister must not only avoid this peril himself, but (as New
Englanders had learned to their dismay) be prepared to counter misreadings.
For this, Chauncy insisted, the unlearned (even unlearned saints) were ill
equipped: "Now let any prudent man be judg in this case, whither he think
that every christian that hath received the sanctifying Spirit of God, is gifted
therby & qualified for the confutation of gainsayers, and the whole work of
the ministry" (43). Chauncy's answer was an emphatic "no."

Nor was this merely a problem of argumentative skill. Chauncy asserted
that it was a problem of reading and interpretation. "How," Chauncy asked,
"shall a minister without the knowledg of the Original tongues, either trans-
late the Scriptures, or when they are translated, maintain them against the
popish vulgar, or other diverse false translations, to be the infallible trueth of
God?" (47). This was a pastoral question, rather than simply a scholarly one,
for failing this, "how shall he comfort the poor soul that saith he is a reprobate, and proves it out of 2 Cor: 13. 5. Because he knows not *that Iesus Christ*
*is in him,* if he knows not what *adokirros* means" (47). Without some knowledge of logic, "how shall a man know when a Scripture is wrested, or falsly
applyed, or a false use is made of it, or a false consequence is drawn out of it,
or a true" (48). Without such knowledge, "especially to hold forth these things
to others he must needs be a shamefull workman, and many times ridiculous,
neither rightly apprehending, nor dividing the word of trueth, that hath no
knowledg how to interpret the Scripture" (48). Once again insisting on the
language of labor and craft, Chauncy dismissed the unschooled as having "no
knowledg of how to interpret the Scripture" (48).

Chauncy made similar claims about other branches of learning, challenging "the unlearned minister, or him that understands not rhetorick, to give any
tolerable sense of . . . [a list of difficult] places of Scripture, and many the like
(farther then they have been opened to them by the learned)" (48). He asserted the interpreter's reliance on human arts and human interpreters for understanding biblical metaphors. While he conceded that "what is necessary to
salvation, may be both understood & preached, without the help of Philosophy," he nevertheless called philosophy "lawfull & usefull" (49). In Chauncy's

view, a minister would be an inadequate workman if he failed to prepare him-self with "humane learning," and could not hope to interpret the Word prop-erly, or to apply it to the comfort of his congregation.[9]

Nor was Chauncy merely telling an audience of academics what they wanted to hear. Expanding his sermon for publication, Chauncy seems to have envisioned an audience of potential opponents among the laity, for he included among his uses not only his justification of a learned ministry, but also "double reproof," both of insufficient gratitude to God for the mercy of the ministry and of the sins committed despite this mercy (16, 18). Chauncy was certainly mindful as well of the lure of Interregnum England for the min-istry's most promising candidates, which had such consequences as the un-successful call by the North Church in Boston of a candidate who lacked a university education.[10] A movement that had earlier objected to inadequately trained ministers now seemed divided about how much education was truly necessary. Chauncy's sermon reveals the willingness even of doctrinal con-servatives to assert the necessity of training, expertise, and artistry, claiming interpretive authority even as they preserved institutional structures that maintained lay power.

## "To Give Subtilty to the Simple"

Though ministers were increasingly willing to stress interpretive expertise in the wake of the Antinomian Controversy, they strove to maintain an uneasy balance between this emphasis and continued assertions of Spirit-assisted lay reading ability. The Native American converts who people John Eliot's narra-tives and guides suggest the persistence of the ministry's sense that Chris-tians—even those who had not been trained to read the Scriptures since child-hood—could learn to read the Bible with the assistance of the Holy Spirit.

In his *Indian Dialogues*, Eliot traces the process by which Native Ameri-cans become Christians.[11] As for English Christians, that process is closely tied to interaction with the biblical text and to the acquisition of literacy. Eliot de-scribes his *Indian Dialogues* as a blend of historical account, prescription, and wishful thinking: "partly historical, of some things that were done and said, and partly instructive, to show what might or should have been said, or that may be (by the Lord's assistance) hereafter done and said, upon the like occa-sion" (61). These narratives present a range of responses to the biblical text. Some potential converts respond with skepticism. In the first dialogue, a kins-man of the Christian Piumbukhou, for example, finds the threat of torment in the afterlife frightening, but remains suspicious of English motives: "May not we rather think that *English* men have invented these stories to amaze us and fear us out of our old customs, and bring us to stand in awe of them, that they might wipe us of our lands, and drive us into corners, to seek new ways of living, and new places too? And be beholding to them for that which is our own, and was ours, before we knew them" (71). To counter this claim, Pium-bukhou offers the biblical text. "The Book of God," he asserts, "is no invention of Englishmen" (71). Indeed, he emphasizes that Englishmen too are converts to Christianity. The Bible, he explains, "is the holy law of God himself, which was given unto man by God, before Englishmen had any knowledge of God; and all the knowledge which they have, they have it out of the Book of God" (71). Now, he invites, "this book is given to us as well as to them, and it is as free for us to search the scriptures as for them. So that we have our instruction from a higher hand, than the hand of man" (71). Drawing on the Reformed tradition in which his teachers were instructed, he renders human instructors secondary to "the great Lord God of heaven and earth, who teacheth us these great things of which we speak" (72). The Bible derives its authority, in Eliot's account, directly from God, and not from the reliability of its human preachers.

Yet along with this claim, Eliot emphasizes the role of the human beings who brought this text to the Indians, including himself. Piumbukhou exhorts his kinsmen to be "thankful to the English, and to thank God for them," for having brought the word of God to his people (72). From this act, he is prepared to generalize, insisting that the English "love us, they do us right, and no wrong willingly. If any do us wrong, it is without the consent of the rulers, and upon our complaints our wrongs are righted" (72). Moreover, Piumbukhou offers more specific praise of Eliot, explaining that "God put it into the heart of one of their ministers (as you all know) to teach us the knowledge of God, and hath translated the holy Book of God into our language, so that we can perfectly know the mind and counsel of God."[12] Though the motives of those who brought the book to his people are relevant, Piumbukhou offers the book itself as the source of authority: "And out of this book have I learned all that I say unto you, and therefore you need no more doubt of the truth of it, then you that the heaven is over our head, the sun shineth, the earth is under our feet, we walk and live upon it, and breathe in the air. For as we see with our eyes these things to be so, so we read with our own eyes these things which I speak of, to be written in God's own book, and we feel the truth therein in our own hearts" (72). Because the knowledge comes from the book itself, rather than from human intermediaries, it is trustworthy, though ultimately Piumbukhou suggests that such authority must be validated by his kinsmen's own feelings as well.

But Eliot's narrative does not imagine immediate triumph for Piumbukhou's message. Instead, his kinswoman suggests at this point that he must be tired and hungry, and that the best response to "long and learned discourses which we do not well understand" is to "stop [Piumbukhou's] mouth, and fill [his] belly with a good supper," so that he will cease to pester them with "gastering and heart-trembling discourses" (72–73). "We are well as we are," she asserts, "and desire not to be troubled with these new wise sayings."[13] In other dialogues, the argument from the biblical text receives an even more skeptical response. Just as Piumbukhou's kinsmen in the first dialogue suggest that the English have made up these ideas, an interlocutor named Sontim suggests that the Bible itself is similarly suspect: "It may be the Englishmen made it, and tell you they are the Words of God" (92). While Sontim does not respond to Piumbukhou's claim that "This book was written long before the Englishmen prayed to God," he does later express willingness to be instructed (92–93, 94).

In the various dialogues, Eliot suggests that instruction of Native American converts followed patterns established for the instruction of their English counterparts, though often that instruction took place over a shorter time period. For example, the story is related of a "young man with us" who is appointed to read selected biblical verses to the potential converts (98–99). Waban, another of Eliot's Christian Indians, explains to Peneovot that while he "cannot yet read the word, yet you must get the help of others, and learn the Word of God by heart" (109). The Word heard and meditated upon is very powerful, asserts Waban: "the meditation on the word will sanctify the heart, and kill corruption, and will mightily help you to subdue it" (109).

Powerful as this is, Waban exhorts Peneovot that he must nevertheless "learn the catechism" so that "by learning to read that, you will learn to read and understand the whole Bible" (109). Peneovot laments the "loss" of beginning to "learn catechism and the Word of God" as a man, rather than as a child, as he might have had he "been brought up among the *praying Indians*" (109). But Eliot's dialogues suggest that the converts' late starts hamper them less than might be feared. For his imagined Indian converts, like the converts of Thomas Shepard's congregation, incorporate biblical imagery into their own language. After his conversion, for example, Peneovot describes himself as "a man that was looking for a shell, and found a pearl of inestimable value" (113). As in the case of Shepard's congregants, Peneovot's facility with biblical images testifies to his transformation, countering accusations that praying Indians were outwardly changed without experiencing genuine conversions.

If the ease with which the Indian converts of the *Indian Dialogues* became biblically literate demonstrated the capabilities of even the most untutored lay reader assisted by the Holy Spirit, Eliot nevertheless emphasized as well the need for professional teachers and preachers among the Indians. In addition to the scholarly labor involved in preparing his Bible translation, Eliot also published *The Logick Primer*, subtitled *Some Logical Notions to initiate the* INDIANS *in the knowledge of the Rule of Reason; and to know how to make use thereof. Especially for the Instruction of such as are Teachers among them.*[14] Just as Chauncy had emphasized the need for ministers learned in rhetoric and the arts who would be able to interpret the Bible properly, and Cotton before him had emphasized the importance of understanding logic, Eliot too suggested that his Praying Indians would need professional Bible interpreters as well. Those interpreters, he argued, must be trained in the arts of logic in order to recognize various sorts of propositions, causes, and modes of scriptural proof. *The Logick Primer* is an elementary logic text, but it is unmistakably academic in tone, emphasizing examples and providing minimal explanation. The text is also firmly grounded in scripture. Eliot drew on the Bible for examples throughout, and justified the enterprise in scriptural terms as well, quoting from Proverbs 1:4 on the title page in affirming his purpose: "To give subtilty to the simple; to the young man knowledge and discretion" (A2r). He emphasized the importance of human interpreters by citing the query of the eunuch in Acts 8:31, who asks, "How can I understand [the words of Isaiah], unless some man should guide me?" (A3r–A3v). In Eliot's understanding, lay readers—even those not immersed from childhood in a biblical culture—could become capable readers with the assistance of the Holy Spirit, but they needed skilled human interpreters to help them in this process.

Like Chauncy's sermon, Eliot's negotiation of the balance between lay ability and the importance of human interpreters was shaped by his awareness of the political situation in both old and New England. On the one hand, he had to emphasize that his Indian converts were genuine Christians, in the face of skepticism on both sides of the Atlantic. And, beyond the local troubles that had afflicted New England's churches, his texts reflect his anxiety about the status of his project amid the shifting political situation in old England. When, after long research and labor, Eliot published his translation of the Bible in 1663, he dedicated the project to Charles II, and sought his new sovereign's favor for his mission:

> Give us therefore leave (*Dread Soveraign*) yet again humbly to Beg the Continuance of your Royal Favour, and of the Influences thereof, upon this poor Plantation, *The United Colonies of* NEW-ENGLAND, for the Securing and Establishment of our Civil Priviledges and Religious Liberties hitherto Enjoyed; and, upon this Good Work of Propagating Religion to these Natives, that the Supports and Encouragements thereof from *England* may be still Countenanced and Confirmed.[15]

Eight years later, in the *Indian Dialogues*, Eliot felt it necessary to emphasize the connection between his mission and the progress of Protestantism, and to

emphasize as well the sovereign's responsibility for that progress. In one dialogue, William explains to Philip Keitasscot about "a certain people who are
called Papists," whose "wicked ministers will not suffer the people to read the
Word of God, and pretend the same reason as you do, because they be ignorant"
(136). Keitasscot is convinced, promising "never [to] hinder [his] people from
the knowledge of the Word of God," and expressing "wonder" both at "those
vile ministers who do so wickedly abuse the people" and at "the sachems"
who "suffer such vile ministers to abuse their people in that manner" (137).
Once again, the relationship between lay power and ministerial authority
was not a simple dyad; rather, it was a triangle which included as well civil (in
this case, royal) authority exerted upon both laity and clergy. New England's
ministers maintained their emphasis on lay access to the Bible, and its centrality to the Protestant project, even as they asserted their own authority as
interpretive professionals.

## "A Matter of Humbling to Us"

Emphasis on interpretive expertise grew even more pronounced during the
controversy surrounding the Halfway Covenant, as New England's churches
wrestled with another unanticipated challenge to their initial expectations.
Even as Anabaptists objected to the practice of infant baptism, a less extreme
question about the practice generated enormous disagreement. New England
churches baptized the children of their members on the theory that the covenant
extended to members and their "seed." But in the 1640s, the churches found
that these baptized children of church members often grew to adulthood and
had children of their own, without themselves experiencing and testifying to
their own regenerate status. Ministers wrestled with the implications of this
phenomenon. Were these "halfway members" insufficiently pious, or excessively scrupulous? Was this a sign of spiritual declension, and if so, how could
it be combated?[16]

Aside from these broader concerns, the children of the so-called halfway
members posed an immediate practical problem. Should the churches baptize
them as well, extending the covenant's reach through the generations? This
was the recommendation of the Synod of 1662, known as the Halfway Synod.
The debate that this proposal stirred and the uneven process by which it was
implemented demonstrate how much had changed in the wake of the colony's
earlier controversies. Throughout the debate, ministers on both sides followed the leads of Cotton and Chauncy, placing new stress on human interpretive authority. They relied heavily on interpretive precedents, emphasized
their own expertise, and lamented the laity's interpretive naïveté. Without

overturning institutional structures that preserved lay power, they emphasized the authority conferred by their own knowledge.[17]

The change was a subtle one, rooted in the chastening that their interpretive expectations had received in the controversies that had troubled the
colony in its first decades. The preface of the *Propositions* put forward by the
Synod of 1662 shows a continued commitment to scriptural principles, yet
also reveals a certain decline in confidence.[18] The ministers affirmed the biblical mission of the community, noting "That one end designed by God's All-
disposing Providence in leading so many of his poor people into this Wilderness, was to lead them unto a distinct discerning and practice of all the Wayes
and Ordinances of his House, according to Scripture pattern, may seem an
Observation not to be despised" (sig. A2r). In a voice much less confident than
had been that of the early migrants, they conceded "That we are fit or able for
so great a Service, the sense of our own feebleness forbids us to think" (sig.
A2r). Indeed, they acknowledged sadly, "It is a matter of humbling to us,
that we have made no better improvement of our Opportunities this way; but
some Fruits God hath given, and is to be praised for" (sig. A2r). The ministers emphasized the interpretive labor necessarily involved in "improv[ing]"
the opportunity God had granted them. No longer was God's word simply revealed "in his Blessed word of truth."[19] Instead, the process of determining
God's will required labor, practice, and human assistance; the ministers hoped
that their endeavors would benefit from all of these:

> For, besides the useful Labours and Contemplations of many of the Lords
> Worthies in other places, and in former times, contributing to our Help, and
> shewing our Principles to be neither novel nor singular, the advantage of
> Experience and Practice, and the occasion thereby given for daily searching
> into the Rule, is considerable. And he that hath made *the path of the just as
> the shining Light,* is wont still to give unto them further Light, as the prog-
> ress of their path requires further Practice, making his *Word a Lanthorn to
> their feet,* to shew them their Way from step to step; though haply some-
> times they may not see far before them. (sig. A2r)

Asserting their allegiance to scripture even in their biblical language, Jonathan
Mitchell and his colleagues emphasized their allegiance to earlier principles,
their reliance on the instruction of their predecessors, and the need for practice and study in order to determine and follow God's will.[20]

Throughout the debates on baptism all parties maintained their allegiance
to scripture. In their preface to the *Propositions* advocating the Halfway Covenant, for example, the elders noted that they had reached their conclusions
only "after earnest Supplications for Divine Assistance, having consulted the

holy Scriptures touching the Questions proposed to them" (sig. A2v). They insisted that the standards they upheld for admission to the Lord's Supper were "Scripture qualifications," and presented their propositions justifying the baptism of the children of baptized but unconverted parents as "briefly confirmed from the Scriptures" (sig. A2v, 1). Moreover, they affirmed that scripture was the ultimate authority, and invited their readers to test their conclusions by a scriptural ruler: "To the Law and to the Testimony we do wholly refer our selves, and if anything in the following Conclusion, be indeed found not to speak according thereunto, let it be rejected" (sig. A2v). Indeed, knowing that their position was opposed by many among the laity and by some of their clerical brethren, they anticipated criticism, and relied on Scripture as arbiter, suggesting that their critics "let the Scriptures be Judge between us all" (sig. A2v).

Though the ministers lamented their limitations, they denied that their position reflected a decline in piety: "What is here offered is far from being any declining from former Principles, it is rather a pursuance thereof; for it is all included in, or deducible from what we unanimously professed and owned in the fore-mentioned *Platform of Discipline*, many years since" (sig. A4r). Even this insistence, though, shows marks of the change. Rather than emphasizing the scriptural precedents for their practice, the second generation of ministers looked back to their predecessors, insisting that they were following the models carved out for them by the founding generation. While they certainly saw these models as scriptural models, the emphasis on the Bible's human interpreters was much more pronounced than in earlier documents.

## INTERPRETIVE PRECEDENTS

Perhaps the most obvious indication of the ministers' increasing willingness to rely on human interpretive authority lies in their increased appeal to the texts of their predecessors. While the texts of the early controversies included only occasional and very spare references to earlier authorities such as Luther, Calvin, and Ames, the texts of the Halfway Covenant debates include extensive quotations from texts by ministers of the first generation. In pages and pages of text, participants attempted to validate their views by drawing on the writings of John Cotton, Thomas Hooker, Thomas Shepard, Richard Mather, Samuel Stone, George Phillips, Peter Prudden, Nathaniel Rogers, and others. Representing the majority position at the 1662 synod, Jonathan Mitchell was especially eager to validate his position in terms of the views of "the Lord's Worthies in *New-England*, who are now with God" (sig. A4v).[21] Referring to this earlier period as the time of New England's "first Purity" and "first and best generation," he looked for precedent not in the apostolic primitive church, but in New England's first churches (sig. A4r, A8v).

Reliance on human models must, of course, be constrained by the ultimate authority of the biblical text. Thus Mitchell acknowledged that "in Matters of Religion, not so much what *hath been* held or practised, as what *should be,* and what the Word of God prescribes, ought to be our Enquiry and our Rule" (sig. A4r). Indeed, he marshaled several prooftexts to emphasize this point, including the biblical precedent that the "People in *Nehemiah's* time are commended for doing as *they found written in the Law,* though from *the dayes* of Joshua *the Son* of Nun, *unto that day, the children of Israel had not done so,* Nehm. 8.14,17."[22] Though there was scriptural precedent for appealing to scripture rather than to custom, the impulse to rely on the example of the founders was quite strong, and Mitchell was eager to establish that extending baptism to the grandchildren of full members reflected not only a scriptural position, but also one consistent with the founders' views. He asserted that scripture would take precedence if the founders' practice diverged from it, but denied that this was the case: "Yet this must not be granted, the contrary being the Truth, *viz.* that the Points herein which may be most scrupled by some, are known to have been the Judgement of the generality of the Elders of these Churches for many years, and of those that have been of most eminent esteem among us" (sig. A4v). In order to demonstrate "the Judgement of the generality of the Elders," Mitchell offered lengthy documentation drawn from the writings of first generation divines. In keeping with what Sargent Bush Jr. has called "the growing acknowledgment of the power of print," Mitchell cited many texts by page number, including Cotton's *Grounds and Ends of the Baptisme of the Children of the Faithful, Of the Holinesse of Church-members,* and *The Bloudy Tenent, Washed, and Made White in the Bloud of the Lambe,* Thomas Hooker's *Survey of the Summe of Church-discipline,* the Cambridge Platform, Phillips's *Reply to a Confutation of Some Grounds for Infants Baptisme,* Shepard's *The Church-membership of Children, and Their Right to Baptisme,* as well as writings of Prudden and Rogers (sig. A4v–A8v).[23]

Despite this ample documentation, Mitchell noted that "in the beginning of these Plantations, and the Infancy of these Churches, there was not so much said touching these things, as there hath been since," but clarified that this was not due to disagreement on fundamental principles (sig. A7r). Rather, "the reason is, Because then there was not the like occasion as since hath been: Few Children of Church-members being then adult, at least few that were then married" (sig. A7r). Nevertheless, "many of the Elders in these Churches, both such as are now living, and sundry who are now deceased, did declare their Judgments as aforesaid, and this many years ago" (sig. A7r).

Mitchell insisted that the relative infrequency of references to this issue in early New England texts reflected the different demographics of the first generation. Because the first generation did not confront the problems faced by their descendants, they did not write extensively about enlarging baptism. Mitchell was nevertheless eager to claim them as supporters, appropriating for his view their interpretive authority as well as the precedent of their New England practices.

Those who opposed the conclusions of the synod also complicated scriptural authority with increased reliance on human interpreters. Like their opponents, they appealed to the biblical text, asserting that the synod advocated an unscriptural innovation. Charles Chauncy presented this position in the *Anti-Synodalia Scripta Americana*, offering a close reading of Christ's institution of baptism, and emphasizing the importance of divine rather than human institution:

> 3. The things practised must be things commanded. 4. Not only some things commanded must be practised, but all things whatsoever. 5. And especially, let the two Pronounes be remembred [*I* and *You*] *I have commanded you;* that is, Christ himself commanded the Apostles, *viz.* for the Churches to the end of the world. These Pronounes are exclusive, first of mens traditions and inventions, and all will-worship: Secondly, of *Mosaical* rites and manners of Administrations in Gospel-times.[24]

God had ordained baptism, "Having left nothing to the prudence of man, or the Pædagogy of *Mosaical* Administrations" (14). Suggesting that their opponents were overstepping human authority and confusing themselves with Christ, they argued that baptism had been established by Christ on a "Congregational" model, in which only members of the congregation should be allowed to have their children baptized (14).

Chauncy and his colleagues objected to their opponents' reliance on local precedent, insisting instead on a return to apostolic models:

> That the shortest and surest way, by the consent of all Divines, to end all controversies, especially about the Worship of God, and the manner of it, is to find out how it was from the beginning, and at the first institution of it: as Christ told the *Jewes* about Marriage, *Math.* 19.8. So we are to doe by considering the first institution of Baptisme by Christ, and by his Apostles, according to his command: If we can find sufficient footing here, then we have found enough for our Consciences to rest in, for nothing can be like this, or added unto this. (14)

They objected strenuously to the proposition that the *"customes of the Churches should be observed,"* noting that the churches' current practice did not necessarily reflect apostolic purity, and that "Custome swerving from Institution, is but *vetustas erroris;* the elder an error or sin is, the worse it is, and more displeasing unto God, as it appears, *Ezek.* 23. 43 and *Ezek.* 25. 15" (17). They cited scriptures in support not only of their position itself, but also in support of their reluctance to rely on precedent. And they emphasized their reliance on divine rather than human authority, "Because every Christian is forbidden to take up Religion, or any way of worship upon trust from man, *Mar.* 7. 7. Yea we are commanded to try all things, and hold fast to that which is good, so that we may abstain from all appearance of evil, 1 *Thes.* 5. 21. 22" (10). "All things" should be tried by a scriptural standard, rather than on the basis of local custom or the interpretive authority of others.

But for those opposed to the synod's conclusions, the rejection of human interpreters was qualified. As they drew their argument to a close, they asserted once again their objection to reliance on human authority: "We might easily abound in alledging other Scriptures and Presidents and testimonies of most approved Divines consonant to this; but this would be, but casting drops into the Sea: Christ saith, *John* 5. 34. *I receive not testimony from man;* This truth and doctrine needs no mans testimony for the confirmation of it, being sufficiently confirmed by his own authority" (18). Here, even as they denied a need for interpretive precedent, they made claims on such precedent, asserting that "other Scriptures and Presidents and testimonies of most approved Divines" "abound[ed]" (18). Moreover, in alleging that the propositions of their opponents lacked scriptural validation, they appealed to earlier texts to support their view. For example, they cited Richard Mather's *Church-Government and Church-Covenant Discussed,* noting that Mather had deemed the new practice unscriptural (4). Similarly, they noted that Thomas Hooker had rejected some of the scriptural grounds cited by their proponents: *"Mr. Hooker* in his survey rejects this place as impertinent to the case in hand, and he alledgeth for his Judgement, *Calvin, Zancy, Junius,* and *Perkins"* (21–22). Their subject remained the scriptural validity of their opponents' claims, but they bolstered their argument by citing not only the first generation ministers, but also major figures of the continental and English Reformations.

Based on such texts, Chauncy and his colleagues asserted that while local precedent would not justify an unscriptural practice, nevertheless local precedent was on their side: "By these and other Testimonies it may appear, that what the Dissenters hold and defend, is the old-way of *New-England,* and what is now pleaded for, and to be introduced, is an innovation" (5). The proposals of the synod were not only unscriptural, but they were also a violation

of the "old-way of *New-England*" (5). And the dissenters affirmed allegiance
to that old—and scriptural—way: "That our selves (and many more of our
brethren in our respective Churches) do account our selves bound by Covenant
and the Oath of God (as that which is the revealed will of God) unto that order, and dispensation of the worship of God (as far as it may be, and we have
light) that hath hitherto been received, and peaceably practised in our churches
above 30 yeares" (10). They celebrated the happy results of that allegiance—
that for those thirty years, "the Lord hath so blessed both our Common-wealth
and Churches, that Jesus Christ did shew himselfe wonderfull amongst us, as
was well held forth openly at *Boston* by many instances of great deliverances
and wonders that the Lord hath wrought in former times for *N. E.*"—and
warned darkly that the "new light" in which their opponents were "glorying" would "prove but glorying in our shame" (10). In addition to citing New
England's long-standing practice, the dissenters tempered their reliance on
scriptural justification by invoking human authority, for example closing
their interpretation of a scriptural passage with the words "and so it is usually expounded by the Learned" (15).

Chauncy's appeals to learning were complex, however, for he appealed to
the authority of expertise and learning, even as he emphasized that learning
itself did not guarantee interpretive authority. For example, he quoted with
approval the Latin of "learned Drusius":

> learned *Drusius* did say well, that, *Laicus cum Scriptura loquens contra to-
> tam Synodum audiendus*, i.e. a mean Lay-man speaking with the Scripture
> is to be heard, though a whole Synod of learned men were against him;
> much more many of Gods faithfull and conscientious people and Ministers,
> having both Christs and his Apostles authoritative institution of the proper
> subjects of Baptism, they should be heard, and their assertions or testi-
> monies not stifled or smothered, though all the Oecumenical Counsels were
> opposite unto them; yea, though an Angel from Heaven should teach other-
> wise; although we will not dare to say, let him be *Anathema*, yet we will say,
> let not his doctrine be received. (15)

Here, Chauncy held the "mean" laity's scripture reading above "a whole
Synod of learned men" (15). At the same time, he carefully contained this
claim, deliberately opposing the "Lay-man speaking with the Scripture" to
revelations of heavenly angels (15). He was not upholding the unlimited authority of the laity; rather, he was holding scripture above clergy. Moreover,
the reference to "learned *Drusius*" itself qualified his claim, resting it upon
the authority of men of learning. On the whole, however, dissenters from the
Halfway Covenant treated scriptural authority in more traditional ways than

did their opponents, emphasizing scripture over its interpreters, as they might very well be expected to do given their opposition to what they saw as unscriptural innovation.

In the aftermath of the controversy, Increase Mather's treatment of the Halfway Covenant focused even more sharply on the founders' views. Titling his text *The First Principles of New-England, Concerning the Subject of Baptisme & Communion of Churches,* Mather took pains "to shew that such *Inlargement of Baptisme,* and that *Consociation of Churches,* which is in the Synod Book asserted is no Apostacy from the first Principles of *New-England,* nor yet any declension from the *Congregational way.*"[25] To show "that *the first Fathers* of this Country were for that *Enlargement of Baptisme,* which the late Synod Book pleads for, And that therefore *such a practice is no apostacy from our Primitive Principles,*" Mather produced extensive and elaborate quotations from multiple texts by the various divines of the first generation (24). He cited early texts by John Cotton, including page references where he could. He drew as well on manuscript texts, including a 1634 letter, as evidence of this view from "Primitive Times of these Churches" (2–4).

Resting on fallible human authority, even of so eminent a divine, posed challenges, however. Both the majority and the dissenters in the Synod of 1662 claimed that the founders shared their views, and such claims were buttressed by the reversals that some of the community's leaders had made in their positions. Increase Mather himself had opposed the expansion of baptism until his father's death in 1669. Shortly thereafter he reversed his thinking to become an ardent advocate of the Halfway Covenant.[26] Drawing on a textual record that betrayed such shifts of opinion, Mather attended to its implications by representing advocates on both sides quoting Cotton's texts back and forth. He imagined, for example, that "against [one of his claims] some may object a passage in Mr. *Cottons Book of the Way of the Churches, pag. 81,*" and responded to this argument by noting that other passages in Cotton's text supported the Halfway Synod's conclusions (6–7). He also raised questions about the authority of the book itself, objecting that "That Book of the way was printed from an *imperfect Copy,* in which respect it is not to be wondered at, if there be therein some passages *contradictory* to Mr. *Cottons known Iudgement.*"[27] As a result, Mather suggested, it was difficult to determine Cotton's intent from the text; indeed, he reported, for this reason "Mr. Co[t]ton himself was much troubled when he saw that Book come forth, and was desirous that the Reader should understand that his Judgement in such things, wherein the *Book of the way* is *discrepant* from that of the *Keyes,* should be sought for, not in the *Book of the Way,* but in that of the *Keys*" (7). So important was this point to Mather that he quoted Cotton's later printed qualms about the text (7). In contrast, Mather cited as more authoritative accounts "extant, under Mr. *Cottons* own hand writing" (6). Nor was Cotton the only divine to receive this detailed reading. Mather devoted similarly close attention to the writings of Thomas Hooker, Samuel Stone, Richard Mather, Thomas Shepard, John Norton, and others, in cases of conflict privileging handwritten accounts as reflecting the divines' genuine opinions. Mather's emphasis on human authority was thus quite extensive and elaborate, marking the ministers' greater reliance on human interpretation.

## "A MEAN LAY-MAN SPEAKING WITH THE SCRIPTURE"

Increasingly articulating their reliance on human interpretive authority, New England ministers emphasized interpretive skill and expertise as grounds for that authority. In his treatise on baptism, Cotton had suggested that lay opponents of infant baptism lacked the sophisticated skills of exegesis necessary for a proper understanding of the biblical text. In the documents of the Halfway Controversy, participants took this complaint even further, retreating from earlier claims about biblical accessibility and instead asserting the necessity for skill and expertise. While the ministers who participated in the controversy left considerable power in the hands of the laity, they nevertheless questioned the laity's ability to understand the situation properly.[28] In his opposition to the principles of the 1662 synod, Chauncy asked why so few of the lay representatives had dissented from the synod's proposals. His answer was that the lay representatives had been bamboozled. First, their ministers' preaching had influenced their opinions: "divers of the Elders preached and practiced, some time before this new Doctrine of late years, who were Members of the Synode" (*Anti-Synodalia*, 5). The clergy had begun to persuade their congregants in advance of the synod, Chauncy argued. Moreover, these efforts at persuasion worked because the laity lacked the the skills of exegesis and logic: "diverse of the Messengers being no Logitians, and so unable to answer Syllogismes, and discern Ambiguities, were over-born by the many opposers. The corruption of man most inclines to walk in the broadest way, though the straight way may be never so clear unto him, and to affect the stronger side, especially when persons that are eminent in place and power, and learning and piety are so linked together; we are ready (as *James* saith) to have the faith of Christ and every truth of Christ in respect to persons" (5). Untrained in logic and thus unable to deal with the biblical text's ambiguities, the lay representatives were unable to recognize the flawed arguments "which if they were all formed into Syllogismes, would appear ridiculous among young Scholars in Universities" (6). Lacking the skills of even beginning students, the laity had instead gone along with "the stronger side" (5). In response, Chauncy explained, he had revised the text that the dissenting ministers had presented to the General Court to make it appropriate to ordinary lay readers, "to many meaner persons and capacities which need to have all things with all possible plainnesse represented unto them" (12). Faced with a laity who had been misled by confusing academic rhetoric, Chauncy set out to explain it to them, but at the same time reminded them of their limitations and of their dependence on his interpretive powers.

Other participants shared Chauncy's awareness of the gap between lay and clerical reading. In his account of the controversy, Increase Mather suggested that "For the most part, when *godly, learned men miss of the Truth*, it is in points which either they have not at all, or not *thoroughly* and *Impartially* studied, when as the *Leaders* in the *Synod mentioned*, had most *industriously*, and not without *prayers* and *Tears* laboured to know the will of the Lord, concerning the Affairs of his *house*, and *Kingdome*."[29] In Mather's view, learning was necessary, and even the learned might "miss of the truth" by failing to study thoroughly. Carefully qualifying Reformed emphasis on scriptural accessibility, Mather joined many of his colleagues in emphasizing that proper Bible reading required not only scriptural gifts, but discipline and learning as well.

Moreover, while the ministers left a good deal of power in the hands of the laity, they did suggest that the laity defer to them in interpretive issues. In the *Propositions*, for example, Mitchell exhorted younger members of the congregation to defer to their elders, emphasizing the institutional authority of the church elders: "*Ye younger, submit your selves unto the elder;* and to that end, *be clothed with humility.* Lye under the Word and Will of Christ, as dispensed and conveyed to you by all his appointed Instruments in their respective places" (sig. A8r). He cautioned the youth, "whose Interest" was perhaps most directly involved in the provisions of the Halfway Covenant, not to respond to its inclusiveness inappropriately: they must "Break not in upon the Lord's Table (or upon the Priviledges of full Communion)" (sig. A8r). Moreover, Mitchell emphasized the need for education and for the development of interpretive skills, admonishing the youth to "Be ordered, and take not upon [themselves] to order the affairs of Gods Family," which is "not the place of those who are yet but in the state of Initiation and Education in the Church of God" (sig. A8r). Determining the dictates of scripture demanded education, and at this point the ministers were willing to assert this demand.

Thus ministers on both sides of the debate were attentive to lay responses, eager to win the support of the laity while at the same time doubtful of the laity's interpretive skills. Meanwhile, many lay members of the churches, like Cotton's Silvester, remained skeptical, testing the Halfway Covenant by scriptural standards and finding it to be an unscriptural innovation.

## NORMALIZING DISSENT

Ministerial responses to churches divided over the Halfway Covenant marked the change that had occurred. When Anne Hutchinson and her allies had questioned their ministers' scriptural grounds, the clergy and magistrates had responded harshly. But during the controversy over the Halfway Covenant, the community responded to dissent in a dramatically different fashion, accepting and even institutionalizing dissent as a temporary (if long-term) and tolerable state of affairs. The documents of this controversy show both an increased tolerance for dissent and a heightened awareness that consensus would be elusive. Combatants on both sides of the debate demonstrated a willingness to tolerate a draw, or at least to acknowledge the sincerity of their opponents.

On the winning side, Mitchell and his colleagues acknowledged the diversity of opinion on the question of extending baptism. "We are not ignorant," Mitchell explained, "of variety of Judgments concerning this Subject; which notwithstanding, with all due reverence to Dissenters, after Religious search of the Scriptures, we have here offered what seems to us to have the fullest Evidence of Light from thence" (*Propositions*, sig. A3v). He believed the majority position to "have the fullest Evidence" of scriptural support, but he remained open to further proofs: "if more may be added, and may be found contained in the Word of God, this shall be no prejudice thereunto" (sig. A3v). Moreover, Mitchell asserted his willingness to accept not only further evidence, but also dissent on this question: "Hence also we are far from desiring that there should be any rigorous imposition of these things (especially as to what is more narrow therein, and more controversal [sic] among godly men)" (sig. A3v).

Mitchell's defense of this position suggests his awareness that it marked a departure for his community. He acknowledged that "To tolerate, or to desire a Toleration of damnable Heresies, or of Subverters of the Fundamentals of Faith or Order, were an irreligious inconsistency with the love of true Religion," maintaining his opposition to toleration as a general principle (sig. A3v–A4r). But within certain narrow parameters, he was now prepared to permit a range of opinions and practices: "But to bear one with another in lesser differences, about matters of a more difficult and controversal [sic] nature, and more remote from the Foundation, and wherein the godly-wise are not like-minded, is a Duty necessary to the peace and welfare of Religion, while we are in the state of Infirmity" (sig. A4r). In some matters that were "difficult," "controversal," and "remote from the Foundation," it was possible that "the state of Infirmity" that beset the earthly church would lead the "godly-wise" to disagree. In such cases, it was not only permissible, but even "a Duty necessary to the peace and welfare of Religion" to "bear one with another" (sig. A4r). Indeed, one must treat his opponents not only with tolerance, but with the respect due to the godly: "In such things let not him that practiseth, *dispise him* that forbeareth; and let not him that forbeareth, *judge him* that practiseth, *for God hath received him*" (sig. A4r). Once again, Mitchell drew on scriptural authority for his position, invoking the language of Romans in his call for toleration.[30] The extensive justification here betrayed some discomfort with this position, or at the very least a need to explain why toleration could now be not only acceptable, but even necessary.[31]

Moreover, Mitchell asserted in the *Propositions* that willingness to tolerate dissent did not imply doubt about the truth: "But as we do not thus speak from doubting of the Truth here delivered (*Paul knows* where the Truth lies, and *is perswaded of it*, Rom. 14.14. yet he can lovingly bear a Dissenter, and in like manner should we). So we do in the bowels of Christ Jesus commend the consideration of these things unto our Brethren in the several Churches" (sig. A4r). Mitchell found biblical justification for the ministers' tolerant position in Paul's tolerance. And just as Paul's toleration did not imply uncertainty about God's will, Mitchell asserted that willingness to tolerate dissent over the Halfway Covenant recognized the *dissenters'* difficulty recognizing truth, and not his own.[32]

The dissenters as well acknowledged that opinions about the extension of baptism were varied. The *Anti-Synodalia*, asserted Chauncy, grew out of the difficulty of identifying who was "appointed by God in holy Scripture to receive" baptism, "that hath been thought difficult to find, and hath cost much labour and dispute to many Divines, and they have still different apprehensions about it; that is here enquired after" (13). Chauncy did not advocate public dissent lightly. Even as he dissented from the majority of his brethren, Chauncy expressed concern about potential disrespect for learned authority. He noted that some might object to publication of the dissent because of concern that "the publishing of these things will trouble the peace of the Churches; they are the troublers of *Israel*, that raise Objections, and hold forth their private Judgments against so many learned men" (3). In response to such concerns, he opened his preface with cautions to dissenters, drawn from the writings of Jeremiah Burroughs: "He that differs in Judgement from wise, learned, and Godly men; 1. Had need to spend much time in prayer and humiliation before the Lord: 2. Preserve due reverence in his heart, and shew due respect to them according to their worth: 3. In all things wherein he can agree, he should be more carefull to manifest all possible observance and respect unto them: 4. In what still his conscience will not suffer him to agree with them, to take it as an affliction to him" (8). But having considered carefully, with "prayers and tears, and much affliction of spirit, and conflicts with sad temptations about it," as well as efforts to preserve "Reverend thoughts, affections and respects in [their] hearts" toward their opponents, Chauncy explained, he and his colleagues felt compelled to present their views (8).

Having prefaced his argument with these caveats, Chauncy expressed optimism that dissent might well prove productive, and might even help to lead his opponents to truth: "Although differences be sad, yet the truth that comes to light by them, may recompence the sadness" (3). Indeed, he suggested, difficulties and differences inhered in the interpretive process: "You cannot beat out a place for a window to let in light, but you must endure some trouble" (3). And though this might be alarming along the way, the results would justify the difficulty: "Children will think the house is pulling down, but the father knows the benefit that will come by it; there will be rubbish and dust raised by this means (as in sweeping houses) but the light that is let in, will easily remove it: So in this controversie" (3). Chauncy asserted that, appearances to the contrary, New England was not being pulled down by this division; when the dust settled, it would be evident that the controversy brought the community clearer access to the light of truth.

The publication of the *Anti-Synodalia* itself indicated a fundamental change in the treatment of dissent in Massachusetts Bay. Both Michael Warner and Grantland S. Rice describe the restricted nature of print culture in early New England. Warner emphasizes the normative function of printed texts in this period, and their role in what he calls "sacred internalization."[33] Rice, however, rejects Warner's account as "a flattened, apolitical conception of writing in seventeenth-century America," and suggests instead that there was a "viable civic print culture in seventeenth-century New England."[34] He concedes "the New England theocracy's effectiveness in suppressing printed commentary within the colonies, an activity which again and again reemphasized the political nature of public writing" (24–25). He emphasizes, however, "the concurrent lapse of censorship enforcement in England," which afforded various dissenters from Roger Williams onward venues for wide publication of their views (24–25).

In the controversy over the Halfway Covenant, however, dissenters were not forced to such lengths to publish their objections. Instead, the General Court permitted the publication of dissenting opinions, leading to what Robert Pope calls "the most controversial series of pamphlets published in New England."[35] He argues that the court's decision to allow publication of dissenting views caused these views to circulate more widely than they would have otherwise, thus "undermin[ing] the 'official' status of the synodical decision and encourag[ing] laymen to resist introduction of the half-way covenant" (55–56). Pope adds that the court's decision to give "its imprimatur in fact, if not in spirit, to the publication of conclusions diametrically opposed to the propositions of the synod . . . probably reflected the ambivalence felt

by many of the deputies toward the recommended innovation" (56).[36] Despite the large majority which had supported the synod's conclusion, "the
members discovered that they faced a renewed attack from an articulate minority which commanded respect in the colony" (56). In some cases, the texts
opposing the synod's conclusions were published with the texts articulating
those conclusions. The title page of one 1662 edition of the *Propositions* indicates that the edition was ordered printed by the General Court, yet it is
printed with the *Anti-Synodalia* "anext" to it, producing a text that testifies
to a new toleration of dissent by its very physical composition.

Moreover, Cooper notes that because individual churches had to consent
to the synod's recommendations before they would be implemented, "opponents directed their tracts on the Half-way Covenant squarely at ordinary
churchgoers," who were left with considerable power over the covenant's
implementation.[37] Though ministers in each church presented their views
to the congregation, the members of the congregation had to ratify the covenant themselves. Faced with conflicting ministerial opinions, some congregants were not easily persuaded. Because churches still sought unanimity on
procedural matters in the 1660s, dissent sometimes delayed or even prevented
adoption of the new procedures even when a majority favored them.[38] In the
First Church of Boston, the aftermath of the synod produced what no previous controversy had: a separation of the church not only into two factions, but
into two churches.[39] By this point, of course, the rhetoric of tolerance had sub-
sided. But the division of power was no longer clear; in earlier controversies,
one faction had ended up controlling the church, while the other was exiled or
excommunicated. In this controversy, the formation of a second church looked
more like a draw, and it constituted recognition that this difference of opinion
would not be resolved in the immediate future. Moreover, as Cooper has
demonstrated, even in the wake of this division, Massachusetts churches affirmed and protected the rights of dissenters within congregations.[40]

In nearby Connecticut, where debate about baptism and church membership raged as well, this crisis resulted in a very pointed institutionalization of
dissent as the status quo.[41] Finding its churches divided, the colony's General
Court in 1664 sought to resolve the conflict by proposing that churches extend church membership to "all children of the church," and that those children "be accepted and acco[un]td reall members."[42] The court even considered
imposing this as a requirement on the churches.[43] It also invited ministers
who opposed the changes to present their views, however, and apparently
those ministers were persuasive, for the court did not pursue its proposals.[44]
But as debates in Connecticut's churches grew increasingly heated, the court
once more intervened, calling for a synod, ordering "every settled minister
in the colony to attend," and inviting four ministers from Massachusetts as

well.[45] The synod convened in May of 1667, but it accomplished almost nothing: in Pope's words, "the meeting was extraordinarily short and it adjourned until the following October without considering a single question."[46] The synod never reconvened.[47]

Instead, the court appointed James Fitch, Gershom Bulkeley, Joseph Elliott, and Samuel Wakeman to meet at Saybrook on June 8, 1668, "to consider of some expedient for our peace, by searching out the rule and thereby cleareing up how farre the churches and people may walke together within themselues and one w[th] another in fellowship and order of the Gospel, not withstanding some various apprehension amonge them in matters of discipline respecting membership and baptisme &c."[48] Nearly a year later, they submitted their recommendations to the court, which in May 1669 announced that "hauing seriously considered the great divisions that arise amongst us about matters of Church Gouernment, for the honor of God, welfare of the churches, and preseruation of the publique peace so greatly hazarded," they could "do no less than . . . approue and countenance" multiple approaches "untill better light in an orderly way doth appeare."[49] Like its Massachusetts neighbor, the court asserted that this was not a fundamental matter, and therefore that while enlarged baptism had been approved by "the Congregationall Churches in these partes for the generall of their profession and practice," "forasmuch as sundry persons of worth for prudence and piety amongst us are otherwise perswaded (whose welfare and peaceable satisfaction we desire to accommodate,) This court doth declare that all such persons being so approved according to lawe as orthodox and sownd in the fundamentalls of Christian religion may have allowance of their perswasion and profession in church wayes or assemblies w[th]out disturbance."[50] Pope characterizes this decision as "revolutionary," noting that

> For more than a generation the *principle* of uniformity had remained sacrosanct in the holy commonwealths, despite the differences in polity that had always existed. Now the Connecticut General Court admitted that the word of God was not yet clear enough on these issues for the state to promulgate and enforce a single "truth." Although it still considered uniformity a desideratum, Connecticut would recognize diversity and tolerate minority views "untill better light in an orderly way doth appeare." Forty years later in the Saybrook Platform the colony thought it had "better light." (94–95)

By 1690, three-quarters of the churches in Massachusetts Bay were following the Halfway Covenant.[51] Although both communities ultimately moved toward general acceptance of these provisions, the debate around the Synod of 1662 itself revealed the extent to which interpretive assumptions had shifted.

Though members of the Massachusetts and Connecticut churches accepted the inevitability of dissent on this issue, many did not generalize from this case to advocate broader practices of religious toleration. In fact, as Stephen Foster explains, divisions that emerged in the course of debate over the Halfway Covenant persisted in later debate about the relationship between the colony and England and about treatment of Baptists, with opponents of the Halfway Covenant tending to oppose accommodation with England and favor toleration of Baptists.[52] Others resisted toleration nearly as forcefully as Nathaniel Ward had in 1645, when he insisted "that God doth nowhere in his word tolerate Christian States, to give Tolerations to such adversaries of His Truth, if they have power in their hands to suppress them."[53] Though they remained unwilling to tolerate dissent generally, however, many participants in the Halfway Controversy acknowledged that this was a case not of dire heresies, but of "lesser differences," and, moreover, many participants perceived dissent as temporary. In each example cited above, those who announced their tolerance also announced their expectation that "truth" would emerge or that "better light" would appear. But these expectations deferred the illumination of the Spirit that they had expected to aid them in interpreting God's will for their community. Determining God's ways was proving a much more complex process than the founders had imagined.

## REAFFIRMING ALLEGIANCE TO SCRIPTURE

This does not mean, however, that earlier models of reading, exegesis, and preaching were abandoned. In their 1680 *Confession of Faith*, the elders and messengers of the Massachusetts Bay churches affirmed once more their allegiance to the biblical text.[54] Drawing on the 1658 *Savoy Declaration* and in turn on the *Westminster Confession* of 1646, choosing "to express [them] selves in the words of those Reverend Assemblyes, that so [they] might not only with one heart, but with one mouth glorifie God," the 1680 synod devoted the first chapter of its *Confession* to a consideration "Of the holy Scripture" (sig. A4v, 1). They asserted that God had chosen to reveal his will to the church through scripture, and that "The Authority of the holy Scripture . . . dependeth not upon the Testimony of any man or Church, but wholly upon God (who is Truth it self) the Author thereof; and therefore it is to be received, because it is the Word of God" (1, 3). They praised the biblical text for "the heavenliness of the Matter, the efficacy of the Doctrine, the majesty of the Style, the consent of all parts, the scope of the whole (which is, to give all glory to God) the full discovery of it makes of the only way of mans Salvation, the many other incomparable excellencies, and the intire perfection thereof," all of which they cited as "Arguments whereby it doth abundantly evidence it self to be the word of God" (4). At the same time, they affirmed the role of the Holy Spirit in the reading process, noting that "notwithstanding [the merits of the text], our full perswasion and assurance of the infallible Truth and Divine Authority thereof, is from the inward work of the holy Spirit, bearing witness by and with the Word in our hearts" (4).

Carefully qualifying the "inward work of the holy Spirit," the ministers noted that "The whole Counsel of God concerning all things necessary for his own Glory, Mans Salvation, Faith and Life, is either expressly set down in Scripture, or by good and necessary consequence may be deduced from Scripture; unto which nothing at any time is to be added, whether by new Revelations of the Spirit, or Traditions of men" (4). Increased caution about revelations of the Holy Spirit is one of the few differences among nearly identical discussions of the Scriptures in the three texts. Where the *Westminster Confession* asserts that the "Supreme Judge by which all Controversies of Religion are to be determined, and all Decrees of Councels, Opinions of Ancient Writers, Doctrines of men, and private spirits, are to be examined; and, in whose Sentence we are to rest, can be no other but the Holy Spirit speaking in the Scripture," both the *Savoy Declaration* and the 1680 *Confession of Faith* back away from the reference to "the Holy Spirit speaking in the Scripture."[55] Perhaps reluctant to encourage "revelations" like those of John Underhill and Anne Hutchinson, the ministers instead emphasized the scripture itself over the Holy Spirit's speech, closing the paragraph by asserting that the "Supream Judge . . . in whose Sentence we are to rest, can be no other, but the holy Scripture delivered by the Spirit; into which Scripture so delivered, our Faith is finally resolved."[56] They left room for no confusion: the Spirit delivers "the holy Scripture," and not any "new Revelations" (6, 4). Though they rejected "new Revelations of the Spirit," the synod's participants "nevertheless . . . acknowledge[d] the inward illumination of the Spirit of God to be necessary for the saving understanding of such things as are revealed in the Word" (4).

Beyond the assistance of the Spirit, the ministers of Massachusetts Bay noted as well "that there are some circumstances concerning the Worship of God and Government of the Church, common to humane actions and Societies, which are to be ordered by the Light of Nature, and Christian Prudence, according to the general Rules of the Word, which are always to be observed" (4–5). In admitting the need for interpretation by deduction and in accordance with "the Light of Nature, and Christian Prudence," the ministers acknowledged as well that "All things in Scripture are not alike plain in themselves, nor alike clear unto all" (5). They insisted once more on the accessibility of "those things which are necessary to be known, believed and observed for salvation," which they found "so clearly propounded and opened in some place of Scripture or other, that not only the learned, but the unlearned, in a due use of the ordinary means, may attain unto a sufficient understanding of them" (5). Nevertheless, they suggested that interpretive expertise might be necessary for some finer points, allowing for the emphasis on training and skill that emerged in the debates over the Halfway Covenant.

Heightened emphasis on the minister's interpretive artistry, however, did not reflect an abandonment of the ideal of the minister as prophet. Even as the seventeenth century drew to a close, ministers articulated their sense that the minister should remain transparent in his preaching. Nehemiah Walter, for example, exhorted his congregation to hear Christ in their ministers' words: "Remember then, when Christ's Ministers speak to you in the Discharge of their Office, tis as *if Christ Himself spake unto you; they represent him in his Prophetical Office;* the Words which they speak according to the mind and will of Christ, are not the words of man, but indeed the words of God."[57] Even as Walter exhorted his congregants to hear Christ, however, he emphasized the minister's office. While Thomas Shepard, in *Of Ineffectual Hearing the Word,* had downplayed the preacher's role, treating the minister as ideally transparent to the voice of Christ, Walter instead devoted attention to the minister's "Prophetical Office." It was to be hoped that the minister would be a prophet, and the congregation would hear Christ's voice, and not the minister's. But later generations of New England's ministers were increasingly willing to proclaim that achieving that kind of prophecy demanded "humane skill" as well as divine assistance.

It would be tempting to close by lamenting the decline of a pure ideal of reading in the Spirit. But I do not mean to join the tradition of Puritanists who, in Emory Elliott's words, suggest that "the questing spirit of the Puritans [ended] with the passing of the founders, the errand unfulfilled, the original idea of purity and perfection unachieved."[58] Certainly, some of the New England readers described above deplored the failure of their interpretive community to meet their expectations. Having envisioned a reading process in which a community of saints reading in the Spirit shared an interpretive consensus, they discovered to their dismay that they were often a divided community of readers. Where they had expected unity, they found instead debate and discord, not only over the content of the biblical text, but even over how it should be read.

Although their disappointment may be poignant, the persistence of their ideal is just as compelling. As the ministers preached the biblical text to their congregants, they wrestled with the complexities of Reformed exegesis and sermon theory, adapting the prescriptions of the previous generation to their own understandings of the relationship between the text and its readers.

Throughout, they maintained the fluidity and flexibility of the text. They did so even when the theoretical formulations that they held dear faced serious practical challenges. Even as Roger Williams asserted the inevitability of misinterpretation, New England's ministers clung to their belief that the text could be understood. Even as they excommunicated Anne Hutchinson, they urged the women of the Boston church to evaluate what they had heard and hold it to a scriptural standard, rather than simply deferring to their ministers. And even as they lamented the role of unskilled lay readers in the debate over the Halfway Covenant, they upheld the prerogative of those unskilled lay readers to shape church polity.

Through all these challenges, New England's early literary theorists clung to their sense of a Bible open to its readers. They revised and reformulated their understanding of the interactions among text, reader, author, and interpreter, reluctantly conceding a need for increased human interpretive authority in the communal reading process. Yet the ministers who claimed increasing authority for their own interpretations did so in limited and subtle ways, resting their interpretive authority on their skill and training, rather than on ministerial privilege or formal institutional control. If New England's literary theorists elevated the status of reading experts, they nevertheless upheld the importance of lay reading and interpretation. Though it proved a source of conflict and struggle, they resisted the impulse to trade the open text for a closed book.

# The Problem of the Texts

In much of the above discussion, I have bracketed the problems posed by the way in which Puritan sermons were preserved and published. Sermons began, of course, as oral texts and became printed books in a variety of ways, sometimes with the minister/author's ongoing supervision and sometimes almost entirely independent of the minister. As a result, these texts vary in the accuracy with which they reproduce the minister's actual sermons, and modern readers can make only educated guesses at which texts best reflect the sermons as preached.

Puritan ministers rarely read their sermons from full manuscripts, as this practice was frowned upon both by preaching manuals and by Puritan audiences.[1] The ministers themselves agreed; in John Cotton's words, "the reading of a mans owne Sermon in stead of preaching will much detract from the life and power of it, and make a man of God unserviceable to his place."[2] While some Puritan ministers wrote out their sermons in advance and then memorized them, most made notes only, and then either memorized their notes or preached from them.[3] Printed versions of sermons were usually prepared from notes, whether those of the minister or those of a listener.[4] Sometimes the minister revised or corrected the edition produced from these notes, and occasionally the printed text was prepared from a manuscript written out before or after the sermon by the minister himself.[5]

But ministers who had emigrated to Holland or New England could not easily correct texts that were being published in London, and texts published in Cambridge and Boston were often published posthumously.[6] Even those texts that ministers corrected for publication sometimes bear far from straightforward relationships with the original preached sermons. Cotton's earliest extant American sermon series, for example, was published three times, under three different titles.[7] In 1654 *The New Covenant* was published, "with Cotton's consent [and] after he had read and corrected it."[8] The 1659 edition, entitled *A Treatise of the New Covenant*, was also corrected by Cotton, but is "a third longer than the first edition."[9] Is the "best" text the one that most closely approximates the sermon as preached, then, or is it the one that most accords with Cotton's final (and perhaps thus most perfect) articulation of his thought on the covenant? Such problems were sometimes aggravated by the ministers' ambivalence about publishing sermons in the first place. Cotton, for example, stressed the preached word over the read word, noting the limited efficacy of the latter: "little hath been done by the Writings of godly men, against the adversaries in this kinde."[10]

The difficulties involved in the texts of Thomas Hooker's ministry are illustrative. The status of the various texts is both complicated and illuminated by the fact that Hooker preached sermons covering the sequence of stages in the regenerative process at least three times in the course of his career.[11] Consequently, scholars can compare various published texts that are revisions of other published texts. Published texts based on sermons delivered earlier in Hooker's career include *The Poor Doubting Christian, The Unbelievers Preparing for Christ, The Sovles Preparation, The Souls Humiliation, The Souls Ingrafting, The Souls Implantation* (later revised as *The Souls Implantation into the Natural Olive*), *The Souls Effectual Calling,* and *The Souls Exaltation.*[12] These sermons seem to have been delivered before Hooker's departure from England, and were responsible for his popularity at Chelmsford.[13]

Late in his career, Hooker revised this sequence of sermon series, producing *The Application of Redemption: The first eight Books, The Application of Redemption: Books Nine and Ten,* and *A Comment upon Christs Last Prayer*, which was described as the *"Seventeenth Book made in New-England."*[14] The clear ordering of these texts, as well as the repetition of topics, provides a basis for comparisons of variant readings, including different editions based on the same delivery of a sermon or sermon series, but prepared from notes taken by different listeners.[15] But the situation remains extremely complicated. Sermons in the iteration delivered at Chelmsford were not all published in sequence; nor does a comparison of various editions clearly reveal one to be more useful than another for a scholar interested in Hooker's sermons as preached.

Competition among Hooker's publishers further complicates matters. Thomas Goodwyn and Philip Nye, publishers of *The Application of Redemption*, preface both volumes with the assertion that their text is far superior to earlier Hooker texts then circulating:

> And whereas there hath been published long since, many Parts and Pieces of this Author, upon this Argument, Sermon=wise preach'd by him here in *England* (which in the preaching of them did enlighten all those Parts) Yet having been taken by an unskilful hand, which upon his recess into those remoter parts of the World, was bold without his privity or consent to print and publish them (one of the greatest injuries which can be done to any man) it came to pass his genuine meaning, and this in points of so high a Nature, and in some things differing from the Common Opinion,

was diverted in those printed Sermons from the fair and cleer draught of his own Notions and Intentions, because so utterly deformed and mis=represented in multitudes
of passages; And in the rest but imperfectly and crudely set forth.[16]

Goodwyn and Nye's sense that previous texts of Hooker's sermons are imperfect
seems plausible. When many of these texts were published, Hooker had already left
England, and was a fugitive from the ecclesiastical courts. Consequently, most texts of
*The Sovles Preparation* bear no mention of Hooker's name.[17] It thus seems quite unlikely that extensive communication would have been possible between the publishers and Hooker. The publisher of *The Sovles Preparation* himself acknowledges this
difficulty, apologizing for the inadequacies of the text he presents: "by reason of the
*Authors* absence," he explains, the sermons of the book "are presented to thy view,
both with some lesser escapes, and in more homely terms, than his judicious eye would
have suffered."[18]

But Goodwyn and Nye's assertion that the publishers of the earlier volumes had
published without Hooker's "privity or consent," thus doing him "one of the greatest
injuries which can be done to any man," is somewhat suspect (C3v). Certainly they
had a stake in proclaiming their texts the sole legitimate versions of Hooker's thought.
In Winfried Herget's words, "a certain amount of sales strategy may be involved in
their epistle to the reader" and in their proclamation that

> Here, in these Treatises, thou *hast* his Heart from his *own Hand*, his own Thoughts
> drawn by his own Pensil. *This is all truly and purely his own, not as preached only,*
> but as *written by himself* in order to the Press; which may be a great satisfaction to all
> that honored and loved him (as who that was good, and knew him, did not?) espe-
> cially those that received benefit by those other imperfect Editions.[19]

In fact, Frank Shuffelton suggests that *The Sovles Preparation*, far from being a pi-
rated text, was written out from Hooker's own sermon notes by Hooker himself.[20]

Moreover, Goodwyn and Nye claim that it was previous publication of his sermons
"by others (in that manner that hath been mentioned)" that "provoked [Hooker] . . .
to go over again the same Materials in the Course of his Ministry amongst them, in
order to the perfecting of it by his own hand for publick Light, thereby to vindicate
both himself and it from that wrong which otherwise had remained for ever irrecom-
pensible" (C3v–C4r). This claim is certainly exaggerated. As Cotton Mather relates,
Hooker advised young ministers that they should "preach over the whole *body of divinity* methodically," suggesting that his repetition came not out of frustration with
the printed texts of his sermons, but rather out of a sense of the proper ministerial
role.[21] Goodwyn and Nye note this as well, a bit later in their preface (C4v–D1r). Nevertheless, Herget is willing to credit some of their claim, noting in her essay "The
Transcription and Transmission of the Hooker Corpus" that "later sermons in the *Application* appear to be closer to the conventions of written style than do the earlier sermons based on auditors' notes" (257).

But even if *The Application of Redemption* is based on Hooker's own written-out version of the sermons, and is thus more accurate in some way, this hardly resolves all difficulties. As a written text, it may be closer to accurately conveying Hooker's ideas, but farther from accurately reproducing the sermons as they were delivered to audiences.[22] Nor is it a text completely free of problems. It does include more careful discussion of certain areas in which Hooker might have been open to doctrinal challenge, and these areas deserve some attention. But in other sections, it is remarkably close to the corresponding texts of the earlier sermon series, in content and language as well as in inaccuracies present.

Certain of these inaccuracies are likely to be editorial rather than authorial. All of the texts contain numerous instances in which a biblical citation given marginally is incorrect. Sometimes these miscitations are easily understandable—a digit is left out of a verse citation, a "9" becomes an "8," or an "11" is read as the Roman numeral "II."[23] In other instances, they are less straightforward—citations from verses that do not exist, such as the marginal reference in *The Sovles Preparation* to "Pro. 2.38."[24] Such inaccuracies are less frequent in the texts of *The Application of Redemption*, largely because the publisher includes very few marginal citations. In any case, these inaccuracies tell less about Hooker's biblical approach than they do about the carelessness of printers, and cannot be taken as indications of Hooker's own biblical patterns.

Such inaccuracies, however, make it more difficult to evaluate other points at which differences between Hooker's biblical translations and published Bibles seem suggestive, for example when he introduces anomalous vocabulary or additional phrases. Similar inaccuracies are found in the texts of many ministers' sermons, and reflect in part the fluidity of allegiance to particular Bible translations, habits of memorization, and the way notes were used.[25] At some points, however, differences between passages quoted by the ministers and Geneva or Authorized texts seem to reveal the ministers' doctrinal and scriptural concerns and priorities. I make my observations about such instances with caution, and with the awareness that some of the textual phenomena that I attribute to the ministers may in fact be the impositions of their various editors. Nevertheless, these phenomena illuminate the ministers' scriptural practices, their doctrinal positions, and their approaches to their preached biblical text. Moreover, while these texts may preserve the actual preached sermons with various degrees of accuracy, they were printed, sold, and read in their day as pieces of devotional literature, and thus warrant consideration in their own right. I have, however, preferred editions that seem to preserve the markings of the sermons' delivery. Thus I have cited Cotton's *Christ the Fountaine of Life*, which is structured as a collection of sermons in a series, more extensively than his *Treatise of the Covenant of Grace*, which has become a treatise, despite maintaining some facets of sermon structure.

The following abbreviations are used in the text and notes for frequently cited works. Full citations are provided on first use in each chapter and in the bibliography. Unless otherwise noted, biblical quotations are drawn from the Authorized Version, specifically the edition published on computer disk by Parsons Technology as *Quickverse 2.0* (1990).

| | |
|---|---|
| *Anti-Synodalia* | [Charles Chauncy,] *Anti-Synodalia Scripta Americana* |
| *AR 9–10* | Thomas Hooker, *The Application of Redemption . . . Ninth and Tenth Books* |
| *Arte* | William Perkins, *The Arte of Prophecying* |
| *BT* | Roger Williams, *The Bloudy Tenent, of Persecution* |
| *CTF* | John Cotton, *Christ the Fountaine of Life* |
| "Examination" | "The Examination of Mrs. Anne Hutchinson at the Court at Newtown" |
| *Faithfvll* | Richard Bernard, *The Faithfvll Shepheard* |
| *IH* | Thomas Shepard, *Of Ineffectual Hearing the Word* |
| *Journal* | John Winthrop, *The Journal of John Winthrop* |
| *Laws* | Richard Hooker, *Of the Lawes of Ecclesiasticall Politie* |
| *Magnalia* | Cotton Mather, *Magnalia Christi Americana* |
| *PDC* | Thomas Hooker, *The Poor Doubting Christian Drawn Unto Christ* |
| *Propositions* | *Propositions Concerning the Subject of Baptism and Consociation of Churches* |
| *PTV* | Thomas Shepard, *The Parable of the Ten Virgins Unfolded* |
| "Report" | "A Report of the Trial of Mrs. Anne Hutchinson before the Church in Boston" |

| | |
|---|---|
| *Short Story* | *A Short Story of the Rise, reign, and ruine of the Antinomians, Familists & Libertines* |
| *SB* | Thomas Shepard, *The Sound Believer* |
| *SP* | [Thomas Hooker,] *The Sovles Preparation for Christ* |
| *Way Cleared* | John Cotton, *The Way of Congregational Churches Cleared* |

Introduction

1. [John Winthrop,] *A Short Story of the Rise, reign, and, ruine of the Antinomians, Familists & Libertines, that infected the Churches of New-England* (1644) [hereafter *Short Story*], in *The Antinomian Controversy, 1636–1638: A Documentary History*, ed. David D. Hall, 2d ed. (Durham: Duke University Press, 1990), 293–94. John Winthrop assembled the documents that were first published anonymously under the title *Antinomians and Familists Condemned by the Synod of Elders in New-England: with the Proceedings of the Magistrates against them, And their Apology for the same* in 1644, then in a second edition with a new title and preface supplied by Thomas Weld as the *Short Story*. Though the texts of the *Short Story* are widely attributed to Winthrop, their authorship is uncertain.

2. Parrington condemned the Puritans as anti-intellectual, illiberal, undemocratic, "hard characters" with "close-fisted natures," whose "social issues" were "likely to be mean and petty," while Mencken blamed Puritans, with their "books of grisly sermons," for American literature's "wholesale and ecstatic . . . sacrifice of aesthetic ideas, of all the fine gusto of passion and beauty, to notions of what is meet, proper, and nice" (Vernon Louis Parrington, *Main Currents in American Thought: An Interpretation of American Literature from the Beginnings to 1920*, vol. 2, *1800–1860: The Romantic Revolution in America* [New York: Harcourt, Brace, 1930], 339; H. L. Mencken, "Puritanism as a Literary Force," *A Book of Prefaces* [New York: Knopf, 1917], 199). Similar accounts are found in Parrington, *Main Currents in American Thought: An Interpretation of American Literature from the Beginnings to 1920*, vol. 1, *1620–1800: The Colonial Mind;* William Carlos Williams, *In the American Grain* (New York: Albert and Charles Boni, 1925); and Van Wyck Brooks, *The Wine of the Puritans* (London: Sisley's, 1908). Darren Staloff's argument in *The Making of an American Thinking Class: Intellectuals and Intelligentsia in Puritan Massachusetts* (New York: Oxford University Press, 1998), 13, is considerably more subtle, but echoes this tradition nonetheless.

3. William Perkins, *The Arte of Prophecying. Or a Treatise Concerning the Sacred and Onely True Manner and Methode of Preaching* (1592, trans. 1607), trans. Thomas Tuke, in *Works* (London, 1609), 737; Richard Bernard, *The Faithfull Shepheard: Or The Shepheards Faithfulnesse: Wherein is for the matter largely, but for the maner, in few words, set forth the excellencie and necessitie of the Ministerie; A Ministers properties and dutie; His entrance into this function and charge; How to begin fitly to instruct his people; Catechising and Preaching; And a good plaine order and method therein: Not so as yet published. Very profitable both for yoong Students, who intend the studie of Theologie (heerein being also declared what Arts and tongues first to be learned, what kinde of Authors to be read and books necessarie in the beginning, and which in the first place) as also for such Ministers as yet have not atteined to a distinct order to studie, write, meditate, and to preach methodically, both for their better course in deliuering the Word, and the peoples vnderstanding in hearing, and memorie in reteining the same* (London, 1607), 20.

4. "The Examination of Mrs. Anne Hutchinson at the Court at Newtown," in *The Antinomian Controversy*, 336.

5. Perry Miller, "The Marrow of Puritan Divinity" (1935), in *Errand into the Wilderness* (Cambridge: Harvard University Press, Belknap Press, 1956), 92.

6. Miller's first book on New England orthodoxy was *Orthodoxy in Massachusetts 1630–1650* (1933; New York: Harper Torchbooks, 1970). For discussion of Miller and his legacy, see Michael McGiffert, "Puritan Studies in the 1960's," *William and Mary Quarterly* 3d ser. 27, no. 1 (January 1970): 36–67; David D. Hall, "On Common Ground: The Coherence of American Puritan Studies," *William and Mary Quarterly* 3d ser. 44, no. 2 (April 1987): 193–229; Charles L. Cohen, "The Post-Puritan Paradigm of Early American Religious History," *William and Mary Quarterly* 3d ser. 54, no. 4 (October 1997): 695–722.

7. Geoffrey F. Nuttall, *The Holy Spirit in Puritan Faith and Experience* (Oxford: Basil Blackwell, 1946).

8. Philip F. Gura, *A Glimpse of Sion's Glory: Puritan Radicalism in New England, 1620–1660* (Middletown, Conn.: Wesleyan University Press, 1984).

9. David D. Hall, *Worlds of Wonder, Days of Judgment: Popular Religious Belief in Early New England* (New York: Knopf, 1989).

10. For example, the January 2000 issue of the *Journal of British Studies* was devoted to "Anglo-American Puritanisms." In that issue, Peter Lake and David Como call attention to the limits of Puritan unity, suggesting through scare quotes and parentheses in their title that the terms "orthodoxy," "consensus," and even "Puritan" cannot be taken for granted: "'Orthodoxy' and Its Discontents: Dispute Settlement and the Production of 'Consensus' in the London (Puritan) 'Underground,'" *Journal of British Studies* 39, no. 1 (January 2000): 34–70. Patrick Collinson notes that "[m]odern historians could have been spared much of their effort to arrive at a 'correct' definition of puritanism if it had been more clearly understood that we are dealing with a term of art and stigmatization which became a weapon of some verbal finesse but not philosophical precision" (*English Puritanism* [1983; London: Historical Association, 1984], 10). See also Patrick Collinson, *The Puritan Character: Polemics and Polarities in Early Seventeenth-Century English Culture* (Los Angeles: William Andrews Clark Memorial Library, 1989).

11. Janice Knight, *Orthodoxies in Massachusetts: Rereading American Puritanism* (Cambridge: Harvard University Press, 1994).

12. Michael P. Winship, "'The Most Glorious Church in the World': The Unity of the Godly in Boston, Massachusetts, in the 1630s," *Journal of British Studies* 39, no. 1 (January 2000): 72.

13. Michael P. Winship, "Reconsiderations: Were There Any Puritans in New England?" *New England Quarterly* 74, no. 1 (March 2001): 118–38. As Winship suggests, I use the term "Puritan" cautiously, not to indicate a rigidly defined set of doctrines and party allegiances, but rather to describe a group of English Protestants who shared certain assumptions about their relationship with the biblical text. Not all of these assumptions were unique to those who were called "Puritan"; on the contrary, many were shared with other Reformed Christians, including those who maintained their allegiance to the established English church. Moreover, those who were identified as "Puritans" often disagreed about a wide range of issues, ranging from soteriology to church polity.

14. Sacvan Bercovitch, *The Rites of Assent: Transformations in the Symbolic Construction of America* (New York: Routledge, 1993), 29–30.

15. Nathan O. Hatch and Mark A. Noll, introduction to *The Bible in America,* ed. Nathan O. Hatch and Mark A. Noll (New York: Oxford University Press, 1982), 4.

16. A notable exception is Jeffrey A. Hammond, who describes "a Puritan aesthetic of commemoration" in *The American Puritan Elegy: A Literary and Cultural Study* (Cambridge: Cambridge University Press, 2000). Taking an anthropological approach to Puritan elegy, Hammond defends Puritan poetry against those who would "patronize" it for its "heartfelt simplicity" (38). To those who compare Puritan poetry with Milton's "Lycidas" and find it wanting, Hammond suggests that Wigglesworth's use of ballad meter in *The Day of Doom* was "fully appropriate for a poem designed to be read aloud in families as a kind of catechism" (44). The sensitivity of Hammond's readings throughout *The American Puritan Elegy* suggests to me that his pleasure in these texts, like mine, is not entirely anthropological, just as my students' puzzled pleasure at reading *The Day of Doom* aloud suggests that the poem's appeal transcends its function as catechism.

17. I welcome Norman S. Grabo's insight that "if we suspend our customary disbelief in an early American critical disposition we will find a much richer range of critical discourse—both theoretical and applied—than we presently allow" ("Running the Gauntlet: Seventeenth-Century Literary Criticism," *ELH* 67, no. 3 [fall 2000]: 697).

18. Hall, *Worlds of Wonder,* 6.

19. John Winthrop, *The Journal of John Winthrop, 1630–1649,* ed. Richard S. Dunn, James Savage, and Laetitia Yeandle (Cambridge: Harvard University Press, 1996), 316.

20. James F. Cooper Jr., *Tenacious of Their Liberties: The Congregationalists in Colonial Massachusetts* (New York: Oxford University Press, 1999).

Chapter 1

1. John Calvin, *Institutes of the Christian Religion* (1559), ed. John T. McNeill, trans. Ford Lewis Battles, The Library of Christian Classics 20–21 (Philadelphia: Westminster, 1960), book IV, chapter i, section 6, p. 1021. Further quotations from the *Institutes* are cited with references for book, chapter, paragraph, and page to this edition.

2. Richard Bernard, *The Faithfvll Shepheard: Or The Shepheards Faithfulnesse: Wherein is for the matter largely, but for the maner, in few words, set forth the excellencie and necessitie of the Ministerie; A Ministers properties and dutie; His entrance into this function and charge; How to begin fitly to instruct his people; Catechising and Preaching; And a good plaine order and method therein: Not so as yet published. Very profitable both for yoong Students, who intend the studie of Theologie (heerein being also declared what Arts and tongues first to be learned, what kinde of Authors to be read and books necessarie in the beginning, and which in the first place) as also for such Ministers as yet have not atteined to a distinct order to studie, write, meditate, and to preach methodically, both for*

*their better course in deliuering the Word, and the peoples vnderstanding in hearing, and memorie in reteining the same* (London, 1607) [hereafter *Faithfvll*], 85.

3. [Andrew Willet and Thomas Cartwright,] *A Christian Letter of Certain English Protestants vnfained fauourers of the present state of religion, authorised and professed in* ENGLAND: *vnto that Reverend and learned man, Mr R. Hoo. requiring resolution in certaine matters of doctrine (which seeme to ouerthrow the foundation of Christian Religion, and of the church among vs) expreslie contained in his fiue books of Ecclesiasticall pollicie* ([Middleburg,] 1599), quoted in Harold Fisch, "The Puritans and the Reform of Prose-Style," *ELH* 19, no. 4 (December 1952): 233.

4. Thomas Nash, *Pierce Penilesse his Supplication to the Diuell. Describing the ouerspreading of Vice, and suppression of Vertue. Pleasantly interlac't with variable delights: and pathetically intermixt with conceipted reproofes* (London, 1592), 17. Harold Fisch discusses this passage as well, noting that "Nashe was, of course, a very partial witness but the statements of the Puritans themselves suggest that, in this respect at any rate, he gives a correct account of the contemporary situation. An extreme sobriety of language was the natural corollary of the Puritan sobriety in dress and diet and everything else associated with the old Adam" (Fisch, "The Puritans and the Reform of Prose-Style," 234–35). I find Puritan preaching, especially that of Thomas Hooker, less sober than does Fisch.

5. Perry Miller, *The New England Mind: The Seventeenth Century* (1939; Cambridge: Harvard University Press, 1954), 332.

6. See, for example, Patrick Collinson, *English Puritanism* (1983; London: The Historical Association, 1984), and *The Puritan Character: Polemics and Polarities in Early Seventeenth-Century English Culture* (Los Angeles: William Andrews Clark Memorial Library, 1989).

7. Recent accounts of Puritan preaching have stressed its complexity and artistry, and qualified our understanding of Puritan plainness. See, for example, Janice Knight, *Orthodoxies in Massachusetts: Rereading American Puritanism* (Cambridge: Harvard University Press, 1994); Teresa Toulouse, *The Art of Prophesying: New England Sermons and the Shaping of Belief* (Athens: University of Georgia Press, 1987); Sandra M. Gustafson, *Eloquence Is Power: Oratory and Performance in Early America* (Chapel Hill: University of North Carolina Press, 2000); Jesper Rosenmeier, "'Clearing the Medium': A Reevaluation of the Puritan Plain Style in Light of John Cotton's *A Practicall Commentary Upon the First Epistle Generall of John*," *William and Mary Quarterly* 3d ser. 37, no. 4 (October 1980): 577–91.

8. William Ames, *The Marrow of Theology* (1623), ed. and trans. from the third Latin edition (1629) John D. Eusden (1968; Durham: Labyrinth, 1983), 194.

9. William Perkins, *The Arte of Prophecying. Or A Treatise Concerning the Sacred and Onely True Manner and Methode of Preaching* (1592, trans. 1607) [hereafter *Arte*], trans. Thomas Tuke, in *Works* (London, 1609), 759.

10. On the high expectations and "highly developed critical acumen" of the colonial laity, see Babette May Levy, *Preaching in the First Half Century of New England History* (New York: Russell and Russell, 1945), 158. Levy notes that "[b]ecause of their feeling of dedication and their augmented sense of the effectuality their preaching ought to possess, the ministers often became almost morbidly concerned with the possible weaknesses of their sermons" (158).

11. Miller, *New England Mind: The Seventeenth Century*, 102–3. Miller lists Keckermann's *Opera omnium quae extant* (Geneva, 1614) as the Keckermann text used by the New England ministers, but Debora Shuger (citing Miller) suggests that Keckermann's more compact *Rhetoricae ecclesiasticae* was "extremely popular in England and New En-

gland during the seventeenth century" (Bartholomaeo Keckermanno, *Rhetoricae ecclesiasticae, sive Artis formandi et habendi conciones sacras, Libri duo: Methodice adornati per
praecepta & explicationes* [Hanover, 1616], cited in Debora K. Shuger, *Sacred Rhetoric: The
Christian Grand Style in the English Renaissance* [Princeton: Princeton University Press,
1988], 112). In Alsted's *Encyclopaedia*, the most relevant chapters are in book 25, which
deals with theology. See especially "De Sacrâ Scripturâ" in the third section, and the entire
sixth section, which is devoted to "Prophetica," or preaching (Johann Heinrich Alsted
[Johannis-Henrici Alstedii], *Encyclopaedia, Septem tomis distincta* [Herborn, 1630]). For
more general discussions of ministers' education, see Levy, *Preaching in the First Half Century of New England History*; Samuel Eliot Morison, *Harvard College in the Seventeenth
Century* (Cambridge: Harvard University Press, 1936); Shuger, *Sacred Rhetoric*; and John
Morgan, *Godly Learning: Puritan Attitudes towards Reason, Learning, and Education,
1560–1640* (Cambridge: Cambridge University Press, 1986).

12. Shuger, *Sacred Rhetoric*, 69; Andreas Hyperius, *The Practis of Preaching, otherwise called the Pathway to the pulpet: conteyning an excellent method how to frame diuine
sermons, & to interpret the holy Scriptures according to the capacitie of the vulgar people.
First written in Latin by the learned pastor of Christes Church, Andreas Hyperius: and now
lately (to the profit of the same Church) Englished by Iohn Ludham, vicar of Wethersfeld.
1577. Hereunto is added an oration concerning the lyfe and death of the same Hyperius: which may serue for a president to all the learned men of his calling in our tyme*,
trans. J. Ludham (London, 1577); Niels Hemmingsen, *The Preacher, or Method of preaching, wrytten in Latine by Nicholas Hemminge and translated into Englishe by I.H. Very
necessarie for all those that by the true preaching of the word of God, labour to pull downe
the sinagogue of Sathan, and to buylde up the Temple of God*, trans. J[ohn] H[orsfall] (London, 1574). Both Hyperius and "Hemingius" are acknowledged by William Perkins as
sources for his *Arte of Prophecying*, at 762.

13. John W. O'Malley recommends specific texts of both works: *De officiis conciona-
tores* in *Supplementa Melanchthoniana*, ed. Paul Drews and Ferdinand Cohrs, vol. 5, pt. 2
(Leipzig, 1929); *Ecclesiastes, sive Concionator Evangelicus*, in *Opera omnia*, ed. J. Clericus,
10 vols. (Leiden, 1703–6), 5:769–1100. See "Content and Rhetorical Forms in Sixteenth-
Century Treatises on Preaching," in *Renaissance Eloquence: Studies in the Theory and
Practice of Renaissance Rhetoric*, ed. James J. Murphy (Berkeley: University of California
Press, 1983), 242–43. On the availability of these works to ministers in New England, see
Arthur O. Norton, "Harvard Text-Books and Reference Books of the Seventeenth Century,"
*Publications of the Colonial Society of Massachusetts* 28 (April 1933): 361–438; see also
Charles F. Robinson and Robin Robinson, "Three Early Massachusetts Libraries," *Publica-
tions of the Colonial Society of Massachusetts* 28 (April 1931): 107–75.

14. For a full discussion of training in general (i.e., secular) rhetoric in New England,
see Morison, *Harvard College*, part 1, 172–93.

15. Ian Breward, editorial preface to *The Work of William Perkins*, Courtenay Library
of Reformation Classics 3 (Appleford, Abingdon, Berkshire, England: Sutton Courtenay
Press, 1970), xi; Levy, *Preaching in the First Half Century of New England History*, 17;
Morgan, *Godly Learning*, 134. Barbara Kiefer Lewalski calls Perkins's *Arte of Prophecying*
"seminal" for the development of the *ars praedicandi*, which emphasized "a method based
directly upon the preacher's special subject," and notes that Perkins's method "was the basis—with some variation—of subsequent Puritan manuals for preachers" (*Protestant Poetics and the Seventeenth-Century Religious Lyric* [Princeton: Princeton University Press,
1979], 218, 219). Everett Emerson notes that *The Arte of Prophecying* "became the defini-
tive treatment of preaching" (*Puritanism in America, 1620–1750* [Boston: Twayne, 1977],
23). Samuel Eliot Morison observes that *The Arte of Prophecying* "was the favorite puritan

manual of the art of preaching, at least to 1660" (*The Intellectual Life of Colonial New England* [1936; Ithaca: Cornell University Press, 1961], 166n. Shuger, too, asserts Perkins's centrality, and finds in him "the purest example of the Protestant version of the passionate plain style" (*Sacred Rhetoric*, 71).

16. Morgan, *Godly Learning*, 137; William Haller, *The Rise of Puritanism, Or, The Way to the New Jerusalem as Set Forth in Pulpit and Press from Thomas Cartwright to John Lilburne and John Milton, 1570–1643* (1938; New York: Harper Torchbooks, 1957), 137. Levy describes *The Faithfvll Shepheard* as an important guide to the method and style of sermon construction (*Preaching in the First Half Century of New England History*, 23). See also Robinson and Robinson, "Three Early Massachusetts Libraries," 126, 155.

17. Miller, *New England Mind: The Seventeenth Century*, 328.

18. *Arte*, 731. Barbara Kiefer Lewalski traces this focus to Augustine's *De Doctrina Christiana* (*Protestant Poetics*, 216).

19. See *Arte*, 731–32.

20. Calvin, *Institutes* I.ix.3, 94–95. For further discussion of Calvin's view of divine authorship of the Bible, see Jackson Forstman, *Word and Spirit: Calvin's Doctrine of Biblical Authority* (Stanford: Stanford University Press, 1962), 59. See also David H. Kelsey, "Protestant Attitudes Regarding Methods of Biblical Interpretation," *Scripture in the Jewish and Christian Traditions*, ed. Frederick E. Greenspahn (Nashville: Abingdon Press, 1982), 137.

21. Allegiance to the "literal" meaning itself raises complications, for the term "literal," as discussed below, was often more polemical than actually descriptive of an approach to reading.

22. Martin Luther, *Dr. Martin Luther's Answer to the Superchristian, Superspiritual, and Superlearned Book of Goat Emser of Leipzig with a Glance at His Comrade Murner* (1521), trans. and intro. A. Steimle, *Works of Martin Luther*, vol. 3 (Philadelphia: Muhlenberg Press, 1930), 333.

23. John R. Knott Jr., *The Sword of the Spirit: Puritan Responses to the Bible* (Chicago: University of Chicago Press, 1980), 17.

24. Calvin, *Institutes* I.vi.1, 70; Forstman, *Word and Spirit*, 77.

25. Luther, *Dr. Martin Luther's Answer*, 333.

26. Harry Caplan traces the development of the fourfold method of exegesis and describes its impact on medieval preaching in "The Four Senses of Scriptural Interpretation and the Medieval Theory of Preaching," *Speculum: A Journal of Medieval Studies* 4 (1929): 282–90.

27. Luther, *Dr. Martin Luther's Answer*, 352.

28. Robert M. Grant and David Tracy note that this flexibility was common among reformed exegetes, who were "eager to insist on the relevance of scripture for their own time, and therefore stress[ed] its literal meaning; but . . . [did] not deny that it . . . [might] have other meanings as well" (*A Short History of the Interpretation of the Bible*, 2d ed. [Philadelphia: Fortress Press, 1984], 103). For a detailed discussion of reformed exegetes' complex views of allegory, see Thomas H. Luxon, *Literal Figures: Puritan Allegory and the Reformation Crisis in Representation* (Chicago: University of Chicago Press, 1995). Charles J. Scalise discusses "literal" meaning in "The 'Sensus Literalis': A Hermeneutical Key to Biblical Exegesis," *Scottish Journal of Theology* 42, no. 1 (1989): 45–65.

29. John R. Knott Jr. notes that the "reasonable amount of freedom of interpretation" offered by Perkins's approach was typical rather than exceptional (*Sword of the Spirit*, 37). Indeed, "[f]or all the talk of the literal sense from Tyndale onwards, there was widespread

recognition that this could often be extended legitimately to include figurative or 'spiritual' meanings" (37).

30. When Anne Hutchinson was examined before the General Court, the participants debated the meaning of the Fifth Commandment and whether Hutchinson had violated it. See "The Examination of Mrs. Anne Hutchinson at the Court at Newtown" [hereafter "Examination"], in *The Antinomian Controversy, 1636–1638: A Documentary History*, ed. David D. Hall, 2d ed. (Durham: Duke University Press, 1990), 313.

31. See Calvin, *Institutes* IV.xxvii.20, 1382–84, in which Calvin considers and rejects several arguments for a literalist reading of the verse.

32. Miller cites Cotton Mather's later rejection of transubstantiation in similar terms: "[T]he doctrine of transubstantiation, he said, was so absurd and irrational that should we accept it we should 'altogether loose all the use of *common sense*, and *Natural Reason*, in those very things which God Himself has made them judges in; and we can be sure of Nothing, all the World must Evaporate into nothing with us'" (*New England Mind: The Seventeenth Century*, 71).

33. Calvin, *Institutes* III.ii.34, 582.

34. Sacvan Bercovitch sees the denial of subjectivity in a system that was in fact so subjective as a key tension in reformed hermeneutics, and ties it to the shift in the focus of hermeneutics "from biblical to secular history" ("Colonial Puritan Rhetoric and the Discovery of American Identity," *The Canadian Review of American Studies* 6, no. 2 [fall 1975]: 132).

35. Bernard's association of logic and the power of the Spirit is consistent with Miller's description of Puritan rationalism. See esp. *New England Mind: The Seventeenth Century*, 66–70.

36. Roland Barthes, "The Death of the Author," *Image-Music-Text*, trans. Stephen Heath (New York: Hill and Wang, 1977), 148.

37. Hutchinson's perplexities about 1 John 2.18 were resolved by "an immediate revelation" of God's "own spirit to [her] soul." See "Examination," 336–37. For fuller discussion of Hutchinson's revelations in the context of Puritan theories of Bible reading, see chapter 7.

38. Kelsey, "Protestant Attitudes Regarding Methods of Biblical Interpretation," 137–38; *Faithfvll*, 29. For a discussion of the *Clavis scripturae sacrae*, see Kathy Eden, *Hermeneutics and the Rhetorical Tradition: Chapters in the Ancient Legacy and Its Humanist Reception* (New Haven: Yale University Press, 1997), 90–100.

39. Forstman, *Word and Spirit*, 60.

40. *Dr. Martin Luther's Answer*, 334.

41. On use of different Bible translations, see Marvin W. Anderson, "The Geneva (Tomson/Junius) New Testament among Other English Bibles of the Period," *The Geneva Bible: The Annotated New Testament 1602 Edition*, ed. Gerald T. Sheppard (New York: Pilgrim, 1989), 5–17; Harry S. Stout, "Word and Order in Colonial New England," *The Bible in America*, ed. Nathan O. Hatch and Mark A. Noll (New York: Oxford University Press, 1982), 19–38.

42. Stout, "Word and Order in Colonial New England," 22–23.

43. Michael Ditmore, "A Prophetess in Her Own Country: An Exegesis of Anne Hutchinson's 'Immediate Revelation,'" *William and Mary Quarterly* 57 3d ser., no. 2 (April 2000): 349–92.

44. Christopher Hill, *The English Bible and the Seventeenth-Century Revolution* (1993; New York: Penguin, 1994), 66.

45. John Cotton, *A Modest and Cleare Answer to Mr. Balls Discourse of set formes of Prayer. Set forth in a most Seasonable time, when this* KINGDOME *is now in Consultation about Matters of that Nature, and so many godly Long after the Resolution in that Point* (London, 1642), [11]. (This page is mismarked as a second page 3.)

46. Bernard suggested that "It is not fit that euerie one be a publike controller of a publike receiued translation. As it may argue some presumption and pride in the Corrector, so it may breed contention, and leaue a great scruple, and cast doubts into the hearers mindes, what reckoning to make of a translation; and it giues great aduantage to the Papists; who heereby labour to forestall many, that they smally account of our translations; which we see can neuer be so well done and generally approued of, but some particular persons will be censuring the same, and that not only in priuate (a thing happely tolerable if the censure bee true, and wisely proceeded in) but also they must needs shew their skill in Pulpits" (16). Bernard conceded that "It is verie necessarie that the translation be most sound," but found it "nothing expedient that euer publike proclaimation bee made of some small defects, that by much prying happely may be noted therein, of euery ordinarie person, but only such faults as needs noting, and that of learned men too" (16).

47. On the use of notes and memorization, see *Faithfvll*, 85–86; *Arte*, 758; Alan Fager Herr, *The Elizabethan Sermon: A Survey and a Bibliography* (New York: Octagon Books, 1969), 35; Levy, *Preaching in the First Half Century of New England History*, 82–83; Edward H. Davidson, "Cotton's Biblical Exegesis: Method and Purpose," *Early American Literature* 17, no. 2 (fall 1982): 119–38. Harry S. Stout describes the ministers' often extensive notes, which were "recorded . . . in leatherbound volumes that closely resembled printed treatises. The number of pages in sermon books varied between thirty and two hundred, and depending on their size could contain three to five hundred words per page. Generally each volume contained one or more series broken down into sermons of six to twelve pages each. In these extended sermon outlines, punctuation was scarce, but thoughts were developed fully in the distinctive text-doctrine-application formula of the plain style sermon. To conserve paper, margins were fully used to make note of scriptural cross-references that could be read during the sermon and to enter abbreviated rhetorical cues like 'doct,' 'reas,' 'use 1,' that could lead the minister through the major 'heads' or divisions of his discourse. The substance of the notes was almost exclusively scriptural exegesis and personal applications." *The New England Soul: Preaching and Religious Culture in Colonial New England* (New York: Oxford University Press, 1986), 34.

48. Perkins lists five causes for repetition and for variation in repetition: (1) "first exegeticall, that is, for exposition sake," (2) "diacritically, or for discernings sake, that places, and times, & persons might be mutually distinguished," (3) "circumscriptiue: or for limitation sake, that the sense and sentence of the place might be truely restrained, according as the minde and meaning of the H Ghost was," (4) "for application sake, that the type might be fitted vnto the truth: and the generall to a certaine speciall, and so contrariwise," (5) "some things are omitted for breuitie sake: or because they doe not agree with the matter at hand" (738–39).

49. See, for example, Cotton's sermon series *Christ the Fountaine of Life*, in which Cotton preaches twelve full sermons on 1 John 5:12, "He that hath the Son hath life, and he that hath not the Son, hath not life" (London, 1651; New York: Arno Press, 1972). I discuss Cotton's unfolding of the biblical text at greater length in chapter 2.

50. Stefan Morawski, "The Basic Functions of Quotation," in *Sign • Language • Culture* (The Hague: Mouton, 1970), 690–705.

51. Richard Sibbes, *The Complete Works of Richard Sibbes*, ed. Alexander Balloch Grosart (Edinburgh: James Nichol, 1862–64), 2:462, cited in Knott, *Sword of the Spirit*, 51.

52. Thomas Shepard, *The Sound Believer* (1645), in *The Works of Thomas Shepard, First Pastor of the First Church, Cambridge, Mass. with a Memoir of His Life and Character*, vol. 1 (1853; New York: AMS Press, 1967; Ligonier, Penn.: Soli Deo Gloria, 1991), 268.

53. *Faithfvll*, 58. See chapter 3 for a fuller discussion of Shepard's approach to preaching.

54. Cotton Mather, *Magnalia Christi Americana; or, The Ecclesiastical History of New-England, from its First Planting, in the Year 1620, unto the Year of Our Lord 1698* [hereafter *Magnalia*], vol. 2 (1702; Hartford: Silus Andrus and Son, 1853); reprinted as *Great Works of Christ in America* (Edinburgh: Banner of Truth Trust, 1979), 61. Mather's description of Danforth's preaching was brought to my attention by Babette Levy's discussion in *Preaching in the First Half Century of New England History*, 93.

55. John Norton, *Abel being Dead yet speaketh; Or, The Life & Death Of that deservedly Famous Man of GOD, M' John Cotton, Late Teacher of the Church of Christ, at BOSTON in New-England* (London, 1658), 24; reprinted in facsimile in *The New England Way*, Library of American Puritan Writings 12 (New York: AMS Press, 1983).

56. In the Authorized Version the biblical verse describes "a certain Jew named Apollos, born at Alexandria, an eloquent man, *and* mighty in the Scriptures." Unless otherwise noted, biblical quotations are taken from the Authorized Version, specifically from the edition published on computer disk by Parsons Technology as *Quickverse 2.0* (1990).

57. Bernard is silent on this question.

58. Stanley E. Fish, *Self-Consuming Artifacts: The Experience of Seventeenth-Century Literature* (Berkeley: University of California Press, 1972), 70.

59. For a discussion of Ramism and Puritan sermon structure, see Miller, *New England Mind: The Seventeenth Century*, 344–49.

60. Miller cites Cotton Mather's description of John Wilson, who apparently preached "in the methodical way" in England, but in New England often structured his sermons much more loosely (*New England Mind: The Seventeenth Century*, 353–54).

61. Everett H. Emerson, introduction to *Redemption: Three Sermons (1637–1656) by Thomas Hooker* (Gainesville, Fla.: Scholars' Facsimiles and Reprints, 1956), xiv.

62. Edward H. Davidson, "'God's Well-Trodden Foot-Paths': Puritan Preaching and Sermon Form," *Texas Studies in Literature and Language* 25, no. 4 (winter 1983): 503, 524.

63. J. W. Blench, *Preaching in England in the late Fifteenth and Sixteenth Centuries: A Study of English Sermons 1450–c. 1600* (Oxford: Basil Blackwell, 1964), 102.

64. Toulouse, *Art of Prophesying*, 22. N. H. Keeble also discusses "the practical bias characteristic of puritan homiletics" in "Richard Baxter's Preaching Ministry: Its History and Texts," *Journal of Ecclesiastical History* 35, no. 3 (July 1984), 552–53.

65. Knott, *Sword of the Spirit*, 6; see also Levy, *Preaching in the First Half Century of New England History*, 94. In exploring John Cotton's rhetoric, Eugenia Delamotte also describes some of the complexities of Puritan exegetical and sermon theory. See Delamotte, "John Cotton and the Rhetoric of Grace," *Early American Literature* 21, no. 1 (spring 1986): 49–74.

66. Patrick Collinson, "The English Conventicle," *Voluntary Religion: Papers Read at the 1985 Summer Meeting and the 1986 Winter Meeting of the Ecclesiastical History Society*, ed. J. Sheils and Diane Wood, *Studies in Church History* 23 (1986): 241.

67. *The Bible, That Is, The holy Scriptures conteined in the Olde and Newe Testament, Translated according to the Ebrew and Greeke, and conferred with the best Translations in diuers Languages. With most profitable Annotations vpon all hard places, and other things of great importance* (1599), reprinted in facsimile as *The Geneva Bible* (Buena Park, California: Geneva Publishing, 1991).

68. Lewis Bayly, *The Practise of Pietie, Directing a Christian how to walke that he may please God*, 3d ed. (London, 1613), 314–15. Charles E. Hambrick-Stowe includes *The Practise of Pietie* among "the devotional manuals widely used in New England" (*The Practice of Piety: Puritan Devotional Disciplines in Seventeenth-Century New England* [Chapel Hill: University of North Carolina Press, 1982], 158).

69. *Christ the Fountaine of Life: Or, Sundry Choyce Sermons on part of the fift Chapter of the first Epistle of St. John* (London, 1651; New York: Arno Press, 1972), 200.

70. "To the Christian Reader," *The Geneva Bible.* For a discussion of these glosses, see Ditmore, "A Prophetess in Her Own Country," 379–80, 389–92. Stout calls the Geneva Bible "the first English translation that could legitimately be characterized as a people's Bible," describing not only its marginal glosses but also its "translation . . . devoid of circumlocutions and Latinisms that would only distract the reader" as well as the physical appeal of a work "issued in a relatively inexpensive single volume, Roman type edition that was conveniently organized into sentence units of 'verses' and 'chapters'" ("Word and Order in Colonial New England," 21).

71. Hill, *The English Bible and the Seventeenth-Century Revolution*, 52.

72. *Arte*, 752–56. Bernard's categories are the same as Perkins's, although he combines those not yet humbled and those humbled as two subheadings under one Roman numeral (8–11). The same categories appear also in Alsted's *Encyclopaedia*, where they match Perkins word for word (1675). All three writers note that each of these audiences must be dealt with differently, according to their needs, and Perkins and Bernard provide specific instructions for each group.

73. Theodore Dwight Bozeman, *To Live Ancient Lives: The Primitivist Dimension in Puritanism* (Chapel Hill: University of North Carolina Press, 1988), 67.

74. John Winthrop, *The Journal of John Winthrop, 1630–1649* [hereafter *Journal*], ed. Richard S. Dunn, James Savage, and Laetitia Yeandle (Cambridge: Harvard University Press, 1996), 316. In October of 1634, the ministers, magistrates, and churches had agreed "that the 4:Lectures did spende too muche tyme, & proved ouer burdensome to the ministers & people," and agreed "to reduce them to 2 dayes" by having ministers alternate weekday lectures from week to week (*Journal*, 130). In 1639, Winthrop reported, the court instructed the church elders to meet with the magistrates and deputies to address the problem. After some dispute, the elders agreed that lectures should "ordinarily" break up early enough to allow those attending to return home before nightfall (*Journal*, 316–18).

Chapter 2

1. Twentieth-century biographies of Cotton include Everett H. Emerson, *John Cotton*, Twayne United States Authors Series 80 (New York: Twayne, 1965); and Larzer Ziff, *The Career of John Cotton: Puritanism and the American Experience* (Princeton: Princeton University Press, 1962). Both of these texts provide some bibliographical information about Cotton's published works. A wealth of information is found as well in *The Correspondence of John Cotton*, ed. Sargent Bush Jr. (Chapel Hill: University of North Carolina Press, 2001). Additional biographical and bibliographical information is available in Janice Knight, *Orthodoxies in Massachusetts: Rereading American Puritanism* (Cambridge: Harvard University Press, 1994); Andrew Delbanco, *The Puritan Ordeal* (Cambridge: Harvard University Press, 1989); Julius H. Tuttle, "Writings of Rev. John Cotton," in *Bibliographical Essays: A Tribute to Wilberforce Eames* (Cambridge: Harvard University Press, 1924), 363–80; and Sargent Bush Jr., "John Cotton's Correspondence: A Census," *Early American Literature* 24, no. 2 (1989): 91–111.

2. John Cotton, *Christ the Fountaine of Life: Or, Sundry Choyce Sermons on part of*

*the fift Chapter of the first Epistle of St. John* [hereafter *CTF*] (London, 1651; New York: Arno Press, 1972), 183. This sermon series is generally dated to Cotton's English ministry, between 1612 and 1632. See Ziff, *The Career of John Cotton,* 263.

3. John Cotton, *A Briefe Exposition With Practicall Observations Upon the Whole Book of Ecclesiastes* (London, 1654), 16.

4. John Cotton, *The Way of Life, Or, Gods Way and Course, in bringing the soule into, keeping it in, and carrying it on, in the wayes of life and peace* (London, 1641), 12, reprinted in facsimile in *The Way of Faith,* Library of American Puritan Writings 13 (New York: AMS Press, 1983).

5. Teresa Toulouse, "John Cotton and the Shaping of Election," in *The Art of Prophesying: New England Sermons and the Shaping of Belief* (Athens: University of Georgia Press, 1987), 32, 38.

6. Knight, *Orthodoxies in Massachusetts,* 150. In addition to the texts cited above, studies of Cotton's preaching include Edward H. Davidson, "Cotton's Biblical Exegesis: Method and Purpose," *Early American Literature* 17, no. 2 (fall 1982): 119–38; Eugenia Delamotte, "John Cotton and the Rhetoric of Grace," *Early American Literature* 21, no. 1 (spring 1986): 49–74; Norman S. Grabo, "John Cotton's Aesthetic: A Sketch," *Early American Literature* 3, no. 1 (spring 1968): 4–10; Alfred Habegger, "Preparing the Soul for Christ: The Contrasting Sermon Forms of John Cotton and Thomas Hooker," *American Literature* 41, no. 3 (November 1969): 342–54; Jeffrey A. Hammond, "The Bride in Redemptive Time: John Cotton and the Canticles Controversy," *New England Quarterly* 56, no. 1 (March 1983): 78–102; Ann Kibbey, *The Interpretation of Material Shapes in Puritanism: A Study of Rhetoric, Prejudice, and Violence* (Cambridge: Cambridge University Press, 1986); Jesper Rosenmeier, "'Clearing the Medium': A Reevaluation of the Puritan Plain Style in Light of John Cotton's *A Practicall Commentary Upon the First Epistle Generall of John,"* *William and Mary Quarterly* 3d ser. 37, no. 4 (October 1980): 577–91; Jesper Rosenmeier, "Eaters and Non-Eaters: John Cotton's *A Brief Exposition of . . . Canticles* (1642) in Light of Boston's (Linc.) Religious and Civil Conflicts, 1619–22," *Early American Literature* 36, no. 2 (2001): 149–81; Prudence L. Steiner, "A Garden of Spices in New England: John Cotton's and Edward Taylor's Use of the Song of Songs," in *Allegory, Myth, and Symbol,* ed. Morton W. Bloomfield, Harvard English Studies 9 (Cambridge: Harvard University Press, 1981), 227–43.

7. Toulouse, *Art of Prophesying,* 38; William Perkins, *The Arte of Prophecying* (1592, trans. 1607), trans. Thomas Tuke, in *Works* (London, 1609), 736.

8. In the Authorized Version, the biblical text reads: "When all Israel is come to appear before the LORD thy God in the place which he shall choose, thou shalt read this law before all Israel in their hearing. Gather the people together, men, and women, and children, and thy stranger that *is* within thy gates, that they may hear, and that they may learn, and fear the LORD your God, and observe to do all the words of this law: And *that* their children, which have not known *any thing,* may hear, and learn to fear the LORD your God, as long as ye live in the land whither ye go over Jordan to possess it" (Deut. 31:11–13). Unless otherwise noted, biblical quotations are taken from the Authorized Version, specifically from the edition published on computer disk by Parsons Technology as *Quickverse 2.0* (1990).

9. The additional verse cited here provides the setting for verses that Cotton has cited earlier: "And Moses commanded them, saying, At the end of *every* seven years, in the solemnity of the year of release, in the feast of tabernacles" (Deut. 31:10).

10. Cotton cites Nehemiah 8:18 and 8:4–8. Nehemiah 8:18 reads: "Also day by day, from the first day unto the last day, he read in the book of the law of God. And they kept the feast seven days; and on the eighth day *was* a solemn assembly, according unto the manner." Nehemiah 8:4–8 reads: "And Ezra the scribe stood upon a pulpit of wood, which they had

made for the purpose; and beside him stood Mattithiah, and Shema, and Anaiah, and Urijah, and Hilkiah, and Maaseiah, on his right hand; and on his left hand, Pedaiah, and Mishael, and Malchiah, and Hashum, and Hashbadana, Zechariah, *and* Meshullam. And Ezra opened the book in the sight of all the people; (for he was above all the people;) and when he opened it, all the people stood up: And Ezra blessed the LORD, the great God. And all the people answered, Amen, Amen, with lifting up their hands: and they bowed their heads, and worshipped the LORD with *their* faces to the ground. Also Jeshua, and Bani, and Sherebiah, Jamin, Akkub, Shabbethai, Hodijah, Maaseiah, Kelita, Azariah, Jozabad, Hanan, Pelaiah, and the Levites, caused the people to understand the law: and the people *stood* in their place. So they read in the book in the law of God distinctly, and gave the sense, and caused *them* to understand the reading."

11. In some of his most overtly polemical preaching, Cotton attacked the Roman Catholic Church. The defeat of Catholicism received significant attention in *The Powring Out of the Seven Vials,* an American sermon series on the sixteenth chapter of Revelation, in which Cotton identified "the lowest and basest Element in the Antichristian world" with "the lowest sort of vulgar Catholiques" (*The Powring Out of the Seven Vials: Or, An Exposition of the Sixteenth Chapter of the REVELATION, with an Application of it to our Times. Wherein is revealed Gods powring out the full VIALS of his fierce Wrath. Very fit and necessary for this present Age* [London, 1645], 3).

12. See John Cotton, *Mr. Cottons Rejoynder,* in *The Antinomian Controversy, 1636–1638: A Documentary History,* ed. David D. Hall, 2d ed. (Durham: Duke University Press, 1990), 78–151.

13. John Norton, *Abel being Dead yet speaketh; Or, The Life & Death Of that deservedly Famous Man of GOD, Mᵣ John Cotton, Late Teacher of the Church of Christ, at BOSTON in New-England* (London, 1658), reprinted in *The New England Way,* Library of American Puritan Writings 12 (New York: AMS Press, 1983), 13.

14. John Cotton, "A Thankful Acknowledgement of God's Providence," ll. 17–19, quoted in ibid., 28–29.

15. Cotton Mather, *Magnalia Christi Americana; or, The Ecclesiastical history of New England, from its First Planting, in the Year 1620, unto the Year of Our Lord 1698* [hereafter *Magnalia*], vol. 1 (1702; Hartford: Silus Andrus and Son, 1853), reprinted as *Great Works of Christ in America* (Edinburgh: Banner of Truth Trust, 1979), 275. Mather bases much of his account on John Norton's biography of Cotton, cited above.

16. In Janice Knight's words, "The preacher makes himself a passive vessel through which the Spirit flows from Bible to saint" (Knight, *Orthodoxies in Massachusetts,* 150).

17. Babette May Levy, *Preaching in the First Half Century of New England History* (New York: Russell and Russell, 1945), 89.

18. See, for example, the treatise "Sinnes deadly Wound," a set of sermons preached on Acts 2:37 and published in *The Way of Life,* 123–97.

19. Norton, *Abel being Dead yet speaketh,* 17.

20. Alan Heimert and Andrew Delbanco, eds., *The Puritans in America: A Narrative Anthology* (Cambridge: Harvard University Press, 1985), 28.

21. John Winthrop reported that "It pleased the Lord to give speciall Testimonye of his presence in the Church of Boston, after mr Cotton was called to Office there: more were converted & added to that Churche, then to all the other Churches in the Baye" (*The Journal of John Winthrop 1630–1649,* ed. Richard S. Dunn, James Savage, and Laetitia Yeandle [Cambridge: Harvard University Press, 1996], 106). Boston church records show eighty members at Cotton's arrival, with forty-four joining between September and December of

1633 and ninety-four new members in 1634. See *Publications of the Colonial Society of Massachusetts* 39:13–22, quoted in ibid., 121 n. 41).

22. Both writers treat the step of actually dividing the text into parts only briefly. Bernard writes that ministers "must know what to teach for the matter, and how for the maner; and so to divide the word aright to the heareres; which is required in all that preach unto the people" (*The Faithfvll Shepheard: Or, The Shepheards Faithfulnesse: Wherein is for the matter largely, but for the maner, in few words, set forth the excellencie and necessitie of the Ministerie; A Ministers properties and dutie; His entrance into this function and charge; How to begin fitly to instruct his people; Catechising and Preaching; And a good plaine order and method therein: Not so as yet published. Very profitable both for yoong Students, who intend the studie of Theologie (heerein being also declared what Arts and tongues first to be learned, what kinde of Authors to be read and books necessarie in the beginning, and which in the first place) as also for such Ministers as yet have not atteined to a distinct order to studie, write, meditate, and to preach methodically, both for their better course in deliuering the Word, and the peoples vnderstanding in hearing, and memorie in reteining the same* [London, 1607], A3v). Perkins devotes the sixth chapter of *The Arte of Prophecying* to "the right deuiding of the word," and treats gathering doctrines out of the text and applying them under the category of division (750–52).

23. [Thomas Hooker,] *The Sovles Preparation for Christ. Or, A Treatise of Contrition, Wherein is discovered How God breakes the heart and woundes the Soule, in the conversion of a Sinner to Himselfe* (London, 1638), reprinted in facsimile as *The Soules Preparation*, Library of American Puritan Writings 15 (New York: AMS Press, 1982), 1. For fuller discussion of Hooker's approach to the biblical text, see chapter 4.

24. The cited texts read: "And if we know that he hear us, whatsoever we ask, we know that we have the petitions that we desired of him. If any man see his brother sin a sin *which is* not unto death, he shall ask, and he shall give him life for them that sin not unto death. There is a sin unto death: I do not say that he shall pray for it. All unrighteousness is sin: and there is a sin not unto death" (1 John 5:15–17)

25. A parallel phenomenon is found in the petihta of the rabbinic darshan. See Joseph Heinemann, "The Proem in the Aggadic Midrashim," *Studies in Aggadah and Folk-Literature*, ed. Joseph Heinemann and Dov Noy. Scripta Hierosolymitana 22 (Jerusalem: Magnes, 1971), 101; David Stern, "Midrash and the Language of Exegesis: A Study of Vayikra Rabbah, Chapter 1," *Midrash and Literature*, ed. Geoffrey H. Hartman and Sanford Budick (New Haven: Yale University Press, 1986), 107.

26. Heimert and Delbanco comment briefly on Cotton's "language of holy paradox" in their introduction to an excerpt from Sermon 8 of *Christ The Fountaine of Life* (*Puritans in America*, 28). For two very different approaches to Cotton's imagery, see Kibbey, *The Interpretation of Material Shapes in Puritanism*, and Steiner, "A Garden of Spices in New England."

27. Knight, *Orthodoxies in Massachusetts*, 150–51.

28. *Magnalia*, 1:275.

29. Toulouse, *Art of Prophesying*, 14; Habegger, "Preparing the Soul for Christ," 350.

30. Levy, *Preaching in the First Half Century of New England History*, 141.

31. Habegger, "Preparing the Soul for Christ," 345.

32. Emerson notes Cotton's description of the text as "a Discourse not unseasonable for this Countrey, wherein men that have left all to enjoy the Gospel, now (as if they had forgotten the end for which they came hither) are ready to leave the Gospel for outward things" (Emerson, *John Cotton*, 93, quoting Cotton, *Briefe Exposition*, 1). Consequently, he dates the work early in Cotton's New England ministry (92). Ziff, on the other hand, dates

this text during Cotton's English ministry, between 1612 and 1632, surmising that Cotton "would have needed the equivalent of his *Brief Exposition* as a basis" for sermons preached on Ecclesiastes in his English ministry, "and since there is nothing in the *Brief Exposition* to indicate its composition after 1633" (*The Career of John Cotton*, 262). The "Epistle Dedicatory" suggests that Anthony Tuckney, who published the treatise, envisioned a lay audience, as do Cotton's introductory remarks (sig. A3r-1).

33. Cotton, *Briefe Exposition*, 3; Emerson, *John Cotton*, 93. Such details do continue to hold the attention of modern biblical scholars, however. See, for example, Robert Gordis's summary of various scholars' explanations for the origins of the name "Koheleth," as well as his own suggestion that "feminine participles were used to denote functionaries or officials and then became masculine proper names" (*Koheleth — The Man and His World: A Study of Ecclesiastes* [New York: Schocken, 1968], 203–4).

34. Cotton, *The Powring Out of the Seven Vials*, 2.

35. John Cotton, *A Modest and Cleare Answer to Mr. Balls Discourse of set formes of Prayer. Set forth in a most Seasonable time, when this* KINGDOME *is now in Consultation about Matters of that Nature, and so many godly* Long *after the Resolution of that Point* (London, 1642), 12.

36. Ibid.

37. See "The Examination of Mrs. Anne Hutchinson at the Court at Newtown," in *The Antinomian Controversy, 1636–1638*, 318–19. See chapter 7 for a fuller discussion of Hutchinson's response to Cotton and his colleagues.

## CHAPTER 3

1. For biographical information on Shepard, see John Albro, *Life of Thomas Shepard*, in *The Works of Thomas Shepard, First Pastor of the First Church, Cambridge, Mass. with a Memoir of His Life and Character*, vol. 1 (Boston: Boston Doctrinal Tract and Book Society, 1853; Ligonier, Penn.: Soli Deo Gloria, 1991), vii–cxcii; Thomas Werge, *Thomas Shepard* (Boston: Twayne, 1987); Michael McGiffert, "Thomas Shepard: The Practice of Piety," in *God's Plot: Puritan Spirituality in Thomas Shepard's Cambridge*, ed. and intro. Michael McGiffert (1972; Amherst: University of Massachusetts Press, 1994), 3–33; George Selement and Bruce C. Woolley, introduction to *Thomas Shepard's "Confessions,"* ed. George Selement and Bruce C. Woolley (*Publications of the Colonial Society of Massachusetts Collections* 58 [Boston, 1981]), 1–28; Samuel Eliot Morison, "Master Thomas Shepard," in *The Builders of the Bay Colony* (1930, revised 1962; Boston: Northeastern University Press, 1981), 105–34; and Babette May Levy, *Preaching in the First Half Century of New England History* (New York: Russell and Russell, 1945). Early accounts include Cotton Mather's biography of Shepard entitled "Pastor Evangelicus; the Life of Mr. Thomas Shepard" (*Magnalia Christi Americana; or, The Ecclesiastical History of New-England, from its First Planting, in the Year 1620, unto the Year of Our Lord 1698* [hereafter *Magnalia*] [1702; Hartford: Silus Andrus and Son, 1853], reprinted as *Great Works of Christ in America*, vol. 1 [Edinburgh: Banner of Truth Trust, 1979], 380–94); and Edward Johnson's discussion of the Cambridge church in *Wonder-working Providence of Sions Saviour in New England* (1653), reprinted as *Johnson's Wonder-working Providence, 1628–1651*, ed. J. Franklin Jameson (1910; New York: Barnes and Noble, 1937). Shepard's autobiography and journal (in *God's Plot*, cited above) also provide useful perspective on the events of his life.

2. Thomas Shepard, *Of Ineffectual Hearing the Word* (1652) [hereafter *IH*], in *The Works of Thomas Shepard*, vol. 3 (1992), 367. This sermon was originally preached in 1641. See Werge, *Thomas Shepard*, 28.

3. Cotton Mather uses the term "notable *text-man*" to describe Samuel Danforth. See

*Magnalia,* 2:61, quoted in Levy, *Preaching in the First Half Century of New England History,* 93.

4. Roland Barthes, *The Pleasure of the Text,* trans. Richard Miller (New York: Hill and Wang, 1975), 8.

5. Thomas Shepard, *The Sound Believer* (1645) [hereafter *SB*], in *The Works of Thomas Shepard,* vol. 1 (1991), 133. The cited texts are Jeremiah 8:6: "I hearkened and heard, *but* they spake not aright: no man repented him of his wickedness, saying, What have I done? every one turned to his course, as the horse rusheth into the battle." Zephaniah 2:1: "Gather yourselves together, yea, gather together, O nation not desired." Although Shepard generally uses the text of the Authorized Version, here his citation is closer to the text of the Geneva Bible, which reads: "Gather your selues, euen gather you, O nation not worthy to be loued" (*The Bible, That Is, The holy Scriptures conteined in the Olde and Newe Testament, Translated according to the Ebrew and Greeke, and conferred with the best Translations in diuers Languages. With most profitable Annotations vpon all hard places, and other things of great importance* (1599), reprinted in facsimile as *The Geneva Bible* [Buena Park, Calif.: Geneva Publishing, 1991]).

As Shepard's quotations are generally closest to the Authorized Version, unless otherwise noted biblical quotations in this chapter are taken from that version, specifically from the edition published on computer disk by Parsons Technology as *QuickVerse 2.0* (Parsons Technology, 1990).

6. See, for example, Theodore Dwight Bozeman's *To Live Ancient Lives: The Primitivist Dimension in Puritanism* (Chapel Hill: University of North Carolina Press, 1988).

7. On the drive for a gathered church of saints, see Edmund Morgan, *Visible Saints: The History of a Puritan Idea* (1963; Ithaca: Cornell University Press, 1965); Geoffrey F. Nuttall, *Visible Saints: The Congregational Way, 1640–1660* (Oxford: Blackwell, 1957). On the relation of conversion narratives in Shepard's own church, see Patricia Caldwell, *The Puritan Conversion Narrative: The Beginnings of American Expression* (Cambridge: Cambridge University Press, 1983). For Shepard's transcriptions of these narratives, see *Thomas Shepard's "Confessions"*; Mary Rhinelander McCarl, "Thomas Shepard's Records of Relations of Religious Experience, 1648–1649," *William and Mary Quarterly,* 3d ser. 48, no. 3 (July 1991): 432–66; and *God's Plot,* 149–225. The conversion narratives of Shepard's congregants are discussed in chapter 5.

8. The text of Zephaniah 1:12 reads: "And it shall come to pass at that time, *that* I will search Jerusalem with candles, and punish the men that are settled on their lees: that say in their heart, The LORD will not do good, neither will he do evil."

9. 1 Chronicles 21:16 reads: "And David lifted up his eyes, and saw the angel of the LORD stand between the earth and the heaven, having a drawn sword in his hand stretched out over Jerusalem. Then David and the elders *of Israel, who were* clothed in sackcloth, fell upon their faces."

10. Deuteronomy 30:1 reads: "And it shall come to pass, when all these things are come upon thee, the blessing and the curse, which I have set before thee, and thou shalt call *them* to mind among all the nations, whither the LORD thy God hath driven thee."

11. The biblical text reads: "When he maketh inquisition for blood, he remembereth them: he forgetteth not the cry of the humble."

12. Jonathan Mitchell, preface to Shepard, *The Parable of the Ten Virgins Unfolded* (1660) [hereafter *PTV*], in *The Works of Thomas Shepard,* vol. 2 (1991), 5. See also the introduction by Phyllis M. Jones and Nicholas R. Jones to the excerpt from *PTV* in *Salvation in New England: Selections from the Sermons of the First Preachers,* ed. Phyllis M. Jones and Nicholas R. Jones (Austin: University of Texas Press, 1977), 132.

13. Elsewhere in the same sermon, Shepard asserts that "There may be an eternal effi-cacy of the word, and yet lie hid, and not felt for a time" (373).

14. McGiffert, "Thomas Shepard: The Practice of Piety," in *God's Plot*, 27. For further exploration of the role of reason in Puritan theology, see Robert Middlekauff, "Piety and Intellect in Puritanism," *William and Mary Quarterly*, 3d ser. 22, no. 3 (July 1965): 457–70; Charles Lloyd Cohen, *God's Caress: The Psychology of Puritan Religious Experience* (Ox-ford: Oxford University Press, 1986).

15. McGiffert, "Thomas Shepard: The Practice of Piety," in *God's Plot*, 27.

16. See *The Antinomian Controversy, 1636–1638: A Documentary History*, ed. David D. Hall, 2d ed. (Durham: Duke University Press, 1990). For fuller discussion of Hutchinson's revelations and their resemblance to prescribed forms of reading, see chapter 7.

17. *IH*, 373. Deuteronomy 4:32 reads: "For ask now of the days that are past, which were before thee, since the day that God created man upon the earth, and *ask* from the one side of heaven unto the other, whether there hath been *any such thing* as this great thing *is*, or hath been heard like it?" Hebrews 12:24 reads: "And to Jesus the mediator of the new covenant, and to the blood of sprinkling, that speaketh better things than *that of* Abel."

18. Barthes, *The Pleasure of the Text*, 8.

19. 2 Thessalonians 1:9 reads: "Who shall be punished with everlasting destruction from the presence of the Lord, and from the glory of his power."

20. 2 Thessalonians 1:10: "When he shall come to be glorified in his saints, and to be admired in all them that believe (because our testimony among you was believed) in that day."

21. Barthes, *The Pleasure of the Text*, 6.

22. I enclose "literal" in quotation marks because, for Reformed exegetes, it was a complex polemical term. Tracing their rejection of fourfold meaning in scripture to Luther, divines like William Perkins insisted that biblical texts could have only one meaning: *"There is one only sense, and the same is the literal"* (*The Arte of Prophecying* [1592, trans. 1607], trans. Thomas Tuke, in *Works* [London, 1609], 737). But the distinction between the literal meaning and other interpretations was often more polemical than actual. Perkins, for ex-ample, expanded his definition of the literal to include the four other means of interpreta-tion as well: "An allegorie is onely a certaine manner of vttering the same sense. The Ana-goge and Tropologie are waies, whereby the sense may be applied" (737). See chapter 1 for fuller discussion of this issue.

23. Thomas Shepard, *The Saint's Jewel; Showing How to Apply the Promise* (1655), in *The Works of Thomas Shepard*, vol. 1 (1991), 289.

24. McGiffert notes that "the *Journal* shows that Shepard found solace most abun-dantly in the Psalms and the Fourth Gospel" ("Thomas Shepard: The Practise of Piety," in *God's Plot*, 13). This observation holds true for Shepard's sermons as well. While Shepard quotes from a wide variety of biblical texts with great frequency, his quotations from John dramatically outnumber quotations from any other book.

25. John T. Frederick, "Literary Art in Thomas Shepard's 'The Parable of the Ten Vir-gins,'" *Seventeenth-Century News* 26, no. 1 (spring 1968): 5; Charles E. Hambrick-Stowe, *The Practice of Piety: Puritan Devotional Disciplines in Seventeenth-Century New En-gland* (Chapel Hill: University of North Carolina Press, 1982), 119.

26. Acts 9:5: "And he said, Who art thou, Lord? And the Lord said, I am Jesus whom thou persecutest: *it is* hard for thee to kick against the pricks." Acts 26:14: "And when we were all fallen to the earth, I heard a voice speaking unto me, and saying in the Hebrew tongue, Saul, Saul, why persecutest thou me? *it is* hard for thee to kick against the pricks."

27. The relevant biblical texts are as follows: John 18:36: "Jesus answered, My king-

dom is not of this world: if my kingdom were of this world, then would my servants fight, that I should not be delivered to the Jews: but now is my kingdom not from hence." John 14:2–3: "In my Father's house are many mansions: if *it were* not *so*, I would have told you. I go to prepare a place for you. And if I go and prepare a place for you, I will come again, and receive you unto myself; that where I am, *there* ye may be also." John 17:23–24: "I in them, and thou in me, that they may be made perfect in one; and that the world may know that thou hast sent me, and hast loved them, as thou hast loved me. Father, I will that they also, whom thou hast given me, be with me where I am; that they may behold my glory, which thou hast given me: for thou lovedst me before the foundation of the world." 2 Cor. 12:2: "I knew a man in Christ above fourteen years ago, (whether in the body, I cannot tell; or whether out of the body, I cannot tell: God knoweth;) such an one caught up to the third heaven." 1 Chron. 29:16: "O LORD our God, all this store that we have prepared to build thee an house for thine holy name *cometh* of thine hand, and *is* all thine own." Eph. 5:1: "Be ye therefore followers of God, as dear children." Matt. 25:31: "When the Son of man shall come in his glory, and all the holy angels with him, then shall he sit upon the throne of his glory." Matt. 25:34: "Then shall the King say unto them on his right hand, Come, ye blessed of my Father, inherit the kingdom prepared for you from the foundation of the world." 1 Pet. 1:3–4: "Blessed *be* the God and Father of our Lord Jesus Christ, which according to his abundant mercy hath begotten us again unto a lively hope by the resurrection of Jesus Christ from the dead, To an inheritance incorruptible, and undefiled, and that fadeth not away, reserved in heaven for you." Note that there are inaccurate citations, and that Shepard sometimes quotes loosely.

28. While such an emendation would seem trivial among Thomas Hooker's often loose biblical appropriations, Shepard is generally considerably more precise. Moreover, Shepard prepared *The Sound Believer* for publication himself, so fewer inaccuracies in this text can be attributed to erring middlemen.

29. Thomas Shepard, *The Autobiography* (1832), in *God's Plot*, 37.

30. McGiffert notes that Shepard's biblical citation is inaccurate, that the quoted text is actually Genesis 18:32 (43 n. 11).

31. McGiffert, "Thomas Shepard: The Practice of Piety," in *God's Plot*, 20.

32. Ibid., 25.

33. Jones and Jones, introduction to *The Parable of the Ten Virgins*, in *Salvation in New England*, 132.

34. For a fuller account of the psychology of Puritan soteriology, see Cohen, *God's Caress.*

35. Shepard, *The Autobiography*, in *God's Plot*, 72.

36. Michael J. Colacurcio offers a subtle and illuminating reading of Shepard's response to this loss in "'A Strange Poise of Spirit': The Life and Deaths of Thomas Shepard," *Religion and Literature* 32, no. 1 (spring 2000): 1–44.

37. Thomas Shepard, *The Journal*, in *God's Plot*, 117.

38. The gospels of Matthew and Mark report Jesus' quotation from the first verse of Psalm 22, which reads: "To the chief Musician upon Aijeleth Shahar, A Psalm of David. My God, my God, why hast thou forsaken me? *why art thou so* far from helping me, *and from* the words of my roaring?" (Ps. 22:1). Matthew 27:46 reads: "And about the ninth hour Jesus cried with a loud voice, saying, Eli, Eli, lama sabachthani? that is to say, My God, my God, why hast thou forsaken me?"; while Mark 15:34 reads: "And at the ninth hour Jesus cried with a loud voice, saying, Eloi, Eloi, lama sabachthani? which is, being interpreted, My God, my God, why hast thou forsaken me?"

39. The cited texts read: "And when Saul inquired of the LORD, the LORD answered him

not, neither by dreams, nor by Urim, nor by prophets" (1 Sam. 28:6); and "And Samuel said to Saul, Why hast thou disquieted me, to bring me up? And Saul answered, I am sore distressed; for the Philistines make war against me, and God is departed from me, and answereth me no more, neither by prophets, nor by dreams: therefore I have called thee, that thou mayest make known unto me what I shall do" (1 Sam. 28:15).

40. David Stern explains that in the midrashic tradition (which shares certain important traits with Puritan interpretation), exegesis served this function, offering "interaction with God's presence through discourse" ("Midrash and the Language of Exegesis: A Study of Vayikra Rabbah, Chapter 1," *Midrash and Literature*, ed. Geoffrey H. Hartman and Sanford Budick [New Haven: Yale University Press, 1986], 121).

41. The biblical text of Isaiah 60:19 reads: "The sun shall be no more thy light by day; neither for brightness shall the moon give light unto thee: but the LORD shall be unto thee an everlasting light, and thy God thy glory." The citation from 1 John 3:1–2 is incorrect, however. The cited text reads: "Behold, what manner of love the Father hath bestowed upon us, that we should be called the sons of God: therefore the world knoweth us not, because it knew him not. Beloved, now are we the sons of God, and it doth not yet appear what we shall be: but we know that, when he shall appear, we shall be like him; for we shall see him as he is." While this idea is similar to that discussed by Shepard, the closest text to the phrase which Shepard quotes here—"see God face to face"—is found in Genesis 32:30: "And Jacob called the name of the place Peniel: for I have seen God face to face, and my life is preserved."

42. Jude 1:15 reads: "To execute judgment upon all, and to convince all that are ungodly among them of all their ungodly deeds which they have ungodly committed, and of all their hard *speeches* which ungodly sinners have spoken against him."

43. Luke 23:34: "Then said Jesus, Father , forgive them; for they know not what they do. And they parted his raiment, and cast lots."

## CHAPTER 4

1. Cotton Mather, *Magnalia Christi Americana; or, The Ecclesiastical history of New England, from its First Planting, in the Year 1620, unto the Year of Our Lord 1698* [hereafter *Magnalia*], vol. 1 (1702; Hartford: Silus Andrus and Son, 1853), reprinted as *Great Works of Christ in America* (Edinburgh: Banner of Truth Trust, 1979), 337. For biographical information on Hooker, see also George Leon Walker, *Thomas Hooker: Preacher, Founder, Democrat* (New York: Dodd, Mead, 1891); Sargent Bush Jr., *The Writings of Thomas Hooker: Spiritual Adventure in Two Worlds* (Madison: University of Wisconsin Press, 1980); Frank Shuffelton, *Thomas Hooker, 1586–1647* (Princeton: Princeton University Press, 1977); George H. Williams, "The Life of Thomas Hooker in England and Holland, 1586–1633," in *Thomas Hooker: Writings in England and Holland, 1626–1633*, ed. and intro. George H. Williams, Norman Pettit, Winfried Herget, and Sargent Bush Jr., Harvard Theological Studies 28 (Cambridge: Harvard University Press, 1975), 1–40.

2. On the rivalry between Cotton and Hooker, see Perry Miller, "Thomas Hooker and the Democracy of Connecticut" (1931), in *Errand into the Wilderness* (Cambridge: Harvard University Press, Belknap Press, 1956), 25–27; see also Shuffelton's observation of an "antagonistic undertone below Hooker's publicly correct and brotherly relationship with Cotton" (*Thomas Hooker*, 258).

3. John Cotton, "On my Reverend and dear Brother, Mr Thomas Hooker . . . ," *A Survey of the Summe of Church Discipline*, by Thomas Hooker (London, 1648), sig. [c4], quoted in Bush, *The Writings of Thomas Hooker*, 11. The full text of the poem is found in George Leon Walker, *History of the First Church in Hartford, 1633–1883* (Hartford: Brown and Gross, 1884), 428.

4. John Winthrop, *The Journal of John Winthrop 1630–1649* [hereafter *Journal*], ed. Richard S. Dunn, James Savage, and Laetitia Yeandle (Cambridge: Harvard University Press, 1996), 691.

5. This praise, like that of Cotton, was offered despite tensions between Winthrop and Hooker. Hooker had been drawn into political conflicts between Thomas Dudley and John Winthrop soon after his arrival in New England, and had experienced further conflicts with Winthrop over the settling of Connecticut. See *Journal*, 72–77, 103–4; Shuffelton, *Thomas Hooker*, 183–85.

6. Bush, *The Writings of Thomas Hooker*, 21.

7. [Thomas Hooker,] *The Sovles Preparation for Christ. Or, A Treatise of Contrition, Wherein is discovered How God breakes the heart, and woundes the Soule, in the conversion of a Sinner to Himselfe* [hereafter *SP*] (1632; London, 1638), reprinted in facsimile as *The Soules Preparation*, Library of American Puritan Writings 15 (New York: AMS Press, 1982), 10.

For discussions of the various printed versions of Hooker's sermons, see Sargent Bush Jr., "A Bibliography of the Published Writings of Thomas Hooker," in *Thomas Hooker: Writings in England and Holland,* 390–425; Winfried Herget, "The Transcription and Transmission of the Hooker Corpus," in ibid., 253–70; and Sargent Bush Jr. "Establishing the Hooker Canon," in ibid., 371–89.

8. Hooker's humor is often mockingly pointed. For example, in a passage from *The Sovles Preparation*, Hooker uses humor as a tool to emphasize the error of those who slight sin and underestimate its seriousness. People, he argues, tend to slight sin for several reasons: "First, in respect of the commonnesse of it, because that every man is guilty of it, wee slight it" (38). Hooker gives an example of this gesture: "what, saith one; Good now, what then, are not all sinners, as well as we? though we have many failings, yet we have many fellowes. If we were drunkards, or whoremongers, then it were somewhat" (38–39). Here, he emphasizes the sophistry of this position with the alliterative pairing of "failings" and "fellowes," inviting his audience to laugh at this error and to distance themselves from it, even as they recognize themselves in the sputtering sinner who thinks his sins trivial because they are common. Then, having drawn the audience in, Hooker turns the sophistry of the sinner back upon him: "Thou sayest true indeed, thou hast many fellowes in thy sins, and thou shalt have share with many fellowes in the punishment to come; there is roome enough in hell for thee and all thy fellowes, hell hath opened her mouth wide; nay the more companions thou hast had in thy sinnes, the more shall be thy plagues" (39). Though there is humor in Hooker's successful redirection of the parallel between "failings" and "fellowes," he emphasizes that this is in fact no laughing matter. While the claim that "there is roome enough in hell for thee and all thy fellowes" seems to continue the banter between Hooker and the sophist-sinner, the final pairing of "companions" and "plagues" asserts the inadequacy of wit and alliteration when "hell hath opened her mouth wide" (39). Having drawn the audience in and set them at ease with wit and humor, Hooker proceeds to drive home his very serious message.

9. Everett H. Emerson, introduction to Thomas Hooker, *Redemption: Three Sermons (1637–1656)*, ed. Everett H. Emerson (Gainesville, Fla.: Scholars' Facsimiles and Reprints, 1956), xiv.

10. John Winthrop chronicles an instance of auditors' enthusiasm for Hooker's sermons. In 1639, Hooker lectured at Cambridge, and Winthrop recorded the occasion in his *Journal*: "Mr. Hooker being to preach at Cambridge, the governour and many others went to hear him, (though the governour did very seldom go from his own congregation upon the Lord's day). He preached in the afternoon, and having gone on, with much strength of

voice and intention of spirit, about a quarter of an hour, he was at a stand, and told the people, that God had deprived him both of his strength and matter, etc., and so went forth, and about half an hour after returned again, and went on to very good purpose about two hours" (*Journal*, 297). As I note in chapter 5, the incident is a useful index not only of sermon length, but also of the eagerness to hear Hooker that apparently kept congregants patiently awaiting Hooker's apparently unpromised return for half an hour.

11. The association of the Word and the sword is found in Ephesians 6:17: "And take the helmet of salvation, and the sword of the Spirit, which is the word of God"; see also Hebrews 4:12: "For the word of God *is* quick, and powerful, and sharper than any twoedged sword, piercing even to the dividing asunder of soul and spirit, and of the joints and marrow, and *is* a discerner of the thoughts and intents of the heart."

12. Thomas Hooker, *The Application of Redemption, By the Effectual Work of the Word, and the Spirit of Christ, for the bringing home of lost Sinners to God, the Ninth and Tenth Books* [hereafter *AR 9–10*] (London, 1657), 195. Book 9 has been reprinted in facsimile from the 1656 edition in Hooker, *Redemption: Three Sermons*. References to book 9 of *The Application of Redemption* cite this edition, as it is the most readily available text, without distinguishing among the 1656, 1657, and 1659 editions, which are identical.

13. The text of Ezekiel 16:2, in both the Geneva and the Authorized versions, reads: "Son of man, cause Jerusalem to know her abominations."

14. See *SP*, 64, and the parallel passage in *AR 9–10*, 197.

15. Thomas Goodwyn and Philip Nye, "To the Reader," *The Application of Redemption, By the effectual Work of the Word, and Spirit of Christ, for the bringing home of lost Sinners to God*, by Thomas Hooker (London, 1657), reprinted as *The Application of Redemption* (New York: Arno Press, 1972), sig. C3r. The same preface appears in the second volume of *AR 9–10*.

16. In *The Arte of Prophecying*, Perkins cautions that "neither the wordes of arts, nor Greeke and Latine phrases and quirks must be intermingled in the sermon. 1. They disturbe the minds of the auditours, that they cannot fit those things which went afore with those that follow. 2. A strange word hindreth the understanding of those things that are spoken. 3. It drawes the minde away from the purpose to some other matter" (*The Arte of Prophecying* [1592, trans. 1607] [hereafter *Arte*], trans. Thomas Tuke, in *Works* [London, 1690], 759).

17. Thomas Hooker, *The Poor Doubting Christian Drawn Unto Christ*, in *Thomas Hooker: Writings in England and Holland, 1626–1633*, Harvard Theological Studies 28 (Cambridge: Harvard University Press, 1975), 152–86. Norman Pettit identifies this as Hooker's "earliest published sermonic text" in his introduction to the text in ibid., 147. On the status of this text, see Pettit, ibid., 147–51; and Winfried Herget, "Preaching and Publication—Chronology and the Style of Thomas Hooker's Sermons," *Harvard Theological Review* 65 (1972): 231–32.

18. See Charles Lloyd Cohen, *God's Caress: The Psychology of Puritan Religious Experience* (Oxford: Oxford University Press, 1986), esp. 25–74; Perry Miller, *The New England Mind: The Seventeenth Century* (1939; Cambridge: Harvard University Press, 1954), 239–79.

19. On the emphasis Puritan preachers placed on uses, see Teresa Toulouse, *The Art of Prophesying: New England Sermons and the Shaping of Belief* (Athens: University of Georgia Press, 1987), 20–23. See also Emerson, introduction to Hooker, *Redemption: Three Sermons*, xv.

20. For discussion of Hooker's preparationist emphasis on human responses to God's grace, see R. T. Kendall, *Calvin and English Calvinism to 1649* (New York: Oxford University Press, 1979), 125–38; Norman Pettit, *The Heart Prepared: Grace and Conversion in Puritan Spiritual Life* (New Haven: Yale University Press, 1966); William K. B. Stoever, "A

*Faire and Easie Way to Heaven": Covenant Theology and Antinomianism in Early Massa-chusetts* (Middletown, Conn.: Wesleyan University Press, 1978); and Janice Knight, *Ortho-doxies in Massachusetts: Rereading American Puritanism* (Cambridge: Harvard University Press, 1994).

21. Lewis Bayly, *The Practise of Pietie, Directing a Christian how to walke that he may please God,* 3d ed. (London, 1613). David D. Hall notes "that first-generation colonists relied on Bayly's *Practice of Piety,* [Arthur] Dent's *The Plain Mans Pathway to Heaven,* and [Henry] Scudder's *Daily Walk"* ("Readers and Writers in Early New England," in *The Colonial Book in the Atlantic World,* ed. Hugh Amory and David D. Hall, vol. 1 of *A History of the Book in America* [Cambridge: Cambridge University Press, 2000], 126).

22. Theodore Dwight Bozeman argues that such identification with the biblical text was central to Puritanism: "[I]n the many forms of biblical nurture sponsored by Puritan interests, the first aim was to abolish objective distance between the precise saint of Eliza-bethan or Stuart times and the world of biblical report; it was to draw the observer within the horizon of action, to promote self-forgetful identification with the presented events" (*To Live Ancient Lives: The Primitivist Dimension in Puritanism* [Chapel Hill: University of North Carolina Press, 1988], 16). Though Hooker's manipulations of biblical identification encouraged self-mindfulness, rather than self-forgetfulness, Bozeman's account of "dra-matic identification" with the biblical text is very illuminating. Alan D. Hodder take a somewhat different approach to Hooker's attempts to engage his audience's identification, emphasizing continuities between Hooker's sermon rhetoric and drama. See Hodder, "In the Glasse of God's Word: Hooker's Pulpit Rhetoric and the Theater of Conversion," *New England Quarterly* 66, no. 1 (March 1993): 67–109. Jessie Schindler explores Hooker's "the-atrics of instruction" in her master's thesis, "A Mirror for Educators: The Puritan Sermon and the Theatrics of Instruction" (M.A. thesis, Columbia University, 1995).

23. John Collins, "The Relation of Mr Collins," in *The Diary of Michael Wigglesworth, 1653–1657: The Conscience of a Puritan,* ed. Edmund S. Morgan (Gloucester: Peter Smith, 1970), 108.

24. The parallel passage in *The Application of Redemption* is found in book 10, p. 199.

25. Andrew Delbanco describes Puritan ministers' increasing concern with spiritual torpor, noting that "[e]ven before the embarkation for America, Puritan sermons contain fewer and fewer catalogues of sinful excess, and more and more demands that a sleeping people be roused" (*The Puritan Ordeal* [Cambridge: Harvard University Press, 1989], 56).

26. Bush, *The Writings of Thomas Hooker,* 20.

27. Ibid., 19.

28. Hooker uses Judas similarly to explain why people do not always recognize how evil sin is, "because we judge not of sinne according to the Word and verdict of it, but either in regard of the profit that is therein, or the pleasure that wee expect therefrom. The Vsurer lookes on his profit that comes by sinne, and the adulterer on his pleasure; and *Iudas* saw the money, but he did not see the malice of his owne heart, nor the want of love to his *Master,* and this made him take up that course which he did; but when he threw away his thirtie pence, the Lord made him see the vilenesse of his sinne; it came clearely to his sight, and therefore he cryed out: *I have sinned in betraying innocent blood"* (*SP,* 19). Here, too, Hooker uses the biblical sinner as both negative and positive exemplar.

29. See *AR* 9–10, 654–57, in which Hooker explores "How to know a right Confession of sin," and 680–84, on "How true hatred of sin discovers itself."

30. Acts 7:51 reads: "Ye stiffnecked and uncircumcised in heart and ears, ye do always resist the Holy Ghost: as your fathers *did,* so *do* ye."

31. Revelations 2:21–22 reads: "And I gave her space to repent of her fornication; and

she repented not. Behold, I will cast her into a bed, and them that commit adultery with her into great tribulation, except they repent of their deeds." Psalm 41:3 reads: "The LORD will strengthen him upon the bed of languishing: thou wilt make all his bed in his sickness."

32. The biblical text, in the Authorized Version, reads: "Let the wicked forsake his way, and the unrighteous man his thoughts: and let him return unto the LORD, and he will have mercy upon him; and to our God, for he will abundantly pardon. For my thoughts *are* not your thoughts, neither *are* your ways my ways, saith the LORD. For *as* the heavens are higher than the earth, so are my ways higher than your ways, and my thoughts than your thoughts."

33. Isaiah 5:19 reads: "That say, Let him make speed, *and* hasten his work, that we may see *it:* and let the counsel of the Holy One of Israel draw nigh and come, that we may know *it!*" The closest matches to the second verse Hooker paraphrases include Psalm 94:11 ("The LORD knoweth the thoughts of man, that they *are* vanity"); 1 Corinthians 3:20 ("And again, The Lord knoweth the thoughte wise, that they are vain"); and Isaiah 66:18 ("For I *know* their works and their thoughts: it shall come, that I will gather all nations and tongues; and they shall come, and see my glory"). See also *SP,* 43, for a dialogue set up between the people described in Jeremiah and the Deuteronomic God.

34. Roland Barthes, *The Pleasure of the Text,* trans. Richard Miller (New York: Hill and Wang, 1975), 6. For further discussion of Barthes's approach to intertextuality, see chapter 5.

35. Shuffelton explains that Mrs. Drake "had in her most querulous moments a deplorable way of using the Scriptures; she would chose texts for guidance by arbitrarily opening her Bible and putting her finger on the page. Whichever text she came upon she presumed applicable to her condition, and she usually labored to put the worst possible interpretation on it. By supplying an ordered method of approaching the word, Hooker was apparently able to direct the misguided procedure of Joanna Drake into a more profitable course and to persuade her to leave off this business of tempting God" (*Thomas Hooker,* 54–55). Shuffelton bases his understanding of Hooker's interaction with Mrs. Drake on *The Poor Doubting Christian,* and on the account in Jasper Hartwell, *The Firebrand Taken out of the Fire. Or, the Wonderfull History, Case, and Cure of Mis Drake* (London, 1654).

36. Hodder, "In the Glasse of God's Word," 69.

37. *Magnalia,*1:337; Shuffleton, *Thomas Hooker,* 107.

38. David D. Hall explores the role of the New England ministry (and the ministers' own understanding of that role) in *The Faithful Shepherd: A History of the New England Ministry in the Seventeenth Century* (Chapel Hill: University of North Carolina Press, 1972).

39. The text of Acts 2:37 reads: "Now when they heard *this,* they were pricked in their heart, and said unto Peter and to the rest of the apostles, Men *and* brethren, what shall we do?"

40. *SP,* 11. Citations for all verses in this paragraph are included in the margin of Hooker's text.

41. The text of Job 36:8–10 reads: "And if *they be* bound in fetters, *and* be holden in cords of affliction; Then he showeth them the transgressions that they have exceeded. He openeth also their ear to discipline, and commandeth that they return from iniquity." Generally, the printers of Hooker's texts did not distinguish between such paraphrases and fuller quotations. Moreover, even the quotations contain inaccuracies, and it is difficult to determine whether such inaccuracies result from incomplete or error-ridden manuscripts or merely from inconsistency or carelessness on the printer's part. The texts of *The Application of Redemption* are not so much more accurate than the Chelmsford texts that they resolve the question definitively.

42. Jer. 8:6. The marginal annotation in *SP* reads, inaccurately, "Ier.8.6.8."

43. The next several pages of *SP* include only about one quotation per page (11–14).

44. Thomas Hooker, *The Application of Redemption, By the effectual Work of the Word, and Spirit of Christ, for the bringing home of lost Sinners to God. The first eight Books* (London, 1657; New York: Arno Press, 1972), 141. This passage is a revised version of the opening of "The Preparing the Heart for to Receive Christ," in T[homas] H[ooker], *The Soules Implantation into the Naturall Olive* (London, 1640), reprinted in facsimile as *The Soules Implantation*, Library of American Puritan Writings 17 (New York: AMS Press, 1981), 29–31.

45. The verse reads: "Behold, I will send my messenger, and he shall prepare the way before me: and the Lord, whom ye seek, shall suddenly come to his temple, even the messenger of the covenant, whom ye delight in: behold, he shall come, saith the LORD of hosts" (Mal. 3:1).

46. The text from Luke 3:4 reads: "As it is written in the book of the words of Esaias the prophet, saying, The voice of one crying in the wilderness, Prepare ye the way of the Lord, make his paths straight." Isaiah 40:3 reads: "The voice of him that crieth in the wilderness, Prepare ye the way of the LORD, make straight in the desert a highway for our God."

47. This discussion appears in "The Soules Ingrafting into Christ," in the previously cited *The Soules Implantation into the Naturall Olive* (133). This is an abridged version of "The Soules Ingrafting into Christ," published in *The Soules Implantation: A Treatise* (London, 1637), reprinted in Hooker, *Redemption: Three Sermons*, edited by Emerson. The parallel text (which has not been changed in the abridgement process) appears on pp. 115–16 of the unabridged text, and on pp. 101–2 of Emerson's collection. See also Emerson's introduction to Hooker, *Redemption: Three Sermons*, xvi, for information on the texts he includes.

Kendall cites a slightly different version of this text, identifying its source as *The Soules Ingrafting into Christ* (London, 1637) (*Calvin and English Calvinism to 1649*, 137). Bush describes the version in *The Soules Implantation: A Treatise* as "a much longer version of this sermon . . . which was in turn reprinted in more carefully edited form in *The Souls Implantation into the Natural Olive* (1640)" ("Bibliography," 401). I quote from the 1637 text of *The Soules Ingrafting into Christ*, which differs slightly from the text as Kendall quotes it.

48. T[homas] H[ooker], *The Soules Ingrafting Into Christ* (London, 1637), 16.

49. See Genesis 28:10–16.

50. The page in *SP* is mislabeled as page 86.

51. Alfred Habegger, "Preparing the Soul for Christ: The Contrasting Sermon Forms of John Cotton and Thomas Hooker," *American Literature* 41, no. 3 (November 1969): 342–54.

52. Ibid., 345. Habegger cites *The Application of Redemption* (London, 1659), 2. This is a reissue of the 1657 edition of *The Application of Redemption . . . The Ninth and Tenth Books*, with the title page reset. The 1657 edition is a reprint of the 1656 text, with title pages identical except for the date. See Bush, "Bibliography," 418–420.

53. Hooker makes a similar declaration early in book 1 of *The Application of Redemption:* "Neither shall we meddle with every particular which the several Texts will offer to our Consideration, but only handle such as concern our purpose" (2).

54. Hooker, *The Application of Redemption*, 141; Hooker, *The Soules Implantation into the Naturall Olive*, 29. The full text of Luke 1:17 reads: "And he shall go before him in the spirit and power of Elias, to turn the hearts of the fathers to the children, and the disobedient to the wisdom of the just; to make ready a people prepared for the Lord."

55. Habegger, "Preparing the Soul for Christ," 345. Kendall suggests that Hooker's listener-centered orientation *did* have limits. Building on Habegger's argument that Hooker privileged preaching the *ordo salutis* over "opening" a biblical text fully, Kendall argues that preaching the *ordo salutis* took precedence over the needs of individual congregants, with Hooker preaching "to his hearers as though they themselves are no further along (or

behind) spiritually than the immediate subject (e.g. 'contrition') he is discussing" (*Calvin and English Calvinism to 1649*, 127–28 n. 13). But Kendall overstates the implications of Hooker's structure for the listener's situation. While it is true that Hooker "does not return to the original phase (the unbeliever's preparation) once he has moved on," the possibility Kendall suggests, that "new people" present in the congregation "would not necessarily be aware of his original premiss" seems unlikely, both in the English and in the New English contexts (ibid.). Moreover, Hooker's goal was not to *explain* Calvinist soteriology, but rather to drive it "home" to his listeners in affective terms. In his approach to the preached text, as in his approach to the biblical text, Hooker stressed the effects of the experience on the hearer or reader, emphasizing affective and spiritual response over intellectual understanding.

56. T[homas] H[ooker], *The unbeleevers preparing for Christ* (London, 1638), 6–7 (second pagination).

57. Cohen, *God's Caress*, 81.

58. Hooker, *The unbeleevers preparing for Christ*, 6.

59. For discussion of the transmission and publication of sermon texts, see the appendix.

60. The text of Job 7:20 reads: "I have sinned; what shall I do unto thee, O thou preserver of men? why hast thou set me as a mark against thee, so that I am a burden to myself?"

61. In the biblical text, the exhortation is to buy "gold tried in the fire," and "annoint thine eyes with eyesalve": "I counsel thee to buy of me gold tried in the fire, that thou mayest be rich; and white raiment, that thou mayest be clothed, and *that* the shame of thy nakedness do not appear; and anoint thine eyes with eyesalve, that thou mayest see" (Rev. 3:18).

62. Hooker, *The Application of Redemption (Books 1–8)*, 144. The text of Isaiah 40:3 reads: "The voice of him that crieth in the wilderness, Prepare ye the way of the LORD, make straight in the desert a highway for our God."

63. The full text of Luke 23:18 reads: "And they cried out all at once, saying, Away with this *man*, and release unto us Barabbas."

64. On page 3 of this text, Hooker discusses various phrases from the verse, and here he omits "to be saved."

65. Hooker's position is not, of course, utterly without biblical sanction. Acts 16:30 does contain the words "to be saved," although the answer that follows does not straightforwardly validate the activity of a preparationist agenda: "And brought them out, and said, Sirs, what must I do to be saved? And they said, Believe on the Lord Jesus Christ, and thou shalt be saved, and thy house" (Acts 16:30–31). Like some of Hooker's seventeenth-century critics, Perry Miller saw Hooker's soteriology as a deviation from Calvinist orthodoxy. See Miller, "'Preparation for Salvation' in Seventeenth Century New England," *Journal of the History of Ideas* 4, no. 3 (1943): 253–86, reprinted in *Ideas in Cultural Perspective*, ed. Philip P. Wiener and Aaron Noland (New Brunswick: Rutgers University Press, 1962), 604–32. More recent (and generally more generous) considerations of preparationist soteriology are offered by Pettit, *The Heart Prepared*; Stoever, *"A Faire and Easie Way to Heaven"*; Cohen, *God's Caress*; Kendall, *Calvin and English Calvinism to 1649*; and Knight, *Orthodoxies in Massachusetts*.

66. Treating the Word as distinct from the words of the biblical text was more typical of radical Puritans. See Nigel Smith, *Perfection Proclaimed: Language and Literature in English Radical Religion 1640–1660* (Oxford: Clarendon Press, 1989), 269.

67. Hooker's approach to the biblical text remains less flexible than that of Conformist churchmen. Richard Hooker, for example, allows "sundry sensible meanes besids" preaching to move the hearts of Christian congregants. See Richard Hooker, *Of the Lawes of Ecclesiasticall Politie, Eyght Bookes* (1593), ed. Georges Edelen, vol. 1 of *The Folger Library*

*Edition of the Works of Richard Hooker,* ed. W. Speed Hill (Cambridge: Harvard University Press, Belknap Press, 1977), vol. 4, chap. 1, sec. 3, p. 418. See also Andrew Delbanco's discussion of this passage in *The Puritan Ordeal,* 34–35.

## Chapter 5

1. David D. Hall, *Worlds of Wonder, Days of Judgment: Popular Religious Belief in Early New England* (New York: Knopf, 1989), 32.

2. Kenneth A. Lockridge, *Literacy in Colonial New England: An Enquiry into the Social Context of Literacy in the Early Modern West* (New York: Norton, 1974), 13; Hall, *Worlds of Wonder,* 32, 262–63 n. 28.

3. Quoted in David D. Hall, "Readers and Writers in Early New England," in *The Colonial Book in the Atlantic World, A History of the Book in America,* vol. 1. (Cambridge: Cambridge University Press, 2000), 120. Similar laws were passed in subsequent years in Connecticut, Plymouth, and New Haven. See ibid., 119.

4. Hall cites Lockridge's assessment of signature literacy, as well as his assumption "that the ability to read was much more widespread than the ability to write" ("Readers and Writers in Early New England," 550 n. 13). The estimate of male literacy at 50 percent is found in Ralph J. Crandall and Ralph J. Coffman, "From Emigrants to Rulers: The Charlestown Oligarchy in the Great Migration," *New England Historic Genealogical Register* 131 (1977): 1–27, cited in ibid. The estimate of nearly 90 percent male signature literacy is derived by Jennifer Monaghan, in unpublished research "done across the life cycle and using records other than wills, [which] tends to indicate a higher rate of signing literacy" (ibid.).

5. Hall, *Worlds of Wonder,* 32, 22.

6. Ibid., 7, 34.

7. Ibid., 32, 36.

8. Ibid., 37, 43.

9. Christopher Hill describes authors' exploitation of expected audience recognition of biblical passages "to combine outspokenness and caution" to communicate revolutionary messages (*The English Bible and the Seventeenth-Century Revolution* [1993; New York: Penguin, 1994], 76–78).

10. Theodore Dwight Bozeman, *To Live Ancient Lives: The Primitivist Dimension in Puritanism* (Chapel Hill: University of North Carolina Press, 1988), 38.

11. Hall, *Worlds of Wonder,* 43.

12. Lewis Bayly, *The Practise of Pietie, Directing a Christian how to walke that he may please God,* 3d ed. (London, 1613). Stephen Foster calls *The Practise of Pietie* "the best-selling manual of all," noting that it "reached at a bare minimum fifty-four editions (eighty-seven thousand copies at least) before 1640" (*The Long Argument: English Puritanism and the Shaping of New England Culture, 1570–1700* [Chapel Hill: University of North Carolina Press, 1991], 91). On Bayly's popularity in New England, see Hall, "Readers and Writers in Early New England," 126.

13. William Ames, *The Marrow of Theology (1623),* ed. and trans. (from the third Latin edition of 1629) John D. Eusden (1968; Durham: Labyrinth, 1983), 254.

14. Charles E. Hambrick-Stowe observes that many sermons "were edited for publication [in Cambridge and Boston] from listeners' notes," and that it "was not uncommon for New Englanders to keep a personal book of sermon notes" (*The Practice of Piety: Puritan Devotional Disciplines in Seventeenth-Century New England* [Chapel Hill: University of North Carolina Press, 1982], 116–17).

15. Thomas Shepard, *The Autobiography* (1832), in *God's Plot: Puritan Spirituality in*

*Thomas Shepard's Cambridge,* ed. and intro. Michael McGiffert. (1972; Amherst: University of Massachusetts Press, 1994), 41.

16. Patrick Collinson, "The English Conventicle," *Voluntary Religion: Papers Read at the 1985 Summer Meeting and the 1986 Winter Meeting of the Ecclesiastical History Society,* ed. J. Sheils and Diane Wood, *Studies in Church History* 23 (1986): 240.

17. Ames, *Marrow of Theology,* 192.

18. John D. Eusden, introduction to Ames, *The Marrow of Theology,* 2.

19. Ibid., 1. Eusden notes that the *Medulla,* in twelve further Latin editions, circulated "widely in England, New England, and on the Continent." An English translation appeared in three printings between 1638 and 1643, and a Dutch translation appeared in 1656 (ibid., 1–2).

20. John Cotton, *Christ the Fountaine of Life: Or, Sundry Choyce Sermons on part of the fift Chapter of the first Epistle of St. John* (1651; New York: Arno Press, 1972), 200.

21. See Collinson, "The English Conventicle," 223–34, on the legal status of the conventicle in seventeenth-century England.

22. *The Book of the General Lawes and Libertyes Concerning the Inhabitants of the Massachusetts* (Cambridge, Mass., 1648), 19; J. Hammond Trumbull and Charles J. Hoadly, eds., *The Public Records of the Colony of Connecticut* (Hartford, Conn., 1859–90), 1:311–12. Both are quoted in Foster, *The Long Argument,* 146, 346 n. 16.

23. Shepard recorded narratives from the 1630s and 1640s in a notebook, which was edited by George Selement and Bruce C. Woolley and published as *Thomas Shepard's "Confessions"* (Publications of the Colonial Society of Massachusetts, *Collections* 58 [Boston, 1981]). Another set of sixteen confessions appeared in 1991, in Mary Rhinelander McCarl, "Thomas Shepard's Records of Relations of Religious Experience, 1648–1649," *William and Mary Quarterly,* 3d ser. 48, no. 3 (July 1991): 432–66. Michael McGiffert's revised edition of Shepard's *Autobiography* prints thirty-three of the confessions as well. See *God's Plot,* 149–225. Unless otherwise noted, narratives below are cited from *God's Plot.*

Rich discussions of the conversion narratives of Shepard's congregants are found in Patricia Caldwell, *The Puritan Conversion Narrative* (Cambridge: Cambridge University Press, 1983); and Charles Lloyd Cohen, *God's Caress: The Psychology of Puritan Religious Experience* (New York: Oxford University Press, 1986). For an excellent discussion of Hutchinson's conversion narrative, see Michael Ditmore, "A Prophetess in Her Own Country: An Exegesis of Anne Hutchinson's 'Immediate Revelation,'" *William and Mary Quarterly* 3d ser. 57, no. 2 (April 2000): 349–92.

24. Thomas Shepard, *The Sound Believer* (1645), in *The Works of Thomas Shepard, First Pastor of the First Church, Cambridge, Mass. with a Memoir of His Life and Character,* vol. 1 (Boston: Boston Doctrinal Tract and Book Society, 1853; Ligonier, Penn.: Soli Deo Gloria, 1991), 123, 128.

25. Caldwell, *Puritan Conversion Narrative,* 171.

26. Ibid., 12. Elizabeth White's *The Experiences of God's Gracious Dealing with Mrs. Elizabeth White* (Boston, 1741) "circulated on both sides of the Atlantic," though there is no evidence that White herself traveled to America (1, 3, 202).

27. Ivy Schweitzer describes "redeemed subjectivity" as "a subjectivity deferred," and illuminates the extent to which this subjectivity was both gendered and "hegemonic." See Schweitzer, *The Work of Self-Representation: Lyric Poetry in Colonial New England* (Chapel Hill: University of North Carolina Press, 1991), 29–30.

28. Joseph Caryl, "To the Reader," in John Cotton, *A Treatise of the Covenant of Grace, As it is dispensed to the Elect Seed, effectually unto Salvation* (London, 1671), A1v.

29. Prov. 31:10, 31:31.

30. See Roland Barthes, *The Pleasure of the Text*, trans. Richard Miller (New York: Hill and Wang, 1975), 12.

31. William Bradford, *Of Plymouth Plantation 1620–1647*, ed. Samuel Eliot Morison (1952; New York: Knopf, 1991), 63.

32. See chapter 6 for a fuller discussion of Puritan typology.

33. Ann Stanford, for example, notes that in "As Weary Pilgrim" Bradstreet "finally accepts, even embraces, the everlasting state she has never seemed quite sure of" ("Anne Bradstreet," *Major Writers of Early American Literature*, ed. Everett Emerson [Madison: University of Wisconsin Press, 1972], 56). Charles E. Hambrick-Stowe reads the poem as describing "the consummation of the saint's personal union with Christ" (*The Practice of Piety*, 19). This promised to come with her death and "the Day of the Lord," which "were so near that in the intensity of her devotions Anne Bradstreet could feel them as present reality" (19). Schweitzer, however, finds in Hambrick-Stowe's reading of the poem's last line a confirmation of her "sense of its resistance to the appropriating discourse of Canticles," a sense that "Bradstreet's calling as the Bride in the final line of the poem is dependent upon a readiness that is not yet fully ripened" (*The Work of Self-Representation*, 179). Similarly, Robert Daly notes Bradstreet's request that God "make [her] ready for that day" as an indication that she is not yet "ready," and contrasts Bradstreet's unreadiness to the preparedness Edward Taylor expresses (*God's Altar: The World and the Flesh in Puritan Poetry* [Berkeley: University of California Press, 1978], 134, 172).

34. Anne Bradstreet, "As Weary Pilgrim" (1669), in *The Works of Anne Bradstreet*, ed. Jeannine Hensley (Cambridge: Harvard University Press, Belknap Press, 1967), 1. 1.

35. Hambrick-Stowe's reading of the poem's final line as a dialogue in which Bradstreet calls "Come, dear Bridegroom" and Christ responds "Come away" suggests that he, too, sees this line as potentially unsettling, though he finds a more orthodox balance by giving the last word to Christ. See Hambrick-Stowe, *The Practice of Piety*, 19.

36. Barthes, *The Pleasure of the Text*, 4.

37. See chapter 3 for a fuller discussion of Shepard's practice of biblical quotation.

38. Thomas Prince, *Extraordinary Events the Doings of God, and Marvellous in Pious Eyes. Illustrated in a sermon at the South Church in Boston, N.E. on the general thanksgiving, Thursday, July 18, 1745. Occasion'd by taking the city of Louisbourg on the Isle of Cape-Breton, by New-England soldiers, assisted by a British squadron* (Boston, 1745), 33. Prince's quotations are from Psalm 126:1–3; Psalm 115:1, 3; Psalm 115:12, 18; 1 Chronicles 29:11–13; 1 Chronicles 16:8–9, 24 (see also Psalm 105:1–2). The significance of the victory at Louisbourg and the reasons for such great thanksgiving are explored by Harry S. Stout in *The New England Soul: Preaching and Religious Culture in Colonial New England* (New York: Oxford University Press, 1986), 233–38.

39. John Winthrop, *The Journal of John Winthrop, 1630–1649* [hereafter *Journal*], ed. Richard S. Dunn, James Savage, and Laetitia Yeandle (Cambridge: Harvard University Press, 1996), 316.

40. Barthes, *The Pleasure of the Text*, 7.

41. John Mason, *A Brief history of the Pequot War: Especially of the memorable Taking of their Fort at Mistick in Connecticut In 1637* (Boston, 1732), 22.

42. Sacvan Bercovitch discusses New England Puritans' insistence that "they were reclaiming what by promise belonged to them, as the Israelites had once reclaimed Canaan" in *The Rites of Assent: Transformations of the Symbolic Construction of America* (New York: Routledge, 1993), 81.

43. See Proverbs 20:26: "A wise king scattereth the wicked, and bringeth the wheel over them."

44. Ann Kibbey discusses this passage in *The Interpretation of Material Shapes in Puritanism: A Study of Rhetoric, Prejudice, and Violence* (Cambridge: Cambridge University Press, 1986), 97. Although Kibbey recognizes biblical sources for the images of conflagration that run through Mason's text, she fails to note Mason's biblical paraphrase here. Focusing on what strikes her as an odd usage of the word "turned," she suggests that Mason may perhaps be "alluding to tropes as turns of meaning, . . . [explaining] that his deity has thus 'turned' the lives of the Puritans": "Mason's eerie description, 'we were like Men in a Dream,' implies a grotesque inversion of referentiality, a sense of having compulsively acted out a scriptural image [of conflagration] whose hypnotic power controlled them" (97).

Reading the reference to dreaming as a description of a "hypnotic power [that] controlled" the Puritans, Kibbey distorts Mason's text. His description is not couched within a frenzied or hypnotic account, but rather within a self-satisfied afterword in which he locates "the Finger of God in all this" (21). He appropriates scriptural language not to signal confusion, but to mark great joy. And while it may seem strange to us that Mason should apply the words of these verses to the Puritan attack on the Pequots at Mystic, it is less "eerie" than it would have been to make up such a phrase to describe the attackers' state of mind.

My reading of the passage, however, is consistent with Kibbey's approach to Puritan rhetoric, and the disturbing richness that results from Mason's manipulation of the biblical text illuminates Kibbey's emphasis on the distinction "between religious and secular events" and on the way that the Pequot War "was rationalized by religion in Puritan society" (2).

CHAPTER 6

1. "The [Salem Church] Covenant of 1629," *The Creeds and Platforms of Congregationalism*, ed. Williston Walker (New York: Scribner's, 1893), 116.

2. John S. Coolidge, *The Pauline Renaissance in England: Puritanism and the Bible* (Oxford: Clarendon Press, 1970), 7.

3. Richard Hooker, *Of the Lawes of Ecclesiasticall Politie, Eyght Books* (1593), ed. Georges Edelen, vol. 1 of *The Folger Library Edition of the Works of Richard Hooker*, ed. W. Speed Hill (Cambridge: Harvard University Press, Belknap Press, 1977), preface, chap. 3, sec. 2, p. 13. Subsequent citations of this work are to book, chapter, section, and page number.

4. On Puritan approaches to reason, see Perry Miller, *The New England Mind: The Seventeenth Century* (1939; Cambridge: Harvard University Press, 1954), 111–206; John Morgan, *Godly Learning: Puritan Attitudes towards Reason, Learning, and Education, 1560–1640* (Cambridge: Cambridge University Press, 1986).

5. For detailed discussion of Puritan understanding of "literal" meaning, see chapter 1.

6. Thomas Cartwright, for example, offers four rules to govern ecclesiastical matters "not particularly mentioned of in the scripture" (quoted from John Whitgift's quotation of Cartwright's text in *The Works of John Whitgift*, ed. John Ayre [Cambridge, U.K.: Parker Society, 1851], 1:176, in Coolidge, *The Pauline Renaissance in England*, 5, 158).

7. Ibid., 1:195, quoted in Coolidge, *The Pauline Renaissance in England*, 6.

8. Coolidge, *The Pauline Renaissance in England*, 11.

9. Edward Cardwell, *Documentary Annals of the Reformed Church of England* (Oxford, 1844), 2:201–2, quoted in Stephen Foster, *The Long Argument: English Puritanism and the Shaping of New England Culture, 1570–1700* (Chapel Hill: University of North Carolina Press, 1991), 128, 343 n. 50.

10. For a discussion of later developments in Anglican views of the Bible, see Gerard

Reedy, *The Bible and Reason: Anglicans and Scripture in Late Seventeenth-Century England* (Philadelphia: University of Pennsylvania Press, 1985).

11. The constraints of this book prevent a detailed exploration of the various English movements that were labeled "Puritan" by their opponents. Detailed studies of English Puritanism include William Haller, *The Rise of Puritanism, Or, The Way to the New Jerusalem as Set Forth in Pulpit and Press from Thomas Cartwright to John Lilburne and John Milton, 1570–1643* (1938; Philadelphia: University of Pennsylvania Press, 1972); Patrick Collinson, *The Elizabethan Puritan Movement* (Berkeley: University of California Press, 1967); William Hunt, *The Puritan Moment: The Coming of Revolution in an English County*, Harvard Historical Studies 102 (Cambridge: Harvard University Press, 1983); John R. Knott Jr., *The Sword of the Spirit: Puritan Responses to the Bible* (Chicago: University of Chicago Press, 1980); Murray Tolmie, *The Triumph of the Saints: The Separate Churches of London 1616–1649* (London: Cambridge University Press, 1977). Coolidge, *The Pauline Renaissance in England*, also considers Puritan views of the Bible. Leonard J. Trinterud's *Elizabethan Puritanism* (New York: Oxford University Press, 1971) is a useful anthology of Puritan writings, and clarifies differences among different groups of Puritans. Geoffrey F. Nuttall traces Puritanism's spiritist leanings, and its relationship to the development of Quakerism, in *The Holy Spirit in Puritan Faith and Experience* (Oxford: Basil Blackwell, 1946). Christopher Hill traces various radical groups in seventeenth-century England in *The World Turned Upside Down: Radical Ideas during the English Revolution* (1972; New York: Penguin, 1975).

12. On the primitivist tendencies of the Puritan movement, see Theodore Dwight Bozeman, *To Live Ancient Lives: The Primitivist Dimension in Puritanism* (Chapel Hill: University of North Carolina Press, 1988).

13. "The Examination of Mrs. Anne Hutchinson at the Court at Newtown" [hereafter "Examination"], in *The Antinomian Controversy, 1636–1638: A Documentary History*, ed. David D. Hall, 2d ed. (Durham: Duke University Press, 1990), 337. Hutchinson quotes from Isaiah 30:20, which reads: "And *though* the Lord give you the bread of adversity, and the water of affliction, yet shall not thy teachers be removed into a corner any more, but thine eyes shall see thy teachers."

Not all of the immigrants to New England came for religious reasons, of course. As Everett Emerson notes, "Just as there were nonreligous reasons for being a Puritan, so there were admittedly several nonreligious reasons for leaving England" (*Puritanism in America, 1620–1750*, Twayne's World Leaders Series 71 [Boston: Twayne, 1977], 31). Among these reasons Emerson includes the disintegration of English agrarian society, economic depression, plague, bad harvests, and political crisis (31–32).

14. John Cotton, "Copy of a Letter from Mr. Cotton to Lord Say and Seal in the Year 1636," in *The New England Way*, Library of American Puritan Writings 12 (New York: AMS Press, 1984), 415.

15. *A Model of Church and Civil Power*, quoted in Roger Williams, *The Bloudy Tenent, of Persecution, for cause of Conscience, discussed, in A Conference betweene Truth and Peace. Who, In all tender Affection, present to the High Court of Parliament, (as the Result of their Discourse) these, (amongst other Passages) of highest consideration* (1644) [hereafter *BT*], in *Publications of the Narragansett Club*, ed. Samuel L. Caldwell, 1st ser., vol. 3 (Providence, 1867), reprinted in *The Complete Writings of Roger Williams*, vol. 3 (New York: Russell and Russell, 1963), 145/261. The number before the slash indicates pagination in the 1644 edition; the number following the slash refers to the 1867 edition. This edition does not indicate a page reference in the original text for prefatory materials.

Bozeman dates *A Model of Church and Civil Power* to 1634 or 1635, and places it among "the fullest and most authoritative" "early formulations of New England Congregational theory" (*To Live Ancient Lives*, 127).

16. Edward H. Davidson, "Cotton's Biblical Exegesis: Method and Purpose," *Early American Literature* 17, no. 2 (fall 1982): 128.

17. John Davenport reports that Cotton made this boast in an attempt to convince him to migrate to New England, which he did in 1637. See Davenport, *A Sermon Preach'd at the Election of the Governour at Boston in New England, May 19th, 1669* (Boston, 1670), 15, quoted in Jesper Rosenmeier, "The Teacher and the Witness: John Cotton and Roger Williams," *William and Mary Quarterly* 3d ser., 25, no. 3 (July 1968): 427.

18. "The [Salem Church] Covenant of 1629," 116.

19. "The Charlestown–Boston Covenant," in *The Creeds and Platforms of Congregationalism*, 131.

20. John Calvin, *Institutes of the Christian Religion* (1559), ed. John T. McNeill, trans. Ford Lewis Battles, vol. 1, Library of Christian Classics 20 (Philadelphia: Westminster, 1960), 115.

21. William Perkins, *The Arte of Prophecying* (1592, trans. 1607) [hereafter *Arte*], trans. Thomas Tuke, in *Works* (London, 1609), 751.

22. John Cotton, *The Bloudy Tenent, Washed And made white in the bloud of the Lambe: being discussed and discharged of bloud-guiltinesse by just Defence* (London, 1647), 29.

23. Larzer Ziff, "Upon What Pretext?: The Book and Literary History," *Proceedings of the American Antiquarian Society* 95 (1985): 304.

24. For a detailed discussion of spiritually illumined reading, see chapter 1.

25. *Arte*, 751.

26. Richard Bernard, *The Faithfvll Shepheard: Or The Shepheards Faithfulnesse: Wherein is for the matter largely, but for the maner, in few words, set forth the excellencie and necessitie of the Ministerie; A Ministers properties and dutie; His entrance into this function and charge; How to begin fitly to instruct his people; Catechising and Preaching; And a good plaine order and method therein: Not so as yet published. Very profitable both for yoong Students, who intend the studie of Theologie (heerein being also declared what Arts and tongues first to be learned, what kinde of Authors to be read and books necessarie in the beginning, and which in the first place) as also for such Ministers as yet have not atteined to a distinct order to studie, write, meditate, and to preach methodically, both for their better course in deliuering the Word, and the peoples vnderstanding in hearing, and memorie in reteining the same* (London, 1607), 41.

27. John Winthrop, *The Journal of John Winthrop* [hereafter *Journal*], ed. Richard S. Dunn, James Savage, and Laetitia Yeandle (Cambridge: Harvard University Press, 1996), 54. According to Dunn and Yeandle's note, Brown (1576?–1660) came from Hawkedon, Suffolk and was "formerly a member of a separatist congregation in London" (54 n. 21). For a discussion of Brown's relationship to the difficulties of the Watertown community, see Philip F. Gura, *A Glimpse of Sion's Glory: Puritan Radicalism in New England, 1620–1660* (Middletown, Conn.: Wesleyan University Press, 1984), 37. See also Timothy L. Wood, "'A Church Still by Her First Covenant': George Philips and a Puritan view of Roman Catholicism," *New England Quarterly* 72, no. 1 (March 1999): 28–41.

28. This did not end the difficulties of the Watertown community, which turned "from religion to politics, as Phillips and Brown, nettled by [Winthrop's] intrusion into their congregational affairs, raised the charge that the magistrates in their court meeting of 3 Feb. had levied taxes without the consent of the people" (*Journal*, 63 n. 65). In November of 1632,

"The Congregation of Waterton dicharged their Elder R: Brown of his office for his vnfitt-
nesse in regarde of his passion & distemper in speche havinge been ofte admonished, & declared his repentinge of it" (*Journal*, 84). Nevertheless, Gura reports that Brown persisted in
his errors for two years, though this does not seem to hold Winthrop's attention (*A Glimpse
of Sion's Glory*, 37). Brown appears only twice more in Winthrop's *Journal*. Winthrop notes
an incident in which three men are drowned in a boating incident near Brown's house (124).
And, in his last appearance in the *Journal*, Brown stands at the head of those who complain
"that the Ensigne at Salem was defaced, viz: one parte of the redd Crosse taken out . . .
muche matter was made of this, as fearinge it would be taken as an Acte of rebellion, or of
like high nature in defacinge the kinges Coulors: tho' the truethe were, it was doone vpon
this opinion, that the redde Crosse was given to the Kinges of England by the Pope, as an
Ensigne of victorye, & so a superstitious thinge & a relique of Antichriste" (131–32).
Dunn and Yeandle note that Brown "served frequently after 1634 as Watertown's deputy to
the General Court" (54 n. 21). Interestingly, when Brown speaks in the transcript of Anne
Hutchinson's examination before the General Court, it is to suggest that an oath might
not be appropriate in the case, as "an oath is of a high nature, and it is not to be taken but
in a controversy" ("Examination," 328). Later he calls for "something more" than censure,
as "the foundation of all mischief and of all those bastardly things which have been overthrowing by that great meeting" (344). See chapter 7 for fuller discussion of this comment.

    29. Edmund S. Morgan, *Roger Williams: The Church and the State* (New York: Har-
court, Brace and World, 1967), 24. Gura dates Williams's radically separatist stance to the
late 1620s, noting that by that time he had "broken from more moderate Puritans like John
Cotton and Thomas Hooker on the question of the use of the Book of Common Prayer" and
"adopted Henry Barrow's position that only individuals who had totally renounced their relationship to the Church of England and then had covenanted together into individual congregations were to be considered members of the visible church" (*A Glimpse of Sion's Glory*,
35). Other discussions of Williams include Perry Miller, *Roger Williams: His Contribution
to the American Tradition* (1953; New York: Atheneum, 1965); Irwin H. Polishook, *Roger
Williams, John Cotton, and Religious Freedom: A Controversy in New and Old England*
(Englewood Cliffs, N.J.: Prentice-Hall, 1967); Hugh Spurgin, *Roger Williams and Puritan
Radicalism in the English Separatist Tradition*, Studies in American Religion 34 (Lewiston,
N.Y.: Edwin Mellen Press, 1989); L. Raymond Camp, *Roger Williams, God's Apostle of Ad-
vocacy: Biography and Rhetoric*, Studies in American Religion 36 (Lewiston, N.Y.: Edwin
Mellen Press, 1989); Donald Skaggs, *Roger Williams' Dream for America*, American Uni-
versity Studies Series 9, vol. 129 (New York: Peter Lang, 1993); Edmund J. Carpenter, *Roger
Williams: A Study of the Life, Times, and Character of a Political Pioneer* (1909; Freeport,
N.Y.: Books for Libraries Press, 1972); Darren Staloff, "John Cotton, Roger Williams, and
the Problem of Charisma," in *The Making of an American Thinking Class: Intellectuals and
Intelligentsia in Puritan Massachusetts* (New York: Oxford University Press, 1998), 26–39.

    30. Gura notes that "[t]he Boston church's willingness to consider Williams, whose ec-
clesiastical views could not have been a secret to them, for the post bespeaks their ecclesiastical liberality" (*A Glimpse of Sion's Glory*, 40).

    31. Morgan, *Roger Williams*, 26.

    32. The Massachusetts General Court had objected to a 1631 attempt to appoint
Williams teacher of the Salem church, suggesting they should approve such appointments;
Williams in turn had found this a troubling instance of state interference in church matters.
See Gura, *A Glimpse of Sion's Glory*, 40. Thus Williams's status in 1633 "was not official; he
did, however preach to the congregation there" (Glenn W. LaFantasie, "The Road to Banish-
ment: Editorial Note," in *The Correspondence of Roger Williams*, ed. Glenn W. LaFantasie,

vol. 1 [Hanover: Brown University Press/University Press of New England, for the Rhode Island Historical Society, 1988], 13–14).

Skelton's separatist stands included refusal to baptize a child born en route with Winthrop's fleet because the child's parents were not yet members of a particular congregation, and denial of the Lord's Supper to John Winthrop and other prominent men on the same grounds. See Gura, *A Glimpse of Sion's Glory*, 36.

33. Miller, *Roger Williams*, 19.

34. LaFantasie, "The Road to Banishment," 14.

35. Winthrop reports that "There were 3: passages cheifly wherat they were muche offended. 1: for that he Chargeth Kinge Iames to have tould a solemne publicke lye: because in his Patente he blessed God that he was the first Christian Prince that had discovered this land. 2: for that he chargethe him & others with blasphemy for callinge Europe Christendom or the Christian world: 3: for that he did personally apply to our present Kinge Charles these 3: places in the Revelation viz: [blank]" (*Journal*, 107). In a letter to John Endecott, Winthrop discusses these scriptural applications: "For the 3: the first place which he applies to our Kinge is Rev: 16: [14] the spiritts of Deuills going forth to the kinges of the earth, which is all one, as if he had sayde, that the Deuill had seduced him to take vp armes with Antech[ris]t against the Lord Jesus: Ch[ris]t. the next is Rev: 17: 12, where settinge downe onely the first words of the 10 Kinges who should giue their power and strengthe to the beast, to make warre with the Lambe (not addinge any more nor so muche as we doe) he makes our Kinge a friend of the Beast and an enemye of Jes[us] Ch[ris]t. the 3 is Rev: 18:19, by which he makes our Kinge one of those, who have comitted Fornication with the whore, and shall bewyle her destruction" (John Winthrop, "John Winthrop to John Endecott," 3 January 1633/34, in *Winthrop Papers*, vol. 3 [Boston: Massachusetts Historical Society, 1943], 147–48; words between square brackets in this passage appear in the *Winthrop Papers*). A marginal note refers Endecott to "Rev: 16: 13, 14, 17: 12. 13. 18:19" (147). Winthrop suggests that "if it be not treason," such a statement is "strange boldnesse," and suggests as well that "if he had loued the peace of these Churches as Paul did those, he would not (for smale or no occasion) have provoked our Kinge against vs, and putt the sworde into his hande to destroye vs" (148).

36. James Savage's edition reads "appeared penitently" in place of "appeared privatly." See John Winthrop, *The History of New England from 1630 to 1649*, ed. James Savage (Boston: Phelps and Farnham, 1835; Salem, N.H.: Ayer, 1992), 1:122.

37. Jesper Rosenmeier, "The Teacher and the Witness," 418; Larzer Ziff, *The Career of John Cotton: Puritanism and the American Experience* (Princeton: Princeton University Press, 1962), 88.

38. Edmund S. Morgan calls John Endecott "one of the most influential" of the New England settlers, but "also [one of] the most headstrong," and notes as well that he was not "a very patient man" (*The Puritan Dilemma: The Story of John Winthrop* [Boston: Little, Brown, 1958], 86–87).

39. "The Charlestown–Boston Covenant," 131.

40. Williams may have participated in some symbolic actions as well. He was, for example, thought to be somehow involved in the defacement of the English flag at Salem. Motivated by the sense that the flag's red cross was an idolatrous remnant of loyalty to the pope, John Endecott seems to have ordered that it be cut out. See LaFantasie, "The Road to Banishment," 17; *Journal*, 142. Other leaders were themselves "doubtfull of the lawfull vse of the Crosse in an Ensigne," though they also objected to Endecott's defacement of the flag (*Journal*, 136). Though Williams's name was not mentioned in the debates about this event, LaFantasie notes that "the Bay authorities appear to have regarded Endecott's act as an overt

expression of the extremism that Williams was nurturing in Salem" (LaFantasie, "The Road to Banishment," 18). In fact, argues Philip F. Gura, "they believed that Williams had instigated the action as part of his attempt to destroy all connections to the Antichrist, whether in a flag or in a corrupt monarch's willingness to claim New England for Christ's work" (*A Glimpse of Sion's Glory*, 41–42).

41. LaFantasie, "The Road to Banishment," 22; Anne G. Myles, "Arguments in Milk, Arguments in Blood: Roger Williams, Persecution, and the Discourse of Witness," *Modern Philology* 91, no. 2 (November 1993): 140.

42. See *Journal*, 164; Myles, "Arguments in Milk, Arguments in Blood," 140. Williams later claimed that Winthrop "privately wrote to [him] to steer [his] Course to the Nahigonset Bay and Indians, for many high and heavenly and public Ends, incowraging [him] from the Freenes of the place from any English Claims or Pattents" (*The Correspondence of Roger Williams*, vol. 2, 610, quoted in *Journal*, 164 n. 81).

43. Roger Williams, *Mr. Cottons Letter Lately Printed, Examined and Ansvvered* (London, 1644), reprinted in *Publications of the Narragansett Club*, vol. 1, ed. Reuben Aldrige Guild (Providence, 1866), 31/315. This section of volume 1 of the *Publications of the Narragansett Club* has two separate page numbers on each page. The number preceding the slash refers to the separate pagination for the section containing a "Letter of John Cotton, and Roger Williams's Reply"; these page numbers appear on the outer corners of each page. The second page number indicates pagination continuous with volume 1 as a whole, and is printed in this edition in brackets on the inner upper corner of each page. This edition does not indicate a page reference in the original text for prefatory material. Where page references are offered to this text with three page numbers, the first number refers to the pagination of the 1644 edition.

44. In the discussion of Williams's views that follows, I draw on texts composed largely after Williams's departure from the Massachusetts Bay colony, relying most heavily on the texts containing his later exchanges with John Cotton. Though some of Williams's positions seem to have become increasingly extreme following his exile, scholars from Edmund Morgan to Anne G. Myles have tended to rely on these texts to illuminate Williams's views in earlier years. See, for example, Myles's note that "Williams's text reproducing these charges was written considerably later than his 1635 trial. Although he went through a series of affiliations and developments in the intervening period, no texts survive from before 1643 that reflect specifically on the conflict. Hence I write here always in reference to Williams's ideas as they existed, more or less completely developed, in 1643–44. Cotton's original letter, however, to which Williams responds, was written shortly after the banishment and later published in England" ("Arguments in Milk, Arguments in Blood," 135 n. 2).

45. Rosenmeier, "The Teacher and the Witness," 410, 415. Rosenmeier's study of the relationship between Williams and Cotton refines further Sacvan Bercovitch's argument about the centrality of typology to the Cotton–Williams debate. See Sacvan Bercovitch, "Typology in Puritan New England: The Williams–Cotton Controversy Reassessed," *American Quarterly* 19, no.2 (summer 1967): 166–91. See also Morgan, *Roger Williams*.

46. Rosenmeier, "The Teacher and the Witness," 415–16.

47. For an excellent overview of typology in New England, see Karen E. Rowe, *Saint and Singer: Edward Taylor's Typology and the Poetics of Meditation* (Cambridge: Cambridge University Press, 1986).

48. Rosenmeier, "The Teacher and the Witness," 416. Many scholars, Perry Miller, Sacvan Bercovitch, and Jesper Rosenmeier among them, have explored the differences between Williams's approach to typology and that of his New England colleagues. Miller argued,

mistakenly, that Williams's interpretations troubled his colleagues because Cotton and the other ministers rejected typology, while Williams embraced it. See Miller, *Roger Williams*, 32. Bercovitch's major reassessment corrects Miller's account, emphasizing that typological issues were central to the controversy not because Cotton and his colleagues rejected typology, but rather because they understood it differently. See Bercovitch, "Typology in Puritan New England."

49. In Anne G. Myles's formulation, "Williams broke with the New England orthodoxy in his insistence that 'fulfillment' meant the complete realization of the types, and hence their cessation in the historical world" ("Arguments in Milk, Arguments in Blood," 137).

50. Roger Williams, *The Bloody Tenent Yet More Bloody* (1652), in *Publications of the Narragansett Club*, ed. Samuel L. Caldwell, 1st ser., vol. 4 (Providence, 1870), 29.

51. Pressing a somewhat subtle distinction, Williams did "acknowledge that what was simply *moral, civill*, and *naturall* in *Israels state*, in their *constitutions, Lawes, punishments*, may be imitated and followed by the *States, Countries, Cities*, and *Kingdomes* of the World," though he emphasized that other forms of law and government were "lawfull" as well (*BT*, 209/364).

52. Morgan, *Roger Williams*, 102.

53. Though Williams often quotes from Old Testament passages as well, he anchors his primary arguments in the New Testament.

54. On the relationship between the visible and invisible churches in New England, see Edmund S. Morgan, *Visible Saints: The History of a Puritan Idea* (1963; Ithaca: Cornell University Press, 1965). Gura notes that New England separatist communities such as those at Plymouth and in Rhode Island did not institute tests for membership, as did many mainstream Massachusetts congregations. Rejecting the Massachusetts notion of visible sainthood, they "rejected all notions that in a fallen world individual congregations had any direct relationship to the universal, invisible church of true believers" (*A Glimpse of Sion's Glory*, 46–47).

55. Miller discusses "that puzzling business of the wheat and the tares," calling Williams's argument that "no church is so distinct from the wilderness of the world that in it, and in it alone, tares may be allowed to grow . . . a good example of his method" (*Roger Williams*, 104–5). In Miller's analysis, Cotton's reading "made perfect sense within the dialectic of Nonseparation," allowing "heretics and disturbers of the theological peace *outside* the church . . . [to] be pounced on by the civil government and mercilessly rooted up, without that agency being in the slightest degree guilty of 'persecution'" (104–5).

56. In *The Bloudy Tenent, Washed and made white in the blood of the Lambe*, published in 1647, John Cotton explains that "*Mr. Williams* sent me about a dozen years agoe (as I remember) a letter, penned (as he wrote) by a Prisoner in *Newgate*, touching persecution for Conscience sake: and intreated my judgement of it for the satisfaction of his friend. I wa not wiling to deny him any office of Christian love, and gave him my poor judgement in a private letter. This private letter of mine he hath published in Print after so many yeares, and there with a Refutation of it" (2).

57. John Cotton, "The *Answer* of Mr. Iohn Cotton of *Boston* in *New-England*, To the aforesaid ARGUMENTS against *Persecution* for Cause of *Conscience*. Professedly mainteining *Persecution for Cause of Conscience*," in *BT*, 8/43.

58. Interestingly, Williams uses "literal" in a way somewhat different from William Perkins's definition as well as from the sensus historicus. For Williams, the literal and the material seem to be related, though his claim for the identity of "literall *Babell* and *Jerusalem*" complicates this sense.

59. Williams, *Mr. Cottons Letter*, 45/108/392.

60. Ibid., 45–46/109/393. Williams shared with many of his contemporaries a conception of hell as separation from God: "Thirdly, their end is the *Ditch*, that bottomlesse pit of everlasting *separation* from the holy and sweet Presence of the *Father* of *Lights, Goodnesse* and *Mercy* it selfe, *endlesse, easelesse*, in *extremity, universality*, and *eternity* of *torments*, which most direfull and lamentable downefall, should strike an holy fear & trembling into all that see the *Pit*, whither these blinde Pharises are tumbling, and cause us to strike (so far as hope may be) by the spirituall eye-salve of the Word of *God* to heale and cure them of this their soule-destroying blindnesse" (*BT*, 56/124). On first-generation Puritan conceptions of sin as privative, see Andrew Delbanco, *The Puritan Ordeal* (Cambridge: Harvard University Press, 1989).

61. Williams, *Mr. Cottons Letter*, 45/108/392.

62. See above, page 125, for Williams's similar claim that historical typology denies the incarnation and wakens Moses from his grave.

63. Williams, *Mr. Cottons Letter*, 5/42/326.

64. Ibid., 5–6/42–43/326–27.

65. Separatism was associated with a range of other extreme positions. Gura in fact argues that "the importance of the Plymouth colonists and the groups that spun off from them to other areas in southeastern Massachusetts and Cape Cod, and of the separatists who settled in Salem in the late 1620s and early 1630s, lies in how their radical position on church and state forwarded other, more heterodox ideas" (*A Glimpse of Sion's Glory*, 31).

66. See Gura's description of the "vexed" question of separatist influence on the development of New England Puritanism, and on English responses to New England rejections of separation (45–48). See also Stephen Foster, *The Long Argument: English Puritanism and the Shaping of New England Culture, 1570–1700* (Chapel Hill: University of North Carolina Press, 1991).

67. John Cotton, *A Letter of Mr. John Cottons Teacher of the Church in Boston, in Nevv-England, To Mr. Williams a Preacher there, Wherein is shewed, That those ought to be received into the Church who are Godly, though they doe not see, nor expressely bewaile all the pollutions in Church-fellowship, Ministery, Worship, Government* (London, 1643), *Publications of the Narragansett Club*, ed. Reuben Aldridge Guild, vol. 1 (Providence, 1866), 6–7/18–19/302–3.

68. *BT*, 28/77–78 Williams identifies his source as Luke 11:51, though the quoted passage is actually Luke 12:51–53. Williams quotes the Authorized Version here. For "division," in verse 51, the Geneva text reads "debate."

69. As John J. Teunissen and Evelyn J. Hinz point out, "Williams found the deeds and words of St. Paul so congenial" precisely because he identified with Paul's status as an outsider: "Like Paul, Williams found himself accused of sedition, mutiny, and civil disobedience; indeed, he found himself banished by his own in much the same way that Paul found his chief persecutors in the Pharisees" ("Roger Williams, St. Paul, and American Primitivism," *The Canadian Review of American Studies* 4, no. 2 [fall 1973]: 123).

70. For a discussion of Williams's use of history to support his argument and the sources of his historical examples, see Hans R. Guggisberg, "Religious Freedom and the History of the Christian World in Roger Williams' Thought," *Early American Literature* 12, no. 1 (spring 1977): 36–48.

71. See chapter 7 on the Antinomian Controversy, in which the relationship between sanctification and justification was central. Though this episode followed Williams's departure from Massachusetts Bay, it preceded the composition of *The Bloody Tenent of Persecution*.

72. See also Williams's accusation "that in such a maintaining a clearnesse of *funda-*

*mentals* or waightier *points,* and upon that ground a persecuting of men, because they sinne against their *consciences,* Mr. *Cotton* measures that to *others,* which he himselfe when he lived in such *practices,* would not have measured to himselfe" (24/71).

73. Williams singles Cotton out for particular attention, exhorting one of the figures in his dialogue to "glance [her] . . . eye on this not unworthy observation, to wit, how fully this worthy *Answerer* hath learned to speake the roaring *language* of *Lyon-like Persecution,* far from the *purity* and *peaceablenesse* of the *Lambe,* which he was wont to expresse in *England*" (96/185–86).

74. In the Authorized Version, Psalms 101:8 reads: "I will early destroy all the wicked of the land; that I may cut off all wicked doers from the city of the LORD."

75. Williams's similarly emphasized actions flowing from misinterpretation when he asserted that "So farre as he [Cotton] hath been a Guide (by preaching for persecution) I say, wherein he hath beene a Guide and Leader, by misinterpreting and applying the Writings of Truth, so far I say his owne mouthes and hands shall judge (I hope not his persons, but) his actions, for the Lord Jesus has suffered by him, Act. 9. 3. and if the Lord Jesus himselfe were present, himselfe should suffer that in his owne person, which his servants witnessing his Truth doe suffer for his sake" (31–32/83).

76. Cotton, *A Letter,* 11/24/308.

77. Williams, *Mr. Cottons Letter,* 26/75–76/359–60.

78. "The [Salem Church] Covenant of 1629," 116.

79. "The Enlarged [Salem Church] Covenant of 1636," in *The Creeds and Platforms of Congregationalism,* 116–17. Williston Walker notes in his introductory essay on "The Development of Covenant and Creed in the Salem Church, 1629–1665" that the covenant was probably renewed at the ordination of Hugh Peter on December 21, 1636 (110–11).

80. Ibid., 111; Gura, *A Glimpse of Sion's Glory,* 43.

81. Cotton, *The Bloudy Tenent, Washed and made white in the blood of the Lambe,* 9, 26.

82. Ibid., 55.

83. On disruption in Salem in the wake of Williams's departure, see Gura, *A Glimpse of Sion's Glory,* 43–44.

## Chapter 7

1. Thomas Weld, preface to [John Winthrop], *A Short Story of the Rise, reign, and ruine of the Antinomians, Familists & Libertines, that infected the Churches of New-England* [hereafter *Short Story*], in *The Antinomian Controversy, 1636–1638: A Documentary History,* ed. David D. Hall, 2nd ed. (Durham: Duke University Press, 1990), 201. Though the *Short Story* is widely attributed to Winthrop, its authorship is uncertain.

2. John Winthrop, *The Journal of John Winthrop 1630–1649* [hereafter *Journal*], ed. Richard S. Dunn, James Savage, and Laetitia Yeandle (Cambridge: Harvard University Press, 1996), 195.

3. Studies that address questions of gender and politics include Lyle Koehler, *A Search for Power: The "Weaker Sex" in Seventeenth-Century New England* (Urbana: University of Illinois Press, 1980); Ann Kibbey, *The Interpretation of Material Shapes in Puritanism: A Study of Rhetoric, Prejudice, and Violence* (Cambridge: Cambridge University Press, 1986); Kai T. Erikson, *Wayward Puritans: A Study in the Sociology of Dissent* (New York: John Wiley, 1966); Ben Barker-Benfield, "Anne Hutchinson and the Puritan Attitude toward Women," *Feminist Studies* 1 (fall 1972): 65–96; Sandra M. Gustafson, *Eloquence Is Power: Oratory and Performance in Early America* (Chapel Hill: University of North Carolina Press, 2000); as well as the less rigorous account by Selma R. Williams in *Divine Rebel: The*

*Life of Anne Marbury Hutchinson* (New York: Holt, Rinehart, and Winston, 1981). Amy Shrager Lang considers Hutchinson's development into monitory and mythic figure in New England literature in *Prophetic Woman: Anne Hutchinson and the Problem of Dissent in the Literature of New England* (Berkeley: University of California Press, 1987). Notable, if problematic, is Emery Battis's *Saints and Sectaries: Anne Hutchinson and the Antinomian Controversy in the Massachusetts Bay Colony* (Chapel Hill: University of North Carolina Press, 1962), in which Battis describes the complex political issues involved in the controversy, but also attributes Hutchinson's religious experiences to hormonal imbalance. Patricia Caldwell considers language issues in the controversy in "The Antinomian Language Controversy," *Harvard Theological Review* 69 (1976): 345–67.

Theological considerations of the controversy have been especially numerous. Recent examples include Michael P. Winship, *Making Heretics: Militant Protestantism and Free Grace in Massachusetts, 1636–1641* (Princeton: Princeton University Press, 2002); Michael P. Winship, "'The Most Glorious Church in the World': The Unity of the Godly in Boston, Massachusetts, in the 1630s," *Journal of British Studies* 39, no. 1 (January 2000): 71–98; Janice Knight, *Orthodoxies in Massachusetts: Rereading American Puritanism* (Cambridge: Harvard University Press, 1994); Stephen Foster, "New England and the Challenge of Heresy, 1630 to 1660: The Puritan Crisis in Transatlantic Perspective," *William and Mary Quarterly* 3d ser., 38, no. 4 (October 1981): 624–60; William K. B. Stoever, *"A Faire and Easie Way to Heaven": Covenant Theology and Antinomianism in Early Massachusetts* (Middletown, Conn.: Wesleyan University Press, 1978); Jesper Rosenmeier, "New England's Perfection: The Image of Adam and the Image of Christ in the Antinomian Crisis, 1634 to 1638," *William and Mary Quarterly* 3d ser., 27, no. 3 (July 1970): 435–59. See also J. F. Maclear, "Anne Hutchinson and the Mortalist Heresy," *New England Quarterly* 54, no. 1 (March 1981): 74–103, as well as Maclear's earlier essay "'The Heart of New England Rent': The Mystical Element in Early Puritan History," *Mississippi Valley Historical Record* 42, no. 4 (March 1956): 621–52. A more recent consideration of Hutchinson's mysticism appears in Marilyn J. Westerkamp, "Anne Hutchinson, Sectarian Mysticism, and the Puritan Order," *Church History* 59, no. 4 (December 1990): 482–96.

Books that consider the Antinomian Controversy in the context of larger arguments include Andrew Delbanco, *The Puritan Ordeal* (Cambridge: Harvard University Press, 1989); Larzer Ziff, *The Career of John Cotton: Puritanism and the American Experience* (Princeton: Princeton University Press, 1962); Norman Pettit, *The Heart Prepared: Grace and Conversion in Puritan Spiritual Life*, Yale Publications in American Studies 11 (New Haven: Yale University Press, 1966); Philip F. Gura, *A Glimpse of Sion's Glory: Puritan Radicalism in New England, 1620–1660* (Middletown, Conn.: Wesleyan University Press, 1984); David S. Lovejoy, *Religious Enthusiasm in the New World* (Cambridge: Harvard University Press, 1985); Darren Staloff, *The Making of an American Thinking Class: Intellectuals and Intelligentsia in Puritan Massachusetts* (New York: Oxford University Press, 1998); James F. Cooper Jr., *Tenacious of Their Liberties: The Congregationalists in Colonial Massachusetts* (New York: Oxford University Press, 1999).

4. Foster, "New England and the Challenge of Heresy," 643. Foster presents a rich discussion of antinomianism in England and New England, and contextualizes its New England manifestations thoughtfully and carefully.

5. *Journal*, 193; Hall, preface to the second edition, in *The Antinomian Controversy*, xiv.

6. In his *Autobiography*, for example, Shepard explains: "when I could not take notes of the sermon I was troubled at it and prayed to the Lord earnestly that he would help me to note sermons. And I see cause of wondering at the Lord's providence therein, for as soon as ever I had prayed (after my best fashion) then for it, I presently the next Sabbath was able to take notes who the precedent Sabbath could do nothing at all that way" (*The Autobiogra-*

*phy,* in *God's Plot: Puritan Spirituality in Thomas Shepard's Cambridge,* ed. Michael McGiffert [Amherst: University of Massachusetts Press, 1994], 41). Winship discusses John Wilson's position to show "the complexity of mainstream Puritan teaching on assurance" ("'The Most Glorious Church,'" 73–74).

7. Hall grounds his analysis in membership statistics found in the Boston Church Records (*Collections of the Colonial Society of Massachusetts* 39: 12–18; Hall, introduction to *The Antinomian Controversy,* 14–15). Michael P. Winship disputes Hall's account, however, arguing that "there is no real indication that Cotton's arrival initiated a colony-wide revival" (*Making Heretics,* 266–7 n. 56).

8. Foster, "New England and the Challenge of Heresy," 656.

9. Ibid., 657.

10. This phrase is used repeatedly in the documents of the controversy. See, for example, John Cotton, *Mr. Cotton's Rejoynder,* in *The Antinomian Controversy,* 128. In the Puritan covenantal system, God first made the covenant of works with Adam, promising to reward Adam's obedience with eternal life. By his sin, Adam abrogated this covenant and corrupted his descendants, rendering it impossible for human beings to achieve salvation by fulfilling the law, and impossible for them to fulfill the Law in the first place. During the Antinomian Controversy, the accusation that one is "going aside in a covenant of works" was used to indicate that one was acting or preaching as if the covenant of works were still an available means of salvation, making it possible for an individual to achieve salvation through righteous action. For detailed discussion of the covenant of works and its place in Puritan covenant theology, see Michael McGiffert, "Grace and Works: The Rise and Division of Covenant Divinity in Elizabethan Puritanism," *Harvard Theological Review* 75, no. 4 (1982): 463–502; John Von Rohr, *The Covenant of Grace in Puritan Thought,* American Academy of Religion Studies in Religion 45 (Atlanta: Scholars Press, 1986); Stoever, *"A Faire and Easie Way to Heaven";* and Charles Lloyd Cohen, *God's Caress: The Psychology of Puritan Religious Experience* (New York: Oxford University Press, 1986).

11. See the editors' comment in *Journal,* 193 n. 22.

12. For a discussion of manuscript exchanges and private conferences as media "through which the godly hammered out their differences, winnowing out the chaff of error from the grain of true doctrine," see Peter Lake and David Como, "'Orthodoxy' and Its Discontents: Dispute Settlement and the Production of 'Consensus' in the London (Puritan) 'Underground,'" *Journal of British Studies* 39, no. 1 (January 2000): 39.

13. For discussion of the ideas of free consent and "general agreement," see Cooper, *Tenacious of Their Liberties.*

14. John Calvin, *Institutes of the Christian Religion* (1559), ed. John T. McNeill, trans. Ford Lewis Battles, vol. 1, Library of Christian Classics 20 (Philadelphia: Westminster, 1960), 115.

15. Larzer Ziff, for example, suggests that Cotton was "a conserver and consolidator rather than a founder" (introduction to *John Cotton on the Churches of New England,* ed. Larzer Ziff [Cambridge: Harvard University Press, 1968], 17).

16. John Norton, *Abel Being Dead, Yet Speaketh; Or, the Life & Death of the deservedly Famous Man of God, Mr John Cotton, Late Teacher of the Church of Christ, at Boston in New-England* (London, 1658), reprinted in *The New England Way,* Library of American Puritan Writings 12 (New York: AMS Press, 1983), 10; Cotton Mather, *Magnalia Christi Americana; or, The Ecclesiastical history of New England, from its First Planting, in the Year 1620, unto the Year of Our Lord 1698* [hereafter *Magnalia*], vol. 1 (1702; Hartford: Silus Andrus and Son, 1853), reprinted in *Great Works of Christ in America* (Edinburgh: Banner of Truth Trust, 1979), 273.

17. Thomas Shepard, letter to John Cotton, in *The Antinomian Controversy*, 27.

18. Reformed exegetes believed in the consistency of the biblical text. They therefore devoted interpretive effort to resolving apparent contradictions in the text. See chapter 1, pages 24–27, for further discussion.

19. John Cotton, letter to Thomas Shepard, in *The Antinomian Controversy*, 31.

20. "The Elders Reply," in ibid., 71.

21. Cotton, *Mr. Cottons Rejoynder*, 117–18.

22. Ibid., 130.

23. See, for example, the opening of "The Elders Reply," which is addressed to "Reverend and Beloved in the God of Love," and which professes great love and honor for Cotton (61).

24. John Cotton, *Sixteene Questions of Serious and Necessary Consequence*, in *The Antinomian Controversy*, 46.

25. Cotton, *Mr. Cotton's Rejoynder*, 105. Michael J. Colacurcio's superb reading of the *Rejoynder* points to several instances in which Cotton is similarly combative. See Colacurcio, "Primitive Comfort: The Spiritual Witness of John Cotton," *ELH* 67, no. 3 (fall 2000): 655–95.

26. Winthrop reports, for example, that "many copies . . . [of the *Sixteene Questions*] were dispersed about" (*Journal*, 206).

27. Winthrop reports that these included "that the Holy Ghost dwelt in a believer as he is in heaven; that a man is justified before he believes; and that faith is no cause of justification," as well as "that the letter of the scripture holds forth nothing but a covenant of works; and that the covenant of grace was the spirit of the scripture, which was known only to believers; and that this covenant of works was given by Moses in the ten commandments; that there was a seed (viz., Abraham's carnal seed) went along in this, and there was a spirit and life in it, by virtue whereof a man might attain to any sanctification in gifts and graces, and might have spiritual and continual(?) communion with Jesus Christ, and yet be damned. After, it was granted, that faith was before justification, but it was only passive, an empty vessel, etc.; but in conclusion, the ground of all was found to be assurance by immediate revelation" (*Journal*, 205–6).

28. Winthrop identifies the speaker who opposed Wheelwright as "one of the church," but Dunn and Yeandle identify him as Winthrop himself (*Journal*, 195 n. 26). For a fuller account of these events, including a discussion of the new Mount Wollaston church, see Winship, *Making Heretics*, 92, 278 n. 28.

29. These papers are discussed by Thomas Shepard in his letter to John Winthrop, c. 15 December 1636, in *Winthrop Papers 1498–1654*, vol. 3 (Boston: Merrymount Press, 1943), 326.

30. Winship also suggests that Shepard did not share Winthrop's interest in pacification, and that he "restrained Winthrop's impulse to moderation" in this instance ("'The Most Glorious Church,'" 89). In fact, he argues that Shepard attempted "to create conflict" (90). Winship joins Foster ("New England and the Challenge of Heresy," 643–44), Stoever ("*A Faire and Easie Way to Heaven*," 30), and Rosenmeier ("New England's Perfection," 440–49) in emphasizing Shepard's role in the controversy.

31. See the editors' comment in *Journal*, 202 n. 48; "Propositions of the Church of Boston" (c. December 1636), in *Winthrop Papers*, 3:324–26.

32. "Propositions of the Church of Boston" (c. December 1636), in *Winthrop Papers*, 3:324.

33. In March, the court fined him for his statements ("The First Month, the 9th Day," in *Records of the Governor and Company of the Massachusetts Bay in New England, Printed by Order of the Legislature*, ed. Nathaniel B. Shurtleff, vol. 1, *1628–1641* [Boston: William White, 1853], 189). In Winthrop's account, the ministers are unnamed: "A. B. and

C" (*Journal*, 210, 210 n. 70). For further discussion of the General Court's proceedings against Greensmith, see below, page 157 and note 41.

34. John Wheelwright, "A Fast Day Sermon" (1637), in *The Antinomian Controversy*, 168.

35. *Journal*, 210; *Short Story*, 293.

36. Wheelwright dismissed charges of sedition as preposterous in *Mercurius Americanus, Mr. Welds his Antitype, Or, Massachusetts great Apologie examined, Being Observations upon a Paper styled, A short story of the Rise, Reign, and Ruine of the Familists, Libertines, &c. which infected the Churches of New-England, &c. Wherein some parties therein concerned are vindicated, and the truth generally cleared* (1645), in *John Wheelwright, Publications of the Prince Society* 9 (Boston, 1896). Historians are divided as to the validity of his complaint. James Savage suggested that "the sermon was not such as can justify the court in their sentence for *sedition* and *contempt*, nor prevent the present age from regarding that proceeding as an example and a warning of the usual tyranny of ecclesiastical factions" (John Winthrop, *The History of New England from 1630 to 1639*, ed. James Savage [1825; Salem, N.H.: Ayer, 1992], 215 n. 3). Michael P. Winship suggests that Wheelwright's doctrine was misrepresented to the General Court, and notes that some suspected that "Wheelwright was being used . . . to rein in Cotton" ("'The Most Glorious Church,'" 90–91). Philip F. Gura, on the other hand, notes that Wheelwright managed to keep "the relation between justification in balance," but still finds Wheelwright's sermon "inflammatory" (*A Glimpse of Sion's Glory*, 62, 250).

37. Battis notes Cotton's concern "that the news of these disturbances might retard the wave of immigration" (*Saints and Sectaries*, 144).

38. Winthrop's use of "the one" and "the other" corresponds to the Latin "hic . . . ille" construction, rather than to modern use of "the former" and "the latter." Thus he takes Cotton's use of "the grace of God towards us" to be justification and "the grace of God within us" to be sanctification. Winship argues that Cotton's sermon may have been much less conciliatory than Winthrop's account suggests. Instead, drawing on a later account by William Coddington, he speculates that Cotton probably delivered "an angry polarizing sermon," and that Wilson followed with "an angry sermon of his own" (*Making Heretics*, 115).

39. The petition is included in *Short Story*, 249–50.

40. Sentencing was in fact repeatedly deferred. At the May meeting of the General Court, sentencing was deferred "because a general day of humiliation was appointed" and because a synod was planned for August (*Journal*, 217). The court also hoped that "being thus provoked by their tumultuous course, and divers insolent speeches, which some of that party had uttered in the court, and having now power enough to have crushed them, their moderation and desire of reconciliation might appear to all" (*Journal*, 217).

41. Greensmith was censured, commited temporarily to the marshal, and fined forty pounds. He later appealed to the king, but the court was unswayed. After repeated refusals, Greensmith eventually paid the fine, but moved to New Hampshire (*Journal*, 228, 210 n. 70; *Records of the Governor and Company of the Massachusetts Bay*, 1:189, 196, 200, 245; *Short Story*, 270, 270 n. 56).

42. *Records of the Governor and Company of the Massachusetts Bay*, 1:189.

43. Ibid., 1:191; *Journal*, 211.

44. Winthrop notes that "The reason was conceived to be because they accounted these as legal preachers, and therefore would not give approbation to their ordination" (*Journal*, 212).

45. As Larzer Ziff explains, the Bostonians had expected this outcome, and had consequently deferred the selection of deputies to the court: "On the day after the election, they sent Vane, Coddington, and Atherton Hough to the Court as deputies, and although an attempt was made to unseat them because of an alleged irregularity in their election, they re-

mained as deputies" (Ziff, *The Career of John Cotton: Puritanism and the American Experience* [Princeton: Princeton University Press, 1962], 128). For proceedings of this session, see "A Generall Court, held at Newetowne, the 2th Day of the 9th Mo, [2 November 1637] @1637," in *Records of the Governor and Company of the Massachusetts Bay*, 1:194–97.

46. *Journal*, 216. Dunn and Yeandle note that "[m]ost of the 'divers writings' mentioned by [Winthrop] have not survived," including a reply by Winthrop to the Antinomians' remonstrance (216 n. 84).

47. Specifically, Winthrop reports that "in these particulars they agreed: 1. That justification and sanctification were both together in time; 2. That a man must know himself to be justified, before he can know himself to be sanctified; 3. That the spirit never witnesseth justification without a word and a work" (*Journal*, 216). Remaining differences were "whether the first assurance be an absolute promise always, and not by a conditional also, and whether a man could have any true assurance, without sight of some such work in his soul as no hypocrite could attain unto" (216–17).

48. *Records of the Governor and Company of the Massachusetts Bay*, 1:196. They also ordered Greensmith "to give satisfaction to the elders & churches, & pay his fine, & certify so much at the next Courte, or else to forfet his bond" (ibid.).

49. See Knight, *Orthodoxies in Massachusetts*, 18; Winship, *Making Heretics* 139–40.

50. See *Hutchinson Papers*, Publications of the Prince Society, vol. 1 (Boston: Prince Society, 1865; New York: Burt Franklin, 1967), 74–113. In the 1865 printing the pages are 63–100.

51. John Cotton, *The Way of Congregational Churches Cleared* (1648) [hereafter *Way Cleared*], in *John Cotton on the Churches of New England*, ed. Larzer Ziff (Cambridge: Harvard University Press, 1968), 266.

52. Cotton's account must be read with some caution, of course, as it represented an attempt to refute charges that the Antinomian Controversy was an inevitable outcome of Congregationalist polity. He thus had a large stake in demonstrating that the Congregational churches could resolve controversies even without formal presbyterian hierarchies.

53. Winthrop describes Davenport's sermon and quotes a portion of the sermon's text, using a loose Bible translation that corresponds precisely neither to the Geneva nor to the Authorized Version of the biblical text.

54. In his *Journal*, Winthrop numbers these errors as "eighty in all," though the *Short Story* catalogues eighty-two errors (*Journal*, 232; *Short Story*, 219–43).

55. Michael Schuldiner notes that the synod produced "compromise statements," though he also describes persistent differences between Cotton's doctrine and that of the other ministers. See Schuldiner, *Gifts and Works: The Post-Conversion Paradigm and Spiritual Controversy in Seventeenth-Century Massachusetts*, National Association of Baptist Professors of Religion Dissertation Series 8 (Macon, Ga.: Mercer University Press, 1991), 81–82.

56. Foster, "New England and the Challenge of Heresy," 643–51.

57. Davenport preached on Philippians 3:16, a verse which recalled the New England churches to the unity they had pledged in their early church covenants: "Nevertheless, whereto we have already attained, let us walk by the same rule, let us mind the same thing."

58. Many Puritan ministers preached sermons in four parts: text, doctrine, reasons, and uses or applications. Wheelwright's "doctrines" would have been the portions of the sermon in which he presented "the sense and understanding" of the passage, "by the Scripture it selfe," and "collect[ed] a few and profitable points of doctrine out of the naturall sense." "Uses" or "applications" applied the biblical text and its insights to the lives of the

congregation. See William Perkins, *The Arte of Prophecying* (1592, trans. 1607), trans. Thomas Tuke, in *Works* (London, 1609), 762.

59. Similar accusations had been lodged against Roger Williams, and Hugh Peter made like allegations against Henry Vane (*Journal*, 203), as did Hutchinson's opponents at her court and church trials. Wheelwright objected that his arrival could not have caused all of the difficulties if, as the magistrates accused, Hutchinson had "vented her Opinions in the ship as she came over," and that there had in fact been "Divisions before Mr. *Wh:* Sermon" (*Mercurius Americanus*, 219).

60. Wheelwright initially planned to appeal his sentence to the king, but agreed the next day to accept a simple banishment (*Short Story*, 257).

61. Others prosecuted by the court included William Balston, Edward Hutchinson, Thomas Marshall, William Dinely, William Dyer, and Richard Gridley. See *Short Story*, 250–78; see also Wheelwright, *Mercurius Americanus*, 191–98; *Journal*, 241 n. 73.

62. See *Short Story*, 250–78; see also Wheelwright, *Mercurius Americanus*, 191–98.

63. This inquiry arose when Underhill petitioned the court for land he had been promised, as he planned to leave the colony for Exeter, New Hampshire (*Journal*, 262). The incident is described in Jane Holmes's confession, as recorded by Thomas Shepard. See *God's Plot*, 176. Foster identifies Holmes as the unnamed "sober, godly woman" of Winthrop's account, and Underhill as the unnamed "wretch" of Holmes's account ("New England and the Challenge of Heresy," 652).

64. Holmes, Confession, 175.

65. It later emerged that Underhill had claimed other alarming and unscriptural revelations as well. Richard Wayte, a fellow soldier in the expedition against the Pequots, reported that Underhill "tould [him] of a Revelation that he had Concerninge the Coopers wife, that it was revealed to him that her Husband should dye, and his wife, and that he should marry the Coopers wife." James F. Cooper, Jr., "The Confession and Trial of Richard Wayte, Boston, 1640," *William and Mary Quarterly* 3d ser., 44, no. 2 (April 1987): 322. Cooper identifies the cooper of Wayte's account as Joseph Febar (322 n. 38).

66. Winship, "'The Most Glorious Church in the World,'" 75–76; Hall, introduction to *The Antinomian Controversy*, 4.

67. "The Examination of Mrs. Anne Hutchinson at the Court at Newtown" [hereafter "Examination"], in *The Antinomian Controversy*, 317.

68. "A Report of the Trial of Mrs. Anne Hutchinson before the Church in Boston" [hereafter "Report"], in *The Antinomian Controversy*, 384.

69. Hugh Peter told Vane "that <before he came,> within less than two years since, the churches were in peace, etc." (*Journal*, 203). See above p. 163 for the very similar accusation made against Wheelwright.

70. Accounts of the controversy emphasizing gender include Mary Beth Norton, *Founding Mothers and Fathers: Gendered Power and the Forming of American Society* (1996; New York: Vintage, 1997); Koehler, *A Search for Power*; Kibbey, *The Interpretation of Material Shapes in Puritanism*; Battis, *Saints and Sectaries*; Lang, *Prophetic Woman*; Westerkamp, "Anne Hutchinson, Sectarian Mysticism, and the Puritan Order"; Lad Tobin, "A Radically Different Voice: Gender and Language in the Trials of Anne Hutchinson," *Early American Literature* 25, no. 3 (1990): 253–70; and Williams, *Divine Rebel*.

71. Several of the accounts which emphasize the significance of Hutchinson's gender also examine broader issues of social and economic power in early New England. These include Norton, *Founding Mothers and Fathers*; Koehler, *A Search for Power*; and Battis, *Saints and Sectaries*. Bernard Bailyn's *New England Merchants in the Seventeenth Century*

(Cambridge: Harvard University Press, 1979) and Darren Staloff's *The Making of an American Thinking Class* also situate the controversy in the context of economic and social issues in the Massachusetts Bay colony.

72. Darren Staloff rejects claims that Hutchinson out-argued her opponents, suggesting instead that she was "outnumbered and outmatched by New England's assembled dialecticians," and "allowed the assembled inner party to publicly demonstrate their superior forensic, dialectical, and biblical skills" (*The Making of an American Thinking Class*, 59–60).

73. Michael Ditmore notes that Hutchinson's "'immediate revelations,' at least during her court testimony, were actually composed mostly of exact scriptural citations and allusions, 'revealing' her self in a pastiche of allusions and quotations" ("A Prophetess in Her Own Country: An Exegesis of Anne Hutchinson's 'Immediate Revelation,'" *William and Mary Quarterly* 3d ser. 57, no. 2 [April 2000]: 360). Ditmore finds Hutchinson's account of revelation more unorthodox than I do, citing especially the "prophetic merging of her own identity with that of the biblical voice of revealed inspiration" (ibid., 350). Hutchinson does not quote Hebrews precisely here. The text of Hebrews 9:16–17 in the Authorized Version reads: "For where a testament is, there must also of necessity be the death of the testator. For a testament is of force after men are dead: otherwise it is of no strength at all while the testator liveth." Hutchinson also cites Jeremiah 46:27–28 and the seventh chapter of Daniel.

74. Calvin, *Institutes*, 1:734.

75. Marilyn J. Westerkamp, "Puritan Patriarchy and the Problem of Revelation," *Journal of Interdisciplinary History* 23, no. 3 (winter 1993): 589.

76. Cotton, *Mr. Cotton's Rejoynder*, 126.

77. John Cotton, *A Treatise of the Covenant of Grace, As it is dispensed to the Elect Seed, effectually unto Salvation. Being The Substance of divers Sermons preached upon Act, 7.8. by that eminently holy and judicious man of God, Mr. John Cotton, teacher of the Church at Boston in N.E.* (London, 1671), 177. Michael J. Colacurcio notes that Cotton "seems to have been preaching" "some version" of this text in 1636, agreeing in his assessment with R. T. Kendall, Larzer Ziff, and Everett H. Emerson that this text represents "the closest we can get to Cotton's preaching in 1636" ("Primitive Comfort," 657, 692 n. 10).

78. Cotton, *Mr. Cotton's Rejoynder*, 141.

79. John Cotton, *Christ the Fountaine of Life: or, Sundry Choyce Sermons on part of the fift chapter of the first Epistle of St John* [hereafter *CTF*] (London, 1651; New York: Arno Press, 1972), 35.

80. Familists, members of the Family of Love, "were followers of Henry Niclaes, born in Münster in 1502, who taught that heaven and hell were to be found in this world" (Christopher Hill, *The World Turned Upside Down: Radical Ideas during the English Revolution* [1972; New York: Penguin, 1975], 26). They believed that human beings could recapture a state of prelapsarian innocence, held property in common, and emphasized the role of the indwelling Spirit in allowing believers to understand the Bible (ibid., 26). Its opponents associated it with "moral sloth" and "social insubordination" (ibid., 326; Christopher Marsh, "'A Gracelesse, and Audacious Companie'?: The Family of Love in the Parish of Balsham, 1550–1630," in *Voluntary Religion: Papers Read at the 1985 Summer Meeting and the 1986 Winter Meeting of the Ecclesiastical History Society*, ed. J. Sheils and Diane Wood, *Studies in Church History* 23 [1986]: 192). For a full discussion of this sect, see Alastair Hamilton, *The Family of Love* (Cambridge, U.K.: James Clarke, 1981). Winship suggests that "contemporaries in New England used the term 'familist' far more than they did 'antinomian' to describe their radical opponents. . . . [W]ithin the casual Puritan classificatory systems of the early seventeenth century, familists were assumed to be antinomians, but antinomians were not necessarily familists. Antinomianism was perceived to bring

with it soul-damning moral laxity; familism, on top of that, brought revelation-driven Mün-
sterian chaos and the abandonment of the Bible, and it was familism that the winning side
in Massachusetts thought they were struggling against, not entirely without reason" (*Making Heretics*, 26–7).

81. Shepard, letter to John Cotton, 28.

82. Thomas Shepard, *Of Ineffectual Hearing the Word* (preached 1641, published
1652), in *The Works of Thomas Shepard, First Pastor of the First Church, Cambridge, Mass.
with a Memoir of His Life and Character*, vol. 3 (Boston: Boston Doctrinal Tract and Book
Society, 1853; Ligonier, Penn.: Soli Deo Gloria, 1992), 365. For further discussion of Shepard's view of divine inhabitation of the Word, see chapter 3. Shepard's mystical view of the
Word may explain Cotton's claim that of the other elders, Hutchinson "esteemed best of
Mr. Shepard" (*Way Cleared*, 240).

83. For an illuminating reading of the glosses Hutchinson would have found, see Ditmore, "A Prophetess in Her Own Country," 379–80, 389–92.

84. Hooker stressed the particular and personal application of the biblical text to the
individual listener and reader. In *The Sovles Preparation for Christ*, for example, he explained that "The word of God is like a sword; the explanation of the text is like a drawing
out of this sword, and the flourishing of it, and so long it never hits: But when a man strikes
a full blow at a man, it either wounds or puts him to his fence: So the application of the
Word is like the striking with the sword, it will worke one way or other, if a man can fence
the blow, so it is: but if not, it wounds" ([Thomas Hooker], *The Sovles Preparation for
Christ. Or, A Treatise of Contrition, Wherein is discovered How God breakes the heart
and woundes the Soule, in the conversion of a Sinner to Himselfe* [1632; London, 1638],
reprinted in facsimile as *The Soules Preparation*, Library of American Puritan Writings 15
[New York: AMS Press, 1982], 64). In *The Poor Doubting Christian Drawn Unto Christ*,
Hooker laid out rules for the Christian reader of scripture. These rules, in keeping with
Hooker's practical approach to the text, explicitly related scripture reading to a particular
purpose; they are "[Four] Rules to Direct a Christian How to Use the Word of God for the
Evidence of His Assurance" (*The Poor Doubting Christian Drawn Unto Christ*, in *Thomas
Hooker: Writings in England and Holland, 1626–1633*, Harvard Theological Studies 28
[Cambridge: Harvard University Press, 1975], 168). For fuller discussion of Hooker's ap-
proach, see chapter 4.

85. See Thomas Hooker, *The Danger of Desertion: or A Farewell Sermon of Mr. Thomas
Hooker, Sometimes Minister of Gods Word at Chainsford in Essex; but now of New En-
gland. Preached immediately before his departure out of old England* (London, 1641).
The quotation included above is taken from the 1657 edition of the sermon, which is ex-
cerpted in *The Puritans in America: A Narrative Anthology*, ed. Alan Heimert and Andrew
Delbanco (Cambridge: Harvard University Press, 1985), 68.

86. Foster, "New England and the Challenge of Heresy," 652.

87. See, for example, Edward Johnson's report that "there was a little nimbled tongued
Woman among them, who said she could bring me acquainted with one of her own Sex that
would shew me a way, if I could attaine it, even Revelations, full of such ravishing joy that I
should never have cause to be sorry for sinne, so long as I live, and as for her part shee had
attained it already" (*A History of New-England, from the English planting in the Yeere
1628 untill the Yeere 1652* [1653, dated 1654], in *Johnson's Wonder-Working Providence
1628–1651*, ed. J. Franklin Jameson [1910; New York: Barnes and Noble, 1959], 134).

88. Ibid., 127.

89. Ibid. For an interesting discussion of this passage, see Sandra M. Gustafson's discussion of the Antinomian Controversy in the prologue to *Eloquence Is Power: Oratory*

*and Performance in Early America* (Chapel Hill: University of North Carolina Press, 2000), esp. 27–28.

90.  Viewing Hutchinson as less independent of the ministry than the characterizations by her opponents might suggest is consistent with Patrick Collinson's suggestion that "a major difference" "between pre-Reformation 'schools of heresy' and post-Reformation conventicles" was "the greater dependence of the latter on the public sermon, and, indeed, on the person and authority of the preacher, whether physically present or represented by the notes of his sermons carried and deployed by the hearers" ("The English Conventicle," in *Voluntary Religion,* 240). Although Hutchinson's comments about her distress at Cotton's migration suggest that she had heard him preach in Lincolnshire, Winship cautions that it is "unknown" whether Hutchinson "actually heard" Cotton preach in England (*Making Heretics,* 38). He explains that historians who claim that she did are drawing on Emery Battis's claim (in *Saints and Sectaries,* 36) that Cotton reported Hutchinson to have occasionally attended his services in Lincolnshire; however, he notes that "the source [Battis] gives makes no mention of this" (*Making Heretics,* 257 n. 47).

91.  Robert Baillie, *The Dissuasive from the Errors of the Time, Vindicated from the Exceptions of Mr. Cotton and Mr. Tombes* (London, 1655), quoted in Hall, notes to the second edition, in *The Antinomian Controversy,* xxi; *Way Cleared,* 286.

92.  See, for example, the opening of Helen Augur's biography, in which Hutchinson listens to Cotton preaching on the Song of Songs: "John Cotton's voice was beautiful. It was warm and silky" (*An American Jezebel: The Life of Anne Hutchinson* [New York: Brentano's, 1930], 1–2).

93.  Lad Tobin suggests that the ministers involved were not only offended, but also jealous: "the antinomian ulcer . . . forced each individual minister to look inward, to measure his own spiritual experience against Hutchinson's, and it is safe to assume that many did not like what they saw" ("A Radically Different Voice," 258). He notes that "they were most furious about her personal criticism of their preaching," citing what he calls "convincing evidence in journals and letters that almost all of Hutchinson's accusers, including Winthrop and Shepard, not only suffered spiritual crises during this period but also that many were privately attracted to—and jealous of—antinomianism" (258). Tobin suggests that "these men resented and envied the intensity of Hutchinson's spirituality and that their punitive behavior was, at least in part, motivated by anger and jealousy" (258). In his words, Hutchinson "made not only her own fantasies and desires public, but also . . . made *their* fantasies and desires public" (258).

94.  Cooper notes that "neither Cotton nor any of his clerical brethren singled out a rebellious laity or congregational liberty as the root of the Antinomian controversy," and finds it "unlikely that the controversy precipitated in the neighboring ministers a crisis in confidence in their own relationships with their congregants" (*Tenacious of Their Liberties,* 53, 49). On the other hand, religious leaders had experience with the dangers of partisanship. Lake and Como describe "an underworld of dispute and debate, of frenzied lay partisanship and activity" in the London Puritan underground in the 1620s ("'Orthodoxy' and Its Discontents," 52).

95.  For fuller discussion of these techniques, see chapter 1.

96.  See, for example, her exchange with John Davenport at the church trial. In this instance, Hutchinson found Davenport's explanation of the distinction between "the *life of the Soule and the Life of the Body,*" supported by references to Ecclesiastes and Isaiah, convincing. "*I am clear in this now,*" she asserted, and she agreed to renounce formerly held "errors" on several related points as a result ("Report," 360).

97.  See, for example, an entry for November 1636, which the editors of the *Journal* an-

notate with the comment that "[w]hen JW wrote this paragraph in November 1636 he seems to have hoped that the Antinomian controversy was blowing over" (*Journal*, 201 n. 43).

98. In her discussion of the Antinomian Controversy, Mary Beth Norton explores the distinction between public and private and suggests its importance, especially in John Winthrop's account of the debate (*Founding Mothers and Fathers*, 378–89). See also Patrick Collinson's discussion of the distinction between public and private religious duties in "The English Conventicle," 224, 234–35.

99. Shepard, letter to John Cotton, 25.

100. Cotton, *Mr. Cotton's Rejoynder*, 119.

101. Maclear notes that Hutchinson's "defensive claim that her views were perplexities rather than convictions may have been genuine, and certainly her mortalist ideas appeared confused and still ill formed" ("Anne Hutchinson and the Mortalist Heresy," 88).

102. Thomas Hooker, letter to John Winthrop, c. October 1637, in *Winthrop Papers*, 3:499.

103. Michael P. Winship argues that "[i]t is hard to read Keayne's notes [of Hutchinson's church trial] and not conclude that in spite of all of the hostilities of the previous months, Winthrop and others in the building genuinely wanted Hutchinson back, and they were prepared to invest a great deal of time and care to get her back" (*Making Heretics*, 206).

104. For a discussion of admonition as a procedure, see David C. Brown, "The Keys of the Kingdom: Excommunication in Colonial Massachusetts," *New England Quarterly* 67, no. 4 (December 1994): 531.

105. Charles E. Hambrick-Stowe notes as well that although "[f]emale leadership of mixed meetings was an innovation that the Massachusetts magistracy firmly brought to a stop after Hutchinson's expulsion. . . . [W]omen's prayer groups continued, though since they caused no further sedition, the record of them is meager" (*The Practice of Piety: Puritan Devotional Disciplines in Seventeenth-Century New England* [Chapel Hill: University of North Carolina Press, 1982], 140).

106. Rosenmeier observes that scholars often relegate Cotton "to the role of prestidigitatious apologizer for New England" ("The Teacher and the Witness: John Cotton and Roger Williams," *William and Mary Quarterly* 3d ser. 25, no. 3 [July 1968]: 409). Perry Miller, for example, describes Cotton as having "bent before the storm and saved his standing in the holy commonwealth at the expense of his consistency." Acknowledging that this may be too severe an assessment, Miller asserts that at the very least Cotton learned "caution" in the Antinomian Controversy, and afterwards did not "speak frankly" ("'Preparation for Salvation' in Seventeenth Century New England," *The Journal of the History of Ideas* 4, no. 3 [1943]: 253–86, reprinted in *Ideas in Cultural Perspective*, ed. Philip P. Wiener and Aaron Noland [New Brunswick: Rutgers University Press, 1962], 622). Maclear argues, on the other hand, that Hutchinson's mortalist views were much more radical than any position Cotton advocated, and that they alarmed him and his colleagues tremendously ("Anne Hutchinson and the Mortalist Heresy," esp. 88–91, 101–3). Gura agrees that by the time of her church trial Hutchinson's positions had evolved into "genuinely radical ideologies": "No longer did the colony's theologians have to split hairs over doctrinal niceties; the opinionists had crossed the line into heresy" (*A Glimpse of Sion's Glory*, 260). Letters written by Cotton in the wake of Hutchinson's exile support the views of Maclear and Gura. In a letter to Wheelwright, for example, Cotton says that when various members of the Hutchinsonian faction claimed that they held "forth noe [m]ore [tha]n their Teacher," he "plainely saw tha[t they] had run a course of hæresie a long tyme together before our Pastours speach in the Court, & before your sermon" (John Cotton to [John Wheelwright], 18 April 1640, *The Correspondence of John Cotton*, ed. Sargent Bush Jr. [Chapel Hill: University of North Car-

olina Press, 2001], 303). See also John Cotton to [Unknown] at Aquidneck, 4 June [1638], in ibid., 276–80.

107. Shepard, *Autobiography*, 74. On Cotton's "long process of distancing himself from his one-time follower," see Norton, *Founding Mothers and Fathers*, 372–73.

108. Brown explains that "[a]lthough [in cases of excommunication] the elders guided proceedings, the congregation had to concur in any sentence" ("The Keys of the Kingdom," 550).

109. Hall notes that Hutchinson "was either pregnant (as contemporaries assumed) or suffering from a hydatidiform mole, as modern medical opinion holds" (notes to the second edition, in *The Antinomian Controversy*, xix). Other discussions of Hutchinson's "monstrous births" include Emery Battis, *Saints and Sectaries*; Anne J. Schutte, "'Such Monstrous Births': A Neglected Aspect of the Antinomian Controversy," *Renaissance Quarterly* 38, no. 1 (spring 1985): 85–106; Valerie Pearl and Morris Pearl, eds., "Governor John Winthrop on the Birth of the Antinomians' 'Monster': The Earliest Reports to Reach England and the Making of a Myth," *Massachusetts Historical Society Proceedings* 102 (1990): 21–37.

110. David D. Hall, "Proceedings of the Boston Church against the Exiles," in *The Antinomian Controversy*, 389. Hall dates the meeting to 1639, but Winship points out that "Robert Keayne's Notebook, the source of this excerpt, was using old-style dating" (*Making Heretics*, 213, 300 n. 8).

111. Robert Keayne, "Robert Keayne's Report of Boston Church Action," in ibid., 392–93.

112. Cooper, *Tenacious of Their Liberties*, 56–67.

113. See Shepard, *Autobiography*, 74. See also Thomas Shepard, *The Parable of the Ten Virgins Unfolded* (1660), in *The Works of Thomas Shepard, First Pastor of the First Church, Cambridge, Mass. with a Memoir of His Life and Character*, vol. 2 (Boston: Boston Doctrinal Tract and Book Society, 1853; Ligonier, Penn.: Soli Deo Gloria, 1991).

## EPILOGUE

1. James F. Cooper Jr. argues that "both the lay rebellion against the clergy and the ministers' assault on lay liberties within individual churches [perceived by many historians who analyze the Antinomian Controversy] were more apparent than real." He contends that "members and their elders inhabited a shared space in matters of church government that ministers defined in such a way as to encourage lay thought and initiative," and that "[t]hese features did not change as a consequence of the Antinomian Controversy" (*Tenacious of Their Liberties: The Congregationalists in Colonial Massachusetts* [New York: Oxford University Press, 1999], 46–47, 67). Darren Staloff, on the other hand, argues that with the defeat of the "merchant Antinomian dissidents of Boston . . . [t]he system of cultural domination and the one-party state it supported had been secured by the class-conscious response of both ministerial intellectuals and magisterial intelligentsia" (*The Making of an American Thinking Class: Intellectuals and Intelligentsia in Puritan Massachusetts* [New York: Oxford University Press, 1998], 72). Michael P. Winship suggests that "a picture of Massachusetts Puritanism, lay and ministerial, reconstituting its unity, albeit in somewhat truncated fashion, after the removal of the exiles" renders overly tidy the "division between socially problematic radicals and mainstream, and it fits neither the conclusion of the Antinomian Controversy nor the dynamic of Puritanism" ("'The Most Glorious Church in the World': The Unity of the Godly in Boston, Massachusetts, in the 1630s," *Journal of British Studies* 39, no. 1 [January 2000]: 95). Janice Knight argues as well that "[t]he magistrates and ministers who emerged victorious in the aftermath of the controversies of the 1630s were not successful in redefining all opposition as heresy; nor were they able to contain or co-opt all expressions of dissent." Rather, she insists, "dissenting preachers like Cotton and Davenport effectively remained both in and out of the game," continuing "to challenge or

modify the policies of the ruling orthodoxy" and perpetuating an alternative orthodoxy that continued to have an impact within American Puritanism and beyond (*Orthodoxies in Massachusetts: Rereading American Puritanism* [Cambridge: Harvard University Press, 1994], 197, 199).

　　2. John Cotton, *A Briefe Exposition With Practical Observations Upon the Whole Booke of Ecclesiastes* (London, 1654). See chapter 2, pages 51–52 for further discussion of this text.

　　3. John Cotton, *The Grovnds and Ends of the Baptisme of the Children of the Faithfull. Opened In a familiar Discourse by way of a Dialogue, or Brotherly Conference* (London, 1647).

　　4. Larzer Ziff, *The Career of John Cotton: Puritanism and the American Experience* (Princeton: Princeton University Press, 1962), 233.

　　5. Charles Chauncy, *Gods Mercy Shewed to his People in Giving Them a Faithful Ministry and Schooles of Learning for the Continual Supplyes Thereof* (Cambridge, 1655).

　　6. See William Ames's discussion of "The Extraordinary Minister of the Church," which "is either for the first instituting of a church, or for the special and extraordinary conservation of a church, or for the extraordinary restoring of a church which has collapsed" (*The Marrow of Theology* [1623], trans. from the third Latin edition of 1629 and ed. John D. Eusden [1968; Durham: Labyrinth, 1983], 182–85).

　　7. For discussion of such objections, see Samuel Eliot Morison, *The Intellectual Life of Colonial New England* (1936; Ithaca: Cornell University Press, 1961), 29, 29 n. 4. Morison notes that Harvard College in the seventeenth century aimed at "higher education in the broadest sense, not a specialized training in Protestant theology," though of course his observation must be read in light of the enterprise of Puritanists in his day to demonstrate the intellectual seriousness of New England Puritans (ibid., 32).

　　8. William Dell, *The Tryal of Spirits Both in Teachers & Hearers Wherein Is Held Forth the Clear Discovery and Certain Downfal of the Carnal and Antichristian Clergie of These Nations Testified from the Word of God to the University-congregation in Cambridge* (1653; London, 1660).

　　9. As Norman S. Grabo explains, Chauncy insisted that "the basis of good reading must be what later came to be called textual criticism" ("Running the Gauntlet: Seventeenth-Century Literary Criticism," *ELH* 67, no. 3 [fall 2000]: 710).

　　10. Stephen Foster, *The Long Argument: English Puritanism and the Shaping of New England Culture, 1570–1700* (Chapel Hill: University of North Carolina Press, 1991), 189. Foster reports that "the General Court forbade him to accept, 'considering the humour of the times in England, inclining to discourage learning'" (189).

　　11. [John Eliot], *Indian Dialogues, For Their Instruction in that great Service of Christ, in calling home their Country-men to the Knowledge of GOD, And of Themselves, and of Iesus Christ* (Cambridge, 1671), in *John Eliot's Indian Dialogues: A Study in Cultural Interaction*, ed. Henry W. Bowden and James P. Ronda (Westport, Conn.: Greenwood Press, 1980).

　　12. Eliot, *Indian Dialogues*, 72. Eliot's modern critics have expressed greater skepticism. James Holstun, for example, acknowledges that Eliot's "justification for colonial domination moves beyond the linguistic racism practiced by many of the earlier colonists," but insists that "on the level of social practice—who translates, what is translated, and to what end— it becomes another instrument of English domination" (*A Rational Millennium: Puritan Utopias of Seventeenth-Century England and America* [New York: Oxford University Press, 1987], 140). George E. Tinker implicates Eliot in "cultural genocide," both through "intentional erosion of Indian culture" and through "its results, the unintentional devasta-

tion of those peoples, all established by thorough confusion of gospel and culture" ("John Eliot: Conversion, Colonialism, and the Oppression of Language," in *Missionary Conquest: The Gospel and Native American Cultural Genocide* [Minneapolis: Fortress Press, 1993], 21). See also Francis Jennings, *The Invasion of America: Indians, Colonialism and the Cant of Conquest* (New York: Norton, 1976).

13. Eliot, *Indian Dialogues*, 73. For further discussion, see James P. Ronda, "'We Are Well As We Are': An Indian Critique of Seventeenth-Century Christian Missions," *William and Mary Quarterly* 3d ser. 34 (1977): 66–82.

14. J[ohn] E[liot], *The Logick Primer. Some Logical Notions to initiate the* INDIANS *in the knowledge of the Rule of Reason; and to know how to make use thereof. Especially for the Instruction of such as are Teachers among them* (Cambridge, 1672).

15. John Eliot, *The Holy Bible containing the Old Testament and the New. Translated into the Indian Language and Ordered to be Printed by the Commissioners of the United Colonies in New-England* (Cambridge, 1663), A4r–A4v.

16. Edmund Morgan suggests that "the very fact that the half-way covenant was needed may be testimony, not to the decline of religion, but to the rise of an extraordinary religious scrupulosity, which still existed in the eighteenth century. The second generation of Puritans may have become so sophisticated in the morphology of conversion that they rejected as inconclusive, religious experiences that would have driven their parents unhesitatingly into church membership" ("New England Puritanism: Another Approach," *William and Mary Quarterly* 3d ser. 18, no. 2 [April 1961]: 241–42). Morgan's suggestion challenges the earlier understanding put forward by Perry Miller in "Declension," book 1 of *The New England Mind: From Colony to Province* (Cambridge: Harvard University Press, 1953), 19–146. Other important considerations of declension include Darrett B. Rutman, "God's Bridge Falling Down: 'Another Approach' to New England Puritanism Assayed," *William and Mary Quarterly* 3d ser. 19, no. 3 (July 1962): 408–21; Robert G. Pope, *The Half-Way Covenant: Church Membership in Puritan New England* (Princeton: Princeton University Press, 1969); Ross W. Beales Jr., "The Half-Way Covenant and Religious Scrupulosity: The First Church of Dorchester, Massachusetts, as a Test Case," *William and Mary Quarterly* 3d ser. 31, no. 3 (July 1974): 465–80; Sacvan Bercovitch, *The American Jeremiad* (Madison: University of Wisconsin Press, 1978); Foster, *The Long Argument*; and Cooper, *Tenacious of Their Liberties*, 88–114.

17. Space constraints prevent me from presenting more than a very brief overview of this controversy here. For fuller accounts, see Pope, *The Half-Way Covenant; The Creeds and Platforms of Congregationalism*, ed. Williston Walker (1893; New York: Pilgrim Press, 1991); Miller, *The New England Mind: From Colony to Province*, 82–104; David D. Hall, *The Faithful Shepherd: A History of the New England Ministry in the Seventeenth Century* (Chapel Hill: University of North Carolina Press, 1972); Emory Elliott, *Power and the Pulpit in Puritan New England* (Princeton: Princeton University Press, 1975); Foster, *The Long Argument*; Rutman, "God's Bridge Falling Down"; Beales, "The Half-Way Covenant and Religious Scrupulosity"; Cooper, *Tenacious of Their Liberties*; Staloff, *The Making of an American Thinking Class*; Lewis Milton Robinson, "A History of the Half-Way Covenant" (Ph.D. diss., University of Illinois, 1963). Because the clergy lost their unanimity, Cooper describes "the Halfway Covenant [as having] generated a crisis in Massachusetts that surpassed all others in the seventeenth century in its breadth and lasting consequences," including a permanent erosion of "clercial authority in church affairs" (*Tenacious of Their Liberties*, 89).

18. *Propositions Concerning the Subject of Baptism and Consociation of Churches Collected and Confirmed out of the Word of God, by a Synod of Elders and Messengers of*

the Churches in Massachusets-Colony in New-England; Assembled at Boston, according to Appointment of the Honoured General Court, In the Year 1662, at a General Court Held at Boston in New-England the 8th of October, 1662 (Cambridge, 1662) [hereafter *Propositions*]. Cotton Mather notes that this text was "Chiefly of [Jonathan Mitchell's] composure" (*Magnalia Christi Americana; or, The Ecclesiastical History of New-England from its First Planting, in the Year 1620, unto the Year of Our Lord 1698*, vol. 2 [1702; Hartford: Silas Andrus and Son, 1853], reprinted as *Great Works of Christ in America* [Edinburgh: Banner of Truth Trust, 1979], 99).

19. "The [Salem Church] Covenant of 1629," in *The Creeds and Platforms of Congregationalism*, 116.

20. The description of "the path of the just as the shining light" is drawn from Proverbs 4:18, while the image of God's word as "a Lanthorn to their feet" is drawn from Psalm 119:105.

21. Hooker had died in 1647, Shepard in 1649, and Cotton in 1652.

22. Other examples are cited as well, including the invitation to "See the like, 2 *Chron. 30. 5, 26. 2 Kings 23.21,22*. they did not tye themselves to former use and custome, but to the Rule of God's written Word; and so should we" (sig. A4r–A4v).

23. Sargent Bush Jr., introduction to *The Correspondence of John Cotton*, ed. Sargent Bush Jr. (Chapel Hill: University of North Carolina Press, 2001), 60; John Cotton, *Of the Holinesse of Church-members* (London, 1650); John Cotton, *The Bloudy Tenent, Washed, and Made White in the Bloud of the Lambe* (London, 1647); Thomas Hooker, *A Survey of the Summe of Church-Discipline. Wherein, The Way of the Churches of NEW-ENGLAND is warranted out of the Word, and all Exceptions of weight, which are not made against it, answered: Whereby also it will appear to the Judicious Reader, that something more must be said, then yet hath been, before their Principles can be shaken, or they should be unsetled in their practice* (London, 1648); George Phillips, *A Reply to a Confutation of Some Grounds for Infants Baptisme: as also, concerning the form of a church, put forth against mee by one Thomas Lamb. Hereunto is added, a discourse of the verity and validity of infants baptisme, wherein I endeavour to clear it in it self: as also in the ministery administrating it, and the manner of administration, by sprinkling, and not dipping; with sundry other particulars handled herein* (London, 1645); Thomas Shepard, *The Church-membership of Children, and Their Right to Baptisme According to that holy and everlasting COVENANT of GOD, established between Himself and the Faithfull and their seed after them, in their Generations: cleared up in a Letter, sent unto a worthy Friend of the AUTHOR, and many Yeares agoe written touching that subject* (Cambridge, 1663).

24. [Charles Chauncy,] *Anti-Synodalia Scripta Americana Or, a Proposal of the Judgment of the Dissenting Messengers of the Churches of New-England Assembled, by the Appointment of the General Court, March 10, 1662, whereof there were several Sessions afterwards* [hereafter *Anti-Synodalia*], printed with *Propositions Concerning the Subject of Baptism and Consocation of Churches; Collected and Confirmed out of the Word of God, by a Synod of Elders and Messengers of the Churches in Massachusetts-Colony in New-England. Assembled at Boston, according to the Appointment of the Honoured General Court, in the Year, 1662* ([Cambridge,] 1662), 13–14.

25. Increase Mather, *The First Principles of New-England, Concerning the Subject of Baptisme & Communion of Churches* (Cambridge, 1673), sig. A4v.

26. In *First Principles*, Mather argued that his own change of opinion validated Cotton's claim to Roger Williams that when people grow in grace they will see the error of separation (sig. A2v–A3r).

27. Mather, *The First Principles of New-England*, 7. Cooper notes that Cotton initially

supported baptism for the grandchildren of full members, but later reversed his position (*Tenacious of Their Liberties,* 89).

28. For a detailed account of the laity's role in the debates over the Halfway Covenant, see Cooper, *Tenacious of Their Liberties,* 88–114.

29. Mather, *The First Principles of New-England,* sig. A2v.

30. Romans 14:3 reads: "Let not him that eateth despise him that eateth not; and let not him which eateth not judge him that eateth: for God hath received him."

31. Such assertions of toleration did not prevent the rhetoric of the controversy from becoming heated. As Cooper notes, "passions intensified on both sides until the rhetoric grew nearly hysterical" (*Tenacious of Their Liberties,* 95).

32. Here, Mitchell's biblical reference is somewhat less apt, for his text suggests that the truth may be somewhat subjective. In Romans 14:14, Paul knows "that *there is* nothing unclean of itself: but to him that esteemeth any thing to be unclean, to him *it is* unclean," suggesting that dissenters are not in fact wrong.

33. Michael Warner, *The Letters of the Republic: Publication and the Public Sphere in Eighteenth-Century America* (Cambridge: Harvard University Press, 1990), 20–21.

34. Grantland S. Rice, *The Transformation of Authorship in America* (Chicago: University of Chicago Press, 1997), 23, 22.

35. Pope, *The Half-Way Covenant,* 55. In 1662, the General Court had instituted censorship of the printing press "For prevention of irregularitjes & abuse to the authority of this country" (Nathan B. Shurtleff, ed., *Records of the Governor and Company of the Massachusetts Bay in New England, Printed by Order of the Legislature,* vol. 4, part 2, *1661–1674* [Boston, 1854; New York: AMS Press, 1968], 62). The court repealed this ruling in 1663, ordering "that the printing presse be at liberty as formerly, till this Court shall take further order" (ibid., 73). In 1665, the court enacted a law "For the preventing of irregularitjes & abuse to the authority of this country by the printing presse," banning any press except in Cambridge, and requiring publications to be screened by court appointees (ibid., 141). The General Court named the president of Harvard College, John Sherman, John Mitchell, and Thomas Shepard, "or any two of them" as censors (ibid., 141). Rice notes that the 1665 law responded to Marmaduke Johnson's attempt to set up a private commercial press (*The Transformation of Authorship in America,* 182 n. 25).

36. Pope, *The Half-Way Covenant,* 56. David D. Hall cites this episode as a "major exception to [the] history of suppression and concealment" in New England, noting that "[s]pokesmen for the majority . . . implied that [unusual] . . . openness was possible because the controversy was not about 'damnable Heresies' but concerned 'lesser differences'" (David D. Hall, "Readers and Writers in Early New England," in *The Colonial Book in the Atlantic World, A History of the Book in America,* vol. 1 [Cambridge: Cambridge University Press, 2000], 130).

37. Cooper, *Tenacious of Their Liberties,* 94.

38. Cooper argues that even after the 1660s, when churches became less stringent about unanimity, communities "rarely imposed decisions upon significant minorities" (ibid., 96).

39. For an account of these events, see Richard C. Simmons, "The Founding of the Third Church in Boston," *William and Mary Quarterly* 3d ser. 26, no. 2 (April 1969): 241–52. See also Cooper, *Tenacious of Their Liberties,* 98–114.

40. Cooper, *Tenacious of Their Liberties,* esp. 106–8.

41. Pope, *The Half-Way Covenant,* 75.

42. Ibid., 77; J. Hammond Trumbull, ed., *The Public Records of the Colony of Connecticut, from 1636–1665 ,* vol. 1 of *The Public Records of the Colony of Connecticut from 1636–1776* (Hartford, 1850; New York: AMS Press, 1968), 388.

43. *The Public Records of the Colony of Connecticut, from 1636–1665* , 1:437–38, quoted in Pope, *The Half-Way Covenant*, 78.

44. Pope, *The Half-Way Covenant*, 78.

45. Ibid., 87.

46. Ibid., 90. Divisions within the Connecticut colony concerned not only baptism but also the larger question of congregational versus presbyterian church polity. See ibid., 82–91.

47. For a full discussion of calls for the synod to reconvene and opposition to it, see ibid., 91–93.

48. Ibid., 93–94; J. Hammond Trumbull, ed., *The Public Records of the Colony of Connecticut, from 1665 to 1678*, vol. 2 of *The Public Records of the Colony of Connecticut from 1636–1776* (Hartford, 1852; New York: AMS Press, 1968), 84.

49. Pope, *The Half-Way Covenant*, 84; *The Public Records of the Colony of Connecticut, from 1665 to 1678*, 2:109.

50. *The Public Records of the Colony of Connecticut, from 1665 to 1678*, 2:109.

51. Cooper, *Tenacious of Their Liberties*, 109–10.

52. Foster, *The Long Argument*, 203.

53. [Nathaniel Ward,] *The Simple Cobler of Aggavvam in America. Willing to help mend his Native Country, lamentably tattered, both in the upper-Leather and sole, with all the honest stitches he can take. And as willing never to bee paid for his work, by Old English wonted pay. It is his Trade to patch all the year long, gratis. Therefore I pray Gentlemen keep your purses* (London, 1647), 3. This text, written in 1645, was published in 1647 under the name of Theodore de la Guard.

54. *A Confession of Faith Owned and Consented unto by the Elders and Messengers of the Churches Assembled at Boston in New-England, May 12, 1680, Being the Second Session of That Synod* (Boston, 1680). This document was produced by the so-called Reforming Synod of 1679 and 1680. The text of the confession itself is almost identical to the 1658 *Savoy Declaration* (*A Declaration of the Faith and Order Owned and Practised in the Congregational Churches in England; Agreed upon and Consented unto by Their Elders and Messengers in Their Meeting at the Savoy, Octob. 12. 1658* [1658; London, 1659]). Both texts draw very heavily on the *Westminster Confession* of 1646 (*The Humble Advice of the Assembly of Divines, Now by Authority of Parliament Sitting at Westminster, Concerning Part of A Confession of Faith Presented by Them Lately to Both Houses of Parliament* [London, 1646]). For fuller discussion of these texts, see *The Creeds and Platforms of Congregationalism*, 340–439. On differences between the *Confession of Faith* and the *Savoy Declaration*, see Foster, *The Long Argument*, 228.

55. *Westminster Confession*, 6.

56. *Confession of Faith*, 6. The text of the *Savoy Declaration* is identical except in the spelling of "Supreme" (3).

57. Nehemiah Walter, *Unfruitful Hearers Detected & Warned: Or A Discourse Wherein the Danger of, and by, Unprofitable Hearing, is laid open and Cautioned against. As it was delivered, in the Course of his Ministry* (Boston, 1696), 50.

58. Elliott, *Power and the Pulpit in Puritan New England*, 6. Elliott notes that "[s]uch a delineation of the process of development of early American thought and culture echoes the bitter charges of the aging first-generation settlers against their sons. Unfortunately, it is an interpretation that fails, as the fathers failed, to understand and appreciate the deeper meaning of the lives of the second and third generations of New England that is exposed in their private and public writings" (6–7).

Appendix

1. Phyllis M. Jones and Nicholas R. Jones, *Salvation in New England: Selections from the Sermons of the First Preachers* (Austin: University of Texas Press, 1977), 17; William Perkins, *The Arte of Prophecying* (1592, trans. 1607) [hereafter *Arte*], trans. Thomas Tuke, in *Works* (London, 1609), 758.

2. John Cotton, *A Modest and Cleare Answer to Mr. Balls Discourse of set formes of Prayer. Set forth in a most Seasonable time, when this* KINGDOME *is now in Consultation about Matters of that Nature, and so many godly* Long *after the Resolution of that Point* (London, 1642), 43.

3. Babette May Levy, *Preaching in the First Half Century of New England History* (New York: Russell and Russell, 1945), 82–83. Harry S. Stout describes the ministers' often extensive notes, which were "recorded . . . in leatherbound volumes that closely resembled printed treatises. The number of pages in sermon books varied between thirty and two hundred, and depending on their size could contain three to five hundred words per page. Generally each volume contained one or more series broken down into sermons of six to twelve pages each. In these extended sermon outlines, punctuation was scarce, but thoughts were developed fully in the distinctive text-doctrine-application formula of the plain style sermon. To conserve paper, margins were fully used to make note of scriptural cross-references that could be read during the sermon and to enter abbreviated rhetorical cues like 'doct,' 'reas,' 'use 1,' that could lead the minister through the major 'heads' or divisions of his discourse. The substance of the notes was almost exclusively scriptural exegesis and personal applications" (*The New England Soul: Preaching and Religious Culture in Colonial New England* [New York: Oxford University Press, 1986], 34).

4. Levy, *Preaching in the First Half Century of New England History*, 83–84. On the practice of notetaking among congregants, see Winfried Herget, "The Transcription and Transmission of the Hooker Corpus," in *Thomas Hooker: Writings in England and Holland, 1626–1633*, ed. and intro. George H. Williams, Norman Pettit, Winfried Herget, and Sargent Bush Jr., Harvard Theological Studies 28 (Cambridge: Harvard University Press, 1975), 253–54. See also W. Fraser Mitchell, *English Pulpit Oratory from Andrewes to Tillotson: A Study of Its Literary Aspects* (New York: Macmillan, 1932), 29–38; Alan Fager Herr, *The Elizabethan Sermon: A Survey and a Bibliography* (New York: Octagon Books, 1969), 67–86; George Selement, "Publication and the Puritan Minister," *William and Mary Quarterly* 3d ser. 37, no. 2 (April 1980): 237–38.

5. Levy, *Preaching in the First Half Century of New England History*, 83–84; Jones and Jones, *Salvation in New England*, 18.

6. Levy, *Preaching in the First Half Century of New England History*, 85.

7. Everett H. Emerson, *John Cotton*, Twayne United States Authors Series 80 (New York: Twayne, 1965), 85.

8. Ibid., 85

9. Ibid., 85–86.

10. John Cotton, *Christ the Fountaine of Life: Or, Sundry Choyce Sermons on part of the fift Chapter of the first Epistle of St. John* (London, 1651; New York: Arno Press, 1972), 184.

11. Sargent Bush Jr. "Establishing the Hooker Canon," in *Thomas Hooker*, 379.

12. Ibid., 379.

13. Winfried Herget, "Preaching and Publication—Chronology and the Style of Thomas Hooker's Sermons," *Harvard Theological Review* 65 (1972): 232.

14. Bush, "Establishing the Hooker Canon," 379, 387. For discussion of the various

printed versions and dating of these texts, see Sargent Bush Jr., "A Bibliography of the Published Writings of Thomas Hooker," in *Thomas Hooker*, 390–425.

15. See Herget, "The Transcription and Transmission of the Hooker Corpus," 256–70.

16. Thomas Goodwyn and Philip Nye, "To the Reader," in Thomas Hooker, *The Application of Redemption, By the effectual Work of the Word, and Spirit of Christ, for the bringing home of lost Sinners to God* (London, 1657), reprinted as *The Application of Redemption* (New York: Arno Press, 1972), sig. C3v. The same preface appears in the second volume of *The Application of Redemption* (*The Application of Redemption, By the Effectual Work of the Word, and the Spirit of Christ, for the bringing home of lost Sinners to God, the Ninth and Tenth Books*, [London: Peter Cole, 1657]).

17. Bush, "A Bibliography of the Published Writings of Thomas Hooker," 398.

18. [Thomas Hooker,] *The Sovles Preparation for Christ. Or, A Treatise of Contrition, Wherein is discovered How God breakes the heart and woundes the Soule, in the conversion of a Sinner to Himselfe* (1632; London, 1638), reprinted in facsimile as *The Soules Preparation*, Library of American Puritan Writings 15 (New York: AMS Press, 1982), sig. A3v. Bush notes in his "Bibliography" that this comment appears in all the editions of *The Sovles Preparation* (398).

19. Herget, "The Transcription and Transmission of the Hooker Corpus," 257; Goodwyn and Nye, "To the Reader," C3v–C4r. See also Jones and Jones, *Salvation in New England*, 20.

20. Frank Shuffelton, *Thomas Hooker, 1586–1647* (Princeton: Princeton University Press, 1977), 155.

21. Cotton Mather, *Magnalia Christi Americana; or, The Ecclesiastical History of New-England, from its First Planting, in the Year 1620, unto the Year of Our Lord 1698* (1702; Hartford: Silus Andrus and Son, 1853), reprinted as *Great Works of Christ in America* (Edinburgh: Banner of Truth Trust, 1979), 1:347; Shuffelton, *Thomas Hooker*, 76.

22. Herget notes that "[t]he extent to which a sermon is written out is not necessarily an indication of its authenticity," explaining that "[a] longer text will certainly be more readable, whereas a shorter text may resemble the notes more closely and can, for example, be more accurate in its Scriptural citations, as a comparison of the two versions of *The Soules Ingrafting* will show" ("Preaching and Publication," 236).

23. In *The Sovles Preparation*, for example, the marginal citation for a quotation from Psalms 50:21 reads: "Psal. 50.2" (20). On page 2, a quotation from Psalms 77:4 is marked "Psal. 74.4."

24. The quotation is from Proverbs 1:22 (Hooker, *The Sovles Preparation*, 51).

25. On the use of notes and memorization, see Richard Bernard, *The Faithfvll Shepheard: Or, The Shepheards Faithfulnesse: Wherein is for the matter largely, but for the maner, in few words, set forth the excellencie and necessitie of the Ministerie; A Ministers properties and dutie; His entrance into this function and charge; How to begin fitly to instruct his people; Catechising and Preaching; And a good plaine order and method therein: Not so as yet published. Very profitable both for yoong Students, who intend the studie of Theologie (heerein being also declared what Arts and tongues first to be learned, what kinde of Authors to be read and books necessarie in the beginning, and which in the first place) as also for such Ministers as yet have not atteined to a distinct order to studie, write, meditate, and to preach methodically, both for their better course in deliuering the Word, and the peoples vnderstanding in hearing, and memorie in reteining the same* (London, 1607), 85–86; *Arte*, 758; Herr, *The Elizabethan Sermon*, 35; Stout, *The New England Soul*, 34. See also Edward H. Davidson, "Cotton's Biblical Exegesis: Method and Purpose," *Early American Literature* 17, no. 2 (fall 1982): 119–38.

Primary Sources

Alsted, Johan Heinrich. *Encyclopædia, Septem tomis distincta*. Herborn, 1630.

Ames, William. *The Marrow of Theology*. 1623. Ed. and trans. from the third Latin edition of 1629 John D. Eusden. 1968. Durham: Labyrinth, 1983.

Baillie, Robert. *The Dissuasive from the Errors of the Time, Vindicated from the Exceptions of Mr. Cotton and Mr. Tombes*. London, 1655.

Bayly, Lewis. *The Practise of Pietie, Directing a Christian how to walke that he may please God*. 3d ed. London, 1613.

Bernard, Richard. *The Faithfvll Shepheard: Or The Shepheards Faithfulnesse: Wherein is for the matter largely, but for the maner, in few words, set forth the excellencie and necessitie of the Ministerie; A Ministers properties and dutie; His entrance into this function and charge; How to begin fitly to instruct his people; Catechising and Preaching; And a good plaine order and method therein: Not so as yet published. Very profitable both for yoong Students, who intend the studie of Theologie (heerein being also declared what Arts and tongues first to be learned, what kinde of Authors to be read and books necessarie in the beginning, and which in the first place) as also for such Ministers as yet have not atteined to a distinct order to studie, write, meditate, and to preach methodically, both for their better course in deliuering the Word, and the peoples vnderstanding in hearing, and memorie in reteining the same*. London, 1607.

*The Bible, That Is, The holy Scriptures coneined in the Olde and Newe Testament, Translated according to the Ebrew and Greeke, and conferred with the best Translations in diuers Languages. With most profitable Annotations vpon all hard places, and other things of great importance*. 1599. Reprint in facsimile as *The Geneva Bible*. Buena Park, Calif: Geneva Publishing, 1991.

Bradford, William. *Of Plymouth Plantation 1620–1647*. 1856. Ed. Samuel Eliot Morison. 1952. New York: Knopf, 1991.

Bradstreet, Anne. "As Weary Pilgrim." 1669. In *The Works of Anne Bradstreet*, ed. Jeannine Hensley. Cambridge: Harvard University Press, Belknap Press, 1967.

Calvin, John. *Institutes of the Christian Religion*. 1559. Ed. John T. McNeill. Trans. Ford Lewis Battles. 2 vols. The Library of Christian Classics 20–21. Philadelphia: Westminster, 1960.

Caryl, Joseph. "To the Reader." In *A Treatise of the Covenant of Grace, As it is dispensed to the Elect Seed, effectually unto Salvation*, by John Cotton. London, 1671.

"The Charlestown–Boston Covenant." In *The Creeds and Platforms of Congregationalism*, ed. Williston Walker, 131. New York: Scribner's, 1893. New York: Pilgrim Press, 1991.

[Chauncy, Charles.] *Anti-Synodalia Scripta Americana Or, a Proposal of the Judgment of the Dissenting Messengers of the Churches of New-England Assembled, by the Appointment of the General Court, March 10, 1662, whereof there were several Sessions afterwards*, printed with *Propositions Concerning the Subject of Baptism and Consociation of Churches; Collected and Confirmed out of the Word of God, by a Synod of Elders and Messengers of the Churches in Massachusetts-Colony in New-England. Assembled at Boston, according to the Appointment of the Honoured General Court, in the Year, 1662*. [Cambridge,] 1662.

Chauncy, Charles. *Gods Mercy Shewed to his People in Giving Them a Faithful Ministry and Schooles of Learning for the Continual Supplyes Thereof*. Cambridge, 1655.

Collins, John. "The Relation of Mr Collins." In *The Diary of Michael Wigglesworth, 1653–1657: The Conscience of a Puritan*, ed. Edmund S. Morgan, 107–23. Gloucester: Peter Smith, 1970.

*A Confession of Faith Owned and Consented unto by the Elders and Messengers of the Churches Assembled at Boston in New-England, May 12, 1680, Being the Second Session of That Synod*. Boston, 1680.

Cotton, John. "The Answer of Mr. Iohn Cotton of Boston in New-England, To the aforesaid ARGUMENTS against Persecution for Cause of Conscience. Professedly mainteining Persecution for Cause of Conscience." In *The Bloudy Tenent, of Persecution, for cause of Conscience, discussed, in A Conference betweene Truth and Peace. Who, In all tender Affection, present to the High Court of Parliament, (as the Result of their Discourse) these, (amongst other Passages) of highest consideration*. 1644. Ed. Samuel L. Caldwell. *Publications of the Narragansett Club*. 1st ser. Vol. 3. Providence, 1867. Reprinted in *The Complete Writings of Roger Williams*. Vol. 3. New York: Russell and Russell, 1963.

———. *The Bloudy Tenent, Washed And made white in the bloud of the Lambe: being discussed and discharged of bloud-guiltinesse by just Defence*. London, 1647.

———. *A Briefe Exposition With Practicall Observations Upon the Whole Book of Ecclesiastes*. London, 1654.

———. *Christ the Fountaine of Life: Or, Sundry Choyce Sermons on part of the fift Chapter of the first Epistle of St. John*. London, 1651. New York: Arno Press, 1972.

———. "Copy of a Letter from Mr. Cotton to Lord Say and Seal in the Year 1636." In *The New England Way*. Library of American Puritan Writings 12. New York: AMS Press, 1984.

———. *The Correspondence of John Cotton*. Ed. Sargent Bush Jr. Chapel Hill: University of North Carolina Press, 2001.

———. *The Grovnds and Ends of the Baptisme of the Children of the Faithfull. Opened In a familiar Discourse by way of a Dialogue, or Brotherly Conference*. London, 1647.

———. *A Letter of Mr. John Cottons Teacher of the Church in Boston, in Nevv-England, To Mr. Williams a Preacher there, Wherein is shewed, That those ought to be received into the Church who are Godly, though they doe not see, nor expressely bewaile all the pollutions in Church-fellowship, Ministery, Worship, Government.* London, 1643. Ed. Reuben Aldridge Guild. *Publications of the Narragansett Club.* Vol. 1. Providence, 1866.

———. *Mr. Cottons Rejoynder.* In *The Antinomian Controversy, 1636–1638: A Documentary History,* ed. David D. Hall, 78–151. 2d ed. Durham: Duke University Press, 1990.

———. *A Modest and Cleare Answer to Mr. Balls Discourse of set formes of Prayer. Set forth in a most Seasonable time, when this* KINGDOME *is now in Consultation about Matters of that Nature, and so many godly* Long *after the Resolution in that Point.* London, 1642.

———. *Of the Holinesse of Church-members.* London, 1650.

———. "On my Reverend and dear Brother, Mr Thomas Hooker. . . ." In *A Survey of the Summe of Church Discipline,* by Thomas Hooker. London, 1648.

———. *The Powring Out of the Seven Vials: Or, An Exposition of the Sixteenth Chapter of the* REVELATION, *with an Application of it to our Times. Wherein is revealed Gods powring out the full* VIALS *of his fierce Wrath. Very fit and necessary for this present Age.* London, 1645.

———. "A Thankful Acknowledgement of God's Providence." Quoted in *Abel being Dead yet speaketh; Or, The Life & Death Of that deservedly Famous Man of God, Mr John Cotton, Late Teacher of the Church of Christ, at Boston in New-England,* by John Norton. London, 1658. Reprint in facsimile, *The New England Way,* 28–29. Library of American Puritan Writings 12. New York: AMS Press, 1983.

———. *A Treatise of the Covenant of Grace, As it is dispensed to the Elect Seed, effectually unto Salvation. Being The Substance of divers Sermons preached upon Act, 7.8. by that eminently holy and judicious man of God, Mr. John Cotton, teacher of the Church at Boston in N.E.* London, 1671.

———. *The Way of Congregational Churches Cleared.* 1648. In *John Cotton on the Churches of New England,* ed. Larzer Ziff. Cambridge: Harvard University Press, 1968.

———. *The Way of Life, Or, Gods Way and Course, in bringing the soule into, keeping it in, and carrying it on, in the wayes of life and peace.* London, 1641. Reprint in facsimile, *The Way of Faith.* Library of American Puritan Writings 13. New York: AMS Press, 1983.

Davenport, John. *A Sermon Preach'd at the Election of the Governour at Boston in New England, May 19th, 1669.* [Boston,] 1670.

*A Declaration of the Faith and Order Owned and Practised in the Congregational Churches in England; Agreed upon and Consented unto by Their Elders and Messengers in Their Meeting at the Savoy, Octob. 12. 1658.* 1658. London, 1659.

Dell, William. *The Tryal of Spirits Both in Teachers & Hearers Wherein Is Held Forth the Clear Discovery and Certain Downfal of the Carnal and Antichristian Clergie of These Nations Testified from the Word of God to the University-congregation in Cambridge.* 1653. London, 1660.

"The Elders Reply." In *The Antinomian Controversy, 1636–1638: A Documentary History,* ed. David D. Hall, 60–67. 2d ed. Durham: Duke University Press, 1990.

[Eliot, John.] *Indian Dialogues, For Their Instruction in that great Service of Christ, in calling home their Country-men to the Knowledge of* GOD, *And of Themselves, and of Iesus Christ.* Cambridge, 1671. Reprint in *John Eliot's Indian Dialogues: A Study in Cultural Interaction,* ed. Henry W. Bowden and James P. Ronda. Westport, Conn.: Greenwood Press, 1980.

E[liot], J[ohn]. *The Logick Primer. Some Logical Notions to initiate the* INDIANS *in the knowledge of the Rule of Reason; and to know how to make use thereof. Especially for the Instruction of such as are Teachers among them.* Cambridge, 1672.

"The Enlarged [Salem Church] Covenant of 1636." In *The Creeds and Platforms of Congregationalism,* ed. Williston Walker, 116–18. New York: Scribner's, 1893. New York: Prilgrim Press, 1991.

Erasmus, Desiderius. *Ecclesiastes, sive Concionator Evangelicus.* In *Opera omnia,* ed. J. Clericus, 769–1100. Vol. 5. Leiden, 1703–6.

"The Examination of Mrs. Anne Hutchinson at the Court at Newtown." In *The Antinomian Controversy, 1636–1638: A Documentary History,* ed. David D. Hall, 311–48. 2d ed. Durham: Duke University Press, 1990.

Goodwyn, Thomas, and Philip Nye. "To the Reader." In *The Application of Redemption, By the effectual Work of the Word, and Spirit of Christ, for the bringing home of lost Sinners to God,* by Thomas Hooker. London, 1657. Reprinted as *The Application of Redemption.* New York: Arno Press, 1972.

———. "To the Reader." *The Application of Redemption, By the Effectual Work of the Word, and the Spirit of Christ, for the bringing home of lost Sinners to God, the Ninth and Tenth Books.* London, 1657.

Hartwell, Jasper. *The Firebrand Taken out of the Fire. Or, the Wonderfull History, Case, and Cure of Mis Drake.* London, 1654.

Hemmingsen, Niels. *The Preacher, or Method of preaching.Wrytten in Latine by Nicholas Hemminge, and translated into Englishe by I. H. Very necessarie for all those that by the true preaching of the word of God, labour to pull downe the Sinagogue of Sathan, and to buylde up the Temple of* GOD. Trans. J[ohn] H[orsfall]. London, 1574.

Hooker, Richard. *Of the Lawes of Ecclesiasticall Politie, Eyght Bookes.* 1593. Ed. Georges Edelen. *The Folger Library Edition of the Works of Richard Hooker.* Ed. W. Speed Hill. Vol. 1. Cambridge: Harvard University Press, Belknap Press, 1977.

[Hooker, Thomas]. *The Soules Implantation: A Treatise.* London, 1637. Reprinted in *Redemption: Three Sermons (1637–1656),* ed. Everett H. Emerson. Gainesville, Fla.: Scholars Facsimiles and Reprints, 1956.

———. *The Sovles Preparation for Christ. Or, A Treatise of Contrition, Wherein is discovered Hovv God breakes the heart, and woundes the Soule, in the conversion of a Sinner to Himselfe.* 1632. London, 1638. Reprint in facsimile, *The Soules Preparation.* Library of American Puritan Writings 15. New York: AMS Press, 1982.

H[ooker], T[homas]. *The Soules Implantation into the Naturall Olive.* London, 1640. Reprint in facsimile, *The Soules Implantation.* Library of American Puritan Writings 17. New York: AMS Press, 1981.

———. *The Soules Ingrafting into Christ.* London, 1637.

———. *The unbeleevers preparing for Christ.* London, 1638.

Hooker, Thomas. *The Application of Redemption, By the effectual Work of the Word, and Spirit of Christ, for the bringing home of lost Sinners to God. The first eight Books.* London, 1657. New York: Arno Press, 1972.

———. *The Application of Redemption, By the Effectual Work of the Word, and Spirit of Christ, for the bringing home of lost Sinners to God. The Ninth and Tenth Books.* London, 1656. Reprinted in *Redemption: Three Sermons (1637–1656),* ed. Everett H. Emerson, 49–64. Gainesville, Fla.: Scholars Facsimiles and Reprints, 1956.

———. *The Application of Redemption, By the Effectual Work of the Word, and the Spirit* of Christ, for the bringing home of lost Sinners to God, the Ninth and Tenth Books. London, 1657.

———. The Danger of Desertion: Or A Farewell Sermon of Mr. Thomas Hooker, Sometimes Minister of Gods Word at Chainsford in Essex; but now of New ENGLAND. Preached immediately before his departure out of old ENGLAND. 1641. London, 1657. In The Puritans in America: A Narrative Anthology, ed. Alan Heimert and Andrew Delbanco, 62–69. Cambridge: Harvard University Press, 1985.

———. Letter to John Winthrop. c. October 1637. In Winthrop Papers 1498–1654, 498–99. Vol. 3. Boston: Merrymount Press, 1943.

———. The Poor Doubting Christian Drawn Unto Christ. In Thomas Hooker: Writings in England and Holland, 1626–1633, 152–86. Harvard Theological Studies 28. Cambridge: Harvard University Press, 1975.

———. Survey of the Summe of Church-discipline. Wherein, The Way of the Churches of NEW-ENGLAND is warranted out of the Word, and all Exceptions of weight, which are made against it, answered: Whereby also it will appear to the Judicious Reader, that something more must be said, then yet hath been, before their Principles can be shaken, or they should be unsetled in their practice. London, 1648.

The Humble Advice of the Assembly of Divines, Now by Authority of Parliament Sitting at Westminster, Concerning Part of A Confession of Faith Presented by Them Lately to Both Houses of Parliament. London, 1646.

Hutchinson, Thomas. Hutchinson Papers, ed. W. H. Whitmore and W. S. Appleton. Publications of the Prince Society, vol. 1. Boston: Prince Society, 1865. New York: Burt Franklin, 1967.

Hyperius, Andreas. The Practis of Preaching, otherwise called the Pathway to the pulpet: conteyning an excellent method how to frame diuine sermons, & to interpret the holy Scriptures according to the capacitie of the vulgar people. First written in Latin by the learned pastor of Christes Church, Andreas Hyperius: and now lately (to the profit of the same Church) Englished by Iohn Ludham, vicar of Wethersfeld. 1577. Hereunto is added an oration concerning the lyfe and death of the same Hyperius: which may serue for a president to all the learned men of his calling in our tyme. Trans. J. Ludham. London, 1577.

Johnson, Edward. Wonder-working Providence of Sions Saviour in New England. 1653. Reprinted as Johnson's Wonder-working Providence, 1628–1651, ed. J. Franklin Jameson. 1910. New York: Barnes and Noble, 1937.

Keayne, Robert. "Robert Keayne's Report of Boston Church Action." In The Antinomian Controversy, 1636–1638: A Documentary History, ed. David D. Hall, 392–93. 2d ed. Durham: Duke University Press, 1990.

Keckermann, Bartholomäus. Opera omnium quae extant. Geneva, 1614.

———. [Title page lists as Bartholomaeo Keckermanno.] Rhetoricae ecclesiasticae, sive Artis formandi et habendi conciones sacras, Libri duo: Methodice adornati per praecepta & explicationes. Hanover, 1616.

Luther, Martin. Dr. Martin Luther's Answer to the Superchristian, Superspiritual, and Superlearned Book of Goat Emser of Leipzig with a Glance at His Comrade Murner. 1521. Trans. and intro. A. Steimle. In Works of Martin Luther, 310–401. Vol. 3. Philadelphia: Muhlenberg Press, 1930.

Mason, John. A Brief history of the Pequot War: Especially of the memorable Taking of their Fort at Mistick in Connecticut In 1637. Boston, 1732.

[Massachusetts]. The Book of the General Lauues and Libertyes Concerning the Inhabitants of the Massachusets Collected out of the Records of the General Court for the

*several years Wherin They Were Made and Established, And now revised by the same
Court and despe[r]sed into an Alphabetical order and published by the same Authoritie
in the General Court held at Boston, the fourteenth of the first month Anno 1647.*
Cambridge, Mass., 1648.

Mather, Cotton. *Magnalia Christi Americana; or, The Ecclesiastical History of New-
England, from its First Planting, in the Year 1620, unto the Year of Our Lord 1698.* 2
vols. 1702. Hartford: Silus Andrus and Son, 1853. Reprinted as *Great Works of Christ
in America.* Edinburgh: Banner of Truth Trust, 1979.

Mather, Increase. *The First Principles of New-England, Concerning the Subject of Baptisme
& Communion of Churches.* Cambridge, 1673.

Melanchthon, Philip. *De officiis concionatores.* In *Supplementa Melanchthoniana,* ed. Paul
Drews and Ferdinand Cohrs. Vol. 5, pt. 2. Leipzig, 1929.

Mitchell, Jonathan. Preface to *The Parable of the Ten Virgins Unfolded,* by Thomas Shepard. 1660. In *The Works of Thomas Shepard, First Pastor of the First Church, Cambridge, Mass. with a Memoir of His Life and Character,* 5–10. Vol. 2. Boston: Boston
Doctrinal Tract and Book Society, 1853. Ligonier, Penn.: Soli Deo Gloria, 1991.

———. *A Model of Church and Civil Power.* In *The Bloudy Tenent, of Persecution, for
cause of Conscience, discussed, in A Conference betweene Truth and Peace. Who, In all
tender Affection, present to the High Court of Parliament, (as the Result of their Discourse) these, (amongst other Passages) of highest consideration.* 1644. Ed. Samuel L.
Caldwell. *Publications of the Narragansett Club.* 1st ser. Vol. 3. Providence, 1867.
Reprinted in *The Complete Writings of Roger Williams.* Vol. 3. New York: Russell and
Russell, 1963.

Nash, Thomas. *Pierce Penilesse his Supplication to the Diuell. Describing the ouerspreading of Vice, and suppression of Vertue. Pleasantly interlac't with variable delights: and pathetically intermixt with conceipted reproofes.* London, 1592.

Norton, John. *Abel being Dead yet speaketh; Or, The Life & Death Of that deservedly Famous Man of God, M<sup>r</sup> John Cotton, Late Teacher of the Church of Christ, at* Boston
*in New-England.* London, 1658. Reprinted in *The New England Way.* Library of
American Puritan Writings 12. New York: AMS Press, 1983.

Perkins, William. *The Arte of Prophecying. Or a Treatise Concerning the Sacred and Onely
True Manner and Methode of Preaching.* 1592. Trans. 1607. Trans. Thomas Tuke. In
*Works.* London, 1609.

Phillips, George. *A Reply to a Confutation of Some Grounds for Infants Baptisme: as also,
concerning the form of a church, put forth against mee by one Thomas Lamb. Hereunto is added, a discourse of the verity and validity of infants baptisme, wherein I
endeavour to clear it in it self: as also in the ministerie administrating it, and the manner of administration, by sprinkling, and not dipping; with sundry other particulars
handled herein.* London, 1645.

Prince, Thomas. *Extraordinary Events the Doings of God, and Marvellous in Pious Eyes.
Illustrated in a sermon at the South Church in Boston, N.E. on the general thanksgiving, Thursday, July 18, 1745. Occasion'd by taking the city of Louisbourg on the
Isle of Cape Breton, by New-England soldiers, assisted by a British squadron.* Boston, 1745.

"Propositions of the Church of Boston." c. December 1636. In *Winthrop Papers 1498–1654,*
Vol. 3, 326. Boston: Merrymount Press, 1943.

*Propositions Concerning the Subject of Baptism and Consocation of Churches, Collected
and Confirmed out of the Word of God, by a Synod of Elders and Messengers of the
Churches in Massachusets-Colony in New-England. Assembled at* Boston, *according*

to Appointment of the Honoured GENERAL COURT, In the Year 1662, At a General Court Held at Boston in New-England the 8th of October, 1662. Cambridge, 1662.

"A Report of the Trial of Mrs. Anne Hutchinson before the Church in Boston." In The Antinomian Controversy, 1636–1638: A Documentary History, ed. David D. Hall, 349–88. 2d. ed. Durham: Duke University Press, 1990.

"The [Salem Church] Covenant of 1629." In The Creeds and Platforms of Congregationalism, ed. Williston Walker, 116. New York: Scribner's, 1893. New York: Pilgrim Press, 1991.

Shepard, Thomas. The Autobiography. 1832. In God's Plot: Puritan Spirituality in Thomas Shepard's Cambridge, ed. and intro. Michael McGiffert, 33–79. 1972. Amherst: University of Massachusetts Press, 1994.

———. The Church-membership of Children, and Their Right to Baptisme According to that holy and everlasting COVENANT of GOD, established between Himself and the Faithfull and their Seed after them, in their Generations: Cleared up in a Letter, sent unto a worthy Friend of the AUTHOR, and many Yeares agoe written touching that subject. Cambridge, 1663.

———. The Journal. In God's Plot: Puritan Spirituality in Thomas Shepard's Cambridge, ed. and intro. Michael McGiffert, 81–134. 1972. Amherst: University of Massachusetts Press, 1994.

———. Letter to John Winthrop. c. 15 December 1636. In Winthrop Papers 1498–1654, Vol. 3., 326. Boston: Merrymount Press, 1943.

———. Of Ineffectual Hearing the Word. 1652. In The Works of Thomas Shepard, First Pastor of the First Church, Cambridge, Mass. with a Memoir of His Life and Character, 361–84. Vol. 3. Boston: Boston Doctrinal Tract and Book Society, 1853. Ligonier, Penn.: Soli Deo Gloria, 1992.

———. The Parable of the Ten Virgins Unfolded. 1660. In The Works of Thomas Shepard, First Pastor of the First Church, Cambridge, Mass. with a Memoir of His Life and Character. Vol. 2. Boston: Boston Doctrinal Tract and Book Society, 1853. Ligonier, Penn.: Soli Deo Gloria, 1991.

———. The Saint's Jewel; Showing How to Apply the Promise. 1655. In The Works of Thomas Shepard, First Pastor of the First Church, Cambridge, Mass. with a Memoir of His Life and Character, 285–97. Vol. 1. Boston: Boston Doctrinal Tract and Book Society, 1853. Ligonier, Penn.: Soli Deo Gloria, 1991.

———. The Sound Believer. 1645. In The Works of Thomas Shepard, First Pastor of the First Church, Cambridge, Mass. with a Memoir of His Life and Character, 111–284. Vol. 1. Boston: Boston Doctrinal Tract and Book Society, 1853. Ligonier, Penn.: Soli Deo Gloria, 1991.

———. Thomas Shepard's "Confessions." Ed. and intro. George Selement and Bruce C. Woolley. Publications of the Colonial Society of Massachusetts Collections 58. Boston, 1981.

———. "Thomas Shepard to John Cotton." In The Antinomian Controversy, 1636–1638: A Documentary History, ed. David D. Hall, 25–29. 2d ed. Durham: Duke University Press, 1990.

Shurtleff, Nathan B., ed. Records of the Governor and Company of the Massachusetts Bay in New England. 5 vols. in 6. Boston, 1853–54. New York: AMS Press, 1968.

Sibbes, Richard. The Complete Works of Richard Sibbes. Ed. Alexander Balloch Grosart. Edinburgh: James Nichol, 1862–64.

Trumbull, J. Hammond, ed. The Public Records of the Colony of Connecticut from 1636–1776. Hartford, 1850–90. New York: AMS Press, 1968.

Tuckney, Anthony. "To the Reader." In *A Brief Exposition With Practical Observations Upon the whole Book of Canticles*, by John Cotton. London, 1655.

Walter, Nehemiah. *Unfruitful Hearers Detected & Warned: Or A Discourse Wherein the Danger of, and by, Unprofitable Hearing, is laid open and Cautioned against. As it was delivered, in the Course of his Ministry*. Boston, 1696.

[Ward, Nathaniel.] *The Simple Cobler of Aggavvam in America. Willing to help mend his Native Country, lamentably tattered, both in the upper-Leather and sole, with all the honest stitches he can take. And as willing never to bee paid for his work, by Old English wonted pay. It is his Trade to patch all the year long, gratis. Therefore I pray Gentlemen keep your purses*. London, 1647.

Weigle, Luther A., ed. *The New Testament Octapla: Eight English Versions of the New Testament in the Tyndale-King James Tradition*. New York: Thomas Nelson and Sons, n.d.

Weld, Thomas. Preface to *A Short Story of the Rise, reign, and ruine of the Antinomians, Familists & Libertines, that infected the Churches of New-England*, [by John Winthrop]. In *The Antinomian Controversy, 1636–1638: A Documentary History*, ed. David D. Hall 201–19. 2d ed. Durham: Duke University Press, 1990.

Wheelwright, John. "A Fast-Day Sermon." 1637. In *The Antinomian Controversy, 1636–1638: A Documentary History*, ed. David D. Hall, 152–72. 2d ed. Durham: Duke University Press, 1990.

———. *Mercurius Americanus, Mr. Welds his Antitype, Or, Massachusetts great Apologie examined, Being Observations upon a Paper styled, A short story of the Rise, Reign, and Ruine of the Familists, Libertines, &c. which infected the Churches of New-England, &c. Wherein some parties therein concerned are vindicated, and the truth generally cleared*. 1645. John Wheelwright, *Publications of the Prince Society* 9. Boston, 1896.

White, Elizabeth. *The Experiences of God's Gracious Dealing with Mrs. Elizabeth White*. Boston, 1741.

Whitgift, John. *The Works of John Whitgift*. Ed. John Ayre. 3 vols. Cambridge, England: Parker Society, 1851.

[Willet, Andrew, and Thomas Cartwright]. *A Christian Letter of certain English Protestants vnfained fauourers of the present state of Religion, authorised and professed in* ENGLAND: *vnto that Reverend and learned man, Mr R. Hoo. requiring resolution in certaine matters of doctrine (which seeme to ouerthrow the foundation of Christian Religion, and of the church among vs) expreslie contained in his fiue books of Ecclesiasticall pollicie*. [Middleburg,] 1599.

Williams, Roger. *The Bloudy Tenent, of Persecution, for cause of Conscience, discussed, in A Conference betweene Trvth and Peace. Who, In all tender Affection, present to the High Court of Parliament, (as the Result of their Discourse) these, (amongst other Passages) of highest consideration*. 1644. Ed. Samuel L. Caldwell. *Publications of the Narragansett Club*. 1st ser. Vol. 3. Providence, 1867. Reprinted in *The Complete Writings of Roger Williams*. Vol. 3. New York: Russell and Russell, 1963.

———. *The Bloody Tenent Yet More Bloody*. 1652. Ed. Samuel L. Caldwell. *Publications of the Narragansett Club*. 1st ser. Vol. 4. Providence, 1870.

———. *The Correspondence of Roger Williams*. Ed. and intro. Glenn W. LaFantasie. 2 vols. Hanover: Brown University Press, University Press of New England, for the Rhode Island Historical Society, 1988.

———. *Mr. Cottons Letter Lately Printed, Examined and Ansvvered*. London, 1644. Ed. Reuben Aldrige Guild. Reprinted in *Publications of the Narragansett Club*. Vol. 1. Providence, 1866.

[Winthrop, John.] *A Short Story of the Rise, reign, and ruine of the Antinomians, Familists & Libertines, that infected the Churches of New-England.* In *The Antinomian Controversy, 1636–1638: A Documentary History,* ed. David D. Hall, 199–310. 2d ed. Durham: Duke University Press, 1990.

Winthrop, John. *The Journal of John Winthrop.* Ed. Richard S. Dunn, James Savage, and Laetitia Yeandle. Cambridge, Massachusetts: Harvard University Press, 1996.

———. "John Winthrop to John Endecott." 3 January 1633/34. In *Winthrop Papers,* Vol. 3, 147–48. Boston: Massachusetts Historical Society, 1943.

———. *The History of New England from 1630 to 1649.* Ed. James Savage. 2 vols. Boston: Phelps and Farnham, 1825. Salem, N.H.: Ayer, 1992.

## SECONDARY SOURCES

Albro, John. *Life of Thomas Shepard. The Works of Thomas Shepard.* Vol. 1. Boston: Boston Doctrinal Tract and Book Society, 1853. Ligonier, Penn.: Soli Deo Gloria, 1991. vii–cxcii.

Amory, Hugh, and David D. Hall. *The Colonial Book in the Atlantic World: A History of the Book in America.* Vol. 1. Cambridge: Cambridge University Press, 2000.

Anderson, Marvin W. "The Geneva (Tomson/Junius) New Testament among Other English Bibles of the Period." In *The Geneva Bible: The Annotated New Testament 1602 Edition,* ed. Gerald T. Sheppard, 5–7. New York: Pilgrim, 1989.

Augur, Helen. *An American Jezebel: The Life of Anne Hutchinson.* New York: Brentano's, 1930.

Barker-Benfield, Ben. "Anne Hutchinson and the Puritan Attitude toward Women." *Feminist Studies* 1 (fall 1972): 65–96.

Barthes, Roland. "The Death of the Author." In *Image-Music-Text,* trans. Stephen Heath, 142–48. New York: Hill and Wang, 1977.

———. *The Pleasure of the Text.* Trans. Richard Miller. New York: Hill and Wang, 1975.

Battis, Emery. *Saints and Sectaries: Anne Hutchinson and the Antinomian Controversy in the Massachusetts Bay Colony.* Chapel Hill: University of North Carolina Press, 1962.

Beales Jr., Ross. W. "The Half-Way Covenant and Religious Scrupulosity: The First Church of Dorchester, Massachusetts, as a Test Case," *William and Mary Quarterly* 3d ser. 31, no. 3 (July 1974): 465–80.

Bercovitch, Sacvan. *The American Jeremiad.* Madison: University of Wisconsin Press, 1978.

———. "Colonial Puritan Rhetoric and the Discovery of American Identity." *Canadian Review of American Studies* 6, no. 2 (fall 1975): 131–50.

———. *The Puritan Origins of the American Self.* New Haven: Yale University Press, 1975.

———. "Typology in Puritan New England: The Williams–Cotton Controversy Reassessed." *American Quarterly* 19, no. 2 (summer 1967): 166–91.

Blench, J. W. *Preaching in England in the late Fifteenth and Sixteenth Centuries: A Study of English Sermons 1450–c. 1600.* Oxford: Basil Blackwell, 1964.

Bozeman, Theodore Dwight. *To Live Ancient Lives: The Primitivist Dimension in Puritanism.* Chapel Hill: University of North Carolina Press, 1988.

Breward, Ian. Editorial preface to *The Work of William Perkins,* by William Perkins. Courtenay Library of Reformation Classics 3, xi–xv. Appleford, Abingdon, Berkshire, England: Sutton Courtenay Press, 1970.

Brooks, Van Wyck. *The Wine of the Puritans*. London: Sisley's, 1908.

Brown, David C. "The Keys of the Kingdom: Excommunication in Colonial Massachusetts." *New England Quarterly* 67, no. 4 (December 1994): 531–66.

Brumm, Ursula. *American Thought and Religious Typology*. New Brunswick: Rutgers University Press, 1970.

Bush Jr., Sargent. "A Bibliography of the Published Writings of Thomas Hooker." In *Thomas Hooker: Writings in England and Holland, 1626–1633*, ed. and intro. George H. Williams, Norman Pettit, Winfried Herget, and Sargent Bush Jr., 390–425. Harvard Theological Studies 28. Cambridge: Harvard University Press, 1975.

———. "Establishing the Hooker Canon." In *Thomas Hooker: Writings in England and Holland, 1626–1633*, ed. and intro. George H. Williams, Norman Pettit, Winfried Herget, and Sargent Bush Jr., 378–89. Harvard Theological Studies 28. Cambridge: Harvard University Press, 1975.

———. Introduction to *The Correspondence of John Cotton*, ed. Sargent Bush Jr., 1–67. Chapel Hill: University of North Carolina Press, 2001.

———. "John Cotton's Correspondence: A Census." *Early American Literature* 24, no. 2 (1989): 91–111.

———. *The Writings of Thomas Hooker: Spiritual Adventure in Two Worlds*. Madison: University of Wisconsin Press, 1980.

Caldwell, Patricia. "The Antinomian Language Controversy." *Harvard Theological Review* 69 (1976): 345–67.

———. *The Puritan Conversion Narrative: The Beginnings of American Expression*. Cambridge: Cambridge University Press, 1983.

Camp, L. Raymond. *Roger Williams, God's Apostle of Advocacy: Biography and Rhetoric*. Studies in American Religion 36. Lewiston, N.Y.: Edwin Mellen Press, 1989.

Caplan, Harry. "The Four Senses of Scriptural Interpretation and the Medieval Theory of Preaching." *Speculum: A Journal of Medieval Studies* 4 (1929): 282–90.

Cardwell, Edward. *Documentary Annals of the Reformed Church of England*. 2 vols. Oxford, 1844.

Carpenter, Edmund J. *Roger Williams: A Study of the Life, Times, and Character of a Political Pioneer*. 1909. Freeport, N.Y.: Books for Libraries Press, 1972.

Cohen, Charles Lloyd. *God's Caress: The Psychology of Puritan Religious Experience*. Oxford: Oxford University Press, 1986.

———. "The Post-Puritan Paradigm of Early American Religious History." *William and Mary Quarterly* 3d ser. 54, no. 4 (October 1997): 695–722.

Colacurcio, Michael J. "'A Strange Poise of Spirit': The Life and Deaths of Thomas Shepard." *Religion and Literature* 32, no. 1 (spring 2000): 1–44.

———. "Primitive Comfort: The Spiritual Witness of John Cotton," *ELH* 67, no. 3 (fall 2000): 655–95.

Collinson, Patrick. *The Elizabethan Puritan Movement*. Berkeley: University of California Press, 1967.

———. *English Puritanism*. 1983. London: Historical Association, 1984.

———. "The English Conventicle." In *Voluntary Religion: Papers Read at the 1985 Summer Meeting and the 1986 Winter Meeting of the Ecclesiastical History Society*, ed. J. Sheils and Diane Wood. *Studies in Church History* 23 (1986): 223–59.

———. *The Puritan Character: Polemics and Polarities in Early Seventeenth-Century English Culture*. Los Angeles: William Andrews Clark Memorial Library, 1989.

Coolidge, John S. *The Pauline Renaissance in England: Puritanism and the Bible.* Oxford: Clarendon, 1970.

Cooper Jr., James F. "The Confession and Trial of Richard Wayte, Boston, 1640." *William and Mary Quarterly* 3d ser. 44, no. 2 (April 1987): 310–332.

———. *Tenacious of Their Liberties: The Congregationalists in Colonial Massachusetts.* New York: Oxford University Press, 1999.

Craig, Raymond Allen. "The Stamp of the Word: The Poetics of Biblical Allusion in American Puritan Poetry." Ph.D. diss. University of California, Davis, 1989.

Crandall, Ralph J., and Ralph J. Coffman. "From Emigrants to Rulers: The Charlestown Oligarchy in the Great Migration." *New England Historic Genealogical Register* 131 (1977): 1–27.

Daly, Robert. *God's Altar: The World and the Flesh in Puritan Poetry.* Berkeley: University of California Press, 1978.

Davidson, Edward H. "Cotton's Biblical Exegesis: Method and Purpose." *Early American Literature* 17, no. 2 (fall 1982): 119–38.

———. "'God's Well-Trodden Foot-Paths': Puritan Preaching and Sermon Form." *Texas Studies in Literature and Language* 25, no. 4 (winter 1983): 503–27.

Delamotte, Eugenia. "John Cotton and the Rhetoric of Grace." *Early American Literature* 21, no. 1 (spring 1986): 49–74.

Delbanco, Andrew. *The Puritan Ordeal.* Cambridge: Harvard University Press, 1989.

Ditmore, Michael. "A Prophetess in Her Own Country: An Exegesis of Anne Hutchinson's 'Immediate Revelation.'" *William and Mary Quarterly* 3d ser. 57, no. 2 (April 2000): 349–92.

Eden, Kathy. *Hermeneutics and the Rhetorical Tradition: Chapters in the Ancient Legacy and Its Humanist Reception.* New Haven: Yale University Press, 1997.

Elliott, Emory. *Power and the Pulpit in Puritan New England.* Princeton: Princeton University Press, 1975.

Emerson, Everett H. Introduction to *Redemption: Three Sermons (1637–1656)*, by Thomas Hooker. Gainesville, Fla.: Scholars' Facsimiles and Reprints, 1956.

———. *John Cotton.* Twayne United States Authors Series 80. New York: Twayne, 1965.

———. *Puritanism in America, 1620–1750.* Twayne's World Leaders Series 71. Boston: Twayne, 1977.

Erikson, Kai T. *Wayward Puritans: A Study in the Sociology of Deviance.* New York: John Wiley and Sons, 1966.

Eusden, John D. Introduction to *The Marrow of Theology*, by William Ames. 1968. Durham: Labyrinth Press, 1983. 1–66.

Fisch, Harold. "The Puritans and the Reform of Prose-Style," *ELH* 19, no. 4 (December 1952): 229–48.

Fish, Stanley E. *Self-Consuming Artifacts: The Experience of Seventeenth-Century Literature.* Berkeley: University of California Press, 1972.

Forstman, Jackson. *Word and Spirit: Calvin's Doctrine of Biblical Authority.* Stanford: Stanford University Press, 1962.

Foster, Stephen. *The Long Argument: English Puritanism and the Shaping of New England Culture, 1570–1700.* Chapel Hill: University of North Carolina Press, 1991.

———. "New England and the Challenge of Heresy, 1630 to 1660: The Puritan Crisis in Transatlantic Perspective." *William and Mary Quarterly* 3d ser. 38, no. 4 (October 1981): 624–60.

Frederick, John T. "Literary Art in Thomas Shepard's 'The Parable of the Ten Virgins.'" *Seventeenth-Century News* 26, no. 1 (spring 1968): 4–6.

Gerrish, B. A. "Biblical Authority and the Continental Reformation." *Scottish Journal of Theology* 10, no. 4 (December 1957): 337–60.

Gordis, Robert. *Koheleth — The Man and His World: A Study of Ecclesiastes.* 1951. New York: Schocken, 1968.

Grabo, Norman S. "John Cotton's Aesthetic: A Sketch." *Early American Literature* 3, no. 1 (spring 1968): 4–10.

———. "Running the Gauntlet: Seventeenth-Century Literary Criticism." *ELH* 67, no. 3 (fall 2000): 697–715.

———. "The Veiled Vision: The Role of Aesthetics in Early American Intellectual History." In *The American Puritan Imagination: Essays in Reevaluation,* ed. Sacvan Bercovitch, 19–33. Cambridge: Cambridge University Press, 1974.

Grant, Robert M., and David Tracy. *A Short History of the Interpretation of the Bible.* 2d ed. Philadelphia: Fortress Press, 1984.

Guggisberg, Hans R. "Religious Freedom and the History of the Christian World in Roger Williams' Thought." *Early American Literature* 12, no. 1 (spring 1977): 36–48.

Gura, Philip F. *A Glimpse of Sion's Glory: Puritan Radicalism in New England, 1620–1660.* Middletown, Conn.: Wesleyan University Press, 1984.

Gustafson, Sandra M. *Eloquence Is Power: Oratory and Performance in Early America.* Chapel Hill: University of North Carolina Press, 2000.

Habegger, Alfred. "Preparing the Soul for Christ: The Contrasting Sermon Forms of John Cotton and Thomas Hooker." *American Literature* 41, no. 3 (November 1969): 342–54.

Hall, David D., ed. *The Antinomian Controversy, 1636–1638: A Documentary History.* 2d ed. Durham: Duke University Press, 1990.

———. *The Faithful Shepherd: A History of the New England Ministry in the Seventeenth Century.* Chapel Hill: University of North Carolina Press, 1972.

———. Introduction to *The Antinomian Controversy, 1636–1638: A Documentary History,* ed. David D. Hall, 3–23. 2d ed. Durham: Duke University Press, 1990.

———. "On Common Ground: The Coherence of American Puritan Studies." *William and Mary Quarterly* 3d ser. 44, no. 2 (April 1987): 193–229.

———. Preface to the second edition in *The Antinomian Controversy, 1636–1638: A Documentary History,* ed. David D. Hall, xviii–xxi. 2d ed. Durham: Duke University Press, 1990.

———. "Readers and Writers in Early New England." In *The Colonial Book in the Atlantic World,* 117–51, vol. 1 of *A History of the Book in America.* Cambridge: Cambridge University Press, 2000.

———. *Worlds of Wonder, Days of Judgment: Popular Religious Belief in Early New England.* New York: Knopf, 1989.

Haller, William. *The Rise of Puritanism, Or, The Way to the New Jerusalem As Set Forth in Pulpit and Press from Thomas Cartwright to John Lilburne and John Milton, 1570–1643.* New York: Columbia University Press, 1938. New York: Harper Torchbooks, 1957. Philadelphia: University of Pennsylvania Press, 1972.

Hambrick-Stowe, Charles E. *The Practice of Piety: Puritan Devotional Disciplines in Seventeenth-Century New England.* Chapel Hill: University of North Carolina Press, 1982.

Hamilton, Alistair. *The Family of Love.* Cambridge: Cambridge University Press, 1981.

Hammond, Jeffrey A. *The American Puritan Elegy: A Literary and Cultural Study.* Cambridge: Cambridge University Press, 2000.

———. "The Bride in Redemptive Time: John Cotton and the Canticles Controversy." *New England Quarterly* 56 no. 1 (March 1983): 78–102.

Hartman, Geoffrey H., and Sanford Budick. Introduction to *Midrash and Literature,* ed. Geoffrey H. Hartman and Sanford Budick. New Haven: Yale University Press, 1986.

Hatch, Nathan O., and Mark A. Noll. Introduction to *The Bible in America,* ed. Nathan O. Hatch and Mark A. Noll. New York: Oxford University Press, 1982.

Hauer, Christian E., and William A. Young. *An Introduction to the Bible: A Journey into Three Worlds.* Englewood Cliffs, N.J.: Prentice-Hall, 1986.

Heimert, Alan, and Andrew Delbanco, eds. *The Puritans in America: A Narrative Anthology.* Cambridge: Harvard University Press, 1985.

Herget, Winfried. "Preaching and Publication—Chronology and the Style of Thomas Hooker's Sermons." *Harvard Theological Review* 65 (1972): 231–39.

———. "The Transcription and Transmission of the Hooker Corpus." In *Thomas Hooker: Writings in England and Holland, 1626–1633,* ed. and trans. George H. Williams, Norman Pettit, Winfried Herget, and Sargent Bush Jr., 253–70. Harvard Theological Studies 28. Cambridge: Harvard University Press, 1975.

Herr, Alan Fager. *The Elizabethan Sermon: A Survey and a Bibliography.* New York: Octagon Books, 1969.

Hill, Christopher. *The English Bible and the Seventeenth-Century Revolution.* 1993. New York: Penguin, 1994.

———. *The World Turned Upside Down: Radical Ideas during the English Revolution.* 1972. New York: Penguin, 1975.

Hodder, Alan D. "In the Glasse of God's Word: Hooker's Pulpit Rhetoric and the Theater of Conversion." *New England Quarterly* 66, no. 1 (March 1993): 67–109.

Holstun, James. *A Rational Millennium: Puritan Utopias of Seventeenth-Century England and America.* New York: Oxford University Press, 1987.

Hunt, William. *The Puritan Moment: The Coming of Revolution in an English County.* Harvard Historical Studies 102. Cambridge: Harvard University Press, 1983.

Jones, Phyllis M., and Nicholas R. Jones. Introduction to *The Parable of the Ten Virgins. Salvation in New England: Selections from the Sermons of the First Preachers,* ed. Phyllis M. Jones and Nicholas R. Jones. Austin: University of Texas Press, 1977.

Keeble, N. H. "Richard Baxter's Preaching Ministry: Its History and Texts." *Journal of Ecclesiastical History* 35, no. 3 (July 1984): 539–59.

Kelsey, David H. "Protestant Attitudes regarding Methods of Biblical Interpretation." In *Scripture in the Jewish and Christian Traditions,* ed. Frederick E. Greenspahn, 134–61. Nashville: Abingdon Press, 1982.

Kendall, R. T. *Calvin and English Calvinism to 1649.* New York: Oxford University Press, 1979.

Kibbey, Ann. *The Interpretation of Material Shapes in Puritanism: A Study of Rhetoric, Prejudice, and Violence.* Cambridge: Cambridge University Press, 1986.

Knight, Janice. *Orthodoxies in Massachusetts: Rereading American Puritanism.* Cambridge: Harvard University Press, 1994.

Knott Jr., John R. *The Sword of the Spirit: Puritan Responses to the Bible.* Chicago: University of Chicago Press, 1980.

Koehler, Lyle. *A Search for Power: The "Weaker Sex" in Seventeenth-Century New England.* Urbana: University of Illinois Press, 1980.

Kristeva, Julia. *Revolution in Poetic Language.* 1974. Trans. Margaret Waller. New York: Columbia University Press, 1984.

———. *Le text du roman: Approche sémiologique d'une structure discursive transforma-tionnelle.* Approaches to Semiotics 6. The Hague: Mouton, 1970.

———. "Word, Dialogue, Novel." 1969. Trans. Alice Jardine, Thomas Gora, and Léon S. Roudiez. In *The Kristeva Reader,* ed. Toril Moi, 34–61. New York: Columbia University Press, 1986.

LaFantasie, Glenn W. "The Road to Banishment: Editorial Note." In *The Correspondence of Roger Williams,* ed. Glenn W. LaFantasie, Vol. 1, 12–23. Hanover: Brown University Press, University Press of New England, for The Rhode Island Historical Society, 1988.

Lake, Peter, and David Como. "'Orthodoxy' and Its Discontents: Dispute Settlement and the Production of 'Consensus' in the London (Puritan) 'Underground.'" *Journal of British Studies* 39, no. 1 (January 2000): 34–70.

Lang, Amy Shrager. *Prophetic Woman: Anne Hutchinson and the Problem of Dissent in the Literature of New England.* Berkeley: University of California Press, 1987.

Levy, Babette May. *Preaching in the First Half Century of New England History.* New York: Russell and Russell, 1945.

Lewalski, Barbara Kiefer. *Protestant Poetics and the Seventeenth-Century Religious Lyric.* Princeton: Princeton University Press, 1979.

Lockridge, Kenneth A. *Literacy in Colonial New England: An Enquiry into the Social Context of Literacy in the Early Modern West.* New York: Norton, 1974.

Lovejoy, David S. *Religious Enthusiasm in the New World.* Cambridge: Harvard University Press, 1985.

Luxon, Thomas H. *Literal Figures: Puritan Allegory and the Reformation Crisis in Representation.* Chicago: University of Chicago Press, 1995.

Lynn, Kenneth S. "Perry Miller." *The American Scholar* 52 (spring 1983): 221–27.

Maclear, J. F. "Anne Hutchinson and the Mortalist Heresy." *New England Quarterly* 54, no. 1 (March 1981): 74–103.

———. "'The Heart of New England Rent': The Mystical Element in Early Puritan History." *Mississippi Valley Historical Record* 42, no. 4 (March 1956): 621–52.

Marsh, Christopher. "'A Gracelesse, and Audacious Companie'?: The Family of Love in the Parish of Balsham, 1550–1630." In *Voluntary Religion: Papers Read at the 1985 Summer Meeting and the 1986 Winter Meeting of the Ecclesiastical History Society,* ed. J. Sheils and Diane Wood. *Studies in Church History* 23 (1986): 191–208.

McCarl, Mary Rhinelander. "Thomas Shepard's Records of Relations of Religious Experience, 1648–1649." *William and Mary Quarterly* 3d ser. 48, no. 3 (July 1991): 432–66.

McGiffert, Michael. "Thomas Shepard: The Practice of Piety." In *God's Plot: Puritan Spirituality in Thomas Shepard's Cambridge,* ed. and intro. Michael McGiffert, 3–33. 1972. Amherst: University of Massachusetts Press, 1994.

———. "Puritan Studies in the 1960's." *William and Mary Quarterly* 3d ser. 27, no. 1 (January 1970): 36–67.

———. Ed. *God's Plot: Puritan Spirituality in Thomas Shepard's Cambridge.* 1972. Amherst: University of Massachusetts Press, 1994.

Mencken, H. L. "Puritanism as a Literary Force." In *A Book of Prefaces.* New York: Knopf, 1917.

Middlekauff, Robert. "Piety and Intellect in Puritanism." *William and Mary Quarterly* 3d ser. 22, no. 3 (July 1965): 457–70.

Miller, Perry. "The Marrow of Puritan Divinity." 1935. Reprinted in *Errand into the Wilderness*, 48–98. Cambridge: Harvard University Press, Belknap Press, 1956.

———. *The New England Mind: The Seventeenth Century*. 1939. Cambridge: Harvard University Press, 1954.

———. *The New England Mind: From Colony to Province*. Cambridge: Harvard University Press, 1953.

———. *Orthodoxy in Massachusetts 1630–1650*. 1933. New York: Harper Torchbooks, 1970.

———. "'Preparation for Salvation' in Seventeenth Century New England." *Journal of the History of Ideas* 4, no. 3 (1943): 253–86. Reprinted in *Ideas in Cultural Perspective*, ed. Philip P. Wiener and Aaron Noland, 604–32. New Brunswick: Rutgers University Press, 1962.

———. *Roger Williams: His Contribution to the American Tradition*. 1953. New York: Atheneum, 1965.

———. "Thomas Hooker and the Democracy of Connecticut." 1931. Reprinted in *Errand into the Wilderness*, 16–47. Cambridge: Harvard University Press, Belknap Press, 1956.

Miller, Perry, and Thomas H. Johnson. Introduction to *The Puritans*, ed. Perry Miller and Thomas Johnson, Vol. 1, 1–79. 2 vols. New York: Harper and Row, 1938.

Mitchell, W. Fraser. *English Pulpit Oratory from Andrewes to Tillotson: A Study of Its Literary Aspects*. New York: Macmillan, 1932.

Morawski, Stefan. "The Basic Functions of Quotation." In *Sign • Language • Culture*, 690–705. The Hague: Mouton, 1970.

Morgan, Edmund S. "New England Puritanism: Another Approach." *William and Mary Quarterly* 3d ser. 18, no. 2 (April 1961): 236–42.

———. *The Puritan Dilemma: The Story of John Winthrop*. Boston: Little, Brown, 1958.

———. *Roger Williams: The Church and the State*. New York: Harcourt, Brace and World, 1967.

———. *Visible Saints: The History of a Puritan Idea*. 1963. Ithaca: Cornell University Press, 1965.

Morgan, John. *Godly Learning: Puritan Attitudes towards Reason, Learning, and Education, 1560–1640*. Cambridge: Cambridge University Press, 1986.

Morgan, Thaïs E. "Is There an Intertext in This Text?: Literary and Interdisciplinary Approaches to Intertextuality." *American Journal of Semiotics* 3, no. 4 (1985): 1–40.

Morison, Samuel Eliot. *Harvard College in the Seventeenth Century*. 2 vols. Cambridge: Harvard University Press, 1936.

———. *The Intellectual Life of Colonial New England*. 1936. Ithaca: Cornell University Press, 1961.

———. "Master Thomas Shepard." In *The Builders of the Bay Colony*, 105–34. 1930. Revised 1962. Boston: Northeastern University Press, 1981.

Myles, Anne G. "Arguments in Milk, Arguments in Blood: Roger Williams, Persecution, and the Discourse of Witness." *Modern Philology* 91, no. 2 (November 1993): 133–60.

Norton, Arthur O. "Harvard Text-Books and Reference Books of the Seventeenth Century." *Publications of the Colonial Society of Massachusetts* 28 (April 1933): 361–438.

Nuttall, Geoffrey F. *The Holy Spirit in Puritan Faith and Experience*. Oxford: Basil Blackwell, 1946.

———. *Visible Saints: The Congregational Way, 1640–1660*. Oxford: Blackwell, 1957.

O'Malley, John W. "Content and Rhetorical Forms in Sixteenth-Century Treatises on

Preaching." In *Renaissance Eloquence: Studies in the Theory and Practice of Renaissance Rhetoric,* ed. James J. Murphy. Berkeley: University of California Press, 1983.

Parrington, Vernon Louis. *1620–1800: The Colonial Mind,* vol. 1 of *Main Currents in American Thought: An Interpretation of American Literature from the Beginnings to 1920.* 3 vols. New York: Harcourt, Brace, 1930.

Pearl, Valerie, and Morris Pearl, eds. "Governor John Winthrop on the Birth of the Antinomians' 'Monster': The Earliest Reports to Reach England and the Making of a Myth." *Massachusetts Historical Society Proceedings* 102 (1990): 21–37.

Pettit, Norman. *The Heart Prepared: Grace and Conversion in Puritan Spiritual Life.* New Haven: Yale University Press, 1966.

———. Introduction to *The Poor Doubting Christian Drawn Unto Christ.* In *Thomas Hooker: Writings in England and Holland, 1626–1633,* 147–51. Harvard Theological Studies 28. Cambridge: Harvard University Press, 1975.

Plett, Heinrich F. "Intertextualities." In *Intertextuality,* ed. Heinrich F. Plett, 3–29. Research in Text Theory 15. Berlin: Walter de Gruyter, 1991.

———. "The Poetics of Quotation." In *Von der berbalen Konstitution zur symbolischen Bedeutung—From Verbal Constitution to Symbolic Meaning,* ed. János S. Petöfi and Terry Olivi. Papers in Textlinguisitics 62. Hamburg: Helmut Buske Verlag, 1988.

Pope, Robert G. *The Half-Way Covenant: Church Membership in Puritan New England.* Princeton: Princeton University Press, 1969.

Porton, Gary G. "Defining Midrash." In *The Study of Ancient Judaism,* ed. J. Neusner. New York: Ktav, 1981.

———. *Understanding Rabbinic Midrash: Text and Commentary.* Hoboken, N.J.: Ktav, 1985.

Rairdin, Craig. *Quick Verse.* Ver. 2.0. King James Version. Computer software. Bible concordance on disk. 1990. IBM PC-DOS 2.11, 680KB, disk.

Reedy, Gerard. *The Bible and Reason: Anglicans and Scripture in Late Seventeenth-Century England.* Philadelphia: University of Pennsylvania Press, 1985.

Rice, Grantland S. *The Transformation of Authorship in America.* Chicago: University of Chicago Press, 1997.

Robinson, Charles F., and Robin Robinson. "Three Early Massachusetts Libraries." *Publications of the Colonial Society of Massachusetts Collections* 28 (April 1931): 107–75.

Robinson, Lewis Milton. "A History of the Half-Way Covenant." Ph.D. diss., University of Illinois, 1963.

Ronda, James P. "'We Are Well As We Are': An Indian Critique of Seventeenth-Century Christian Missions." *William and Mary Quarterly* 3d ser. 34, no. 1 (January 1977): 66–82.

Rosenmeier, Jesper. "'Clearing the Medium': A Reevaluation of the Puritan Plain Style in Light of John Cotton's *A Practicall Commentary Upon the First Epistle Generall of John.*" *William and Mary Quarterly* 3d ser. 37, no. 4 (October 1980): 577–91.

———. "Eaters and Non-Eaters: John Cotton's *A Brief Exposition of . . . Canticles* (1642) in Light of Boston's (Linc.) Religious and Civil Conflicts, 1619–22," *Early American Literature* 36, no. 2 (2001): 149–81.

———. "New England's Perfection: The Image of Adam and the Image of Christ in the Antinomian Crisis, 1634 to 1638." *William and Mary Quarterly* 3d ser. 27, no. 3 (July 1970): 435–59.

———. "The Teacher and the Witness: John Cotton and Roger Williams." *William and Mary Quarterly* 3d ser. 25, no. 3 (July 1968): 408–31.

Rowe, Karen E. *Saint and Singer: Edward Taylor's Typology and the Poetics of Meditation.* Cambridge: Cambridge University Press, 1986.

Rutman, Darrett B. "God's Bridge Falling Down: 'Another Approach' to New England Puritanism Assayed." *William and Mary Quarterly* 3d ser. 19, no. 3 (July 1962): 408–21.

Scalise, Charles J. "The 'Sensus Literalis': A Hermeneutical Key to Biblical Exegesis." *Scottish Journal of Theology* 42, no. 1 (1989): 45–65.

Schindler, Jessie. "A Mirror for Educators: The Puritan Sermon and the Theatrics of Instruction." M.A. essay, Columbia University, 1995.

Schuldiner, Michael. *Gifts and Works: The Post-Conversion Paradigm and Spiritual Controversy in Seventeenth-Century Massachusetts.* National Association of Baptist Professors of Religion Dissertation Series 8. Macon, Ga.: Mercer University Press, 1991.

Schutte, Anne J. "'Such Monstrous Births': A Neglected Aspect of the Antinomian Controversy." *Renaissance Quarterly* 38, no. 1 (spring 1985): 85–106.

Schweitzer, Ivy. *The Work of Self-Representation: Lyric Poetry in Colonial New England.* Chapel Hill: University of North Carolina Press, 1991.

Selement, George. "Publication and the Puritan Minister." *William and Mary Quarterly* 3d ser. 37, no. 2 (April 1980): 219–41.

Selement, George, and Bruce C. Woolley. Introduction to *Thomas Shepard's "Confessions,"* ed. George Selement and Bruce C. Woolley. *Publications of the Colonial Society of Massachusetts Collections* 58 (1981): 1–28.

Sensabaugh, George F. *Milton in Early America.* Princeton: Princeton University Press, 1964.

Shuffelton, Frank. *Thomas Hooker, 1586–1647.* Princeton: Princeton University Press, 1977.

Shuger, Debora K. *Sacred Rhetoric: The Christian Grand Style in the English Renaissance.* Princeton: Princeton University Press, 1988.

Skaggs, Donald. *Roger Williams' Dream for America.* American University Studies Series 9. Vol. 129. New York: Peter Lang, 1993.

Smith, Nigel. *Perfection Proclaimed: Language and Literature in English Radical Religion 1640–1660.* Oxford: Clarendon Press, 1989.

Spurgin, Hugh. *Roger Williams and Puritan Radicalism in the English Separatist Tradition.* Studies in American Religion 34. Lewiston, N.Y.: Edwin Mellen Press, 1989.

Staloff, Darren. *The Making of an American Thinking Class: Intellectuals and Intelligentsia in Puritan Massachusetts.* New York: Oxford University Press, 1998.

Stanford, Ann. "Anne Bradstreet." In *Major Writers of Early American Literature,* ed. Everett Emerson. Madison: University of Wisconsin Press, 1972.

Stein, Michael. "Tevye's Art of Quotation." *Prooftexts: A Journal of Jewish Literary History* 6, no. 1 (January 1986): 79–86.

Steiner, Prudence L. "A Garden of Spices in New England: John Cotton's and Edward Taylor's Use of the Song of Songs." In *Allegory, Myth, and Symbol,* ed. Morton W. Bloomfield, 227–43. Harvard English Studies 9. Cambridge: Harvard University Press, 1981.

Stern, David. "Midrash and Indeterminacy." *Critical Inquiry* 15, no. 1 (autumn 1988): 132–61.

———. "Midrash and the Language of Exegesis: A Study of Vayikra Rabbah, Chapter 1." In *Midrash and Literature,* ed. Geoffrey H. Hartman and Sanford Budick, 105–24. New Haven: Yale University Press, 1986.

Stoever, William K. B. *"A Faire and Easie Way to Heaven": Covenant Theology and Antinomianism in Early Massachusetts.* Middletown, Conn.: Wesleyan University Press, 1978.

Stout, Harry S. *The New England Soul: Preaching and Religious Culture in Colonial New England.* New York: Oxford University Press, 1986.

———. "Word and Order in Colonial New England." In *The Bible in America,* ed. Nathan O. Hatch and Mark A. Noll, 19–38. New York: Oxford University Press, 1982.

Teunissen, John J., and Evelyn J. Hinz. "Roger Williams, St. Paul, and American Primitivism." *Canadian Review of American Studies* 4, no. 2 (fall 1973): 121–36.

Tinker, George E. "John Eliot: Conversion, Colonialism, and the Oppression of Language." In *Missionary Conquest: The Gospel and Native American Cultural Genocide,* 21–41. Minneapolis: Fortress Press, 1993.

Tobin, Lad. "A Radically Different Voice: Gender and Language in the Trials of Anne Hutchinson." *Early American Literature* 25, no. 3 (1990): 253–70.

Tolmie, Murray. *The Triumph of the Saints: The Separate Churches of London 1616–1649.* London: Cambridge University Press, 1977.

Toulouse, Teresa. *The Art of Prophesying: New England Sermons and the Shaping of Belief.* Athens: University of Georgia Press, 1987.

Trinterud, Leonard J., ed. *Elizabethan Puritanism.* New York: Oxford University Press, 1971.

Tuttle, Julius H. "Writings of Rev. John Cotton." In *Bibliographical Essays: A Tribute to Wilberforce Eames,* 363–80. Cambridge: Harvard University Press, 1924.

Walker, George Leon. *History of the First Church in Hartford, 1633–1883.* Hartford: Brown and Gross, 1884.

———. *Thomas Hooker: Preacher, Founder, Democrat.* New York: Dodd, Mead, 1891.

Walker, Williston. "The Development of Covenant and Creed in the Salem Chutch, 1629–1665." In *The Creeds and Platforms of Congregationalism,* ed. Williston Walker, 93–115. New York: Scribner's, 1893. New York: Pilgrim Press, 1991.

Warner, Michael. *The Letters of the Republic: Publication and the Public Sphere in Eighteenth-Century America.* Cambridge: Harvard University Press, 1990.

Werge, Thomas. *Thomas Shepard.* Boston: Twayne, 1987.

Westerkamp, Marilyn J. "Anne Hutchinson, Sectarian Mysticism, and the Puritan Order." *Church History* 59, no. 4 (December 1990): 482–96.

———. "Puritan Patriarchy and the Problem of Revelation." *Journal of Interdisciplinary History* 23, no. 3 (winter 1993): 571–95.

Williams, George H. "The Life of Thomas Hooker in England and Holland, 1586–1633." In *Thomas Hooker: Writings in England and Holland, 1626–1633,* ed and intro. George H. Williams, Norman Pettit, Winfried Herget, and Sargent Bush Jr., 1–40. Harvard Theological Studies 28. Cambridge: Harvard University Press, 1975.

Williams, Selma R. *Divine Rebel: The Life of Anne Marbury Hutchinson.* New York: Holt, Rinehart, and Winston, 1981.

Williams, William Carlos. *In the American Grain.* New York: Albert and Charles Boni, 1925.

Winship, Michael P. *Making Heretics: Militant Protestantism and Free Grace in Massachusetts 1636–1641,* Princeton: Princeton University Press, 2002.

———. "'The Most Glorious Church in the World': The Unity of the Godly in Boston, Massachusetts, in the 1630s." *Journal of British Studies* 39, no. 1 (January 2000): 71–98.

———. "Reconsiderations: Were There Any Puritans in New England?" *New England Quarterly* 74, no. 1 (March 2001): 118–38.

Wood, Timothy L. "'A Church Still by Her First Covenant': George Philips and a Puritan View of Roman Catholicism." *New England Quarterly* 72, no. 1 (March 1999): 28–41.

Ziff, Larzer. *The Career of John Cotton: Puritanism and the American Experience.* Princeton: Princeton University Press, 1962.

————. Introduction to *John Cotton on the Churches of New England,* by John Cotton. Cambridge: Harvard University Press, 1968.

————. "Upon What Pretext?: The Book and Literary History." *Proceedings of the American Antiquarian Society* 95 (1985): 297–315.